D1608052

the handbook of INTERNATIONAL CORPORATE GOVERNANCE

a definitive guide

an Institute of Directors publication

London and Sterling, VA

First published in Great Britain and the United States in 2004 by the Institute of Directors and Kogan Page Limited.

120 Pentonville Road
London N1 9JN
United Kingdom
www.kogan-page.co.uk

22883 Quicksilver Drive
Sterling VA 20166-2012
USA

© The Institute of Directors, 2005

The views expressed in this book are those of the individual authors and are not necessarily the same as those of the Institute of Directors.

ISBN 0 7494 4060 0

British Library Cataloguing-in-Publication Data

A CIP record for this book is available from the British Library.

Library of Congress Cataloging-in-Publication Data

Institute of Directors
   The handbook of international corporate governance: a country-by-country guide/Institute of Directors.
      p. cm
   Includes bibliographical references and index.
   ISBN 0-7494-4060-0
   1. Corporate governance—Handbooks, manuals, etc. 2. Corporate governance—Law and legislation—Handbooks, manuals, etc. 3. Comparative management. I. Waring, Kerrie, 1970-II. Title.
   HD2741.P54 2004
   330'.03--dc22
                                        2004009948

Typeset by Datamatics Technologies Ltd, Mumbai, India
Printed and bound in Great Britain by Scotprint

Contents

Contents

About the
Editors

Institute of Directors

The IoD is a politically independent membership organization established in the United Kingdom in 1903 and granted a Royal Charter in 1906. The Institute's motto is 'enterprise and integrity' and it supports, represents and sets standards for over 53,000 professional directors from a broad variety of entities. The IoD has over 20 years of director training, certification and accreditation expertise in the United Kingdom and overseas. In 1999 it launched the Chartered Director initiative – the world's leading professional qualification for directors underpinned by a rigorous test of knowledge, understanding, experience and probity.
www.iod.com

Kerrie Waring

Kerrie is the International Professional Development Manager at the Institute of Directors in the UK with responsibility for building and promoting the IoD's work in director and board effectiveness via publications, training programmes and lectures. Her consultancy work has included clients in Europe, Africa, the Middle East and South East Asia.

Chris Pierce

Chris has been associated with many of the major board development initiatives in the UK and overseas over the last decade.

He developed the first examination for company directors in the UK, and is a regular speaker at international corporate governance conferences and has written extensively on director and board development issues.

In 2003 Kerrie and Chris were the co-writers of the Global Corporate Governance Forum (a joint World Bank and Organisation for Economic Co-operation and Development initiative) Toolkit on *Building Director Training Organisations*.

List of Contributors

Argentina
Marcos E J Bertin, Member of the Executive Committee of the Instituto Argentino para el Gobierno de las Organizaciones (IAGO), Buenos Aires

Enrique A Pelaez, Professor in Company Law, Universidad Argentina de la Empresa (UADE), Buenos Aires

Armenia
Gagik Poghossian

Australia
Robert Elliott, Policy Manager, Company Secretary, Legal Counsel, Australian Institute of Company Directors, Sydney

Brazil
Paulo Diederichsen Villares, Chairman of the Brazilian Corporate Governance Institute (IBGC), São Paulo

Leonardo Mayerhofer Viegas, Co-founder of the Brazilian Corporate Governance Institute (IBGC), São Paulo

China
Dr Daochi Tong, Deputy Director General, Department of Listed Companies Supervision, China Securities Regulatory Commission (CSRC)

Colombia
Paolo Gutierrez Velandia, Partner, CG Corporate Governance Consultants, Bogota

Hong Kong
Carlye Wai-Ling Tsui, Chief Executive Officer, Hong Kong Institute of Directors, Hong Kong

India
Mahendra Chouhan, Chairman, Mahendra and Young Knowledge Foundation, Mumbai

Indonesia
Dr Anugerah Pekerti, Associate Faculty Member, Indonesian Institute for Corporate Directorship, Jakarta

Marcelino Pandin, Vice Chairman, Indonesian Institute for Corporate Directorship, Jakarta

Japan
Nobuyuki Nakama, Professor of Management Studies, Teikyo University, Tokyo

Kenya
Karugor Gatamah, Centre for Corporate Governance, Nairobi

New Zealand
Peter Webb, Director of Research and Policy, Institute of Directors in New Zealand, Wellington

Philippines
Jesus P Estanislao, President and CEO, Institute of Corporate Directors, Makati City

Cesar Villanueva, Institute of Corporate Directors, Makati City

Romania
Gratiela Iordache, Executive Director of the Romanian Shareholders Association, Bucharest

Russian Federation
Igor Belikov, Director of the Russian Institute of Directors, Moscow

Igor Kostikov, Former Chairman of the Federal Commission for Securities Markets, Moscow

South Africa
Richard Wilkinson, Fomer Director, Institute of Directors in Southern Africa, Johannesburg

Philip Armstrong, Managing Director, ENF Corporate Governance Advisory Services, Johannesburg

Spain

Alejandro Plaza, Vice Secretary, Institute de Consejeros-Administradores, Madrid

Juan Alvarez-Vijande, CEO, Institute de Consejeros-Administradores, Madrid

Fernando Igartua, Chairman, Instituto de Consejeros-Administradores, Madrid

Sebastian Azerrad, Lawyer, Gomez-Acebo & Pombo Abogados, S.C.P., Madrid

Sri Lanka

Ajith Nivard Cabraal, Principal Consultant, Cabraal Consulting Group Ltd, Colombo

Turkey

Dr Melsa Ararat, Executive Director, Corporate Governance Forum of Turkey, Sabanci University, Istanbul

UK

Patricia Peter, Corporate Governance Executive, Institute of Directors, London

Ukraine

Dr Alexander V Merterns, Academic Vice President, International Institute of Business, Kiev

Alexander Y Okunev, Director of Corporate Governance Centre, International Institute of Business, Kiev

USA

Dr Roger W Raber, President and CEO, National Association of Corporate Directors, Washington DC

Alexandra R Lajoux, Editor in Chief and Senior Research Analyst, National Association of Corporate Directors, Washington DC

Uzbekistan

Kahramon Juraboev, Director, Business Solutions Management Consulting Company, Tashkent

Hasan Jamolov, Head of Finance Department, Tashkent Finance Institute

Foreword

Charting the International Corporate Governance Agenda

Corporate governance has become an issue of international concern. The headlines may be dominated by events in the USA, but in developing and emerging markets corporate governance is at the head of the agenda. The issue is getting high-profile support from international bodies such as the World Bank and OECD. In the wake of the Asia crisis it was recognized that high standards of corporate governance are needed to underpin the international financial architecture and meet development goals. Despite two decades of globalization, liberalizing of trade, and rapid growth in some regions, there are still 1 billion people living on less than $1 a day and twice that number without access to electricity and clean water. World Bank President James Wolfensohn has commented 'the governance of the corporation is now as important to the world economy as the government of countries'.

Sir Adrian Cadbury explained well how corporate governance touches on both public and private concerns:

> In its broadest sense, corporate governance is concerned with holding the balance between economic and social goals and between individual and communal goals. The governance framework is there to encourage the efficient use of resources and equally to require accountability for the stewardship of those resources. The aim is to align as nearly as possible the interests of individuals, of corporations and of society.
>
> (Sir Adrian Cadbury, Foreword, Corporate Governance and Development, by Stijn Claessens, Global Corporate Governance Forum, 2003)

Corporate governance, simply put, is the rules of the game for a company in its relations with its shareholders, its lenders, and other stakeholders in the business community and society at large. Lenders and investors need to be assured that the basic principles of corporate governance are in place and will be followed – that a company's dealings with shareholders are fair and transparent; that the board of directors is held accountable; and that the company deals responsibly with stakeholders. Getting this right is key to a company's integrity, efficiency, long-term growth and profitability.

OECD's own policy statement on corporate governance is equally clear on why the issue matters:

> Corporations create jobs, generate tax income, produce a wide array of goods and services... and increasingly manage our savings and secure our retirement income. Amidst growing reliance worldwide on the private sector, the issue of corporate governance has similarly risen in prominence.
>
> (Preface, OECD Principles of Corporate Governance, 1999)

Ultimately, the private sector can spur the growth that will tackle poverty – but that in turn needs investment – and investors at home or abroad won't invest unless they have corporate governance protections in place. This recognition has led to an international consensus that corporate governance systems, though different in form, must achieve credible standards of transparency, accountability, fairness and responsibility – the four principles that underpin the reform effort worldwide.

That consensus was highlighted by the United Nations International Conference on Financing for Development in Monterrey, Mexico, signed by 75 heads of state from the developed and developing worlds. The text acknowledged that corporate governance reform was vital for developing countries seeking to attract investment:

Private international capital flows... are vital complements to national and international development efforts... To attract and enhance inflows of productive capital, countries need to continue their efforts to achieve a transparent, stable and predictable investment climate... special efforts are required in priority areas such as... corporate governance.

The driving economic trends which set the stage for the convergence of the corporate governance agenda were led by liberalization of capital flows, and the associated trends in technology which allowed rapid trading of funds between markets. According to World Bank figures, at the start of the 1990s private sector flows to developing markets were in the order of $69 billion – about level with the public sector lending from international agencies. By the end of the 1990s, private flows to developing markets were five times larger – topping the $300 billion mark including foreign direct investment, portfolio equity and bonds. Institutional funds from OECD member countries provided the lion's share of these funds. With their own restrictions upon investing in equity and corporate paper being relaxed and asset classes no longer confined to government bonds, US pension and mutual funds have led the trend into new markets, seeking diversification and the higher rates of growth that emerging market economies promised. The trend was accelerated by privatization worldwide – shifting assets from public to private ownership and seeking new rounds of investment in the process. OECD figures show that over $800 billion was raised in privatization worldwide during the early and mid-1990s.

Whilst the growth in volume of global investment and lending looked impressive, it became painfully apparent that these flows were channelled through a fragile financial system – and one that was shown at the end of the 1990s to be devastatingly vulnerable. The financial crisis of 1997–98, which started with the collapse of the Thai Baht and ended with the bailout of the New York hedge fund industry, showed the devastation that mobile money could wreak upon markets and whole economies which had not developed the infrastructure and macroeconomic prudence and regulation to ensure stability. The shocks to macroeconomic finances, employment, inflation and collapse in lending to business as the banking sector convulsed caused whole economies to lose the gains of a generation in terms of growth.

The shock waves from the Asia crisis reached Western markets, and 'contagion' became the new term for integrated capital markets susceptible to infection in a borderless world. The shocks were felt from Russia, to New York, to Brazil. Those markets least integrated were the most protected. Much of India, South Asia and China were unaffected.

The capital that had poured into developing markets had ignored the governance agenda – the poor standards of accounting and auditing, the conflicts of interest and related party transactions between companies and banks, the lack of independent boards to oversee management and protect minorities. In short, corporate governance was weak but that had been ignored in the dash to growth. The Asia crisis brought corporate governance to the attention not only of the developing countries suffering the effects, but also to the G7 which put corporate governance reform at the centre of international effort to strengthen the rules governing the workings of the international capital markets. Rt Hon Gordon Brown, Chancellor of the UK Treasury, whilst chairing the G7 at the height of the crisis, put the spotlight on corporate governance and argued forcefully that poor transparency in both the corporate and financial sector, exacerbated by the weak accountability of the boards charged with oversight of management, had exacerbated both the severity and extent of the crisis. Brown called upon the World Bank to help ensure that corporate governance reform was implemented across the developing world in order to help prevent systemic crises, but also to promote domestic economic stability. He pointed to the work of the OECD in developing a framework for corporate governance reform and urged the World Bank to cooperate with the OECD in taking their Principles of Corporate Governance into the international community. The stage was set for the founding of the Global Corporate Governance Forum under a Memorandum of Understanding signed by World Bank President James Wolfensohn and OECD Secretary General Donald Johnston in June 1999. The Memorandum also agreed cooperation in the organization of a series of regional roundtables to promote dialogue on the OECD Principles of Corporate Governance, and to form a Private Sector Advisory Group which would promote partnership with the business community in the reform effort. The first roundtable meetings were held the same year in Korea and Russia. This initiative represented a coordinated effort by developed and developing countries to agree a consensus on the importance of corporate governance, acknowledging the need for extensive dialogue at regional level between the public and private sector. Under the initiative corporate governance roundtables were set up with local partners and international support in Asia, Eurasia, Latin America, Russia and South Eastern Europe. The model was set by the first meetings in Korea and Russia – a discussion between leading public and private sector players on the framework of the OECD Principles of Corporate Governance, leading to the development of 'white papers' which set out priorities for reform and built an alliance for promoting corporate governance improvement. In parallel, the Commonwealth developed its own Principles of Good Business Practice and launched an ambitious programme for establishing national taskforces, and issuing codes of best practice, building upon pioneering work in member countries such as South Africa. The US Chamber of Commerce's own international outreach through the Center for International Private Enterprise, working in Latin America, the former Soviet Union and the Middle East provided support to business associations promoting corporate governance reform as a solution to endemic corruption, inefficiency and chronic underinvestment. The state was set for the development of an international alliance in favour of corporate governance reform to promote sustainable private sector growth.

The OECD's own work in the field of corporate governance pre-dated the Asia crisis. A number of member countries had launched significant reform programmes domestically in the wake of corporate scandals, notably the UK with its Cadbury Committee, the USA Business Roundtable reports on corporate governance and other initiatives such as the Vienot report in France and the Peters committee in the Netherlands.

The OECD had commissioned a report from a group of private sector leaders, chaired by Ira Millstein, from the USA, to consider whether there were any common themes to the reform agenda in OECD countries, and whether there was a need to develop policy guidance in the area of corporate governance. The Business Sector Advisory Group (BSAG) included opinion leaders in corporate governance from leading OECD member countries: Sir Adrian Cadbury from the UK, Michel Albert of France, Dieter Feddersen of Germany and Isikio Taikkei from Japan. They met, discussed, debated and had public consultations over an 18-month period, producing a short report focusing upon the common ground between the very different corporate governance regimes represented in the BSAG.

The group concluded that the purpose of corporate governance reform in each market was the same: to improve access to capital and promote competitiveness. In other words, the group articulated the business case for corporate governance at the level of the firm. The group also concluded that regardless of the different structures, traditions and legal frameworks in their countries, an effective corporate governance system had to reflect four underlying principles: transparency, accountability, fairness and responsibility. The principles reflected the focus upon the need to access capital and promote competitiveness, not to conform to any particular standard or form in corporate governance.

At the time this was a radical conclusion, as until that point much of the debate on convergence in international standards focused around the rivalry between the Anglo-American model versus the insider-orientated systems of Germany, France and Japan. The idea that form was less important than function relieved a burden from the reform debate. The idea that function would reflect four underlying principles and that this would be the focus of the conversion, rather than an individual model, was also radical and set the stage for moving away from the stale debate that had gone back and forth over two decades about the merits of different systems.

This breakthrough also allowed OECD as an inter-governmental think tank to consider developing guidance for its members as to how the four principles could be put into practice.

The Asia crisis had prompted a rethink in the development community which had viewed the twin policies of privatization and liberalization as the panacea to the need for sustained economic growth worldwide. For development institutions such as the World Bank the message was clear. Having unleashed the fosrces of the market, some means of taming the corporation would be needed to protect developing countries vulnerable to economic crisis and ensure that the newly liberalized capital markets were directed within an agreed system of minimum rules of the game. The Financial Stability Forum was the G7's response, and one of their first initiatives was to agree that the world needed to agree upon minimum standards and codes for critical elements of the world's integrated capital markets. Of the twelve standards and codes that were agreed, three related to the private sector: accounting and auditing, insolvency and corporate governance.

All three were intimately related. The World Bank and IMF were charged with carrying out country assessments to identify strengths and weaknesses benchmarked against international guidelines in each area, which were intended to shore up the International Financial Architecture. Again, the international community turned to the OECD's Principles of Corporate Governance as the benchmark.

The wide range of international effort is an impressive development over a relatively short period. The initiatives under way show innovation in the face of tough resistance and progress with scarce resources. In political environments where vested interests are strong, and capacity is weak, notably in the professions, such as directors, accounting and audit and investors, who can take the governance agenda forward, there has been marked progress.

As the international corporate governance agenda has moved forwards, the question of standards has been at the centre. Given the international variety of circumstances, of objectives, of corporate forms, of history and tradition, how and when could there be a convergence of standards on corporate governance?

The recent experience of developing markets has shown that there is an intelligent adaptation process at work, where the standards devised and promoted by the international community are being considered, and integrated into local circumstances, but emphasis has been upon the adaptation, not adoption, process. For developing markets where institutions are weak, markets are not open, law and regulation are untested or unwritten, vested interests prevail, the challenges of corporate governance reform are immense. The achievements of the groups making progress are all the more impressive for that.

The developing regions are aware that there will not be any second prize in the race to attract capital, especially domestic investors, and they cannot expect markets to be more indulgent about their problems, or forgiving of their difficulties. The 2002 Investor Opinion Survey carried out by McKinsey in cooperation with the Global Corporate Governance Forum showed investors marking the progress of developing countries with the same standards as developed countries. If an investor can put money into Brazil, the UK or Indonesia's power sector, then the same rules apply: accounting standards, board composition, shareholder protections, all matter. If the business environment is tough or corrupt, then these may matter even more.

The prize is access to capital – developing countries are taking the international framework of best practice and adapting it to local circumstances. The potential to improve access to capital is proving to be a powerful incentive for the reformers, who have had to learn difficult lessons along the way about how to implement corporate governance reform in the face of tough local conditions. That experience is now being shared across borders through the Global Corporate Governance Forum's regional and international networks, and associated series of roundtables and related forms which now cover the main regions of developing and emerging markets: Asia, Latin America, Africa, Caribbean, Eurasia, South Eastern Europe and Russia, with a number of country workshops having started in the Middle East.

The crafting of the rules was done in more amenable circumstances. The OECD Principles of Corporate Governance, now adopted as the international standard, were drafted by countries where resources are plentiful, the rule of law can be taken for granted, and capacity is plentiful. For the developing world none of this can be assumed. These countries are having to tackle the corporate governance agenda without the institutions, professions or democratic processes which make reform manageable. The impressive range of innovation, commitment, effort and risk-taking in reform across the developing world shows that change is possible, but difficult. If the promise of developing an international financial architecture is to be realized then these countries need to be provided with the support they deserve. Likewise, developing countries need to be given a seat at the table in deciding the global international standards and codes that shape financial flows, to ensure relevance and ownership of international standards. The OECD's decision to invite developing countries into the review discussion of their Principles of Corporate Governance is an important precedent.

Dialogue is important, but ultimately, talk must lead to action. A pressing need in every market has been to develop the pool of independent and competent directors to serve on the boards of companies. This is a critical element in the reform process. Law, regulation, best practice guidelines, will come to nothing if directors are not qualified and confident to carry out their professional role. The question developing countries face is: how can we provide the professional training and support that directors need in meeting their responsibilities? To help address the need for practical advice in corporate governance reform, the Global Corporate Governance Forum brought together representatives from leading organizations in 17 countries into an international peer review group, which provided the experience, model documents and advice on how to build an organization to promote director professionalism. The result is a toolkit, which was launched at the OECD high-level working meeting and consultation in Paris in November 2003 and is already being used in more than a dozen developing and developed countries worldwide.

The Forum commissioned the UK Institute of Directors' international team as consultants for this project. They played a key role in putting the toolkit together, and gave generously of their time and experience, both personally and for the UK IoD.

I am delighted that Chris and Kerrie are continuing their research in the field of international corporate governance. The publication of this collection marks a milestone in corporate governance thinking by using a common framework to describe the state of corporate governance laws and practices amongst a large and varied group of countries across the globe. I am sure that this book will be a valuable resource for the growing international community concerned with corporate governance.

Anne Simpson
September 2004

Anne Simpson

Anne Simpson is the former manager of the Secretariat at the Global Corporate Governance Forum which was founded by the World Bank and OECD to support developing and emerging markets in their corporate governance reform efforts. The Forum's Private Sector Advisory Group brings together leaders in corporate governance reform from the business sector worldwide with an investor taskforce whose members represent global assets of over $3 trillion. Prior to joining the World Bank in 1999, Anne was a joint managing director of corporate governance specialists Pensions and Investment

Research Consultants Ltd, based in London, during which time she served as a member of the Ad Hoc Taskforce which advised the OECD on the development of its Principles of Corporate Governance. She is the author of a number of publications on corporate governance, including (with Jonathan Charkham) *Fair Shares: the future of shareholder power and responsibility*, Oxford University Press, 1999.

Additional Acknowledgements

We would like to express our sincere thanks to everyone who has contributed to this book including: Valerie Church, Karen Jones, Anna Burmajster, Alexandra Jungk, Tammy Nicholls, Marieta Alexis and Roger Glanville.

Collating the material from around the world, writing and editing this book has been an interesting undertaking. We would particularly like to thank our friends, colleagues and associates participating in national, regional and international corporate governance organizations and networks such as the Global Corporate Governance Forum, Commonwealth Association for Corporate Governance, the Organisation for Economic Co-operation and Development, the World Bank and the International Finance Corporation.

Introduction

Over recent years, a series of high-profile companies have experienced spectacular collapses in their share prices and substantially eroded market and public confidence. Behind the Enron, Worldcom and Parmalat headlines have been the same basic story: bad governance.

Today, there are renewed calls for improved integrity and oversight of management, greater use of internal and external audit functions, higher levels of disclosure and transparency and greater engagement with institutional investors.

This book emanated from the recognition that there is not yet a definitive guide on corporate governance on a country-by-country level. There have been some excellent studies focused on selective groups such as the European Commission's *Comparative Study of Corporate Governance Codes Relevant to the European Union and its Member States* (2002) and the OECD's *Regional Roundtable Corporate Governance White Papers*. However, there still does not appear to be a single reference guide providing consistent information enabling the reader to compare regimes on a truly international scale.

The chapters have been developed by over thirty contributors who have kindly provided expert opinion and practical perspectives of corporate governance in their respective countries. Each chapter follows a consistent format covering key issues with useful contacts and recommendations for further reading. The key sections outlined in each chapter are as follows:

- corporate structure and ownership;
- legal framework;
- legal, regulatory and institutional bodies;
- board structure;
- codes, standards and good practice guidelines;
- disclosure and transparency;
- shareholder rights and stakeholder relations; and
- director development activity.

Corporate Structure and Ownership

For many developed countries, ownership patterns have changed dramatically over the past decade with less individual share ownership, increased foreign investments and more collective institutional shareholding, such as those from pension funds and insurance companies. In many developing countries the level of government control within the corporate sector is a significant factor. For example, there is heavy state influence in South Africa where state-owned enterprise control around a quarter of the country's capital stock.

Legal Framework

Most countries rely on a combination of legislative, regulatory and self-regulatory processes underpinning the corporate governance framework. Many have implemented appropriate legal and regulatory mechanisms to suit business, political and cultural norms but the level of enforcement of such mechanisms differ greatly. In lesser-developed countries, one of the biggest obstacles is lack of enforcement through an effective regulatory system. In most countries, few legal actions have been pursued through the court system and few of the regulators have taken action against companies that have failed to comply with minimum listing rule requirements.

In more developed markets, the US Sarbanes–Oxley Act 2002 (SOX), which extends to companies with a listing in the US, is having a dramatic effect. SOX was drafted within a short period of time largely in response to the Enron and Worldcom scandals. It imposes criminal sanctions on Chief Executive Officers and Chief Financial Officers who knowingly sign off false financial statements. As a consequence, any company listed in the US is faced with increased administrative costs to comply with SOX. There is concern that the consequences of increased legislation will deter some companies from listing – or encourage others to de-list. That said, SOX has encouraged a move to enhance transparency as a needed response to corporate scandals for the benefit of companies and shareholders alike.

In the UK the current debate is focused on the draft regulations for an Operating and Financial Review (OFR) which the Department of Trade and Industry plan to make mandatory for all publicly listed companies from 1 January 2005. The OFR is intended to meet EU directives and is another call for improved transparency – this time in relation to strategy and performance.

Legal, Regulatory and Institutional Bodies

International bodies, governments, financial institutions, public and private sector bodies are encouraging corporate governance debate and spearheading initiatives on a national, regional and global scale. Better regulatory and non-regulatory corporate governance frameworks and enforcement mechanisms are being implemented through tougher company legislation and non-mandatory Corporate Governance Codes.

An emphasis on director professionalism is increasing the role of national Institutes of Directors – the IoD in the UK has over 53,000 members and the number of directors undertaking corporate governance courses have doubled over the last two years. Today, the IoD model is replicated in many countries around the world to assist corporate governance reform. This proliferation has led the IoD in the UK to co-operate with other leading bodies to create a Global Director

Development Circle (GDDC). This aims to be the internationally recognized body for organizations aiming to meet the development needs of directors through research, education, dialogue and advocacy.

Board Structure

Much of the debate surrounding corporate governance relate to issues such as the separation of the role of the chairman and the chief executive officer, the establishment of audit, remuneration and nomination committees and the increased number of independent non-executive directors on the board.

Today there is increased scrutiny on the role and effectiveness of board directors – both executive and non-executive. Whilst global recommendations for an increased number of independent non-executive directors is widely accepted, this is accompanied with concerns over the availability of individuals who fulfil new 'independence' criteria. On top of this, added time pressure and increased threats of litigation are deterring high quality candidates from taking board positions.

Codes, Standards and Good Practice Guidelines

There is a growing proliferation of national codes, standards and guidelines. These are often loosely based on the OECD Principles and are designed to promote the importance of properly functioning boards of directors. In some cases, the development of national codes has followed a crisis in the corporate or banking sector. In others, there has been more general recognition of the need to assist legislative and regulatory authorities in their corporate governance reform efforts.

The development of a national code is often initiated by government through a committee – as in the case of the UK's Combined Code of Corporate Governance. In other countries, it is entirely private-sector led. The 1992 and 2002 King reports, which outlined the standards for South Africa, were instigated by the Institute of Directors of Southern Africa. The King Committee was chaired by the former judge and businessman Mervyn King and was made up of businessmen, lawyers, accountants, auditors, company secretaries and regulators, among others.

Disclosure and Transparency

Increasingly, international developments are influencing accounting standards and auditing. Auditor competency regarding how they conduct their duties in relation to non-audit services is highlighting a trend for more training in this area.

There is general consensus for more transparency in areas such as internal audit, control and risk management. This extends the need for improvements in non-financial disclosure particularly in relation to areas of corporate social responsibility.

Shareholder Rights and Stakeholder Relations

In many countries, particularly in the UK and the US, institutional investors are becoming increasingly active and influencing board decisions in areas such as directors' remuneration, nomination and service contracts. There is far less shareholder influence in companies based in developing countries. In many situations majority shareholders with a high degree of control through family holdings, have a significant effect on minority shareholder rights. Often controlling shareholders can extract private benefits from a company at the expense of other shareholders who can do little to stop frequent abuse. Many of these countries are now using the OECD Principles of Corporate Governance as a guide for improving the rights and equitable treatment of shareholders.

Director Development Activity

There is growing emphasis upon the effectiveness in which boards conduct their duties in directing management performance for improved shareholder value. Key to this process is the professionalism in which directors utilise their attributes, experience and knowledge in the boardroom. Consequently there is a growing impetus to improve the standards of individual director and board performance through education, certification and evaluation with national Directors' Institutes delivering training programmes.

This book recognizes that 'one size does not fit all' and seeks to emphasize the development needs of countries at various stages of economic development. For the purpose of this book we have used the World Bank definitions of lesser-developed, developing and developed regions. The book aims to provide a relevant and up-to date reference and to this end we hope that it is found useful by those who are interested in the key issues surrounding corporate governance.

Kerrie Waring and Chris Pierce
September 2004

Part 1

Developed
Countries

Australia

1

Table 1.1

Population	20 million (2002)
Gross National Income (GNI)	US $386 billion (2002)
GNI per capita	US $19,740 (2002)
Total number of companies	1 million (approx)
Number of companies listed on the Stock Exchange	1,500 (approx, Australian Stock Exchange)
Market capitalization	US $35.4 billion (2001)
Key corporate laws	● Corporations Act (2001)
Key corporate governance codes	● Australian Stock Exchange listing rules and guidance notes (2003)
	● Australian Securities and Investment Commission guidance notes

1.1 Corporate Structure and Ownership

There are approximately one million registered companies in Australia. This figure includes all private or proprietary companies, approximately 1,500 public companies listed on the Australian Stock Exchange (ASX) and other public but non-listed corporate entities.

Australia also has a new form of company that is specifically designed to create greater flexibility for small businesses, being the one-person (one director/one shareholder) company introduced by the Corporations Law Simplification Act of 1995. Unlike many of the other legal forms for conducting a business, corporations or companies are regulated in Australia on a national basis under the Corporations Act 2001.

Australian listed companies generally have a unitary board structure with a balance of executive and non-executive directors and a separate chief executive and chairman. The composition of Australian corporate boards varies somewhat between corporate forms (eg large public listed companies, government enterprises and small private companies, including one-person companies). However, the recent focus on local and international corporate collapses has led to a refocusing on 'best practice' for board structure, composition and corporate governance generally.

It is widely recognized that the underlying best practice principles of good corporate governance generally apply to all corporate forms. As such there has been a degree of convergence and harmonization across corporate forms in this area. The nature of boards and how they operate in Australia is expected to continue to change. This is a positive process of continual improvement to create and sustain an environment to optimize performance, create shareholder value and protect the assets of the enterprise.

1.2   Legal Framework

Australia operates under a federal system having six states and two territories, all with their own governments, in addition to the Commonwealth Government of Australia.

The role of the states and territories vis-à-vis the Commonwealth government, courts and regulators is complex and has recently been challenged constitutionally in the High Court of Australia. As a result, individual states' powers over corporations (traditionally the role of the states and territories under the Australian Constitution) have been referred to the Commonwealth, resulting in the enactment of the Corporations Act 2001. Whilst this piece of federal legislation is the primary legislation regulating companies and their directors and officers, it is important to be aware that a range of other federal and state legislation also impacts upon companies and their directors and officers. Some examples of these other areas of legislation include the Trade Practices Act, environmental laws, occupational health and safety, equal opportunity, taxation and privacy. In addition, the Commonwealth Criminal Code that came into effect on 15 December 2001 places a premium on corporate legal compliance. Risk management and corporate compliance are now central features of the organization of a company and the conduct of its directors and officers.

Australia operates under a common law system that entails courts interpreting legislation in particular factual circumstances to develop a body of precedent or common law. Judges interpret previous cases in Australia, and increasingly from overseas, in a constant process of review and adaptation. The list of federal and state legislation, rules and guidelines affecting directors and their companies is ever increasing and constantly changing. Not only are the regulatory settings constantly reviewed by the courts at common law, but also the legislative settings are continually being reviewed and amended by the federal, state and territory parliaments of Australia.

Possibly as a reaction to some of the corporate excesses in Australia during the 1980s, the 1990s in Australia saw a sustained period of legislative amendment, with an emphasis on economic outcomes:

- *The Corporate Law Reform Program Act 1999* introduced a statutory business judgement rule, rewrote many of the provisions about directors' duties, revolutionized the rules on takeovers and fundraising, and clarified some issues about accounting standards and the rules generated by accounting standards setting bodies.

- *The Financial Services Reform Act 2001* introduced standardized regulation for all people and companies that deal in financial products, or that give investment advice.

- *The Corporations Law Simplifications Act 1995*, amongst many other reforms, provided for a new form of company in Australia, the one-person company consisting of one director and one shareholder, with the aim of providing greater flexibility for small businesses to incorporate in Australia.

- *The Corporate Law Economic Reform Program (CLERP)*. The program is an ongoing process of government consultation and resultant law reform. CLERP 9 and its CLERP (Audit Reform & Corporate Disclosure) Bill, 2003 is currently before the parliament with a proposed 1 July 2004 commencement date. Many of the governance issues discussed here are covered in the proposed legislation.

1.2.1 Personal Liability of Directors

The Federal Government's Corporations and Markets Advisory Committee is currently considering the personal liability of directors, whether through the common law or by statutes, and whether these potential liabilities could result in a disincentive for persons accepting or continuing to hold directorships and directors engaging in entrepreneurial but responsible risk taking. Also to be covered in the reference will be the impact of increasing director's liability on the availability of professional indemnity insurance and the consequences of rising premiums.

1.3 Legal, Regulatory and Institutional Bodies

Many of the individual stakeholder groups within Australia have developed their own sets of corporate governance principles, policies, guidelines and background papers on various specific sub-issues in governance, which are influential in setting the corporate governance agenda and determining acceptable best practice and principles.

Apart from legislative and mandatory provisions, the focus on self-regulatory, best practice codes and guidelines highlights how active the Australian corporate governance stakeholder groups and/or peak bodies are. At the same time, however, the broad spectrum of corporate governance stakeholder groups indicates the difficulties, yet importance, of getting the balance between self-regulation and external legislation and regulation right. Balancing the conformance and performance aspects of any corporate governance system is the foundation of an effective and high performance, transparent and accountable market economy.

Any discussion of the current corporate governance system in Australia would be remiss in not explicitly recognizing the vital role played by the Australian media. Australia is fortunate in having a vibrant business, and increasingly corporate governance, focused media that is highly educated, fiercely independent and investigatory in nature. The media forms a vital role in the overall corporate governance system in Australia, particularly in the areas of disclosure and accountability.

1.3.1 Australian Securities and Investments Commission (ASIC)

The Australian Securities and Investments Commission (ASIC) replaced the Australian Securities Commission on 1 July 1998 as the body responsible for not only enforcing corporate law (including the administration of the Corporations Act 2001), but also for regulating certain aspects of the insurance and superannuation industries. The ASIC has also recently taken on the role of regulating some consumer protection laws in Australia, a duty previously the domain of the Australian Competition and Consumer Commission.

1.3.2 Australian Stock Exchange (ASX)

The Australian Stock Exchange (ASX), through its listing rules, regulates the behaviour of ASX listed companies. In addition to the ASX listing rules, which are mandatory, the ASX has a suite of guidance notes to assist listed companies to comply with both the spirit and the letter of the rules.

1.3.3 Australian Institute of Company Directors (AICD)

Another source of influence in the setting of self-regulatory or voluntary corporate governance principles in Australia includes the Australian Institute of Company Directors' 'Duties and Responsibilities of Directors and Officers' (17th Edition) and 'Corporate Practices and Conduct' (3rd Edition) which was produced by a working group, chaired by Henry Bosch AO, including the:

- Australian Institute of Company Directors;
- Australian Society of Certified Practising Accountants;
- Business Council of Australia;
- Law Council of Australia (Business Law Section);
- Institute of Chartered Accountants in Australia; and the
- Securities Institute of Australia.

1.3.4   Australian Shareholders Association (ASA)

The Australian Shareholders Association has produced policy papers on corporate governance.

1.3.5   Securities Institute of Australia (SIA)

The Securities Institute of Australia has produced best practice guidelines for analysts.

1.3.6   Australasian Investor Relations Association (AIRA)

The recently formed Australasian Investor Relations Association produces guidelines on corporate governance for their constituency.

1.3.7   Standards Australia (Stds Aust)

A new development in the Australian corporate governance scene is Standards Australia's development of 'Good Governance Principles'.

1.3.8   Investment and Financial Services Association (IFSA)

The IFSA published the 'Corporate Governance Guide for Fund Managers and Corporations', known as 'The Blue Book', which is influential in the area of corporate governance.

1.4   Board Structure

1.4.1   Composition

In order to achieve diversity and to handle the increasing workload (especially with the increasing use of committees with a majority or totality of independent non-executive directors) the issue of total board size becomes crucial. The 'Boards of Directors Study in Australia and New Zealand 2002' shows that both the median and average board size across its entire sample stood at 7 directors. Fifty-two per cent of the companies sampled for the study had between 4 and 7 directors, whereas only 5 per cent had fewer than 4 directors and 10 per cent had 12 or more directors. Of the top 50 listed companies 38 per cent have 12 or more directors. The larger the company by revenue, the larger the board size. These statistics have been relatively static in Australia for many years but an overall reduction in board size can be noted over decades.

The prevailing trend is to appoint more non-executive directors than executive directors by a factor of almost three to one. The percentage of non-executive directors amongst top 50 listed companies is 77 per cent. The proportion of executive directors generally decreases as company revenues increase. Analysed by industry, information technology and industrial companies have boards which tend to have a higher proportion of executive directors and the finance sector tends to have the lowest proportion of executive directors on their boards.

1.4.2 Independence

What is really sought is 'independence of mind', however, as a 'proxy' for this goal it is generally accepted in Australia that an independent director is a director who is not a member of management (a non-executive director) and who:

- is not a substantial shareholder of the company or an officer of, or otherwise associated directly with, a substantial shareholder of the company;

- has not, within the last three years, been employed in an executive capacity by the company, or another group member, or been a director after ceasing to hold any such employment;

- is not a principal of a professional adviser to the company, or another group member;

- is not a material supplier or customer of the company, or other group member, or an officer of, or otherwise associated directly or indirectly with, a significant supplier or customer;

- has no material contractual relationship with the company, or another group member, other than as a director of the company; and

- is free from any interest, and any business, or other relationship which could, or could reasonably be perceived to, materially interfere with the director's ability to act in the best interests of the company.

It is suggested that no director qualify as 'independent' unless the board affirmatively determines that an independent director has no material relationship with the listed entity. The board should disclose this determination in the annual report, and on a continuous disclosure basis as changes occur. A director should promptly provide in writing all information required by the board to make such a determination.

The Australian Stock Exchange (ASX) listing rules recommend that:

- Every company should have an effective board that should lead and control the company. The board should meet regularly and have a formal schedule of matters specifically reserved to it.

- There should be a procedure agreed by the board, for directors in furtherance of their duties, to take independent professional advice if necessary, at the company's expense.

- All directors should bring an independent judgement to bear on issues of strategy, performance, resources, key appointments, standards of conduct and compliance.

- All directors should commit sufficient time to their role to meet their mandate and, in this context, all directors should consider the number and nature of their directorships and calls on their time from other commitments.

- There should be a clear allocation of functions between the board and management. This should be produced in writing and should be clearly understood by both management and members of the board. It should be reviewed annually. The board's functions are both supervisory (of management) and to contribute to the performance of the company. The board should be supplied, in a timely manner, with information in a form and of a quality appropriate to enable it to discharge its duties.

- The chairman of the company should be an independent non-executive director. If the chairman is not an independent director, there should be a 'lead independent director'.

- The board should include a balance of executive and non-executive directors (including independent non-executive directors) such that no individual or small group of individuals can dominate the board's decision making. The board needs a membership with a balance of detailed knowledge of the day-to-day operations of the company, industry expertise, and members who can bring an external, questioning perspective and a diversity of experience, expertise and community connections.

- A majority of the board should be non-executive directors. At least one-third of the board should be independent non-executive directors, and there should be no fewer than two independent directors. It is recognized that smaller, regionally based or closely held companies (such as subsidiaries or companies with substantial private ownership) may have difficulty in meeting this goal because of the requirements of the majority shareholders for board representation. However, having regard to the concentration of ownership and influence in these companies, the role of the independent directors is even more important in being able to champion views different to management and ensuring proper compliance procedures in the interests of minority shareholders. It is also recognized that the balance of executive and non-executive directors on a board may also be different, depending upon the stage the company is at in its life cycle and what kind of business it is engaged in.

1.4.3   Diversity

It is recognized in Australia that good governance also dictates that a well-constituted board should reflect diversity through a broad matrix of gender, skills, age and experience. In addition to individual director characteristics, the skills mix, synergy or 'chemistry' amongst all board members is also recognized as being crucial. The challenge is to find the right balance between diversity and collegiality so as to maximize the performance of the board.

Approximately 9 per cent of all Australian directors are female; this percentage jumps to 14 per cent in top 50 companies ranked by market capitalization. It is interesting to note that for committees of boards of directors, 17 per cent of the positions are held by female directors. Of the top 100 listed companies 91.7 per cent of board seats are held by men and 8.3 per cent by women. Although this represents a substantial imbalance, it is nevertheless an improvement on the split in 1995 when 96.1 per cent of directorships were held by men and only 3.9 per cent by women. Twelve per cent of top 100 Australian companies have 2 female directors, 51 per cent have 1 female director and 37 per cent have none.

Whilst many commentators have been calling for greater diversity in age of Australian boards of directors, there does not appear a significant reduction in the average or median age of Australian directors. Again from the 'Boards of Directors Study in Australia and New Zealand 2002' the average age is between 58 and 60 years across all industries. There is very little variation in average ages of directors in Australia per industry, company revenue or location.

However, the average age of directors serving on boards varied quite significantly depending upon whether the director held an executive (approximately 52 years) or non-executive (approximately 59 years) position. The non-executive directors' higher average age reflects the fact that it is less common in Australia, compared to the USA and UK, for non-executive directors to be serving chief executive officers (CEOs) and chief financial officers (CFOs) of other listed companies. Only 10 per cent of executive directors in top 100 companies by market capitalization in Australia also held a non-executive position on the board of another top 100 company. Non-executive directors of Australian companies are more likely to be former business executives.

1.4.4 Separation of the Roles of Chairman and Chief Executive

The PRO:NED 'Non-Executive Directors and Chief Executives Remuneration and Board Governance Survey Report 2002' indicates that 89 per cent of all boards have a non-executive chairman. The trend to separate the chief executive and chairman is increasing; the 1999 figure was 85 per cent. The executive chairman is found most often in private companies, with 22 per cent having an executive chairman. Public companies were reported to have an executive chairman on 12 per cent of boards. The executive chairman is rarely found on government boards (2 per cent).

1.4.5 Committees

The percentage of boards operating in Australia with one or more board committees continues to increase, with 61 per cent of boards having one or more committees, an increase from the 1999 finding of 58 per cent and the 1995 figure of 53 per cent.

The main board committees found in Australian companies are the audit committee (often including the work of compliance and risk), remuneration/compensation committee and nomination committee. Many other specific board committees are used less frequently and include corporate governance committees, occupational health and safety committees, environment committees, restructuring committees and so on, depending on the company and the board's particular current needs.

Not all listed entities have a separately designated audit committee, as a number of companies have their entire board undertake this role. However, recent amendments to the Australian Stock Exchange listing rules will make audit committees mandatory for the top 500 listed companies.

Of the top 50 listed companies, 100 per cent had an audit committee, 84 per cent had a remuneration committee and interestingly, and rapidly increasing, 10 per cent had specifically established a corporate governance committee, indicating the priority now placed on governance issues.

1.4.6 Compensation

The determination of remuneration packages and policies for executives and non-executives is a key issue in the context of corporate governance, not only in Australia, but worldwide. The ultimate aim is to remunerate executives and non-executives in a way that ensures that they are motivated to achieve the outcomes and objectives sought by the owners/shareholders. Getting this right is fundamental to sustained company performance and shareholder returns.

When companies are owned by a diffuse group of shareholders, as is the usual case in listed companies in Australia, there can be greater scope for a misalignment of interests between both executives and non-executives, and the owners/shareholders of the company. Further complicating the challenge of structuring effective remuneration packages has been the increasingly competitive and global market for high quality executives and non-executives.

Australia has recently seen a dramatic rise in equity-based components of remuneration packages and the total size of these packages, particularly executive remuneration packages. Simultaneously the nature and structure of remuneration packages have become increasingly complex, less well understood, more generous than perhaps intended or necessary, and more open to abuse and misuse.

There has been increasing angst in the broader community about the growth in and size of, particularly, executive salaries. Unfortunately the general community, and often the business media, do not understand or differentiate between executive and non-executive remuneration issues.

1.5   Codes, Standards and Good Practice Guidelines

Corporate governance principles in Australia are derived from a diverse range of sources both international and domestic. These principles range from the mandatory to optional guidelines indicating 'good practice', and are developed by or promulgated through a range of bodies from the Organization for Economic Cooperation and Development (OECD) and the World Bank Group to Australian governments and regulators. International and local stakeholder groups, including institutional investors, industry bodies and the professions, also actively contribute to the development and refinement of corporate governance principles operating in Australia.

On the international front, the OECD's corporate governance principles and the World Bank Group, through its Global Corporate Governance Forum (GCGF), are influential. So too are the international investor groups such as the International Corporate Governance Network (ICGN) and individual players such as Calpers and Hermes. International corporate governance ratings services are becoming increasingly influential in Australia (eg Standard & Poors, Deminor and Governance Metrics International).

Australia is keen to ensure that its corporate governance framework is internationally competitive and generally in line with international 'good practice'. However, the largest influence on Australia's corporate governance principles is domestic, whilst still keeping one eye on international developments.

Of Australia's mandatory or legislative corporate governance principles, the Corporations Act 2001 takes primacy. Of Australia's quasi-legislative codes of corporate governance practice and principles, the most influential are the Australian Securities and Investments Commission guidance notes and Australian Stock Exchange listing rules and guidance notes.

Australia has a regulatory system that has the power to impose a range of obligations upon companies and their directors and officers. The regulatory bodies impacting corporate life in Australia have a spectrum of tools at their disposal to direct corporate behaviour, ranging from mandatory rules setting strict duties, responsibilities and obligations to guidance notes and 'good practice' guidelines.

An interesting recent initiative is the establishment of the Australian Stock Exchange's Corporate Governance Council, which has brought together all major stakeholders in the corporate governance debate in an effort to develop and agree on a set of best practice corporate governance standards for Australian listed companies. In attempting to focus its activities the Council has identified a number of topical issues in Australian corporate governance as follows:

- board composition and independence;
- controlling shareholders and nominee directors;
- competencies of directors;
- remuneration;
- trading policies for employees and directors;
- integrity of financial reporting;
- risk oversight and management;
- corporate code of conduct/ethics;
- shareholder participation;
- short-term versus long-term issues;
- corporate social responsibility and the triple bottom line;
- corporate governance in the public sector;
- personal liability of directors;
- insider trading.

The ASX Corporate Governance Council has developed the following corporate governance principles, saying the corporate governance framework developed by public listed companies should:

- **Respect the rights of shareholders** and facilitate the exercise of shareholder rights.

- **Make timely and balanced disclosure** of all material matters regarding the Company.
- **Safeguard integrity in financial reporting** – Include a structure to independently verify and safeguard the integrity of the Company's financial reporting.
- **Recognize and manage risk** – Establish a sound system of internal control and risk oversight and management.
- **Lay solid foundations for management and oversight** – Clearly set out the respective roles and responsibilities of board and management.
- **Promote ethical and responsible decision making** – Include mechanisms to promote ethical and responsible decision making.
- **Structure the board to add value** – Include a board of an effective composition and size to adequately discharge its responsibilities and duties.
- **Encourage enhanced performance** – Include a structure to review and encourage enhanced board and management effectiveness.
- **Remunerate fairly and responsibly** – Include a mechanism designed to ensure that the level and composition of remuneration is sufficient and reasonable and its relationship to corporate and individual performance is defined.
- **Recognize the legitimate interests of stakeholders.**

1.5.1 Corporate Governance in the Public Sector

The Uhrig Review aims to bring best practice in corporate governance to the public sector in Australia. Finally, the development by Standards Australia of a series on corporate governance aims to provide a blueprint for the development and implementation of a generic governance framework suitable for a wide range of entities, including the public sector.

1.6 Disclosure and Transparency

1.6.1 Compensation

The key focus of the debate in Australia regarding remuneration has been on disclosure, transparency and sound processes for the determination of remuneration policies. Whilst the debate on this issue in Australia has been vigorous, certain fundamental best practice principles on remuneration are clear:

- Remuneration policy should be designed in a manner that motivates recipients to pursue the long term growth and success of the company.
- There should be a clear relationship between performance and remuneration – poor performance should not be rewarded.
- No individual should be involved in directly deciding his/her own remuneration.
- Companies are expected to disclose sufficient information on the remuneration of board members and key executives for investors to properly assess the costs and benefits of the remuneration plans and particularly the contribution of incentive schemes, such as stock options schemes, to performance.

Given the importance of transparency and disclosure in this area, it is generally agreed that the following information should be disclosed in a company's annual report:

- The broad structure and objectives of remuneration policies and their relationship to company performance.
- The quantum and components of remuneration for each of the highest paid (non-director) executives and of all directors. All monetary and non-monetary components of remuneration, including but not restricted to salary, fees, non-cash benefits, bonuses, profit share, superannuation contribution, other payments in relation to retirement from office and the value of shares issued and options granted, should be disclosed.
- Statements on the expected outcomes of the remuneration structures.
- The economic impact of the remuneration strategies and the cost to shareholders. Including, but not restricted to, earnings per share after dilution, and the proportion of future shareholder value that equity-based compensation plans would provide to executives and their employees.

Remuneration disclosures should be made in one section of the annual report using tabular formats, with appropriate explanatory notes, and obviously must reflect the appropriate accounting standards. This would provide shareholders with meaningful information on the application of the board's remuneration policies in the context of the performance of the company.

Whilst there is not clear support for shareholders voting on remuneration policies, there is support for the 'remuneration report to shareholders' to be a standard item on the agenda of annual general meetings.

Companies should also publicly disclose executive employment agreements, preferably immediately following their entering into force, and certainly no later than their company's next general meeting. Disclosure should include a summary of the main elements and terms of the agreement, including termination provisions.

A final disclosure issue currently being debated in Australia is whether executives should give advance public notice of their intention to dispose of equity holdings in the company. In this regard, it is generally agreed that:

- companies structure remuneration packages to appropriately motivate and retain executives, including the use of appropriate vesting periods for equity holdings;

- all listed companies have in place clearly articulated and publicized trading windows, during which time shareholders will be aware that trading on the part of executives and employees of the company is likely to take place;

- listed companies establish policies for the board to be advised of all material sales by executives and for the board to determine whether the intended sale is driven by a disclosable event, and if this is the case to appropriately disclose the executive's intention to sell.

Shareholders clearly have an interest in potential equity dilution resulting from compensation practices. Equity-based remuneration should be made through plans previously approved by shareholders.

It is generally well accepted in Australia that, in order to achieve 'good practice' in the area of remuneration, all publicly listed companies should have a remuneration committee. The remuneration committee should be a committee of the board and be accountable to the board.

The role and responsibilities of remuneration committees include:

- Being responsible for developing policies on executive remuneration and of setting the remuneration packages of executive officers in relation to the performance objectives of the company.

- Establishing a transparent framework for developing remuneration policies and agreeing packages.

- Being responsible for all aspects of executive remuneration, including all components of remuneration, terms of contracts, retention and termination agreements.

- Exercising independent judgement in determining types and levels of compensation.

- Taking responsibility for ensuring that remuneration policies are fair and reasonable in the context of attracting, retaining and motivating executive officers in light of the company's financial position.

- The remuneration committee should have its own charter. The charter should make clear the committee's purpose and responsibilities, and outline the processes for regular (annual) review of the remuneration committee.

- The remuneration committee should seek external professional advice as needed and should select and appoint appropriate consultants.

- The chairman of the board should ensure that the remuneration committee has direct access to independent external advice.

- The remuneration committee should comprise wholly independent non-executive directors experienced in remuneration matters, or at the least, members with the capacity to make well-informed decisions with reference to recent developments in remuneration policy.

In most instances, it is highly likely that an appropriate remuneration package will involve a balance between cash and equity-based pay and will involve short-term and long-term performance incentives, with a significant component related to long-term performance incentives. It is not appropriate here to provide indications of what is an appropriate proportion of remuneration to be paid as cash or equity stock, as different companies face different challenges and objectives at different points in time. Remuneration packages need to reflect these unique circumstances and the diverse goals of companies.

There is widespread consensus in Australia that a significant part of executive remuneration should be linked to performance. The success of performance-based schemes in stimulating performance depends less on the type of scheme chosen than on the design of the scheme, the targets adopted and the measurement and quantitative relationship between performance targets and compensation. Incentive schemes should be designed around appropriate performance benchmarks that measure relative performance and provide rewards for materially improved company performance.

Another hot issue in the remuneration area in Australia at present is the question of termination payments. Termination payment arrangements should be agreed in advance, including detailed provisions regarding payments in case of early termination, except for removal for misconduct. Termination agreements should be publicly disclosed. Agreements should include a clear articulation of performance expectations, so as to avoid subjective debates on the matter at a later time. Whilst companies must take into account their legal and contractual obligations, termination payments should not reward poor performance.

The term of a contract should be taken into account when agreeing remuneration, including termination payments. Consideration should be given to the consequences of an appointment not working out, the costs and other impacts of early termination. The incorporation of early termination provisions, 'probation' periods or definite terms with specific early termination provisions should be considered. The combination of long terms and termination payments should not be a guarantee for executives to be paid regardless of, or indeed in spite of, performance.

As in the rest of the world, the issue of stock options and their expensing is being heavily debated in Australia currently. Since options represent a cost to shareholders, not expensing them creates a distortion. Treating one type of compensation as 'free', while expensing others, creates an uneven playing field and distorts pay practices. While the accounting treatment of options is controversial and valuation techniques difficult, the mood in Australia is generally for the expensing of stock options.

1.6.2 Audit

Audit committees are an essential mechanism in ensuring the integrity of financial reporting. They oversee the process of the audit (both internal and external) and respond to the board. The issue of whether or not all public companies should have audit committees is currently being discussed in Australia. The need for an audit committee is often decided on a cost–benefit analysis. The counter argument is that the cost of insuring the integrity of financial reporting is part of the cost of listing, and that all investors deserve the same level of integrity in reporting, irrespective of the size of listed company.

Whilst the size of some listed entities may place constraints on their ability to put in place an audit committee, all listed companies should offer the same level of integrity in reporting. It is generally agreed that the top listed entities be required to have an audit committee and all other listed entities are required either to have an audit committee or to disclose the mechanisms in place to achieve the level of integrity of reporting had an audit committee been in place. It is believed that this approach will lead to the market determining the acceptability of the mechanisms that individual listed entities put in place to enhance the integrity of their reporting.

Without compromising the overall responsibility of the board, the audit committee may be assigned a number of tasks associated with the preparation, final review and overall integrity of the reporting and auditing process. Without limiting the role of audit committees, the following list is indicative of the tasks expected:

- Auditor independence – one of the key responsibilities of the audit committee is the oversight of the independence of auditors.

- Recommendation of external auditors to the board – the audit committee should make recommendations to the board for appointing the auditor with due consideration to their independence on an ongoing basis. Such recommendations should be included in the report of the audit committee.

- Appointment criteria for auditors – a number of relevant criteria should be used to determine the appropriateness of the appointment of auditors. These criteria should ensure that the credibility and integrity of the audit process are enhanced and facilitate enhanced shareholder confidence.

- Recommendation of internal auditor to the board – it is generally recognized that listed entities benefit from an internal audit function. The audit committee should be responsible for the hiring and firing of the chief internal audit executive. The chief internal audit executive is to agree on the scope of the internal audit with the audit committee. The internal audit function must be independent of the external auditor.

- Ensure rotation of external audit partners – audit committees should disclose their policy and procedures in the determination and appointment of audit firms and the rotation of audit partners as often as necessary to ensure independence (no less than every five years).

- External audit and non-audit fees each financial year – the provision of non-audit services by the external audit firm gives rise to a threat to independence due to an increased risk of 'fee reliance'. The audit committee should be responsible for approving all non-audit services after having been satisfied that independence is not compromised. Each non-audit service should be considered separately and a review of the level of non-audit services, on an ongoing basis, undertaken to ensure that independence is maintained and the required disclosures are made in the financial report. Specifically, the audit committee should ensure that the following services are provided independently of the external audit service provider: record keeping; information systems design and implementation; appraisals or valuation services; actuarial services, internal audits, management and human resource services; broker/dealer and investment banking services; legal or expert services related to audit services and other services the board determines to be impermissible.

- Internal audit and other non-audit fees each financial year – the internal auditor must not provide operational (non-audit services) or external audit services to the company for which they are internal auditor. The audit committee should be the final arbiter on provision of non-audit services to ensure that independence is maintained in appearance and fact.

- Performance assessment of internal and external auditors – it is part of the oversight function of the audit committee to assess the performance of all of the aspects of the audit of financial reports.

Such performance assessments of the internal and external auditors, including independence, should be included in the audit committee report.

- Committee reporting – the audit committee should present a balanced report to the board of directors as a sub-committee of that board. The report should be available in full at the AGM and on shareholder request. A summary report should be included in the annual report. The report should contain all matters relevant to the role and responsibilities of the audit committee, including results from the work of internal and external auditors, reviews of performance, recommendations for changes to the annual report, review of risk management procedures and the assessment of the independence of the external auditors.

In order to meet their delegated responsibilities and report to the board, the audit committee must be given certain rights:

- access to internal and external auditors without management being present;
- access to management – there need to be clear reporting lines established between the audit committee and management. This would allow the audit committee to seek information and answers directly from management, without going to the board. Audit committees should be given all rights necessary to perform their role, including access to management and the right to seek answers and explanations.

In order to enable the integrity of financial reporting, the audit committee should be of sufficient size, independence, and technical expertise and meet often enough to undertake its roles and responsibilities. The following are seen as minimum requirements:

- Audit committee charter – the audit committee should have a clearly defined charter within which it operates, setting out the role and responsibilities, composition, structure and membership requirements, and should be assigned the necessary power and ability in order to achieve its charter.
- Independence of audit committee members – the independence of the audit committee from the board, the CEO/CFO and the auditor is vital to the integrity of the audit process and facilitates

the oversight of both the internal and external audit functions. It is increasingly being regarded as 'good practice' that all members of the audit committee be independent non-executive directors.

- Size of audit committee – it is considered 'good practice' that all audit committees should have at least three members and, beyond that, should determine the most appropriate size necessary to meet the role and responsibilities assigned to it.

- Technical expertise – audit committee members should have the technical expertise to undertake their duties, without being so closely related to the preparation and audit functions that their objectivity is affected. It is generally recognized that 'good practice' supports the need for at least one member to have 'financial expertise' and all members to be 'financially literate'. 'Financially literate' is broadly equated to the ability to read and understand basic financial statements, whilst 'financial expertise' ordinarily comprises past employment experience, or certification in finance or accounting.

- Frequency of audit committee meetings – a balance should be achieved between the effective and efficient operation of the audit committee, and the cost constraints of the entity. The committee should, however, meet as often as is required to meet the roles and responsibilities as defined in the charter, but at least twice a year is seen as a minimum.

Clearly, the needs of investors are far greater than the mere presentation of the financial position at a fixed point in time, and the past performance of the entity. As such, additional reporting by management is required as to the direction and activities of the entity. Currently the Corporations Act 2001 in Australia requires the financial report to include a review of operations and activities in the directors' report, being the Management Discussion and Analysis section. The current feeling is that this form of reporting falls well short of the needs of the shareholders and potential investors for decision making. It is hoped that the current Corporate Law Economic Reform Program (CLERP) will address these deficiencies by reforming the law by adopting the approach in the 'Guide to Review of Operations and Financial Condition'.

Sign-off of accounts by the chief executive officer (CEO)/chief financial officer (CFO) – public accountability is based on the principle of making those responsible for decisions and outcomes account for their actions. The ultimate responsibility for the decisions that impact the performance, position and cash flow of a company must lie with the directors, but some responsibility for the preparation of the financial report must rest with the principal accounting officer. Currently in Australia there is no formal recognition of the responsibility of the CEO or CFO for the financial reports, even though the board clearly relies on them in determining compliance with accounting standards, presentation of a true and fair view and ensuring the necessary information systems and internal control structures are in place. It should, however, be noted that many entities in Australia have internal processes for management sign-off in place. It is currently being recommended that formal CEO/CFO sign-off be introduced. This proposition is gaining increasing acceptance. Such CEO/CFO sign-off should be included in the financial statements and should include certification that:

- financial statements and the notes thereto are prepared in accordance with accounting standards;
- financial statements present a true and fair view, and where they don't, adequate further disclosure has been provided to present a true and fair view;
- the information system is adequate for the financial reporting needs of the entity;
- the internal control structure is in place and is operating effectively and efficiently in all material respects;
- all material matters necessary for board consideration were provided to the board in a timely manner.

The integrity of financial reporting is not just about following the rules, but presenting a full picture to the shareholders that allows them to make their own decisions. To this end all reporting, financial or otherwise, should be balanced and understandable.

In the area of reporting, Australia's listed companies operate under a continuous disclosure regime, as well as the more common, periodic reporting regime of other jurisdictions. Publicly listed companies in Australia must report, as soon as possible to the Australian Stock Exchange, any matter that would reasonably be expected to have a material impact on their company's market price. As of 1 January

2003 several new Australian Stock Exchange listing rules in relation to continuous disclosure, corporate governance and periodic financial reporting apply to listed entities. Briefly, these amendments include:

- Enhancement of the continuous disclosure obligations in relation to disclosure as a result of market speculation. There is now a duty to avoid a 'false market'. This approach reflects that taken under the federal government's latest stage of corporate law reform, Corporate Law Reform Program, which also requires listed entities to respond to external speculation (eg media speculation).

- In related amendments, the Australian Stock Exchange has modified the relevant limb of the carve-out provisions, which allow corporations not to continuously disclose information which is, amongst other things, confidential, to provide that information must be confidential and the Australian Stock Exchange must be satisfied that confidentiality has in fact been maintained.

The new listing rules will have their most significant impact on pre-transaction discussions where details of a proposed transaction are leaked before the transaction is announced. Given the changes, it is now very important for listed companies to review their continuous disclosure procedures and carefully consider their position where:

- media reports or market speculation, in relation to a transaction involving the listed entity, creates a 'false market' in the entity's securities;

- the Australian Stock Exchange queries the entity in relation to a potential 'false market' situation;

- the entity or Australian Stock Exchange determines that a correcting release must be made to correct a 'false market' situation;

- the entity considers a trading halt is more appropriate than disclosure, to correct a 'false market'; or

- the entity considers they may have 'lost' confidentiality in relation to a material disclosure item, for example where an 'intelligent guess' has been made by a media speculator in relation to a prospective transaction.

1.6.3 Risk Oversight and Management

Risk is an integral part of business, but needs to be commensurate with an adequate level of return. Therefore, risk oversight and management are not just about accountability and the mitigation of hazards, but about identifying and optimizing opportunities to create value. Risk management is integral to strategic planning and much of its responsibility lies with management as opposed to the board. However, certain aspects of risk oversight and management are relevant to the board, including:

- maintaining a sound system of internal control;
- approving the risk management framework (including the risk profile);
- defining risk parameters for management, based on the company's willingness or 'appetite' to take risk;
- clarifying thresholds such as 'material' and 'significant' that dictate when board participation is required;
- reviewing and disclosing the effectiveness of internal controls.

Disclosure of the board's policy on risk oversight and management that addresses these points can assist investors/shareholders to make more informed investment decisions, based on a risk profile that they are prepared to accept.

1.6.4 Corporate Codes of Conduct/Ethics

It is generally agreed to be 'good practice' that the CEO, CFO and any employee, officer or director who has the opportunity to influence the integrity, strategy and operation of the business and its financial performance needs to be bound by a corporate code of conduct. The company needs to have an internal review mechanism in relation to compliance with and effectiveness of their code. The company needs to have a policy in place for waivers of the code and disclosure of any actual waivers given. Full disclosure of the waiver policy and waivers will inhibit casual waivers and ensure waivers are accompanied by sufficient controls to protect the company.

1.6.5 Trading Policies for Employees and Directors

In view of Australia's insider trading laws, current public perceptions and the need to build trust between investors and management, all public companies should have a trading policy in place and provide clear guidance to their directors and management about their obligations under the law. The purpose of the policy should be clearly stated and provide for appropriate steps to be taken to ensure that all directors and employees are aware of, and fully understand, the prohibitions under law and their obligations under it.

Who are the 'insiders' for the purpose of the policy? The board of directors, the chief executive officer and chief financial officer should all be regarded as persons who are likely to possess 'inside' information, and therefore are the persons who should have appropriate restrictions applied to them under the company's trading policy. In addition, those persons who are closely involved in material transactions that the company may enter into should also have restrictions placed on them from time to time, where appropriate. Beyond that, it should be left to companies themselves to determine which of their other employees should be restricted from trading, based on the size of the company and the nature of its activities. The trading policy should clearly identify the employees or groups of employees who are restricted from trading (the 'designated employees').

What limits should the policy place on trading? Some companies explicitly prohibit insiders from engaging in frequent and regular trading for short-term benefits, ie employees must not actively 'deal' in the company's security stock.

It is common practice in Australia for companies to introduce either 'trading windows', where there is a general restriction on trading except for certain specified periods (eg immediately after the publication of financial results), or 'black-outs', where there is no general restriction but a period of no trading might be imposed to coincide with market sensitive events (eg the company is in negotiations for a strategic acquisition).

Australian 'good practice' in this area is that the trading policy should require designated employees to provide notification of all intended trading to an appropriate, senior member of the company, eg the chairman of the board. The policy should identify the person who will review the notification of proposed trading by designated employees, and also who will review the notification of proposed trading by the chairman (or other senior company member). The trading policy should require subsequent confirmation of trading that has occurred.

Use of 'trading windows' and 'black-outs' is encouraged, but it should be left to the companies themselves to decide which (if either) of these should be adopted, having regard to the size of the company and the nature of its activities. If 'trading windows' or 'black-outs' are adopted, full details of their application and the relevant times should be set out in the policy.

The trading policy should state clearly if it includes any discretion to be used in respect of trading by designated employees in specific circumstances (eg financial hardship), and full details of the circumstances where the discretion may be used and the basis upon which it is applied.

Trading policies should disclose whether or not the company prohibits designated employees from trading in financial products issued over the company's securities by third parties or trading in associated products. If so, the trading policy should clearly state the level of trading and the timing of disclosure of such trading to shareholders. Finally the trading policy should require the maintaining of a register of trades conducted by designated employees, for the purpose of monitoring adherence to the policy, and disclosure should be made in each annual report of the aggregate total of securities held by designated employees.

The Australian Corporations Act requires an annual report to contain details of, amongst other things, the relevant interests of directors in securities of the company or related bodies corporate, or contracts under which directors may acquire securities.

1.6.6 Insider Trading

The federal government's corporations and markets advisory committee is also currently considering submissions on its insider trading discussion paper, which may well result in recommendations to the government to amend the legislative settings with regard to this area of corporate governance.

1.6.7 Other Issues

Whilst Australia is literally an island, it is not metaphorically an island in the field of governance. Regional and wider global activities and initiatives will certainly impact Australia in the near future. Some of these initiatives and activities which could have an impact on the Australian corporate governance scene include:

- the adoption of International Accounting Standards;
- the impact on Australian companies listed in the United States of the Sarbanes–Oxley Act 2002 and other legislative and stock exchange listing rule amendments;
- the outcome of the UK Higgs Report into non-executive directors;
- the OECD's corporate governance principles;
- the activities of the Global Corporate Governance Forum;
- the rise of corporate governance ratings services (eg Standard & Poors, Deminor and Governance Metrics International);
- the continuing rise in the power of the institutional investor, both domestic and international, and their peak associations such as the International Corporate Governance Network (ICGN), in the international field, and the Investment and Financial Services Association (IFSA) within Australia.

1.7 Shareholder Rights and Stakeholder Relations

1.7.1 Participation

It has long been recognized in Australia that effective corporate governance relies on the active participation of all the various stakeholder groups. Much effort has been invested in attempting to increase the participation of shareholders, both institutional and especially individual, through law reform, guidance notes and education campaigns.

Some specific areas that are currently being reviewed in this area are:

- simplification of notices of and resolutions for general meetings;
- short form notices of meetings;
- guidelines for bundled resolutions;
- electronic communication of material on meetings to members and beneficial shareholders, fund managers and investment managers;
- voting at general meetings by proxy and otherwise, including a simplified model proxy form;

- the transmission of proxies electronically;
- the ability to vote early at meetings;
- web-casting of general meetings;
- web-casting and telephone conferencing of foreshadowed presentations to analysts, or other presentations by the chair or company;
- electronic dissemination of annual reports.

This is a very active area of review in Australia currently; however, space limitations prohibit a more detailed analysis here. The above sections reflect the work of the seven Australian Stock Exchange Corporate Governance Council's working groups that have inputted into the Australian Stock Exchange Corporate Governance Council's 'Principles of Good Corporate Governance and Best Practice Recommendations' which were launched in March 2003.

1.7.2 Controlling Shareholders and Nominee Directors

Particular problems for good governance arise when significant shareholders are present, or are represented, on the boards of listed companies. An even more difficult situation arises when the CEO is a major shareholder. The problem has been aptly described by Henry Bosch in the following extract:

> *Since it is often possible for directors who own substantial blocks of shares personally, or who are the nominees of those who do, to present plausible and apparently objective arguments in support of their own interest, it is frequently difficult for independent directors to oppose them, particularly if they have less detailed knowledge of the company's affairs. Since independent directors often owe their positions to the controlling shareholders it is not unknown for them to suppress any misgivings they may have about arguments which happen to work in favour of the individual interests of controllers.*
>
> *Such considerations have frequently led to abuses of governance. Listed companies whose boards include nominee directors, or directors who own substantial blocks of shares, present particular risks for investors, and our legal/governance system has, as yet, done little to address the problem.*

1.7.3 Short- versus Long-term Issues

There are a myriad of intense pressures to take a short-term view in today's business world. The tenure of CEOs is falling, professional investors'/fund managers' performance periods, media immediacy, the increasingly competitive business environment, and the increasing pace of change in the business world generally and particularly the focus on short-term returns are some examples, all of which can lead to an unhealthy and unbalanced corporate approach. The tendency of the largest shareholders in corporations to be investors/traders rather than owners for the long haul can lead companies to pay less attention to long-term strategy and growth than is optimal. This in turn can be contrary to the interests of the longer-term shareholders (eg superannuation trustees and many individual shareholders). The concepts, proposed by the recent USA National Association of Corporate Directors (NACD) Blue Ribbon Commission on 'Public Trust and Private Enterprise', to establish compensation arrangements for portfolio managers that encourage a long-term rather than a short-term focus, are extremely interesting and topical.

1.7.4 Corporate Social Responsibility (CSR) and the Triple Bottom Line

The recently fashionable doctrine of 'corporate social responsibility', and particularly the notion of the 'triple bottom line', poses an emerging threat to good corporate governance which, if it lasts, could be serious. Without clear accountability, good governance is impossible. However, there can be no clear accountability unless management understands that it is accountable to the board for delivering explicitly defined results, and that its performance can be monitored and assessed; and unless the board understands that it is similarly accountable to shareholders. The sole common interest to all shareholders is the ongoing prosperity of the company, and while there can be many ways of achieving this objective and many different strategies, the creation of wealth in perpetuity is the sole final criterion.

This issue was considered by the Senate Standing Committee on Legal and Constitutional Affairs, which concluded:

> *It is the shareholders' investment that creates the company. Directors' fiduciary duties are premised on this fact and are designed to protect that investment. If company law were to impose new and at times conflicting duties (such as looking after interests which may be directly opposed to those of the corporators), directors' fiduciary duties could be weakened perhaps to the point where they would be essentially meaningless. In general, requirements aimed*

at securing responsible corporate behaviour are therefore best provided in other than company law.

This does not mean that it is in shareholders' interests for companies to disregard the environment and the societies in which they operate. On the contrary, it is always necessary, in the long-term interests of the company, to have regard to the legitimate interests of genuine stakeholders. Indeed, many opportunities for increasing short-term profit have to be subordinated for longer-term consideration. Moreover, all companies must have regard to their reputations and to their relationships with governments and the societies in which they operate and, in the present climate of opinion, this will certainly mean having some regard to environmental and social considerations – up to the point at which it ceases to be in their long-term interests to do so. However, to elevate environmental or social considerations to a par with the creation of wealth – to argue that companies have an independent social responsibility – is to undermine good governance.

Australia's legal and cultural approach to corporate governance and directors' duties is based on the shareholder rather than stakeholder model. Directors are the stewards of the owner's investments. These issues have also recently found their way into heated debates in Australia on whether companies should make political and philanthropic donations on behalf of and with their owner's money. Most owners/shareholders in Australia express the view that they invest their money in a company for that company to maximize the returns on their investment and any focus on other 'bottom lines' that do not maximize these returns is to be discouraged and could be seen as a misuse of shareholder funds in law. With regard to political and philanthropic donations many shareholders express the view that they, personally, will make the donations they feel appropriate and it is not up to the companies in which they invest to do so, except where this behaviour will increase the shareholder's returns.

Corporate social responsibility/triple bottom line and issues of sustainability are all increasing in their prominence and, with the finalization of the global reporting initiative (GRI), are set to continue as topical issues in the corporate governance landscape of Australia.

1.8   Director Development Activity

Director development is a very active field in Australia and is addressed through a number of different methods, including education, mentoring, induction programmes and so on. Similarly, the provision of these various modes of director development can be provided by a wide range of suppliers, including the companies on whose boards the directors sit, professional associations and institutes, professional advisory, regulators and market setters, the government and the media.

Given the rapid globalization of business and the boom of the Internet as an educational tool and for information and research, Australian directors have access to both Australian and international providers (eg global governance newsletters, electronic e-mail services and magazines are rapidly becoming more and more common as a mechanism for director development in Australia).

Director education and more formal training in Australia is largely provided by the Australian Institute of Company Directors' (AICD's) 'Company Director Course'. In financial year 2002/2003, the AICD's company director course attracted 1,700 students. Further, the AICD has developed a broad suite of core education and professional development courses and seminars offering basic skills training, through to advanced theory, generic through to specialized and face-to-face through to distanced learning programmes, which in total in financial year 2002/2003 attracted over 30,000 participants.

Henry Bosch AO in his contribution entitled 'The Changing Face of Corporate Governance' to the *UNSW Law Journal* volume 25 (p 282) states:

> *Development of the board consulting industry is a further indication of the increased seriousness with which corporate governance is being taken in the board room. Hundreds of companies and other organizations now seek assistance from specialists on an ad hoc or regular basis, about many aspects of their affairs, such as the role and function of the board, board composition and the recruitment of new directors and the reviews of board performance.*

> *There can be no doubt that a large number of directors are giving a great deal more thought to their functions and their effectiveness,... and there has been very considerable progress in improving Australian corporate governance, particularly in making boards conscious of their responsibilities and in making them aware that they are accountable to shareholders and must hold management accountable to them. There can also be no doubt that the process of creating awareness is accelerating and that many boards, and individual directors, are increasingly feeling competitive pressures on them to know more about governance and to make their boards perform better.*

1.8.1 Competencies of Directors

Boards should identify and report the existing skills, knowledge and experience of all directors. This should include a listing of qualifications relevant to the director's duties and responsibilities. Boards should also, at a minimum, indicate that they have:

- conducted an analysis of the skills, knowledge and characteristics required of directors specific to the company, the competitive environment, and the medium- to long-term issues relevant to the industry (to assist in this process, boards may wish to engage external consultants);

- identified and committed to processes for managing the introduction, development and maintenance of appropriate board and individual director competencies and performance assessment.

There is vigorous debate around the definition of competence and how it might be applied in expectations of director's performance. To this end, it is beneficial to clearly articulate and separate: skills, knowledge and experience (competence); and ethics, values and character (personal attributes).

It is generally agreed that the following initiatives are important to the development of 'good practice' procedures in director nomination, induction, assessment and evaluation:

- Nomination – the processes associated with the appointment and re-nomination of directors should be the role of a nomination committee. The exact composition and responsibilities of this committee may vary between boards, but the broad guiding principles of the committee should be recorded and referred to key stakeholders. The committee should have a minimum of three members and the majority should be independent directors. The committee should have a charter, which would outline its scope, composition, role, membership, attendance at meetings etc – and the board should make this charter available to shareholders. The charter should include information on the committee processes and activities that ensure board composition, including director competency and diversity in skill, is appropriate to enable the board to respond to the current and future needs and strategies of the company. The nomination committee should consider the medium-to long-term needs of the business in developing the appropriate board composition.

- Induction – the exact process may vary between boards, but there must be an effective and thorough induction procedure (it should not merely be a 'quick chat with the CEO' or 'tick the box' exercise). The induction procedure should provide the directors with a comprehensive introduction to the company to assist them to become an active and fully participative director as soon as possible. Nomination committees should be accountable for ensuring that an effective induction process occurs. Boards should have an agreed process for reviewing the efficacy of the induction process at regular intervals. The induction process should include business, operational and strategic information, access rights and protocols.

- Assessment and evaluation – assessment of the individual directors and collective board performances should occur in agreed time frames, against appropriate objectives and against both measurable and qualitative indicators. The board and each individual director should be briefed on their performance by the chair. The chair and the board performance should be reviewed by the board as a whole. The nomination committee may take responsibility for these activities to ensure consistency of objectives, with regard to competency and skill mixes and the adoption of these over time, to remain relevant to company needs. The relevant group undertaking these activities may involve external bodies regarding board members' professional development, activities or 'good practice' evaluation. If so, disclosure of this should be made.

1.9 Useful Contacts

- Australian Institute of Company Directors (AICD) – www.company directors.com.au
- Australasian Investor Relations Association (AIRA) – www.aira.org.au
- Australian Securities and Investments Commission – www.asic.gov.au

- Australian Shareholders Association (ASA) – www.asa.asn.au

- Australian Stock Exchange – www.asx.com.au

- Business Council of Australia (BCA) and its Chief Financial Officer wing – the Group of 100 – www.bca.com.au

- Certified Practicing Accountants of Australia (CPA) – www.cpaaustralia.com.au

- Chartered Secretaries Australia (CSA) – www.csaust.com

- Institute of Chartered Accountants in Australia (ICAA) – www.icaa.org.au

- Investment and Financial Services Association Limited (IFSA) – www.ifsa.com.au

- The Law Council of Australia – www.lawcouncil.asn.au

- Securities Institute of Australia (SIA) – www.securities.edu.au

- Standards Australia – www.standards.com.au

1.10   Further Reading

ASX Corporate Governance Council 'Principles of good corporate governance and best practice recommendations'

Australian Stock Exchange (2003) *Principles of good corporate governance and best practice recommendations*, ASX Corporate Governance Council

Baxt, R (2002) *Duties and Responsibilities of Directors and Officers* (17th edition), Australian Institute of Company Directors, Sydney

Bosch, H (1995) *Bosch Report: Corporate Practices and Conduct.* Product of Working Group composed of Australian Institute of Company Directors, Australian Society of Certified Practicing Accountants, Business Council of Australia, Law Council of Australia

Fichling, J and Stapledon, G (2001) *Governance in the Top 100 Companies*

Freehill Solicitors (2003) *New ASX Listing Rule Changes*, electronic client newsletter

Investment and Financial Services Association, *Corporate Governance Guide for Fund Managers and Corporations* (known as 'The Blue Book'), IFSA

Investment and Financial Services Association (1999) *A Guide for Investment Managers and Corporations* ('The Blue Book', first issued by the Australian Investment Managers' Association), third edition

Korn Ferry International (2002) *Boards of Directors Study*, Korn Ferry International, Sydney

Senate Standing Committee on Legal and Constitutional Affairs, Parliament of Australia (1989) *Company Directors' Duties: report on the social and fiduciary duties and obligations of company directors*, Parliament of Australia

Standards Australia:

- *Good Corporate Principles*
- *Fraud and Corporate Control*
- *Organizational Codes of Conduct*
- *Corporate Social Responsibilities*
- *Whistle-Blowing Systems for Organizational Systems*

Uhrig Review Report

1.10.1   AICD Publications

Many corporate governance publications are available from the AICD National Office at:

> Level 25
> Australia Square
> 246–278 George Street
> Sydney
> NSW 2000
> Tel. (02) 8248 6600
> E-mail: aicd@companydirectors.com.au

Notable examples are:

- A guide for board appointments (Due diligence series)
- A guide for directors & officers liability insurance (Due diligence series)
- Audit committees: best practice guide (2001)
- Business planning: do it yourself: a work book for the practical director and business manager by Graham Hubbar (2002)
- Code of conduct (1998)
- Commonsense corporate governance by John B. Reid (2002)
- Conversations between chairmen: Plunkett's progress by Henry Bosch (1997)
- Conversations with a new director by Henry Bosch (1997)
- Corporate practices and conduct (1995) 3rd ed
- Directors' right of access to company documents (1996)
- Duties and responsibilities of directors and officers by Bob Baxt (2002)
- Employee share scheme guidelines (2000)
- Executive share and option scheme guidelines (2000)
- Future direction: the power of the competitive board by Ivor Francis
- Managing proxies and the role of the chairman by Andrew Lumsden (1998)
- Non-executive director remuneration guidelines (1997)

2

France

Table 2.1

Population	59.4 million (2002)
Gross Domestic Income (GDI)	US $1.3 trillion (2002)
GDI per capita	US $22,010 (2002)
Number of companies listed on Euronext	1,900 estimated (2003)
Market capitalization	US $1,451 billion (2001)
Key corporate laws	● Civil Code
	● Commercial Company Acts (1966)
	● Financial Security Act (2003)
	● Bouton Report (2002)
	● New Economic Regulation Act (2001)
Key corporate governance codes	● Bouton Report (2002)
	● Viénot II Report (1999)
	● Viénot I Report (1995)

2.1   Corporate Structure and Ownership

Corporate governance first emerged in France in the mid 1990s when domestic financial scandals, such as Credit Lyonnais, shook the investment community. Reform efforts were pursued in light of the privatization of state-owned enterprises, growth in foreign ownership, and a decrease in cross-shareholdings.

The privatization of government-owned entities has had a big influence on ownership structures in France, however the state still has a wide degree of control with shares in approximately 1,500 companies. Concentrated ownership in companies is common with single-majority shareholders and family-block holders often dominating voting.

There are a number of different varieties of legal entity in France, the main types being:

- The société anonyme (SA): large public companies which may be governed by either a unitary (Consiel d' administration) or two-tier board (Consiel de surveillance) system. The unitary system comprises of a board and a director general (CEO) and the two tier system comprises a management board and a supervisory board.

- The société á responsabilité limitée (SARL): closely held limited liability companies having 50 or fewer shareholders. They are not required to have a board of directors.

- The société en commandité par actions: limited partnerships used by large family controlled companies to retain control while accessing equity.

- The société par actions simplifée (SAS): large private commercial bodies that have more flexible management and administration than société anonyme.

2.2 Legal Framework

The law in France determines that large public companies (SA) may choose the 'status' of its board structure. Many of the significant changes in French corporate law came about from the publication of the Vienot reports on corporate governance in 1995 and 1999, which largely focused on board structures, composition and roles of the CEO and Chairman.

The most recent reforms in corporate law in France have occurred through the New Economic Regulation Act (2001). This Act:

- allowed a company with a single board of directors to separate the functions of the president (chairman of the board) and the director general (CEO):

- improved transparency by identifying the shareholders, (especially foreign shareholders);

- increased executive remuneration reporting by stipulating the disclosure of total packages in annual reports;

- strengthened minority shareholder interests by reducing many of the thresholds from 10 per cent to 5 per cent for the minority shareholders to exercise certain rights;

- allowed for voting electronically and by videoconference.

The Financial Security Act (2003) requires that the president of the board of directors and the director general must communicate all information to all directors in order for them to fulfil their duties. They must also provide in the annual report to shareholders information regarding the preparation and organization of board meetings; the company's internal control procedures and limitations on the powers of the chief executive.

2.3 Legal, Regulatory and Institutional Bodies

2.3.1 The Authorité des Marchés Financiers (AMF)

The AMF was set up in autumn 2003 after the merger of the main market authorities, the Consiel des Marchés Financiers and the Commission des Opérations de Bourse (la COB). The AMF is responsible for investigating issuers and protecting shareholders. It issues regulations, supervises markets, conducts investigations, refers cases to courts and can impose sanctions. The AMF issues a report annually on information contained within the annual reports of listed companies.

2.3.2 The Haut Consiel de Commissariataux Comptes

The Financial Security Act (2003) created the Haut Consiel de Commissariataux Comptes, a high council of statutory auditors. This body is in charge of monitoring the audit profession through:

- developing ethical rules for auditors;
- determining the independence of statutory auditors;
- implementing relevant regulations.

2.3.3 Euronext

Euronext was formed in September 2000 when the exchanges of Amsterdam, Brussels and Paris merged. The group expanded at the beginning of 2002 with the acquisition of LIFFE (London International Financial Futures and Options Exchange) and the merger with the Portuguese exchange BVLP (Bolsa de Valores de Lisboa e Porto). Today, Euronext is Europe's leading cross-border exchange, integrating trading and clearing operations on regulated and non-regulated markets for cash products and derivatives.

2.4 Board Structure

There are three types of board structure in France for both public and private companies:

1. A unitary system with a board of directors and a combined Chairman and CEO;
2. A unitary system with a board of directors and separated functions for Chairman (President) and CEO (Directeur General); and
3. A Two Tier system with a management board and a supervisory board.

The vast majority of large public companies in France have opted for a unitary board structure with less than 5 per cent of companies with a two-tier structure.

A board in France must be composed of at least 3 directors and no more than 18 directors. At least two thirds of the board of large listed companies in France must be comprised of non-executive directors.

The NRE Act (2001) also encourages that an individual can only hold Chairmanships in up to five companies. Directors are restricted to serving on five boards, unless on the board of an affiliated unlisted company, and the term of office does not normally exceed six years.

In addition, it is possible for employee union representatives to attend board meetings and offer advisory suggestions.

Directors on boards in France are committed to share qualifications stipulating a number of shares to be allocated to the director in order to serve on the board.

The Viénot Reports (1995 and 1999) recommended that all listed companies should have an audit, compensation and nomination committee. The Bouton Report (2002) recommended that the audit committee should have sub-committees for risk management and financial statements. Other specialist committees such as a strategy committee were also recommended as good practice. The work of each committee should be reported in the annual report to shareholders.

2.4.1 Unitary System

A unitary board is appointed by the shareholders at the general meeting. If the articles require it, a specified percentage of directors may be elected by the employees of certain public limited companies. In large public companies shareholders must appoint at least one employee shareholder representative to the supervisory board if employees hold at least 3 per cent of the company's share capital.

The board has broad powers to act in the name of the company and has responsibility for supervising the operations of the company. It has the power to dismiss the president, the general managers and top executive officers.

Under the NRE Act (2001) the board appoints the Chairman (président du consiel d'administration) and must determine how much executive power to delegate to him or her. This position often combines the position of chairman and chief executive.

2.4.2 Two Tier System

The two tier system comprises a supervisory board and a management board. The supervisory board exercises control over the management board that is responsible for managing the company. In a two tier system the shareholders elect the supervisory board (consiel de serveillance) at the general meeting. The members of the supervisory board subsequently appoint a management board (directoire) and the (chairman) président du directoire for a specified period.

The supervisory board comments at the annual general meeting on the annual report and accounts presented by the management board. No supervisory board members can be executive managers within the company, but former executive managers can serve on the supervisory board.

2.5 Codes, Standards and Good Practice Guidelines

France has been addressing corporate governance reform through a series of non-binding regulation and legislation. The business environment is continuously adapting in light of the changing ownership structures from concentrated cross-shareholdings of corporations, banks and insurance companies to high levels of foreign ownership. Individual directors themselves are increasingly focusing on personal and company-wide performance both in terms of shareholder value and individual performance incentives.

The Viénot Reports (1995 and 1999) and the Bouton Report (2002) have laid extensive sets of guidelines promoting accountability and transparency in France. Whilst regulatory frameworks are clearly necessary for setting standards and compliance mechanisms for the corporate community, the challenge now is to enhance board processes and individual behaviours to ensure effective board accountability, integrity and transparency.

Marc Viénot led the first corporate governance code in France, which was published in 1995. The Viénot committee was composed of Chief Executives of fourteen leading French public companies in association with the Association Française des Entreprises Privées (AFEP), an association of private companies and the Mouvement des Enterprises de France (MEDEF), a French business confederation. At the time, the committee reported that the current law and regulation in France was sufficient to support good governance practices in French listed companies. The view altered in 1999 when the Viénot committee produced a second report recommending legislative changes, a number of which were enacted in new legislation known as the New Economic Regulation Act (2001).

In September 2002 a report from a working group chaired by Daniel Bouton (President of Societe Generale Bank) was published to address:

...whether there was a satisfactory match between the expectations of investors and financial markets, on the one hand, and the body of rules, standards and practices in respect of companies on the other.

The report developed recommendations for large public companies and focused on:

- the role of the supervisory functions and audit;
- adequacy of accounting practices;
- quality of financial information, effectively of internal and external controls, shareholder relationships and the role of other stakeholders.

One of the key recommendations from the Bouton Report emphasized that all boards should have a majority of independent members. This follows from the second Viénot report in 1999 stating that having genuinely independent directors in sufficient numbers on boards of directors and board committees was an essential factor in guaranteeing that the interests of all the shareholders are taken into account in company decision making.

2.6 Disclosure and Transparency

Whether a unitary or a two tier system, the board must ensure integrity of the financial reporting system and compliance with relevant laws and regulations. Board members may be individually and jointly responsible for any breaches.

In large public companies, the president of the board of directors or supervisory board must provide information in the annual report to shareholders regarding:

- the preparation and organization of board meetings;
- the company's internal control procedures;
- limitations on the powers of the CEO.

International Financial Reporting Standards are being implemented in France with the aim for full compliance by 2005. Publicly listed companies are required to disclose turnover at the end of each quarter with financial statements. The Bouton report raised the importance of reporting on non-financial material items and listed companies are required to disclose in their annual reports how they take into account the social and environmental consequences of their activities.

All large public companies in France appoint two independent statutory auditors for a six year term. The auditors are proposed for appointment by the board and approved by the shareholders and may be re-appointed. In August 2003 a law was passed on financial security to increase the independence of statutory auditors. It requires that auditors cannot:

- hold an interest in the audited company or with any person who holds a controlling interest in the auditing company;
- provide any services not directly linked to the auditing services;
- audit a company already benefiting from the services of another affiliate of the statutory auditor if these services are not directly linked to the audit services.

According to a recent report by Standard & Poors, transparency and disclosure practices of French companies included in the S&P 350 index suggests that France's disclosure levels are among the highest in the world, based on 98 information items examined.

2.7   Shareholder Rights and Stakeholder Relations

In France, the premise of 'one share, one vote' is not applied and it is not uncommon for shareholders to be given greater voting rights if the shares have been held for a period of time specified in the statuts (articles).

A general meeting must be held annually to approve the financial statements. The supervisory body must present a written report on the company's situation and discuss business developments.

The following decisions are referred to shareholders at general meeting:

- approving the financial statements;
- approving the dividend;

- electing and dismissing members of the supervisory board;

- dismissing members of the management board;

- approving the remuneration of the members of the supervisory board;

- approving the auditors;

- approving the issuing of company bonds;

- approving mergers and acquisitions.

The NRE Act (2001) prevents companies from fixing minimum share-holding for attendance at general meetings. Shareholders with more than 5 per cent of the shares may address written questions to the chairman of a supervisory board concerning an event that may affect the continuity of the company. Shareholders holding more than 5 per cent of the shares can also petition a court to appoint an expert to review and report on the operations of the company.

If a shareholder owns one-third of a listed company's shares in most cases they will be required to make a public bid for all outstanding voting stock. Shareholders must notify the Authorite des Marches Financiers (AMF) within 5 days if they cross the threshold of 5 per cent, 10 per cent, 20 per cent, 33.3 per cent or 50 per cent of the share capital or voting rights of a listed company and must disclose the total number of shares and voting rights.

2.8　Useful Contacts

- Paris Bourse – www.bourse-de-paris.fr

- European Corporate Governance Institute – www.ecgi.org

- Bank of France – www.banque-france.fr

- Council on Financial Markets – www.cmf-france.org

- Marche a terme International de France – www.matif.fr

- Institute of Directors France – www.iod.com/france

- European corporate governance network – www.ecgn.org

2.9   Further Reading

AFEP-MEDEF (2003) *The Corporate Governance of Listed Corporations*, AFEP-MEDEF, Paris

AFG/ASFFI Commission on Corporate Governance (1998) *Recommendations on Corporate Governance*, AFG-ASFFI, Paris

Bouton, D (2002) *Pour un Meilleur governement des enterprises cotées*, MEDEF-AFEP, Paris

Conceil National du Patronat Français (CNPF) and Association Français des enterprises privees (1995) Viénot 1 Report, Paris

Gregory, H (2002) *Comparative study of corporate governance codes relevant to the European Union and its member states*, Internal Market Directorate General, European Commission, Brussels

Mesnooh C (2002) *Corporate Governance in France*, Corporate Finance

Mouvement des enterprises de France (MEDEF) formerly CNPF and Français des enterprises privees (1999) Paris

Ploix H (1997) *Corporate governance: legal aspects, method, responsibilities*, Montchrestien, Paris

3

Germany

Table 3.1

Population	82 million (2002)
Gross National Income (GNI)	US $1.9 trillion (2002)
GNI per capita	US $22,670 (2002)
Total number of companies	N/A
Number of companies listed on the stock exchange	1,043 (1999)
Market capitalization	US $1,257 billion (2001)
Key company laws	● The Fourth Financial Market Promotion Act (2002)
	● Law on Registered Shares and the Relief of the Exercise of Voting Rights (NaStraG) (2001)
	● Corporate Governance Rules for Quoted German Companies (German Panel Rules, 2000)
	● Law on Control and Transparency in the Corporate Sector (KonTraG) (1998)
Key corporate governance codes	● Amendments to the Cromme Code (2003)
	● The German Corporate Governance Code (Cromme Commission 2002)
	● German Code of Corporate Governance (The Berlin Initiative Code, 2000)

3.1   Corporate Structure and Ownership

There are two types of incorporated companies in Germany:

- Gesellschaft mit besehrankte Haftung (GmbH) – companies with limited liability;
- Aktiengesellschaft (AG) – joint stock companies with shares that are widely held.

Most of German industry is in the form of unquoted AGs and GmbHs. Small businesses with fewer than 500 employees account for two-thirds of the workforce and produce about one-half of the gross national product.

Voting power in Germany has traditionally been highly concentrated. According to Barca and Becht (2001):

> *DAX companies are generally either majority controlled by a large block-holder or by banks via proxy votes. More than 50% of all listed companies are controlled by a single majority block and only 17.4% are without a block-holder with at least a veto minority (25%).*

However, in recent years there has been a widening of share ownership due to the privatization of large state-owned enterprises. For example, the privatization of Deutsche Telekom led to 4.5 million new private shareholders in 2002. Foreign holdings of shares tend to be concentrated in the major companies.

In Germany growth occurs organically or through mergers. Hostile takeovers are very rare.

3.2   Legal Framework

The key laws relating to corporate direction and control in Germany are:

- Eifulrungsgetz zum Burgerlichen Gesetzbuch (EGBGB) – the Introductory Act to the Civil Code;
- Burgerliches Gesetzbuch (BGB) – the Civil Code;
- Handelsgesetzbuch (HGB) – the Commercial Code;

- Handelsregisterverfugung (HRV) – the ordinance on the implementation and operation of the commercial register;

- Insolvenzordnung – the Insolvency Act;

- Gesetz betreffend die Gesellschaften mit beschrankter Haftung (GmbHG) – the law on limited liability companies;

- Aktiengesetz – the Stock Exchange Corporation Act;

- Gesetz zur Kontroll und Tranzparenz in Unternehmem-abereich (KonTraG) – the law on control and transparency in the corporate sector (1998);

- Gesetz zur Namensaktie und zur Erleichterung der Stimmrechtsausubung – the law on registered shares and the relief of the exercise of voting rights (2001);

- The fourth financial market promotion Act (Viertes Finanzmartktforderungsgesetz) 2002 – the law concerning the supervisory board's access to information and the independence of the company's auditors;

- The Capital Raising Promotion Act (Kap AE G);

- The Law on Limited Liability Partnership (Kap CoRiLiG).

3.3 Legal, Regulatory and Institutional Bodies

3.3.1 Amtsgericht – Handelsregister

The sole government entity responsible for enforcing company laws is the Amtsgerricht – Handelsregister (District Court – Commercial register), which enforces registration and de-registration of company-related entries.

3.4 Board Structure

Certain German limited liability companies (GmbH) and all joint stock companies (AG) have a two-tier board structure that has: a supervisory board that supervises the management of the company (*Aufsichtsrat*); and a management board that manages the company (*Vorstand*).

3.4.1 The Supervisory Board (Aufsichtsrat)

The supervisory board appoints, supervises, advises and, when necessary, dismisses members of the management board. The Aufsichtsrat is involved in decisions of fundamental importance to the enterprise. Both the representatives elected by the shareholders and representatives of the employees are equally obligated to act in the company's interests. The supervisory board never has more than two former members of the management board in order to ensure its independence from the management board.

Supervisory board members are not allowed to hold directorships or similar positions or engage in advisory tasks for important competitors of the company. Each member of the supervisory board must inform the chairman of the supervisory board of any conflicts of interest resulting from consultancy or directorship functions with clients, suppliers, lenders or other business partners. The chairman of the supervisory board must inform the supervisory board of any personal conflicts of interest. In its report, the supervisory board shall inform the general meeting of any conflicts of interest which have occurred, together with how they were resolved.

The supervisory board, in consultation with the management board, commissions the auditor, but the shareholders' meeting formally appoints the auditor.

The supervisory board has responsibility for:

- appointing, dismissing and remunerating the management board;
- approving distributions of profit (the management board proposes profit allocation for the supervisory board to approve);
- ensuring the integrity of the company's accounting, audit and financial reporting systems. The supervisory board participates in the preparation of the annual financial statements and oversees the audit.

The supervisory board is required to serve the interests of the company as a whole. Members of the supervisory board who violate their duties are liable to the company for any resulting damages.

Members of the supervisory board have a responsibility for individual management board members' liability to:

- diligently gather facts;

- avoid conflicts of interest; and

- act in good faith in the company's best interests.

The management board forwards the auditor's report to the supervisory board together with its drafts of the annual financial statements and annual report. The supervisory board examines the annual financial statements, the annual report and the proposal for profit allocation. It subsequently submits a written report on its examination to the annual shareholders' meeting.

The members of the supervisory board have responsibility for managing the business with the care of a diligent and prudent manager. They must not disclose confidential information and secrets of the company, in particular trade and business secrets, which have become known to them as a result of their service on the supervisory board. Violation of the duty of confidentiality constitutes a criminal offence.

If the company is listed, German insider trading laws are applicable. Members of the supervisory board are considered to be primary insiders, according to the Securities Trading Act (Wertpapierhandelsgesetz).

A supervisory board typically meets three or four times a year.

3.4.2 The Management Board (Vorstand)

The management board is responsible for independently managing the company and is jointly accountable for management of the enterprise. The management board coordinates the enterprise's strategic approach with the supervisory board and discusses the current state of strategy implementation with the supervisory board on a regular basis. The management board is required to act in the company's interests and undertakes to increase the sustainable value of the enterprise.

The management board reports to the supervisory board on the following issues:

- the intended business policy and the future strategy of the company (in particular finance, investment and personnel plans);

- the profitability of the company (in particular, the return on equity);

- the state of business and the condition of the company; and

- transactions which may have a material impact upon profitability or liquidity.

The management board prepares resolutions for the general meeting and submits to the general meeting the annual financial statements and the general meeting approves the appropriation of net income and ratifies the acts of the management and supervisory boards, elects the shareholders' representatives to the supervisory board and the auditor.

The management and supervisory boards report on the company's corporate governance in the annual report. This includes explanations of any deviations from the Cromme Code of Corporate Governance (2002).

During their employment members of the management board are subject to a strict non-competitive requirement.

All members of the management board are required to disclose conflicts of interest to the chairman of the supervisory board and inform the other members of the management board without any delay.

The management board is responsible for ensuring that internal risk is managed appropriately. The management board is responsible for taking suitable measures to establish a risk-monitoring system aimed at early recognition of developments that might endanger the future existence of the company (Stock Corporation Act, Section 91).

The management board is required to ensure that the company is in compliance with all applicable laws and regulations. If members of either board fail to exercise due care and diligence, they are liable to the company for damages.

In large AGs there must be a board member in charge of labour matters known as the Arbeitsdirektor.

In 1998 the management board's responsibilities were increased by the introduction of the Act on the Control and Transparency of Companies (Gesetz zur Kontrolle und Transparenz im Unternehmensbereich – 'KonTraG'). This law requires that the management board must report to the supervisory board on finance, investment, and personnel planning, and mandates that adequate internal monitoring and control structures are in place. It further requires that external auditors examine and verify whether the management board has adequately implemented monitoring activities.

The German Code of Corporate Governance (2000) states that individual management board members should be allocated particular spheres of responsibility for which they have been deemed competent, either as: a spokesperson (without authority to make decisions outside of the board as a whole); or head of a department (with authority to make decisions in their area of responsibility).

All of a company's major functions, products and markets should be represented on the management board.

The chairman of the management board sets the agenda for the meetings of the management board. Each member of the management board may add to the agenda points for discussion and decision through the chairman.

The management board normally reaches decisions unanimously. If this cannot be achieved, a decision is made by simple majority after a waiting period of at least 24 hours. The chairman of the management board may defer a majority decision with a veto. The veto may be overruled at the next management board meeting by a majority of members.

Aktiengesellschaft (AGs)

All AGs have a management board that has direction and management responsibilities.

Gesellschaft mit besehrankte Haftung (GmbHs)

- Small GmbHs. The board structure of small GmbH companies (ie those with under 500 employees) is straightforward and simple. All small GmbH companies have a managing director (Geschaftsfuhrer) who is accountable to the shareholders.

- Large GmbHs. All large GmbHs (over 500 employees) must have a supervisory board. This is true even if all of the shares are owned by one person.

3.4.3 Composition

Supervisory Board (Aufsichtsrat)

The size of the supervisory board is related to the number of employees within the company and the articles of association of the company. There must be at least 20 members of the supervisory board.

The members of the supervisory board are elected by the shareholders at the general meeting. The Cromme Code of Corporate Governance emphasizes the role that employee co-determination plays in German corporations.

In GmbH companies with 500 or more employees, or AG companies with fewer than 2,000 employees, shareholders select two-thirds of the supervisory board and the employees select the other third.

In AG companies with 2,000 or more employees, employees select one-half of the supervisory board and shareholders select the other half, including the chairman.

The chairman of the supervisory board is elected by the shareholders and normally has a casting vote.

Both the representatives elected by the shareholders and representatives of the employees are equally obligated to act in the company's interests.

Members of the supervisory board for large listed companies are frequently selected from retiring management board members, bank representatives and business partners.

Management Board

The supervisory board elects the management board. Members of the management board are typically appointed for five years.

Management boards of the largest publicly listed AGs are typically composed of between five and ten members and must have a member responsible for labour matters and human resources (Arbeitsdirektor). Smaller companies tend to have smaller management boards of three to five members representing the founding shareholders, but no labour representation.

3.4.4 Committees

The committees often comprise the chairman and vice-chairman of the supervisory board and two or three other members. These committees will normally include employees' representatives. The supervisory board for large companies normally has the following committees:

- a business committee for managerial key policy issues;

- a personnel committee for all matters affecting the personnel of the management board and, if necessary, a committee pursuant to the Co-determination Act 1976;

- an investment and finance committee;

- an audit committee; and

- a corporate governance committee.

3.4.5 Compensation

Board compensation is not a contentious issue in Germany. There are few stock option schemes for tax reasons and the performance of members of the boards is not generally related to either organization or share performance.

Directors typically obtain the majority of their remuneration as basic salary. The remaining third is composed of annual bonuses and benefits.

Compensation of the members of the management board is determined by the supervisory board on the basis of performance assessment.

3.5 Codes, Standards and Good Practice Guidelines

The system of corporate governance in Germany has emphasized the relationship between boards and its key stakeholders.

3.5.1 The Berlin Initiative Code (2000)

The Berlin Initiative Code of Conduct aimed to improve the quality of board governance. The Berlin Initiative Group was chaired by Prof Axel Werder and consisted of members of German management and supervisory boards, academics and an attorney. The group conducted a survey of the DAX 100 and from the findings recommended best practice for internal corporate governance.

It defined the role of the management board as:

- giving direction to the company;

- assembling infrastructure for the process of wealth creation;

- determining the general course of the company's activities by identifying specific goals and by formulating strategies to achieve such goals;

- putting planning and control systems in place;

- deciding important matters;

- conducting crisis management;

- communicating with the supervisory body as well as with the shareholders;

- supervising the successful execution of board decisions; and

- checking the efficiency of control systems and the quality of delegated decisions.

The Code states that the management board should follow three general guidelines:

- all management board measures should be subject to the principle of legal permissibility;

- all management board measures should be subject to the principle of economic usefulness; and

- the management board should be aware of social responsibility to a reasonable extent and take account of the ethical considerations without which a social market economy cannot survive.

The Code states that members of the supervisory and management boards owe a duty of loyalty to the company. The Code recommends that members should not pursue their own interests if they conflict with the interests of the company, and even the appearance of conflict is to be avoided. Members of the supervisory and management boards may neither directly nor indirectly take advantage of the company's business opportunities, assist competitors or undertake commercial transactions with the company which do not correspond with normal market conditions. All members of the supervisory board should acknowledge in writing the rules applicable for insider dealings as well as the company guidelines for the sale and purchase of shares in the company. Any participation by members of the management board in other companies should be revealed to the chairman of the supervisory board and examined for potential conflict of interests.

The chairman of the supervisory board should be asked to give prior approval to any director's acceptance of a position on the supervisory board of another company, as well as engaging in significant ancillary activities.

The management board can appoint a compliance officer who may issue guidelines for the sale and purchase of shares in the company and who assures their observance.

3.5.2 The German Panel Rules (2000)

The German Panel on Corporate Governance was made up of ten members who recommended rules for quoted companies. The objective of the rules was to improve accountability to shareholders. In addition, the rules aimed to improve quality of board governance.

The rules recommended that the supervisory board establish the following committees:

- General committee: This committee deals with strategy and planning issues for both the supervisory and managerial boards. Its functions include:
  - advising the management board on strategy and planning;
  - preparing information for the supervisory board;
  - assessing the internal state of the company; and
  - reviewing corporate governance rules and their compliance;
- Personnel committee: This committee addresses:
  - recruitment to the management board;
  - management succession planning;
  - remuneration of management board members;
  - performance evaluation of the management board members; and
  - granting of loans;
- Nomination committee;
- Market and credit risk committee;
- Mediation committee;
- Accounts and audit committee.

3.5.3 The Cromme Commission Code of Corporate Governance (2002)

The Baums Commission (2001) was initiated by the German chancellor who requested a report on the Management and Control of Companies and on the Modernization of the Stock Corporation Law. The report recommended the development of a German Code of best practice in Spring 2002.

This led to a commission chaired by Dr Gerhard Cromme (the retired chief executive and current supervisory board chairman of ThyssenKrupp), comprised of twelve members representing the German business sector and members of the legal, financial and academic communities. The Cromme Commission produced the German Corporate Governance Code which comprises three layers of corporate governance:

1. A description of the legal stipulations concerning management and supervision.
2. 'Shall recommendations' – companies that do not comply with these recommendations have to state this in their annual report and/or their Web site.
3. 'Should suggestions' – these suggestions do not require an obligatory statement in the case of non-compliance.

The Code introduced an annual obligation for all listed companies to disclose whether they have complied with the Cromme Commission Code's recommendations, including a description of which rules of conduct have not been complied with.

The Code introduced a duty for auditors to note whether or not the information has been provided; and a duty to disclose and file the compliance statement with the commercial register.

3.6 Disclosure and Transparency

The accounting principles in Germany are based upon commercial prudence. Large reserves in the balance sheet accounting for risk are common.

The German Society of Investment Analysis and Asset Management (DVFA) have developed a scorecard for German Corporate Governance which serves as a practical analytical tool for financial analysts and investors. Items included on the scorecard include:

- Corporate governance commitment. This checks the extent of how embedded the principles of corporate governance are within a company. (10%)

- Shareholders and the general meeting. This covers the equal treatment of shareholders. (12%)

- Cooperation between management board and supervisory board. This evaluates the communication arrangements between the management and supervisory boards. (15%)

- Management board. This evaluates the compensation elements and deals with conflicts of interest. (10%)

- Supervisory board. This evaluates the compensation elements and deals with conflicts of interest, qualification standards for members and expert committees (particularly the audit committee). (15%)

- Transparency. This considers the equal and regular information provision to shareholders. (20%)

- Reporting and audit of the annual financial statements. This reviews the international accounting and auditing standards. (18%)

3.7 Shareholder Rights and Stakeholder Relations

There is no legal obligation for a GmbH to have an annual general meeting. However, general meetings are mandatory for AG companies. It is not uncommon for 70 per cent or more of the voting shareholders to be involved in a general meeting.

A one share, one vote principle is used in Germany.

Investors must inform the company when they acquire 5 per cent of the share capital.

Annual meeting dates and agendas must be published four weeks before the meeting. Shareholders have ten days to submit proposals.

The company then must send the agenda containing any shareholder proposals to the registered shareholders and custodians. Proxy voting is permissible but can be complex to arrange.

The shareholders' meeting is the supreme body of the company and makes fundamental decisions. The powers of the shareholders' meeting are defined by the Stock Exchange Corporation Act (Aktiengesetz or AktG) and the articles of association. The powers include the following:

- election of the supervisory board members, to the extent that they are not delegated to the supervisory board or must be elected by the employees under the relevant co-determination laws;
- removal of supervisory board members elected by the general shareholders' meeting;
- approval of the annual financial statements;
- the discharge of responsibility of the members of the management board and supervisory board;
- distribution and retention of profits;
- appointment of auditors, including the appointment of special auditors;
- consent to acts of the management board that are submitted by the management board to the shareholders' meeting for approval;
- amendments to the articles of association;
- capital increases and decreases;
- dissolution or transformation of the company; and
- consent to conclusion or enterprise agreements, mergers and consolidations.

Certain corporate decisions require varying percentages of shareholder approval:

- **Sale of all or substantially all assets/liquidation:** The sale of all, or substantially all, of the assets, as well as the liquidation of a company, requires at least a seventy-five per cent majority of those voting at the annual shareholders' meeting. Minority shareholders participate pro rata.

- **Transformation,** ie a change in the corporate form (Umwandlung): A transformation requires at least a seventy-five per cent majority of those voting at the annual shareholders' meeting. Minority shareholders are entitled to compensation either in shares or in cash.

- **Merger or amalgamation (Verschmelzung)**: A merger requires at least a seventy-five per cent majority of the general assemblies of all companies directly involved. Concurring minority shareholders are entitled to compensation in shares and, if applicable, cash. Dissenting minority shareholders are entitled to compensation in cash.

Each shareholder can demand information from the management board at a general meeting regarding matters relating to the company, insofar as this is necessary to make a reasonable decision on the matters on the agenda. The management board may only refuse to provide such information in rare cases, eg if providing the information would lead to a substantial disadvantage to the company.

3.7.1 Employees

The Works Constitution Act (1972) is concerned with the representation of workers' interests at plant level and covers most organizations in Germany.

The size of the works council is dependent upon the size of the organization. Members are elected by the workforce for a period of four years. Members are not required to be members of a union.

Works councils are involved in co-determination (ie the right to participate in decisions). They exist to promote trust and cooperation between employers and employees.

Councils meet every three months. The councils deal with issues relating to the conditions of employment. Issues involve working hours, overtime, flexible working, pay, incentives and safety at work. Councils negotiate agreements with their employers.

Works councils do not have the right to call a strike and must deal with disagreements through established conciliation procedures.

In companies of more than 100 employees there must also be an economic committee. The economic committee has rights to information involving the economic and financial information of the company.

3.8   Director Development Activity

There are few director development activities currently being undertaken in Germany.

3.9   Useful Contacts

- Bundesaufsichtsamt fur den Wertpapierhandel – www.bawe.de
- Bundesbank – www.bundesbank.de
- Deutsche Boerse – www.deutsche-boerse.com
- Dusseldorf Exchange – www.rwb.de
- German Society of Capital Market Experts (DVFA) – www.dvfa.de

3.10   Further Reading

Barca, F and Becht, M (2001) *The Control of Corporate Europe*, Oxford

Baums (2001) Baums Commission Report

Berlin Initiative Group (2000) German Code of Corporate Governance, www.gcgc.de

Cromme (2002) Cromme Code, German Corporate Governance Kodex

Cromme (2003) Amendments to the Cromme Code

Deutsche Schutzvereingung fur Werpaierbesitz (June 1998) *DSW Guidelines*

German Ministry of Justice (1998) *Drittes Finanzmarktförderungsgesetz*

German Panel on Corporate Governance (2000) Corporate Governance Rules for German Quoted Companies

KonTraG (1998) *Gesetz zur Kontrolle und Transparez im Unternehmensbereich*, German Ministry of Justice

Van den Berghe, L and De Ridder, L (1999) *International Standardization of Good Corporate Governance: Best Practices for the Board of Directors*, Kluwer Academic Publishers, Holland

Van den Berghe, L (2002) *Corporate Governance in a Globalising World: Convergence or Divergence? A European Perspective*, Kluwer Academic Publishers, Holland

Hong Kong

4

Table 4.1

Population	6.8 million (2003)
Gross National Income (GNI)	$167.6 billion (2002)
GNI per capita	$23,900 (2003)
Number of registered companies	503,111 (2002)
Number of companies listed on the stock exchange	852 Main Board (2003)
	185 Growth Enterprise Board (2003)
Market capitalization	$711 billion (2003)
Key corporate laws	● Companies Ordinance
	● Securities and Futures Ordinance
Key corporate governance codes	● Stock Exchange of Hong Kong Listing Rules
	● Stock Exchange of Hong Kong Code of Best Practice (to be replaced on 1 January 2005 by Code of Corporate Governance Practices)

4.1 Corporate Structure and Ownership

Hong Kong is the twelfth largest banking centre in the world in terms of external transactions. It is the tenth largest stock market in terms of market capitalization and is the seventh largest financial centre in terms of foreign exchange turnover.

There are half a million limited liability companies incorporated in Hong Kong. Out of this total, about 7,000 are public, of which over 1,000 listed on the Hong Kong Stock Exchange of Hong Kong. The rest are private.

About 98 per cent of the business entities are SMEs (small and medium enterprises). Companies which have been incorporated overseas but have established a place of business in Hong Kong must be registered under the Companies Ordinance. The number of companies with regional headquarters and offices in Hong Kong, but incorporated elsewhere is 3,207.

4.1.1 Family Control

As with many other Asian economies, family-controlled interests remain a prevalent characteristic of the market in Hong Kong influencing shareholding patterns and board composition. Some estimate that the proportion of family-controlled listed companies is between 70 and 90 per cent. The growth and success of such companies has essentially been derived from the leadership and determination of one person or one family who not only holds a significant portion of the shareholding but who is also involved with the day-to-day management of the business. The prevalence of family-controlled interests among listed companies has raised concerns about checks and balances, particularly when shareholders have other business interests and when dealings between a listed company and its controlling shareholders may affect the overall interest of all shareholders.

Large private companies are in the main aware of their responsibility to practise good corporate governance. Some of them may seek to be listed as they progress and have thus the foresight to put proper governance practices in place in paving the way for listing. The smaller companies, constituting a majority of the companies in Hong Kong, are encouraged to follow the larger companies in the pursuit of corporate governance practices.

4.1.2 Non-profit-distributing Organizations

The non-profit-distributing organizations are encouraged and, indeed, required to practise good corporate governance, as they are accountable for the spending of public funds. The Hospital Authority was one of the earliest public organizations to introduce governance concepts from the Authority to the hospitals in its mammoth network.

In 2001–02, the Social Welfare Department of the Government of Hong Kong developed and implemented a lump-sum grant system stipulating conditions on corporate governance among welfare agencies that receive collectively a public grant of over HK $6 billion (circa US $0.77 billion) per annum. The Education Commission has also specified a structure and functions of a School Management Committee for each school to comply with, in order to put in force the stewardship role in school management. The Arts Development Council and the Leisure and Cultural Services Department of the Government of Hong Kong have, likewise, actively promoted corporatization programmes and corporate governance responsibilities among the publicly funded arts companies.

4.1.3 Banks and Investors

The Banking Ordinance restricts any bank from owning a significant part of a company, thereby restricting the banking sector from owning a significant part of the corporate sector. Banks, however, play a significant role in corporate governance as lending decisions are influenced by the borrowers' practice of good business culture, provision of reliable financial information, exercising of prudent risk management and proper internal controls.

Institutional investors, life insurers, pension funds, the government as holder of equities and foreign direct investments in Hong Kong all contribute as forces inducing high standards of corporate governance. Although they do not aim to influence the corporate governance of individual firms directly, their investment decisions are steered towards companies that adhere to best corporate governance practices. Although their investment may not be substantial enough to warrant a controlling interest in a company, they do, on occasion, exercise their rights as minority shareholders. Fund managers, in particular, are willing to pay premium prices for good corporate governance.

4.2 Legal Framework

As a Special Administrative Region (SAR) of China and a former British territory, Hong Kong operates under a constitution in the form of Basic Law, a jurisdiction with a legislature based on English and Common Law. Directors on boards have similar responsibilities as directors in the UK.

The main legislation relating to corporate governance in Hong Kong includes the following: Companies Ordinance (including the Companies (Amendment) Ordinance 2003, effective 13 February 2004); and the Securities and Futures Ordinance (effective 1 April 2003).

In the early 1990s, Hong Kong took cognizance of the published Cadbury Report and commenced monitoring of corporate governance developments in both the public and private sectors. The 1990s saw successive legal and regulatory reforms in Hong Kong, including changes to the Listing Rules, particularly with the release of Code of Best Practice as an appendix to the Listing Rules, enactment of the Securities Disclosure Ordinance and the establishment of an Insider Dealing Tribunal.

All companies in Hong Kong are regulated by the Companies Ordinance which addresses the following key areas of corporate governance:

- company formation;
- maintenance of capital and organization of capital structure;
- financial and non-financial disclosure; and
- corporate administration, including for example company meetings and resolutions, preparing and filing of annual returns, etc.

4.2.1   Review of Companies Ordinance, 2001

In February 2001, the Standing Committee on Company Law Reform (SCCLR) published a report on the Overall Review of the Companies Ordinance. The review is focused on improving corporate governance in Hong Kong and recommended amendments to the Companies Ordinance classified into the following categories:

- shareholders' rights;
- directorship requirements; and
- technical matters.

The first batch of these amendments is contained in the Companies (Amendment) Bill 2002 and the eventually enacted Companies (Amendment) Ordinance 2003. The major amendments include:

- new definitions of manager, reserve director and shadow director;
- the establishment of one person and one director companies;
- the requirement of a minimum of one director for private companies and a minimum of two directors for other companies;
- the requirement to separate the director and company secretary in private one-director companies;
- removal of directors by ordinary as opposed to special resolution;
- giving shareholders the capability to change directors' authority by special resolution;
- making directors liable for the acts and omissions of their alternates;
- extending the provisions regarding financial assistance to directors.
- permitting companies to indemnify and purchase insurance for their directors and officers in various statutorily specified circumstances;
- reducing the threshold for circulating shareholders' proposals;
- giving shareholders a personal right to sue to enforce the terms of a company's memorandum and articles of association; and
- removing the need for a company to seek court approval to reduce its nominal capital in certain statutorily specified circumstances.

The remaining phases of the review will be the subject of further companies amendment bills as part of a continual exercise to keep pace with world trends, culminating in a bill to restructure and rewrite the entire Ordinance.

4.2.2　The Securities Ordinance

The Securities and Futures Ordinance administered by the Securities and Futures Commission (SFC) consolidates all 10 securities and futures-related ordinances into a single law, and aims to establish a regulatory framework to meet with international best practice to enhance market efficiency and transparency.

The Ordinance widens the investigative and disciplinary power of the SFC (eg with a Market Misconduct Tribunal (MMT) to handle insider dealing and other specified market misconduct). The Ordinance also allows the SFC to seek explanations of the accounting records from listed companies and have the right to access the working papers of the company's auditors.

The Ordinance lowers the disclosure threshold from 10 per cent of shareholdings in a company to 5 per cent and reduces the time limit for disclosure from five days to three business days. The Ordinance stipulates a clear statutory right of persons who suffer losses as a result of market misconduct to take civil actions and claim compensation for loss.

4.2.3 Latest Developments of the Listing Rules and Related Code

On 30 January 2004, Hong Kong Exchanges and Clearing (HKEx) announced extensive rule changes in the areas of corporate governance, initial listing criteria and continuing obligations, which became effective on 31 March 2004. HKEx also released an Exposure Paper on Draft Code on Corporate Governance Practices and Corporate Governance Report. This draft code is undergoing public consultation inviting the market to comment and react on the timing for implementing the draft Code and the detailed wording of the Code.

The draft Code provides support for listed company boards to improve their corporate governance practices. It is a non-mandatory code, but it is two-tiered as follows:

- First tier: Code Provisions on a comply-or-explain basis; however, non-compliance is not considered a breach of the Listing Rules;

- Second tier: Recommended Best Practices, where companies are not required to explain non-compliance.

The Code provisions cover the following:

- Section A: Directors;

- Section B: Directors' Remuneration;
- Section C: Accountability and Audit;
- Section D: Delegation by the Board;
- Section E: Communication with Stakeholders.

Comments on the Draft Code were required on or before 31 March 2004 and target publication date of the Code would be end of June 2004, with the following effective dates:

- by 1 January 2005: all Code provisions and related disclosure obligations, with a few exceptions;
- by 1 July 2005: Code provisions on internal control and related disclosure obligations.
- encouragement of early adoption.

In the new scheme, listed companies must include a Corporate Governance Report in their annual reports.

4.3   Legal, Regulatory and Institutional Bodies

Financial turmoil in October 1987 led the Hong Kong government to establish the Hong Kong Monetary Authority and the Securities and Futures Commission. The government also reorganized the Stock Exchange of Hong Kong and beefed up the Listing Rules.

4.3.1   Financial Services and the Treasury Bureau, Government of Hong Kong SAR

The policy responsibility of the Financial Services and the Treasury Bureau is, *inter alia*, to maintain and enhance Hong Kong's status as a major international financial centre, ensuring, through the provision of an appropriate economic and legal environment, that Hong Kong's markets remain open, fair and efficient. While market regulatory functions are performed by independent statutory regulators, the Bureau facilitates and coordinates initiatives to upgrade overall market quality and to ensure that Hong Kong's regulatory regime meets the needs of modern commerce. The Bureau aims to maintain and promote Hong Kong as a major international financial centre.

4.3.2 Standing Committee on Company Law Reform (SCCLR)

The Standing Committee on Company Law Reform (SCCLR) was established in 1984 to ensure that Hong Kong's Companies Ordinance remains responsive to the day-to-day needs of the business sector and the community at large. Its members include lawyers, accountants, company secretaries, businessmen, academics, representatives of government departments and regulatory bodies.

4.3.3 Companies Registry

The Companies Registry is the Government department responsible for administering and enforcing the Companies Ordinance. The department's specific functions are to:

- provide facilities to allow the promotion of companies, limited partnerships, trust companies and registered trustees;
- incorporate these enterprises;
- register overseas companies;
- de-register defunct, solvent private companies;
- register all documentation required by the various ordinances governing these enterprises; and
- provide the public with facilities to search for the information held by the Registry on the various statutory registers, microfilmed or computerized records.

4.3.4 Securities and Futures Commission (SFC)

The SFC, an independent statutory body, is responsible for administering the laws governing the securities and futures markets in Hong Kong and facilitating and encouraging the development of these markets. The following four groups regulated by the SFC:

- securities and futures dealers, financiers, advisers, service providers, traders, asset managers and their representatives;
- Hong Kong Exchanges and Clearing Limited;
- listed companies; and
- participants in trading activities.

The SFC prescribes a host of guidelines and codes, in particular the Takeovers and Merger Codes, which is non-statutory codes designed to afford fair treatment for shareholders who are affected by takeovers, mergers and repurchases.

4.3.5 Hong Kong Exchanges and Clearing Limited (HKEx)

Hong Kong Exchanges and Clearing Limited (HKEx) is the holding company of The Stock Exchange of Hong Kong Limited (SEHK), Hong Kong Futures Exchange Limited (HKFE) and Hong Kong Securities Clearing Company Limited. HKEx went public in June 2000 following the merger of the SEHK, HKFE and related three clearing houses. HKEx is a recognized exchange operator and performs its public duty to ensure orderly and fair markets, prudent risk management by listed companies that is consistent with the public interest and in particular, the interests of the investing public.

4.3.6 Hong Kong Monetary Authority (HKMA)

The Hong Kong Monetary Authority issued non-mandatory corporate governance guidelines for the Banking Ordinance setting out minimum standards that locally incorporated authorized institutions must comply with.

4.3.7 Hong Kong Institute of Directors (HKIoD)

The Hong Kong Institute of Directors (HKIoD) is Hong Kong's premier body representing professional directors working together to promote good corporate governance and to contribute towards advancing the status of Hong Kong, both in China and internationally. The Hong Kong Branch of the UK Institute of Directors (IoD) was set up in 1991. With the return of sovereignty of Hong Kong to China in July 1997, the Hong Kong Branch of the IoD converted to The Hong Kong Institute of Directors (HKIoD) as an independent body while continuing to maintain an affiliation with the IoD in the UK. The Institute has a membership approaching 900 practising directors from a diversity of companies and industries. The HKIoD is consulted by government and regulators and responds with collectively considered views on issues affecting corporate governance and economic development.

4.3.8   The Hong Kong Society of Accountants (HKSA)

The Hong Kong Society of Accountants (HKSA) is a professional body that has taken a proactive stance to promote corporate governance since 1995. The HKSA has a corporate governance committee and has published guidelines on disclosure in annual reports and guidelines on directors' business review. The Society's annual Best Corporate Governance Disclosure Awards set benchmarks for excellence in disclosure.

4.3.9   Hong Kong Institute of Company Secretaries (HKICS)

The Hong Kong Institute of Company Secretaries (HKICS) is a professional body with the objectives of promoting and advancing the interests of Company Secretaries in Hong Kong, working closely with various authorities and contributing in debating issues of corporate governance. The HKICS organizes a conference on Corporate Governance every two years.

4.4   Board Structure

4.4.1   Composition

Most listed companies on the HKEx have between 10 and 12 directors on their boards. Companies in Hong Kong may exercise discretion in maintaining boards with different mixes of executive and non-executive directors. For listed companies, the Listing Rules have been amended to increase the minimum number of Independent Non-Executive Directors (INEDs) from two to three, with a transitional period for compliance ending on 30 September 2004, complemented by the Code on Corporate Governance Practices recommending the appointment of INEDs to constitute one-third of the board. It is worth noting that by complying with the mandatory minimum requirements of three INEDs, listed companies with a board of 11 members or fewer will practically have at least one-third of their board represented by INEDs.

There is, however, some scepticism relating to the true independence of directors in Hong Kong owing to the nature of the business community being relatively small and inter-related. The fact that many companies are family controlled also decreases the possibility of having INEDs.

The amended Listing Rules require confirmations of independence from existing INEDs with reference to the new guidelines on independence and stipulate that at least one INED must have appropriate professional qualifications or accounting or related financial management expertise.

4.4.2 Separation of the Role of Chairman and Chief Executive

The case of an executive holding the dual roles of chairman and chief executive is prevalent in Hong Kong. However, there is a trend to separate these roles, particularly in major companies. The separation of the roles of chairman and chief executive in Kowloon Canton Railway Corporation was a high-profile example drawing public attention. The new code on Corporate Governance Practices and amended Listing Rules recommend the segregation of the two roles and require disclosure in the annual reports whether these two roles are segregated.

4.4.3 Remuneration

There have been concerns regarding the level of remuneration for executive directors of listed companies, the correlation of their remuneration with company performance and the related scrutiny mechanisms in Hong Kong. The Listing Rules mandate disclosure of directors' remuneration on an individual named basis, of a general description of the remuneration policy and long-term incentive schemes and of the basis on which INEDs are remunerated. The general opinion is that INEDs are woefully under-remunerated, which affects quality and performance. In addition, the Code on Corporate Governance Practices includes the establishment of a Remuneration Committee comprised of a majority of INEDs.

4.5 Codes, Standards and Good Practice Guidelines

In its 2002 Survey on Corporate Governance in Emerging Markets, Crédit Lyonnais Sécurités Asia ranked Hong Kong and Singapore as markets with the highest levels of corporate governance in Asia. Meanwhile, a survey on attitudes to corporate governance in China and Southeast Asia by the Association of Chartered Certified Accountants in 2002 found that over 60 per cent of Chief Financial Officers in the Mainland of China, Hong Kong and Singapore had increased their awareness of the need for good corporate governance, while 60 per cent of the boards had taken action to review the corporate governance systems of their particular companies.

4.5.1 Corporate Governance Review, Standing Committee on Company Law Reform (SCCLR)

In early 2000, the Financial Secretary asked the SCCLR to undertake an overall review of corporate governance in Hong Kong. The SCCLR established Directors, Shareholders and Corporate Reporting Sub-Committees to undertake the review. As part of the review, the SCCLR commissioned four consultancy reports by the City University of Hong Kong and the Chinese University. Two of these were surveys required to establish external and internal bench-marks. The first was a comparative survey and analysis of the development of corporate governance standards in other comparable jurisdictions, including Australia, Singapore, Taiwan, the United Kingdom and the USA. The second was a survey of the attitudes of international institutional investors towards corporate governance standards in Hong Kong. The review covered unlisted as well as listed companies.

Phase I of the Review was completed in early 2001 and a Consultation Paper published in July 2001. Issues covered included:

- directors' duties;
- connected transactions;
- nomination and election of directors;
- shareholders' remedies including the introduction of a statutory derivative action;
- accounting and auditing standard setting process;
- establishment of a body to investigate financial statements; and the
- revision of audited financial statements.

Action to implement reforms, which do not require legislative amendments, has been taken in conjunction with the Hong Kong Society of Accountants and the Stock Exchange of Hong Kong. Some of the reforms requiring legislative amendments, namely the strengthening of shareholders' remedies, have been included in the Companies (Amendment) Ordinance 2003.

Phase II of the Review was completed in late 2002 and a Consultation Paper published in June 2003. Issues covered include:

- audit, nomination and remuneration committees;
- structure of the board and the role of non-executive directors;
- directors' qualifications and training;
- directors' remuneration;
- company general meetings;
- proxies;
- responsibilities, liabilities and independence of external auditors; and
- corporate regulation.

Appropriate follow-up action will be taken in the light of the comments received as a result of the consultation exercise.

4.5.2 Listing Rules, Hong Kong Exchanges and Clearing Ltd (HKEx)

The Securities and Futures Commission and Hong Kong Exchanges and Clearing Limited have been working on the enhancement of requirements in corporate governance among listed companies. Regulations and listing requirements compatible with international standards and practices are being introduced after consultation with the market followed by public education.

The Listing Rules of the Stock Exchange of Hong Kong stipulate mandatory requirements regulating corporate processes and actions of listed companies to ensure the protection of shareholders' rights and the proper disclosure of information to the public. They also contain a set of guidelines and minimum standards on the fulfilment of corporate governance duties by directors of a listed company.

Over the years, the Listing Rules have undergone dynamic changes. They included a complete revamp in 1991, the introduction of the Code of Best Practice for directors and the requirement for independent non-executive directors (INEDs) in 1993, expansion of disclosure requirements in financial statements in 1994, 1998 and 2000 and proposals relating to corporate governance issues that were published for consultation in 2002 and concluded in 2003 for the Listing Rules amendment, effective in 2004 and Code of Corporate Governance Practices effective in 2005.

4.6   Disclosure and Transparency

Private companies are beginning to realize the need for internal controls in their development from merely surviving competition to achieving growth and profitability. The call for strategic direction sends them on the way to keeping up to date and implementing proper practices of corporate governance. Whilst listed companies and non-profit-distributing organizations are regulated or supervised, private companies practise corporate governance out of voluntary initiatives.

4.6.1   Corporate Reporting

Companies in Hong Kong are required to maintain and disclose their financial information in accordance with Hong Kong accounting standards and auditing standards, which are in turn based on the International Accounting Standards and International Standards on Auditing respectively.

Companies listed on the Growth Enterprise Market Board of the HKEx have to comply with quarterly reporting as they may not have a proven profit track record upon their initial listing. The issues of quarterly reporting requirements for companies listed on the Main Board have been debated seriously. In the light of the developments in major markets elsewhere, in particular in the UK, the European Union's proposal of introduction of quarterly reporting in its member states from 2005 onwards and experience gained after amendments to the Listing Rules and the introduction of the Code on Corporate Governance Practices HKEx will further review the appropriateness of requiring Main Board listed companies to adopt quarterly reporting by 2005.

In the new scheme, listed companies must include a Corporate Governance Report in their annual reports. This report has three levels of disclosure requirements:

- mandatory disclosure requirements, non-compliance of which is a breach of the Listing Rules;

- a summary of the Code provisions relating to the company's corporate governance practices (comply or explain);

- practices that are recommended.

The Companies Ordinance requires that every company should keep proper books of accounts giving a true and fair view of the company's financial statements. Directors may be liable to fines or imprisonment if this rule is not upheld. In addition, a report by the directors must be attached to the balance sheet in the annual report providing information such as:

- the principal activities of the company;

- the names of directors;

- the amount which the directors recommend should be paid as a dividend;

- the amount of donations;

- significant changes in the fixed assets of the company; and

- management contracts.

4.6.2 Audit Committee

The new Listing Rules mandate an audit committee to be set up by each listed company, comprising non-executive directors only with at least three members, a majority of INEDs, one of whom must be qualified or experienced in financial management expertise, and chaired by an INED.

4.6.3 Transparency and Disclosure

The Securities and Futures Ordinance requires notification to the Stock Exchange on stringent change of interest by any person or entity. In addition, any director or chief executive is required by law to inform the listed company of relevant interests. A listed company is required by law to keep a register of this information made available for public scrutiny. The Listing Rules also stipulate disclosure in the annual report of a listed company of significant holdings of each director and of any shareholder.

4.7   Shareholder Rights and Stakeholder Relations

Shareholder activism has increased in recent years and drawn the attention of minority shareholders to the significance of transparency, shareholder rights and corporate governance. Marking the emergence of shareholder activism was the election of a high-profile advocate of minority shareholders to the board of HKEx.

The Listing Rules and the Takeovers Code are continually reviewed, particularly in the introduction of equitable treatment for all share-holders. Conversion of family businesses to well-structured and well-governed modern companies is slowly under way. In a survey conducted by Grant Thornton in 2001, findings indicated that owner-managers of businesses are now receptive to transferring shares to outsiders, allowing management successors from outside and using professional services to assist in business development.

The Companies Ordinance contains provisions which aim to ensure that the rights of the shareholders of a company are protected.

4.8   Director Development Activity

Directors' qualifications and training were included in the recent Corporate Governance Review by the Standing Committee on Company Law Reform (June 2003). Whilst recognizing the importance of improving and maintaining director professionalism, the Committee recommends in its consultation paper that:

> *It would not be either practical or desirable to make directors' training and qualifications mandatory at this stage. However, the SCCLR recognize that, in practice, there are non-executive directors who do not know what responsibilities they have to the company. As a matter of principle, all directors should be required to have an appropriate knowledge of company law, the listing rules, and the Hong Kong Code. In view of this the Hong Kong Code should contain a requirement that a listed company has to disclose what arrangements are made to train its directors, particularly new NEDs, on both an initial and continuous basis, with particular reference to knowledge of company law, the Listing Rules and the Hong Kong Code. Listed companies would be required to disclose in their annual reports either their compliance or reasons for non-compliance with this requirement in the Code.*

4.8.1   Universities

Out of the eight universities in Hong Kong, those with a business school place great emphasis on corporate governance, which has become an essential part of the curriculum for Masters of Business Administration and Doctorate in Business Administration programmes. The Open University of Hong Kong has a Master's degree course in Corporate Governance, while the other universities are contemplating the establishment of such a course.

4.8.2   Hong Kong Institute of Directors (HKIoD)

Dedicated to continually empowering directors in the enhancement of standards of corporate governance, The Hong Kong Institute of Directors (HKIoD) offers professional development programmes for directors. These are designed on the basis of its definition of Core Competencies for Directors, covering knowledge and skills in corporate business functions, the role and responsibilities of the director and the board, development of the board and business ethics as well as personal qualities expected of a director.

The Institute's professional development programmes include formal classroom training, professional talks, speaker meetings, workshops and publications. The Institute offers training programmes in English, Cantonese and Putonghua leading to a diploma by different paths, either by credits accumulation or by enrolment to a packaged course within a short period of time with an intense programme. The Hong Kong Productivity Council, a major multi-disciplinary organization, which has integrated corporate governance in its offering of training programmes, is a frequent partner of the HKIoD on such initiatives.

The Hong Kong Institute of Directors, with support and promotion from the regulators, has embarked on training programmes directed at skills required to discharge the responsibilities of INEDs. The HKIoD also offers a board appointment service facilitating matching of companies with candidates on the Institute's register of qualified members for director appointment. There has been increasing emphasis on the training of INEDs and in ensuring that they understand their role and nature of independence in protecting minority interests. The general concern is that there is a limited supply of qualified INEDs in the Hong Kong market.

In May 2002, the Institute published its position with regard to training and education for directors, stipulating the core elements for director training, particularly in regard to listed companies. This paper was considered by the Directors Sub-Committee of the Standing Committee on Company Law Reform, the Securities and Futures Commission and the Hong Kong Exchanges and Clearing Ltd.

The publications *Guidelines for Directors* and *Guide for Independent Non-Executive Directors* of The Hong Kong Institute of Directors, published in both English and Chinese, have been circulated to over 1,000 readers and 1,500 readers respectively.

The Institute's latest publication, *Guidelines on Corporate Governance for SMEs in Hong Kong*, has been produced with endorsement and financial support from the SME Development Fund administered by the Trade and Industry Department. Since publication, the guidelines are deemed practical and useful for the SMEs, which constitute a vast majority of business entities, ranging from single proprietorships to listed companies. The publication focuses on corporate governance in five categories of SMEs according to their scale of operation, the integration of management practices with governance practices and the issues of family businesses and solutions.

In addition, The Hong Kong Institute of Directors has chosen to promote, inspire, educate and encourage good corporate governance by means of awards. Directors Of The Year Awards were first launched in 2001 and have developed into an annual event organized by the Institute together with over 50 partners as a community-wide consultation with nominations of candidates open to the public. The Awards are divided by organization types of listed companies, private companies as well as statutory/non-profit-distributing organizations and categorized by executive directors, non-executive directors and collective boards.

Planned projects for imminent implementation by The Hong Kong Institute of Directors include the development and publication of scorecards on major listed companies in Hong Kong and the introduction of accreditation of directors through the requirement for annual continuing professional development among members of the Institute so as to initiate a self-disciplined culture.

4.9   Useful Contacts

- Companies Registry – www.info.gov.hk/cr

- Financial Services and the Treasury Bureau – www.info.gov.hk/fstb/fsb

- Hong Kong Exchanges and Clearing Limited (HKEx) – www.hkex.com.hk.

- Hong Kong Institute of Company Secretaries (HKICS) – www.hkics.org.hk

- The Hong Kong Institute of Directors (HKIoD) – www.hkiod.com

- Hong Kong Monetary Authority (HKMA) – www.info.gov.hk/hkma

- Hong Kong Society of Accountants (HKSoA) – www.hksoa.org.hk

- Securities and Futures Commission (SFC) – www.hksfc.org.hk

- Standing Committee on Company Law Reform (SCCLR) – www.info.gov.hk/cr/scclr/index.htm

4.10   Further Reading

'About the SFC', 'Bills, Legislations & Codes' and 'Takeovers & Mergers' in http://www. hksfc.org.hk/eng/html/index.html (May 2003). Internet: Securities and Futures Commission

Cheng, M C (2002) *Corporate Governance and Related Reforms for East Asia – A Presentation to the Concurrent Session 3 of the 14th General Meeting of Pacific Economic Cooperation Council by Moses M C Cheng, Chairman, HKIoD,* The Hong Kong Institute of Directors, Hong Kong

The Hong Kong Institute of Directors (1995) *Guidelines for Directors*

The Hong Kong Institute of Directors (2003) *Guide for Independent Non-Executive Director,* 2nd edn

The Hong Kong Institute of Directors (2003) *Guidelines on Corporate Governance for SMEs in Hong Kong*

Hong Kong Society of Accountants (2001) *Corporate Governance Disclosure in Annual Reports, HKSA, Hong Kong*

Hong Kong Society of Accountants (2002) *Guide for Effective Audit Committee*

Hong Kong Stock Exchange (2004) *Listing Rules and Exposure Paper on Draft Code on Corporate Governance Practices & Corporate Governance Reporting*

Key Statistics in http://www.info.gov.hk/cr/key/index.htm (May 2003). Internet: Companies Registry, Government of the Hong Kong SAR

Securities and Futures Commission (2001). Corporate Governance in the Special Administrative Region of Hong Kong in *Corporate Governance in Asia – A Comparative Perspective*, Centre For Cooperation with Non-Members, OECD, Paris, pp 223–47

Standards & Poors, Web information on Corporate Governance in Hong Kong, Standards & Poors, Hong Kong

Standing Committee on Company Law Reform (2001) *Corporate Governance Review by The Standing Committee on Company Law Reform – A Consultation Paper on proposals made in Phase I of the Review*, Standing Committee on Company Law Reform, Hong Kong

Thornton, G (2002) *The Family and the Business Survey*, University of Hong Kong, Hong Kong

Tsang, J and Gul, F A (2002) *Corporate Governance Regimes in Other Jurisdictions in Connection with the Corporate Governance Review in Hong Kong*, University of Hong Kong, Hong Kong

Japan

Table 5.1

Population	127.2 million (2003)
Gross National Income (GNI)	$4.3 trillion (2002)
GNI per capita	$33,550 (2002)
Total number of companies	N/A
Number of companies listed on the Stock Exchange	N/A
Market capitalization	$2,745.8 billion (2001)
Key corporate laws	● Commercial Law
Key corporate governance codes	● Revised Corporate Governance Principles (2001)

5.1 Corporate Structure and Ownership

Japanese corporate governance was once considered as a model of growth and prosperity in the 1980s, with a focus on the dramatic recovery of its economy after it had been completely destroyed by the Second World War. Collaboration and mutual trust among management, employees, banks, suppliers, clients and the community was a feature of the Japanese corporate culture. Cross-holding of shares was viewed as developing good relationships, and protected the company from hostile takeovers. It also ensured that the executive management was monitored by key interested parties, especially by the main bank.

Since the mid-1990s, the influence of corporate governance has changed slightly. This was as a consequence of the slowing down of the Japanese economy, whilst the US economy appeared to be bullish, associated with the successful corporate restructuring. Corporate governance in Japan has recently focused on improving business performance, and additionally globalization, involving:

- the change in the source of fund raising from banks to the international financial markets;
- the shift of manufacturing factories overseas; and
- the removal of trade barriers.

The above factors have triggered the dissolution of the traditional relationships among interested parties, especially with banks, employees and investors/shareholders.

With the changing environment the Anglo-American standards and methods of implementing corporate governance have been gradually introduced into Japan. This influence can be seen particularly in the increasingly market value oriented management movement towards greater disclosure, board structures, and shareholder relations. Despite such influences, however, most Japanese companies are enhancing corporate governance in their own ways and not necessarily following the Anglo-American model. This is because the latest company law reforms in Japan permit a significant flexibility to each company in the manner in which they operate and ensure fairness and equity.

5.1.1 Cross-shareholding

Cross-shareholding has been a prominent feature of corporate governance structures in Japan. Individual companies formed groups called Keiretsu with each member company owning equity in the other companies in the group. This has been changing, and according to the ratings agency, Standard & Poors:

> *cumulative shareholdings of banks fell to 8.7 per cent of the total market capitalization of Japan's five exchanges as of March 31 2002, compared with a level*

of roughly 15 per cent until the mid-1990s. In contrast individual investors' shareholdings have grown to 19.7 per cent, thereby becoming a more important aggregate shareholder than the banking sector. Foreign ownership was 18.3 per cent as of March 2002 and has shown growth in recent years. While the domestic corporate sector remains the leading source of share ownership, showing the continuous importance of cross shareholdings in Japan, the growth of individual and foreign ownership has resulted in the proportion of domestic corporate ownership dropping to 21.8 per cent at March 2002 from over 25 per cent prior to fiscal 1999. These changes have had an important influence on the corporate governance debate in Japan.

5.1.2 Family-owned Companies

Many companies like Toyota, Honda, Matsushita, Kikkoman and Daiei were established as family companies and then became public. There are still many, especially young companies, which are controlled by a family with a significant share ownership.

As with any other company, both professional auditors and statutory auditors are required to conduct strict reviews of corporate actions to prevent conflicts of interest in related transactions with family companies or closely held companies.

5.1.3 Government-linked Companies

Many public service industries were initiated by the government such as the railways, highways, postal services, steel, utilities supplies, telephone, oil and gas, tobacco, salt and so on. Many of them were made public so that they could be self-sustainable and competitive, but still there are some owned by state and local governments which are a financial burden for taxpayers.

Examples of current targets of governance improvement among state-owned enterprises ('SOE') are Postal Services and the Highway Corporation. The governance structures of each industry have been reviewed so that management can aim for 'the long-term sustainable growth' of the corporation without a significant amount of subsidies from taxpayers and without being adversely influenced by bureaucrats and outside parties. Traditionally, top executives of these SOEs were appointed from top bureaucrats. They are now appointed from experienced top business executives, though there is strong opposition from traditional beneficiaries.

5.2 Legal Framework

The relevant legislation in Japan containing corporate governance principles include:

- the Company Law;

- the Exceptional Rule of Commercial Law for Corporate Auditing;

- the Securities Trade Law;

- the Law Forbidding Private Monopoly and Ensuring Fair Trade (Anti-Trust Law);

- the Manufactured Product Liability Law;

- the Environmental Standards Law; and

- the Labour Laws. These include the Labour Standards Law, Employment Security Law, Labour Union Law, Labour Relation Arbitration Law and the Equal Employment Opportunity Law, etc.

Company Law stipulates the director's duties to serve the company in good faith and to avoid conflict of interest and misconduct.

Statutory auditors must be elected by the shareholders' meeting and the majority must be from independent outsiders in big companies. Auditors may attend the board meetings, call board meetings, sue directors for misconduct and inspect subsidiaries.

The duties imposed by the Company Law on directors are owed by them to the company in good faith and in compliance with regulations, articles of incorporation and the decisions of shareholders' meetings. These duties are enforceable in the same way as any fiduciary duty owed to the company. Naturally, loyalty to the company is assumed and transactions of directors with the company must be approved by the other members of the board, to avoid conflict of interest.

It is clear that the duties imposed by the Company Law on directors are owed by them 'to the company'. The duties to the company have not been sufficiently recognized as duties to the shareholders. Traditionally, Japanese management has been seeking long-term stable growth of the company which shall be contributed first to employees, then other stakeholders, including creditors. In particular, the duty owed to creditors will take legal precedence over that owed to shareholders.

Directors are responsible for overseeing the conduct of the other directors as stipulated in Section 260 of the Company Law, and in principle, all directors are liable for misconduct of the board, unless otherwise expressed at the board meeting (Section 266). However, there are slight differences in the amount of liability for violation of regulations and the articles of incorporation. The shareholders' meeting may approve stipulating in the articles of incorporation that the maximum amount of liability will be limited to the amount equal to 6 years' compensation for representative directors, 4 years' for the other executive directors and 2 years' for non-executive outside directors, unless there has been bad faith or gross negligence on the part of the director. Despite such stipulation in the articles of incorporation, shareholders with 3 per cent ownership may block such exemption.

5.2.1　The Business Judgement Rule

Directors are not liable for losses as long as they made necessary efforts in good faith. However, damage by lack of appropriate oversight to subordinates would impose a penalty on executives. Further, even though they are not legally liable, executive directors normally assume moral responsibility for the results of the business, and either retire or reduce their compensation voluntarily.

5.3　Legal, Regulatory and Institutional Bodies

5.3.1　Financial Service Agency (FSA)

The FSA was constituted by the Cabinet Office Establishment Law and the FSA Establishment Law in January 2001. It is responsible for supervising financial market activity in Japan. The FSA is directed by the Minister for Financial Services and a Commissioner who reports to the Minister. The FSA is responsible for conducting financial market intelligence, research, planning, training and professional development, reviewing legal issues, setting accounting and auditing principles, as well as the supervision of financial institutions and securities trades.

5.3.2 Securities and Exchange Surveillance Commission (SESC)

The SESC was established to monitor compliance with securities law following a stock market scandal in 1992. The SESC has 360 staff under three commissions. Members are appointed by the prime minister with the consent of both Houses of Representatives and Councillors, and they may not be dismissed against their will during their three years' tenure to ensure their independence. The primary mission of the SESC is to protect investors and maintain the integrity of the securities markets. For this purpose SESC conducts inspections of securities companies, daily surveillance of securities markets and investigations of securities fraud.

Besides the SESC, there are two important deliberative councils in the FSA. The **Financial Deliberative Council** was established for the improvement of financial systems by the FSA Establishment Law and by Cabinet Ordinance in June 2000, nominated by the Prime Minister and endorsed by both Houses of Representatives and Councillors. **The Corporate Accounting Standards Deliberative Council** (CASDC) was established in 1952 by Cabinet Ordinance and is nominated by the FSA Commissioner. The Council serves as an advisory organ for the Prime Minister and the FSA Commissioner and has a decisive role on Accounting and Auditing Principles. Further, the **Financial Accounting Standards Foundation** (FASF) was established by private financial and business sector representatives in July 2001. The FASF embodies the Accounting Standards Board of Japan (ASBJ) which independently develops accounting standards and guidelines, and functions as contact with IASB. It is understood that the FASF will replace the CASDC.

It should be also noted that in Japan, other ministries provide 'Administrative Guidance' regarding poor governance practices which cause illegal conduct of executives or employees. Further, it is reported that the Ministry of Economy, Trade and Industry have requested Tokyo Stock Exchange and related agencies to make disclosure mandatory of three figures:

- average payout time of loan;
- interest coverage ratio; and
- shareholders' equity ratio.

5.3.3   Tokyo Stock Exchange (TSE)

In December 2002, the TSE established an Advisory Committee for Corporate Governance. However, the TSE does not intend to establish rigid rules or 'best practice' nor make it compulsory to report deviations. The TSE considers that listed companies know the importance of corporate governance and what investors are requesting, and they should engineer the best system by themselves.

5.3.4   Nippon Keidanren (Japan Business Federation)

The Nippon Keidanren has a role to play in corporate governance developments in Japan but it is resistant to Anglo-American style regimes focused on independent non-executive directors.

5.4   Board Structure

Since the latest reform of the Company Law, effective from 1 April 2003, the structure of the board of directors in Japan has become very flexible in three different ways.

The first is the traditional unitary board where important decisions need action by the entire board and cannot be delegated to an individual or a group of directors. Unless otherwise expressed at the board, all directors are equally responsible for decisions and are held liable for misconduct of the board.

The second structure permits the board of big companies to establish an 'important assets committee', which is an executive committee comprising three or more executive directors. Such a committee can only be established where the board has ten or more members and at least one non-executive independent director. The committee, if formed, is empowered to approve matters otherwise reserved for action by the entire board.

In the two structures outlined above, the statutory auditors are not board members and they are elected at the shareholders' meeting to oversee directors.

In the third structure, a company may provide in its articles of incorporation for the establishment of audit, nomination and compensation committees of the board, each with a majority of independent outside directors who have not worked for the company or its subsidiaries in the past. If the company adopts this system, it may dispense with the current requirement by the Company Law to maintain statutory auditors, but must employ an executive officer. Executive officers may be either directors or non-directors. In this structure, the role of the board of directors is important to strategic policy and the overseeing of executive officers, and includes the nomination and remuneration of executives.

There are not many companies which apply the second and the third structures. According to a survey by the Tokyo Stock Exchange (TSE) announced on 27 January 2003, about 4.3 per cent of companies show interest in the second structure and 4.7 per cent such as Sony, Hitachi, Hoya and ORIX in the third structure, while 64–65 per cent do not have a plan to change and are staying in the first structure.

According to Standard & Poors when examining board structures in Japan:

> Board membership is frequently offered as a reward to long-serving, loyal employees. This system has two noteworthy implications: board size can tend to expand, and the balance of power can be tilted in favour of senior management as opposed to board directors. Boards have traditionally been quiescent and have surrendered most of their authority to company presidents on a range of matters, including hiring and firing top executives, executive pay and severance packages, as well as other management decisions. Even though the board of directors theoretically has the ultimate authority to oversee the activities of a company on behalf of shareholders, in practice, boards in Japan have conventionally not been equipped with adequate governance power or capabilities to carry out this role satisfactorily.
>
> Increasingly, the board's supervisory functions are being separated from the day-to-day operating functions of the company, aimed at ensuring the board takes charge of the former and that executive management is responsible for the latter. This separation of roles would ensure that a single person does not hold the chairpersonship of both the board of directors and the executive board, other than in exceptional circumstances.

5.4.1 Size

According to a survey by the *Nikkei*, a Japanese leading economic paper, the average number of directors on a board in Japan is about 15 as of June 2002, a reduction of 25 per cent from 1999. A similar survey by the Keizai-Doyukai (Association of Corporate Executives) shows that 74 per cent of respondents had 15 directors or less. A few years ago, 30–40 directors was not unusual, while now there are many which have only 7 or fewer, and those with more than 30 account for only 6 per cent.

5.4.2 Composition

Separation of the role of the chairman and the executive officers is not clear, as in most cases the chairman is also a representative director, and in many cases the chief executive chairs the board meeting. Because directors are usually promoted from the employees, non-executive outside directors are still in a minority. Notwithstanding such traditional practice, however, the Keizai-Doyukai survey indicated that about 55 per cent of companies now have non-executive outside directors. Further, according to a public opinion poll in April 2002 by the Nikkei BP, about 70 per cent of people consider that the law should force companies to have non-executive outside directors, though such opinion was opposed by the Nippon Keidanren (Japan Business Federation), which claimed that it must be left to the discretion of each company and that there are not many qualified candidates.

An outside director does not always mean an independent director in Japan. In many cases they are from main banks, trading partners and main shareholders, though genuine independent directors are gradually increasing.

5.4.3 Committees

A recent survey by the Tokyo Stock Exchange revealed that 4.7 per cent of the companies are planning to move to the committee system, establishing three committees, namely remuneration, nomination and audit, and 65 per cent have no plans to do so. A remaining 24 per cent are still undecided. Although legally the committee system was effective from April 2003, many companies are still hesitant to move to the system.

It is noteworthy, however, that the Keizai-Doyukai announced a policy proposal in July 2002 for 'Corporate Governance Reform for Competitiveness', advocating the necessity of three committees. Meanwhile, as a practical step towards the committee system, there are a few that are establishing an outside advisory committee or board.

Audit Committee

The proposed plan in the revised Commercial Law is to have an audit committee comprising members of the board of directors. They would replace the statutory auditors who are elected by shareholders meeting separately from directors. The proposed plan may achieve better communication between executive directors and audit committee members, while the traditional way may be preferable to maintain the independence of auditors.

Keidanren considers that having the present system involving statutory auditors elected by shareholders is more effective than having a committee of outsiders elected by the board, and that enforcing the interplay between statutory auditors, professional accounting auditors and in-house internal audit departments should work better.

Compensation Committee

In Japanese Company Law, the compensation for directors and auditors must be approved at the shareholders' meeting. There are not many cases of compensation committees, though there are a few exceptions like Sony, Hitachi, ORIX, Daiwa Securities, Kikkoman and Hoya Glass. On the other hand, there are a few cases of companies establishing an advisory committee outside the board and inviting genuine independent persons.

There are some self-restraints in Japan which keep compensation at a modest level and make people think that compensation committees are unnecessary.

Japanese tax regulations permit the monthly salary of directors to be charged to an expense account, while a bonus is considered to be distribution of income after tax. If the monthly salary is excessively high in comparison to regular practice or to similar companies, such an excessive portion cannot be charged as an expense. Such regulation prevents a big fluctuation of income for directors based on performance.

Further, there is not much interest or concern about the level of compensation of top business executives, as their annual income is always compared with those of their employees and peers in similar industries.

Those incomes exceeding 20 million yen (about US $170,000) are disclosed to the public and the media lists the income of each top executive. Most top executives would not like to be seen as greedy by receiving top compensation even though the performance of the company is among the best; thus very few top executives are receiving one million US dollars or more.

Nomination Committee

A nomination committee ensures a formal and transparent board nomination process. However, this committee is not popular in Japan. According to a TSE survey, 2.4 per cent listed companies have a nomination committee and another 3.8 per cent are planning to have one. One of the reasons for its unpopularity is that the nomination of executives, especially of the succeeding CEO, is a source of power for the CEO to control human resources in the company, as executives are usually promoted from employees and not from outsiders. Further, in many of the big companies with a long history, there are tacit understandings that the CEO changes every 4–6 years. However, to make the process of selecting the executive transparent, an advisory board is established in a few companies, which reports to the CEO or board of directors.

Compliance Committee and Whistle-blowing

'A single lie shall terminate a company' is a lesson from the recent misconduct of management and employees in such cases as Snow Brand and Nippon Rain. In most cases in Japan, top executives must assume moral responsibility even in cases of misconduct by lower management.

As a countermeasure for such risk, on top of strengthening the auditor role, a compliance committee is becoming more common for most big companies. The latest TSE survey shows 55.9 per cent of companies have or are planning to establish this committee.

Another measure is to make whistle-blowing easier by such means as employing intermediaries to whom employees or whistleblowers can report misconduct without having their name known. However, no whistleblower protection law has yet been introduced.

5.5　Codes, Standards and Good Practice Guidelines

Japan does not have a formal Code of Corporate Governance issued by a regulatory body or any of the stock exchanges. However, the

Japan Corporate Governance Forum, a voluntary body comprising both academia and business executives, has been advocating the necessity of good corporate governance practices since 1996 and issued 'Corporate Governance Principles' in 1998 and revised in 2001.

There are no established rules for the implementation and review procedures of corporate governance. However, the Governor of the Tokyo Stock Exchange (TSE) sent a letter to all listed companies in 1998 requesting that they keep the TSE informed of any reforms to their corporate governance. The Financial Deliberative Council of FSA announced on 6 August 2002 the necessity to make mandatory, in the near future, a disclosure of corporate governance status in the 'Security Report' for each listed company.

5.6   Disclosure and Transparency

Disclosure and transparency are enforced by the Commercial Law, the Securities Trade Law, and Accounting and Audit Principles.

Corporate accounting and disclosures are regulated by the FSA, supported by the Corporate Accounting Deliberative Commission. Financial disclosure requirements are specified in the Securities Trade Act, and reports from listed companies are open to the public and also available through the Internet by EDINET (Electronic Disclosure for Investors' Network). Further, the SESC monitors market manipulation, insider trading and falsified financial statements. The requirements include key financial statements such as the balance sheet, income status, main business transactions and auditing reports. Disclosures are required semi-annually for key figures, and once per year a 'Security Report' with a business summary and full details of liabilities and assets, the accounting method and the opinions of both professional accounting firms and statutory auditors must be produced. Also, disclosure of cash flow analysis is required for investors to judge long-term sustainability as a going concern.

One of the current accounting issues is the evaluation of fixed assets at market value or value on a discounted cash flow basis, rather than value on the acquisition cost basis. This principle will be applied in 2005.

Another ongoing issue is to examine the valuation allowance of deferred tax assets, or operating losses carried forward for tax purposes, that may not be realized.

According to Standard & Poors:

> *An emphasis on disclosure has developed in recent years alongside the collapse of several companies associated with poor disclosure in Japan. Because of the closed keiretsu business network, it has not been common business practice to make information publicly available in a timely manner. Instead, companies have offered information to a closed inner circle of major shareholders, which typically includes the company's main bank, and regulators. A rapid erosion of the cross-shareholding system and the recent influx of many foreign institutional investors have fuelled pressure for more public disclosure of information by Japanese corporations.*

> *The Commercial Code requires large Japanese corporations to report a balance sheet and profit and loss statement prior to the AGM. The SEL requires companies to submit copies of financial documentation to the local regulator, the stock-exchange authorities, and the company's principal office twice a year.*

5.6.1 Creative Accounting

The frequent disclosures to investors increases the pressure on chief financial officers to manage corporate earnings and expectations. There is room for manipulation, such as changing accounting methods of depreciation, amortization of fixed assets and development expenses and evaluation of credits and liabilities. Also, transactions between family companies are often found to have been manipulated. The motivation for this manipulation varies from avoiding a short-term fluctuation of income to concealing business failure or poor governance. The tax authority and professional auditors are very strict in keeping the principles of accounting consistency and conservatism and in examining the reasons for any changes.

The most critical current issue for banks and insurance companies is that the FSA has begun to examine the evaluation of credits to poorly performed companies and long-term assets. As a result of these reviews by the FSA, many banks and insurance companies have had to devalue their bad loans and consequently the disclosure of financial status has been clarified. Further, many banks have decided to increase equity by issuing new shares.

5.6.2 Audit

A big company must be audited by a professional auditor along with the statutory auditor or an audit committee (in the case where it has such a committee). Also, most big companies have an internal audit department that reports to the executive director. Usually they support both statutory auditors and professional auditors. A close interplay among the three audit functions is enhanced.

Appointment of the professional auditors must be approved at the shareholders' meeting, after first being approved by statutory auditors. In enforcing the independence of professional auditing, the Japan Institute of Certified Public Accountants (JICPA) is reviewing outside auditing rules and the system by:

- establishing an overseeing function in the association;
- shorter rotation intervals of auditors;
- multiple persons to audit a big company; and
- a strict firewall between auditing and consulting work.

5.6.3   Internal Control

The primary responsibility of internal control is owed by directors to the company. For this purpose, most companies have the internal control division reporting to the top executive director.

A revision of Auditing Principles by the CADC (recommended by the JICPA), announced on 25 January 2002, makes it mandatory to evaluate the internal control system of a client and assess potential risks in due consideration of the business as an ongoing concern. If professional auditors find misconduct of executives, it must be reported to the statutory auditors or audit committee. If they fail to report, they are also liable for misconduct.

5.7   Shareholder Rights and Stakeholder Relations

5.7.1   Shareholders

Maximizing value for shareholders has not necessarily been a concern of management. Usually a modest and long-term stable dividend was considered to satisfy shareholders. The main source of funds of the company was mostly from bank borrowing, and the majority of shareholders were financial institutions and business partners by cross-holding, whose incentives for shareholding are good business relationships rather than dividends. In other words, the majority of shareholders preferred good business terms to their rights as shareholders. However, as a result of sources of funds changing from banks to securities markets nowadays the market value for shareholders has become one of the first priorities of management.

According to the Standard & Poors country assessment on Japan:

> *The Commercial Code provides shareholders with the right to appoint and dismiss board members at Annual General Meetings (AGMs), to seek reports from management and auditors, and to vote on changes in corporate structure. Each shareholder has a single vote per share. Still relatively concentrated ownership structures in Japan have not made it possible for small shareholders as a group to have a large impact on management. The Commercial Code does not guarantee the pre-emptive rights of shareholders. A board of directors has the authority to decide whether the company gives such rights to shareholders.*

Three per cent of shareholders are empowered to call general meetings and review the company books. Three hundred units or 1 per cent ownership is required, to propose an agenda item for the general meeting. Also, by one or more units of ownership, shareholders can file legal action against the misconduct of directors. Shares held by subsidiaries, with ownership of 25 per cent or more, must be excluded from quorum of shareholders' meetings.

5.7.2 Stakeholders

The stakeholders include financial institutions such as banks, creditors, suppliers, consumers, employees and the community. None of these stakeholders would exercise any powers over a company as long as the company is run successfully and there is continued growth and increased profits.

Where, however, there are signs of poor performance and governance becomes suspect, a main bank which has extended the largest loan or which has the largest loan balance owing to it can exert influence on the company by reviewing the investment plans and income status of the company. This is true even though financing normally involves consortiums of many financial institutions, as the main bank is expected to take on the role of oversight over the management and to extend such necessary advice as may be needed to ensure that the company is prudently run. It is noteworthy that the influence of main banks has been on the decline as companies have increasingly sought alternative funds directly from the securities market and less from banks.

The labour unions and employees of the company are another influential group in the company and can influence management. Given the tradition of lifetime employment, along with which comes seniority in promotion and compensation, the management of a company and its employees behave as if they are one family. They watch the actions of management and question those actions where there is poor performance. As an indication of the tradition of treating the work environment as a family, it is common for the management to cut their own salary before they request the cooperation of employees in the event of a downturn or a restructuring.

Employees are protected by the Labour Laws, consumers by the Manufactured Product Liability Law and the community and public by the Anti-Trust Law as well as by the Environmental Law. These laws not only protect stakeholders but also contribute in allowing them to discuss with management any issues related to them.

Consumers, distributors, sales agents and the communities are becoming more and more influential. The influence they exert on companies to ensure better corporate governance is more passive, but is increasingly seen to be effective. For example, there have been several cases where consumers have refused to buy the products of scandalous companies involved in illegal or immoral conduct, and this has even driven some companies into bankruptcy.

Because of these relations with stakeholders, both professional auditors and statutory auditors have had to extend their audits to review the relationships and potential risks as well as examining the accounts, such as the loan balance and the accounts payable and receivable.

5.8   Director Development Activity

In 2000, the Japan Management Association created a partnership with the Institute of Directors in London to run director development programmes in Tokyo. The development programme comprises eight courses of 1, 2 or 3 days' duration. The courses cover:

- Role of Company Director
- Director and the Law

- Strategic Business Direction
- Finance
- Effective Marketing Strategy
- Directing and Leading Change
- Board Decision Making
- People Mean Business.

An examination to assess the knowledge and understanding of delegates attending the programme is held twice a year.

5.9 Useful Contacts

- Accounting Standards Board of Japan – www.asb.or.jp
- Corporate Governance Forum – www.jcgf.jp
- Financial Accounting Standards Foundation – www.asb.or.jp
- Financial Services Agency (FSA) – www.fsa.go.jp
- Japan Management Association (JMA) – www.jma.or.jp
- Japan Securities Dealers Association (JSDA) – www.jsda.or.jp
- Keizai-Doyukai (Association of Corporate Executives) – www.doyukai.or.jp
- Nippon Keidanren (Japan Business Federation) – www.keidanren.or.jp
- Securities and Exchange Surveillance Commission (SESC) – www.fsa.go.jp/sesc
- Tokyo Stock Exchange (TSE) – www.tse.or.jp

5.10 Further Reading

Corporate Governance Forum of Japan (1998) *Corporate Governance Principles – A Japanese View*, Corporate Governance Forum, Tokyo

Japan Corporate Governance Forum (2001) *Revised Corporate Governance Principles*, Japan Corporate Governance Forum, Tokyo

Developed countries

Keidanren, Japan Federation of Economic Organizations (1997) *Urgent Recommendations Concerning Corporate Governance* [Keidanren Report], Keidanren, Tokyo

Kosei Nenkin Kikin Rengokai (1998) *Report of the Pension Fund Corporate Governance Research Committee, Action Guidelines for Exercising Voting Rights,* Pension Fund Association, Tokyo

An earlier version of this chapter was published in *Corporate Governance Compliance,* edited by K. Anandarajah, in Singapore in 2002

6

New Zealand

Table 6.1

Population	4,022,000 (2003)
Gross National Income (GNI)	US $53.1 billion (2002)
GNI per capita	US $13,710 (2002)
Total number of companies	300,000 (approx)
Number of companies listed on the Stock Exchange	220 NZX (New Zealand Exchange)
Market capitalization	US $18.7 billion (2001)
Key corporate laws	<ul><li>Companies Act (1993)</li><li>Financial Reporting Act (1993)</li></ul>
Key corporate governance codes	<ul><li>NZX Listing Rules and Best Practice Code</li><li>Securities Commission's Principles for Corporate Governance</li></ul>

6.1   Corporate Structure and Ownership

There are approximately 150 New Zealand incorporated companies and 70 overseas companies listed on the stock exchange now called the New Zealand Exchange (NZX). Of the New Zealand incorporated companies, many have majority or cornerstone shareholders based overseas. The total number of companies registered in New Zealand, both listed and unlisted, and including all one-person and family companies, is a little under 300,000. As is therefore apparent, the New Zealand corporate scene is dominated by small to medium-sized enterprises.

As in many developed countries, the limited liability company in New Zealand has been the most significant business structure over the last century. This is given legislative recognition in the Companies Act 1993 which states that one of the purposes of the Act is:

> *To reaffirm the value of the company as a means of achieving economic and social benefits through the aggregation of capital for productive purposes, the spreading of economic risk, and the taking of business risks.*

One or more individuals (the shareholders) can incorporate a company by applying to, and filing, the appropriate forms with the relevant government agency known as the Companies Office of which the administrative head is the Registrar of Companies. From the time of incorporation the company is legally distinct from its shareholders, has legal personality in itself and can accordingly sue and be sued, hold property, enter into transactions, incur liability and generally act as if it were a natural person. Unless the company's constitution provides that the shareholders' liability is unlimited (which is unusual), in general terms shareholders' liability is limited to any amount unpaid on their shares.

The affairs of the company are managed by, or under the supervision of, a single board of directors who may also, but need not, be shareholders. The directors have powers conferred on them by the constitution and by the Companies Act. Particularly in the case of smaller companies, directors are often also employees of the company and take an active part in the company's management. With larger companies, of necessity directors usually assume a largely monitoring role of the performance of management. Again with larger companies, whose affairs can be more complex and time-consuming, it is not uncommon for directors to delegate some of their functions to board committees where matters under consideration can be dealt with more comprehensively and expeditiously.

6.2 Legal Framework

Central to the governance of New Zealand companies are the Companies Act 1993 and the Financial Reporting Act 1993 which are part of a general reform of company law that took place in the 1990s. New Zealand's company law has its origins in the Joint Stock Companies Act 1856 (UK), and the Companies Act 1993's immediate predecessor was closely modelled on the Companies Act 1948 (UK).

6.2.1 Companies Act 1993

The Act introduced many innovations, including:

- a non-mandatory constitution in place of memorandum and articles of association;
- the abolition of the par value of shares and the enabling of companies to purchase and finance the purchase of their own shares;
- a solvency test to be passed if the company is to pay dividends or make other distributions, acquire its own shares, provide financial assistance or redeem shares;
- the retention of shareholder control over major transactions;
- the strengthening of shareholder remedies;
- the streamlining of amalgamation procedures;
- the simplification and clarification of liquidation procedures; and
- the widening of the ability of companies to indemnify and insure their directors and employees.

The Act also extends the definition of director, which, for some purposes, may now include de facto directors, shadow directors, and shareholders who participate in decisions normally made by the directors.

One of the most significant features of the Act is the spelling out, for the first time, of directors' statutory duties. These largely reflect the previous position at common law and essentially are:

- When exercising powers or performing duties, directors must act in good faith and in what they believe to be the best interests of the company. There are exceptions for subsidiary companies, joint venture companies, and employee benefits on the closing down of the company.
- A director must exercise powers for a proper purpose.

- Directors are charged with complying with the Companies Act and the company's constitution, and with ensuring that the company does this also.

- Directors must not engage in reckless trading, which is defined in the Act as agreeing to or causing or allowing conduct likely to create a substantial risk of serious loss to the company's creditors.

- When exercising powers or performing duties, directors are charged with exercising the care, diligence and skill that a reasonable director would exercise in the same circumstances.

- Directors who are interested in transactions to which the company is a party must make disclosure to the board and cause the interest to be noted in the company's interests register required by the Act to be maintained.

- The disclosure or use of confidential information by directors or employees is prohibited.

- Directors who have price-sensitive information may acquire or dispose of their shares in the company only if the consideration paid or received reflects the fair value of the shares. This requirement does not apply to the directors of listed companies to whom the insider trading provisions of other legislation, namely the Securities Markets Act 1988, apply.

As well as the above responsibilities the Act imposes many additional obligations on directors. Furthermore, extra duties are able to be included in the company's constitution.

Directors failing to comply with the Act may be criminally liable with penalties increasing with the seriousness of the offence. Defaulting directors may also be subject to civil actions for losses sustained by other parties.

6.2.2   Financial Reporting Act, 1993

In a further departure from its predecessors, the Companies Act 1993 does not contain any requirements relating to the contents of the financial statements of companies. These requirements are now in the Financial Reporting Act 1993 which applies to a number of other entities in addition to companies.

Under the Financial Reporting Act it is the responsibility of directors to ensure that financial statements are prepared within five months of the company's balance date. The requirements for the financial statement's contents depend on whether or not the company is classified as exempt; that is, normally, the very smallest companies.

The financial statements of reporting companies must be prepared in accordance with generally accepted accounting practice. In addition, directors must ensure that the financial statements present a true and fair view of the company's affairs. Subject to certain exceptions, the Companies Act requires that the financial statements be audited.

6.3 Legal, Regulatory and Institutional Bodies

6.3.1 Securities Commission

The Securities Commission, established by the Securities Act 1978, governs the issue of securities to the public. These principles are:

- directors should observe and foster high ethical standards;
- there should be a balance of independence, skills, knowledge, experience and perspectives among directors so that the board works effectively;
- the board should use committees where this would enhance its effectiveness in key areas while retaining board responsibility;
- the board should demand integrity both in financial reporting and in the timeliness and balance of disclosures on entity affairs;
- the remuneration of directors and executives should be transparent, fair and reasonable;
- the board should regularly verify that the entity has appropriate processes that identify and manage potential and relevant risks;
- the board should ensure the quality and independence of the external audit process;
- the board should foster constructive relationships with shareholders that encourage them to engage with the entity;
- the board should respect the interests of stakeholders within the context of the entity's ownership type and its fundamental purpose.

While not being legally obliged to do so, companies, particularly those that are publicly listed, are expected to report to their shareholders, preferably in their annual report, on how the principles have been achieved.

6.3.2 Commerce Commission

The Commerce Commission was established by the Commerce Act 1986. It controls business acquisitions that might lead to market dominance, and oversees fair trading.

6.3.3 Overseas Investment Commission

The Overseas Investment Commission was established by the Overseas Investment Act 1973. It administers regulatory restrictions on the overseas ownership of companies.

6.3.4 NZX (Formerly the New Zealand Stock Exchange)

For over 100 years the New Zealand Stock Exchange has facilitated and regulated New Zealand's stock market. Today, the same Exchange has a new role that embraces every aspect of the capital markets, from educating and empowering new investors to encouraging new listings and changing attitudes towards investment. To do this effectively, it has recently implemented broad change within the organization, resulting in the name: NZX. While the stock exchange remains at the heart of the business, NZX has a mandate in place to strengthen the capital markets' infrastructure, consolidate and promote New Zealand's markets, and introduce new trading and information products.

6.3.5 Institute of Directors in New Zealand (Inc.)

The Institute of Directors in New Zealand (Inc.) is a professional body for New Zealand company directors whose objectives are to: 'Promote excellence in corporate governance, to represent directors' interests and facilitate their professional development in support of the economic well-being of New Zealand.'

The Institute makes a significant contribution to corporate governance by:

- providing a forum for professional exchange;
- maintaining a Code of Proper Practice for Directors;
- offering a Board Appointment Service;

- offering a Web-based evaluation service;

- issuing best practice guidelines for its members;

- facilitating the professional development of company directors through education and training;

- being affiliated with professional bodies for directors throughout the world;

- being represented on and making representations to bodies effecting changes that influence corporate governance.

6.4   Board Structure

6.4.1   Composition

The mix of executive and independent directors naturally varies from company to company. A reasonably recent survey of larger companies found that New Zealand boards have an average of one executive and six non-executive directors, although it was unclear how independent those non-executive directors are. It is the view of the Institute of Directors in New Zealand that there should be a majority of non-executive directors on the boards of listed and other widely held companies, and the majority of these directors should be independent, and that even small companies would bene-fit from having an independent non-executive director with suitable experience.

Another survey has disclosed that:

- both executive and non-executive directors typically hold office for at least five years;

- it is not common for companies to have a formal retirement policy for their directors but where a policy does exist the usual retirement age is 66 to 70 years; and

- the proportion of female directors on boards is currently around 13.8 per cent trending upwards each year.

Under the Companies Act the number of directors on the board can be as low as one. But as a general rule, taking account of the relatively small size of New Zealand companies in international terms, a board having between six and eight members is usually found to be the most appropriate in the case of medium to large companies if optimum board efficiency is to be achieved. The many smaller companies in the country can normally operate quite satisfactorily with a lower number. Under the NZX Listing Rules, the minimum number of directors for a listed company is three.

6.5 Codes, Standards and Good Practice Guidelines

Being based on the UK model, New Zealand companies have many of the same characteristics as those in that country. Those parties having interests in companies are its shareholders, directors, creditors, employees, customers and suppliers and, more indirectly, the general public and the government. Some parties have rights and duties directly as a function of company law, and some have obligations imposed by contract. Other interests have economic or political impact.

The directors manage, or supervise the management of, the company's affairs. They receive payment by way of directors' fees or, if they are executive directors, remuneration under the terms of their employment contract with the company. Because of the control they have over the company's affairs, they owe the stringent duties to the company, described earlier in the chapter.

The directors are accountable to the shareholders for the company's performance. Subject to anything to the contrary in the company's constitution, the directors are appointed, and can be removed, by the shareholders although, in practice in the case of listed and other large companies, directors are normally appointed by the board in which event shareholders confirm the appointment at the company's next annual meeting.

The essential functions of a New Zealand board of directors are typically as set out in the Principles of Corporate Governance published in 1999 by the Organization for Economic Cooperation and Development (OECD), namely:

- reviewing corporate strategy, major plans of action, risk policy, annual budgets and business plans, setting performance objectives, monitoring implementation and corporate performance, and overseeing major capital expenditures, acquisitions and divestitures;

- selecting, compensating, monitoring and, when necessary, replacing key executives and overseeing succession planning;

- reviewing executive remuneration;

- monitoring and managing potential conflicts of interest of management, board members and shareholders, including misuse of corporate assets and abuse in related party transactions;

- ensuring the integrity of the company's accounting and financial reporting systems, including the independent audit, and that appropriate systems of control are in place; in particular, systems for monitoring risk, financial control, and compliance with the law;

- monitoring the effectiveness of the governance practices under which the board operates and making changes as needed;

- overseeing the process of disclosure and communications.

In addition to the OECD principles relating to the responsibilities of the board, the following governance standards are referred to in the latter sections of this chapter:

- disclosure and accountability; and

- shareholder rights and stakeholder relations.

6.5.1   Securities Commission's Principles for Corporate Governance

At the request of the government the Commission has, after public consultation, identified and published a set of principles of corporate governance for New Zealand supported by guidelines for achieving them.

6.5.2   NZX (formerly the New Zealand Stock Exchange)

The NZX Listing Rules include corporate governance obligations, and the adoption of a Best Practice Code.

The corporate governance obligations comprise such matters as:

- an extended definition of independent director;

- a requirement for a minimum percentage of independent directors on the board; and

- mandatory audit committees with a minimum percentage of independent directors.

The Best Practice Code comprises such matters as:

- the adoption of codes of ethics;
- separation of the roles of board chairman and chief executive officer;
- continuing director education;
- components of director remuneration;
- regular board and individual evaluations;
- the establishing of remuneration and nomination committees; and
- the board's relationship with the external auditors.

Listed companies are required to state in their annual report whether and, if so, how their own corporate governance practices materially differ from the Code.

6.5.3 Code of Proper Practice for Directors, Institute of Directors in New Zealand

The Institute of Directors in New Zealand has developed a *Code of Proper Practice for Directors* for the purpose of providing guidance to New Zealand directors to assist them in carrying out their duties and responsibilities in accordance with the highest professional standards. The guidance offered is more on moral and ethical responsibilities than on those imposed by law.

The subject matter includes:

- the directors' fundamental duty to act in the company's best interests;
- ensuring the directors and the company act lawfully and with high standards of commercial morality;
- the avoidance of conflicts of interest;
- the diligent application by directors to their work;
- keeping up to date with political, legal and social trends;

- observing confidentiality;

- restrictions on insider trading; compliance with the spirit as well as the letter of the law;

- the holding of regular directors' meetings;

- authorities reserved to the board;

- separation of the roles of the board chairman and chief executive officer;

- the balance of executive and non-executive directors on the board;

- the presentation to shareholders of balanced and understandable information;

- the duties of the chairman;

- the roles of non-executive and executive directors;

- board committees in general; and

- audit committees.

The Institute also produces Best Practice Guidelines that are intended to be of practical value to directors in performing their role. The guidelines are regularly reviewed and kept up to date with current law and practice. So far, almost 40 guidelines have been issued on topics such as conflicts of interest; director remuneration; the chairman's duties; key competencies for directors; accepting board appointments; effective board meetings; and not-for-profit boards.

6.5.4 Current Corporate Governance Issues

There are currently many factors influencing corporate governance issues in New Zealand, including:

- the increased visibility of directors' legal duties and responsibilities following the introduction of the Companies Act 1993 and related legislation;

- the recent overseas corporate scandals such as Enron and WorldCom and, closer to home, in Australia, HIH Insurance and One.Tel;

- the recent perceived poor performance of several high-profile New Zealand boards;

- an increase in the size of management funds in relation to individual investors in New Zealand;

- a growing awareness by institutional investors of their responsibilities to the beneficiaries whose funds they represent;

- the relatively small pool of sought-after directors in New Zealand;

- the large number of listed New Zealand companies having substantial overseas shareholders;

- a general rise in the expectations of investors, and indeed of society as a whole, consequent on ever-improving information and communications technologies resulting in a greater awareness of events and trends in the wider world; and

- following on from improvements in educational systems, a more questioning approach by investors and society as a whole to previously accepted ideas.

The main governance issues themselves are:

- increased shareholder activism;

- the short-term outlook of some institutional investors resulting from pressure on institutional managers to produce continuing good results (and sometimes earn themselves bonuses) notwithstanding the state of local and world stock markets;

- the availability to non-executive directors of options to acquire shares in their companies;

- the entitlement of non-executive directors to retirement or termination payments;

- mandatory qualifications and/or continuing education for directors;

- the balance between executive and independent directors on a board and on key board committees;

- the combination of the roles of chairman and chief executive officer;

- the provision by auditors of non-audit services;

- the emphasis in governance matters on conformance rather than keeping a balance with company performance; and

- the relevance of corporate social responsibility to the business world.

6.6   Disclosure and Transparency

Every company is required by the Companies Act to prepare an annual report about the company's affairs and send it to shareholders each year. The information to be contained in the annual report includes, in relation to the company's last accounting period:

- a description of any material change in the nature or class of business of the company or any of its subsidiaries;

- financial statements complying with the Financial Reporting Act;

- particulars or entries in the interests register;

- the total remuneration and value of other benefits received by each director or former director;

- the number of employees or former employees, not being directors, who received remuneration and other benefits exceeding NZ $100,000 per annum, in bands of NZ $10,000;

- the amount of donations made by the company;

- the names of the directors and of any changes; and

- the amount payable to the auditor both as audit fees and fees for other services provided.

A number of these disclosure requirements may not be appropriate for smaller companies where shareholders are involved in management and are aware, on a day-to-day basis, of the company's operations. For that reason, some details may be dispensed with if all shareholders agree.

The NZX Listing Rules currently require that a listed company's annual report contains, in addition, particulars of:

- the 20 largest shareholders;

- the number of shares held by each director;

- the spread of shareholdings;

- the company's current credit rating; and

- any corporate governance policies, practices and processes adopted or followed by the company and how, if at all, they materially differ from the NZX Best Practice Code referred to earlier in this chapter.

The NZX also requires listed companies to issue half-yearly reports to their shareholders, mainly of a financial nature.

Listed companies are further subject to a regime of continuous disclosure of material information that is not generally available to the market, as recently introduced by the Securities Markets Amendment Act 2002. And the Securities Markets Act (Disclosure of Relevant Interests by Directors and Officers) Regulations 2003 obliges directors and officers of listed companies to disclose their relevant shareholdings to the NZX.

The Companies Act requires every company to file an annual return with the Registrar of Companies where it is available for public inspection and which specifies, in particular, the company's current capital structure and, in the case of unlisted companies, any changes in shareholdings over the past year.

Issues of new shares and debt securities to the public are regulated by the Securities Act 1978 which requires extensive disclosure of information to potential investors in a prospectus registered with the Registrar of Companies. The Act also contains restrictions on advertisements of public offerings.

There is a general requirement under the Companies Act that all companies appoint an auditor at their annual meeting. It is, however, possible for a company to determine by unanimous shareholder resolution that no auditor be appointed for the year. This exception does not apply if the company is a subsidiary of an overseas company, is a company 25 per cent or more controlled from overseas, or is an issuer under the Financial Reporting Act (including listed companies). The auditor must be a member of the Institute of Chartered Accountants of New Zealand, or of an approved overseas association.

6.7 Shareholder Rights and Stakeholder Relations

The shareholders are the owners of the company. They contribute share capital to pay for their shares which, subject to any restrictions in the company's constitution, are transferable. They have enforceable rights against the company, the company's directors and each other.

The shareholders receive the profits of the company as distributions. Distributions generally vary in size depending on how profitable the company is in any given year. Distributions are usually made as cash dividends.

Shareholders carry the greatest risk of loss in the event of the company's failure. They rank last in priority for the income and, on a return of capital, rank behind creditors and most other interests.

6.7.1 Shareholder Rights

The Companies Act specifies that a share in a company is personal property and that, subject to any restrictions in the company's constitution, is transferable by entry in the company's share register which the Act requires the company to maintain. Under the NZX Listing Rules, no restrictions on transfers are permitted in the constitutions of listed companies.

Within a limited period after each balance date the company is required by the Act to prepare and send to its shareholders the annual report referred to earlier in this chapter, following which the company must (unless at least 75 per cent of shareholders holding at least 75 per cent of the voting shares decide otherwise) hold an annual meeting at which shareholders have the right (as they have at all other shareholder meetings) to question the company's management. The Act allows for shareholders to vote on all resolutions at a company meeting, subject to anything to the contrary in the constitution.

Powers reserved to shareholders by the Act include changes to the constitution, approval to a major transaction (that is, in general terms, transactions by which the company acquires or disposes of assets, or incurs liabilities, with a value greater than half the value of the existing assets), approval to an amalgamation with another company, and placing the company into liquidation. These powers can only be exercised by a special resolution (that is, by at least a 75 per cent majority vote). Subject to the Act and to the constitution, and in the case of listed companies to restrictions in the NZX Listing Rules, the company's board has the power to issue shares after incorporation at any time, to any person and in any number it thinks fit.

Under the Act, written notice of the date, time and place of a shareholders' meeting must be given to shareholders not less than 10 working days before the meeting and must state the nature of the business to be transacted at the meeting in sufficient detail to enable shareholders to form a reasoned judgement in relation to it. The notice must also contain the text of any special resolution. Shareholders are permitted by the Act to give written notice to the board, within prescribed time limits, of agenda items. Voting at shareholder meetings can be in person or by proxy with equal effect.

New Zealand has a Takeovers Code applying to target companies that are, or were in the previous 12 months, listed on the NZX, or have 50 or more shareholders and NZ $20 million or more in assets. One of the Code's main features is that a person who holds or controls less than 20 per cent of the voting rights in the target company cannot exceed 20 per cent without making an offer for the remaining shares. Nor may a person who already holds 20 per cent increase that percentage without making an offer in accordance with the Code. There are three exceptions to this rule:

- purchases or issues of shares approved by target company shareholders (excluding interested parties) in accordance with procedures set out in the Code;

- a person holding or controlling 50 per cent but less than 90 per cent of the target company's voting shares can increase that holding by up to 5 per cent of the total voting shares in any 12 month period; and

- a person holding or controlling 90 per cent or more of the target company's voting shares can increase that holding without restriction.

A further feature of the Code is the requirement that all shareholders be treated equally, with no premium for control.

6.7.2 Equitable Treatment of Shareholders

Within any class of share, all shareholders normally have the same voting rights. These voting rights are usually contained in the company's constitution or in the terms of issue of the shares, both of which are public documents registered, and available for inspection, at the Companies Office. Under the Companies Act, companies must issue to shareholders, on request, a statement that sets out:

- the class of share held, the total number of shares of that class issued and the number held;
- the rights and restrictions attaching to the shares held; and
- the relationship of the shares held to the other classes of shares.

No changes in voting rights within a class or between classes can be made without a special resolution of the interest groups affected.

Votes are usually cast by custodians or nominees as directed by the beneficial owner of the shares.

Proceedings at general shareholder meetings are prescribed by the Companies Act subject, where permitted by the Act, to the contents of the company's constitution. Within any class of share these proceedings allow for the equitable treatment of all shareholders. The Act does not make it unduly difficult or expensive to cast votes.

The Securities Markets Act 1988 imposes civil liability (at the time of writing, the government is looking to introduce criminal liability as well) on an insider of a company which has issued shares to the public, including a listed company, who, while in possession of inside information about the public issuer, trades in its securities. No action can be brought if the insider sells or buys in accordance with certain procedures specified by the Securities Markets Act to be operated by the public issuer. In the case of companies other than public issuers the Companies Act requires directors of the company with inside information to pay, or be paid, as appropriate, the fair value of shares bought or sold by the director.

The Companies Act requires board members who are materially interested in a transaction to which the company is a party to disclose that interest to the board and cause the interest to be entered in the interests register.

6.7.3 Stakeholder Relations

In addition to its shareholders, a company's creditors, employees, customers, suppliers, and sometimes even the general public, are often referred to as the company's stakeholders.

A number of remedies are available to creditors under the Companies Act and various statutes and regulations. The conditions of employees' employment by the company are protected by the Employment Relations Act 2000 and the Holidays Act 1981, their safety in the workplace by the Health and Safety in Employment Act 1992, and anti-discrimination by the Human Rights Act 1993. Customers and suppliers have the protection of the Commerce Act 1986 and the Fair Trading Act 1986, while the general public has, in addition to those two Acts, the benefit of the Resource Management Act 1991 under which companies and their directors can be held responsible for damage to the physical environment.

Sanctions against failure by companies to comply with their obligations to stakeholders are provided not only by the law but also by competition in the marketplace.

6.8 Director Development Activity

The number of educational and training courses available for New Zealand directors has grown over recent times as directors and their companies have become increasingly aware of the need to enhance their knowledge and skills to enable them to keep in step with continually rising legal and social demands. A variety of courses are available, including:

- the professional development programmes organized by the Institute of Directors in New Zealand;
- courses offered by the business and management schools run by New Zealand universities;
- correspondence business courses both within and outside New Zealand; and
- international courses conducted by major universities and business schools in the USA, UK and Europe.

Conferences and seminars on topics of special interest to directors or of relevance to the industries in which they work are often run, both in New Zealand and overseas, by professional organizations.

The Institute of Directors in New Zealand is dedicated to improving boardroom performance through education and information. The Institute offers a wide range of courses ranging from those of an introductory nature to a five-day residential programme. Recent course subjects have included financial reporting and analysis, board reporting and committee operations, chairing the board, developing an effective business strategy, governance and information technology, and takeovers. The Institute also regularly provides targeted relevant tailored programmes for organizations in both the private and public sectors.

Keeping up to date also means keeping informed. Specialist publications assist directors by informing them of developments in management, law, industry, the economy, politics, and in public expectations and opinion. The Institute of Directors encourages directors to read its monthly journal containing articles designed to inform directors about important relevant issues and to generate interest and stimulate readers in areas of concern. Directors are also encouraged by the Institute to read the regular financial publications available both locally and overseas, especially in Australia, and the business sections of the regional daily newspapers.

6.9   Useful Contacts

- Commerce Commission – www.comcom.govt.nz
- Companies Office – www.companies.govt.nz
- Institute of Directors in New Zealand – www.iod.org.nz
- Listed Companies Association Inc – www.listedcompanies.org.nz
- NZX – www.nzx.com
- Overseas Investment Commission – www.oic.govt.nz
- Securities Commission – www.sec-com.govt.nz
- Takeovers Panel – www.takeovers.govt.nz

Spain

7

Table 7.1

Population	41,837,894 (2003)
Gross National Income	US $821 million (2002)
GNI per capita	US $19,615 (2002)
Total number of companies	115,326 (2002)
Number of companies listed on Stock Exchange	• Total 566 (2003)
	– 248 Madrid Stock Exchange
	– 135 Barcelona Stock Exchange
	– 24 Bilbao Stock Exchange
	– 24 Valencia Stock Exchange
	– 13 New Market
	– 122 Continuous Market (including Ibex 35)
Market capitalization	US $512 million (April 2003)
Key corporate laws	• Transparency Act (2003)
	• Joint Stock Companies Act (1989)
	• Securities Market Act (1988)
Key corporate governance codes	• Aldama Report (2003)
	• Olivencia Code (1998)

7.1 Corporate Structure and Ownership

There are two main types of limited corporations in Spain: joint stock company (Sociedad Anónima); and limited liability company (Sociedad de Responsabilidad Limitada). Additionally, there are other types of companies such as the general partnership (Sociedad Colectiva) in which the liability of the partners is unlimited, or the limited partnership (Sociedad Comanditaria) which has a mix of limited and unlimited liability partners.

7.1.1 Joint Stock Companies

The joint stock company is governed by Royal Decree 1564/1989 of 22 December which adopted the revised text of the Corporate Law in accordance with the reform introduced by Law 19/1989 of 25 July.

The share capital cannot be less than €60,101.21 and at incorporation a minimum of 25 per cent of the total share capital must be paid up.

7.1.2 Limited Liability Companies

The limited liability company is a commercial corporation whose capital is divided into 'participations'. They are governed by Law 2/1995, 3 March. Participations are much like shares of a joint stock company but there are no certificates and they may not be called shares. Furthermore, there is no limit on the number of partners and the share capital may not be less than €3,005.

Unlike joint stock companies, directors may exercise their duties with no other limit than the period of time indicated in the company by-laws. A limited liability company may have a sole director, various directors acting jointly or severally or a board of directors.

There are over 115,000 companies in Spain and of these some 560 are companies listed on the different stock markets such as Madrid, Barcelona, Bilbao and Valencia.

7.1.3 Ownership

The Olivencia Code noted that many Spanish listed companies by pointing out that the major part of these companies are controlled by a major shareholder or by a group of significant ones.

The Joint Stock Companies Act (1989) provides for a system of proportional representation of shareholders on the Board of Directors but it has not been used by listed companies because the dispersion of shareholders. However, this system could be used to appoint the external independent directors.

7.2   Legal Framework

As a result of several financial scandals in the USA and Europe, the Spanish regulators have started to propose alternatives to restore market confidence. The start of these proposals commenced in 1998 with the 'Olivencia Code' which proposed improvements to listed companies' corporate governance practices.

This approach involves self regulation. The Olivencia Code created a framework but circumstances have made the Government promote the Aldama report based on the principles of 'comply or explain'.

The Commission for the Development of Transparency and Security in Markets and Listed Companies, commonly known as the 'Aldama Commission', produced its report at the beginning of 2003 and suggested the continuance of the development of self-regulation and recommended that the legislative body enact certain additional regulations.

Some of the recommendations have been included in the 'Transparency Act' 26/2003 of 17 July such as:

- duties of information and transparency;
- definition and regime for the duties of directors, particularly with regard to conflict of interests; and
- the obligation to provide a set of mechanisms with regard to corporate management, including the need for drafting regulations governing the board of directors and general shareholders' meeting.

Consequently, the self-regulation approach has been changed so that non-compliance with corporate information publication obligations and with directors' duties will be considered a breach of law.

The legal framework of Spain is a civil law system. The sources of Spanish legal regulation are legislation, custom and general principles of law, in that order.

The fundamental legal standard of the State is the 1978 Constitution. Its hierarchical superiority over other legal standards leads to special difficulties for its repeal or reform.

The Spanish state model is formed on the basis of 'autonomous regions'. The regions have different degrees of political autonomy but according to article 149 of the Constitution, the state retains certain fields of competence such as mercantile, penal and penitentiary legislation. Spanish courts must apply Community law to the cases brought before them and must solve conflicts between Community and National regulations.

The most relevant legislation related to companies and their governance involves the following.

7.2.1 The Joint Stock Companies Act

This was approved by Legislative Royal Decree 1564/1989, of 22 December, which includes the following sections:

- general provisions (name, commercial nature, minimum capital, nationality, etc);
- company formation;
- capital contributions;
- shares;
- company bodies;
- amendment of articles of incorporation and increase and reduction of capital;
- annual accounts;
- altering a company's status, merger and splitting;
- winding up and liquidation;
- bonds issuance.

7.2.2 Other Legislation

- Securities Market Act 24/1988 of 28 July
- Transparency Act 26/2003 of 17 July
- Bankruptcy Act 22/2003 of 9 July (in force as from September 2004)

- Royal Decree 1197/1991 of 26 July, ruling Public Tender Offers, amended by Royal Decree 432/2003 of 11 April

- Measures for the Reform of the Financial System Act 44/2002 of 22 November

- Order 3722/2003 of 26 December of the Ministry of Economy

- Circular 1/2004 of 17 March of the Securities Market Commission

7.3 Legal, Regulatory and Institutional Bodies

7.3.1 Securities Market Commission (Comisión Nacional del Mercado de Valores)

The Securities Market Commission (CNMV) is the agency in charge of supervising and inspecting the Spanish stock markets and the activities of all its participants.

The purpose of the CNMV is to ensure the transparency of the Spanish market, the correct formation of prices in them, and to protect investors.

To this end, the CNMV focuses particularly on improving the quality of disclosure of information to the market. Particular efforts are made in the area of auditing and in developing new disclosure requirements relating to remuneration schemes for directors and executives that are linked to the price of the shares of the company where they work. Considerable efforts are also made to detect and pursue illegal activities by unregistered intermediaries and the use of privileged information.

7.3.2 Bank of Spain

The implementation of Stage Three of the Economic and Monetary Union (EMU) on 1 January 1999, together with the institution of the European System of Central Banks (ESCB) and the European Central Bank (ECB), have meant that several of the functions traditionally performed by the national central banks of the euro-zone countries have had to be redefined.

In the exercise of the functions arising from its status as an integral part of the ESCB, the Bank of Spain follows the guidelines and instructions emanating from the ECB and adopts the necessary regulations for the exercise of its functions.

7.3.3   Directorate General of Insurance and Pension Funds (DGS)

This institution is accountable to the Ministry of the Economy and is in charge of controlling compliance insurance activities. It controls mergers, acquisitions and other transactions between insurance companies. Additionally, the DGS must control and supervise the insurance brokerage activities and activity compliance.

7.3.4   Spanish Stocks and Markets (Bolsas y Mercados Españoles – BME)

This institution encompasses companies that direct and manage the securities markets and systems in Spain. It brings together, under a single activity, a decision-taking and coordination unit, the Spanish equity, fixed-income and derivatives markets and their clearing and settlement systems.

The four Governing Companies of the four Spanish Stock Markets joined the Spanish Financial Market Holding in June 2002. The BME Group, the Barcelona, Bilbao, Madrid and Valencia stock exchanges, MF, Iberclear and FC&M.

BME is the Spanish markets' response to the new international financial environment, where investors, intermediaries and firms demand an ever-expanding range of services and products within a framework of security, transparency, flexibility and competitiveness.

By uniting these organizations the Spanish markets have a structure that covers the entire value chain in securities markets from trading to settlement, including the provision of information and data-processing services. The size and structure permits a more efficient use of resources, cost reduction and the streamlining of services. Thanks to this position, BME is set to play a key role within the European Stock Market.

7.3.5   AIAF

AIAF, the fixed income market, is the Spanish market for the issue and contracting of fixed income securities and assets of private companies and institutions, creating, together with the Stock Market, the Public Debt Market and the Futures and Options Market. This market was established in 1987. The AIAF is an official Organized Secondary Market, whose governing company is AIAF Mercado de Renta, Fija, SA, and the number of members is 94.

7.3.6 MEFFSA

These markets are organized by the Spanish Market of Financial Futures (Mercado Español de Futuros Financieros – MEFF). MEFF is the Spanish Official Exchange for Financial Futures and Options. Its main activity is the trading, clearing and settling of futures and options contracts on the Spanish ten-year Notional Bond, on the equity index IBEX 35 and on S&P Europe 350 and sector indices. MEFF is an official exchange and therefore is fully regulated, controlled and supervised by the Spanish authorities (Securities Market Commission and Ministry of Economy). Any resident or non-resident entity or natural person can be a client and can trade at MEFF, buying or selling futures and options.

7.3.7 Iberclear

Iberclear is the Spanish Central Securities Depository which is in charge of both the Register of Securities, held in book-entry form, and the Clearing and Settlement of all trades from the Spanish Stock Exchanges, the Public Debt Market, the AIAF Fixed Income Market, and Latibex – the Latin American stock exchange denominated in euros.

Iberclear was established as a limited company in the 'Reform Measures Of The Financial System' Law 44/2002, 22 November.

7.3.8 Instituto de Consejeros-Administradores (ICA)

The ICA is a non-profit organization, with the prime object of professionalizing the functions of boards of directors. Among the purposes of the Institute is the promotion, diffusion and establishment of international models on corporate governance practices, the implementation of the highest standards of professional regulations, as well as training in order to improve director professionalism.

Furthermore, it issues opinions on the specific regulations that may affect corporate governance, and participates in the defence and representation of directors' interests.

7.4   Board Structure

The Joint Stock Companies Act requires that the appointment of directors and the determination of their number shall be adopted by a resolution of the general shareholders' meeting. When management is entrusted jointly to more than two persons, they shall constitute a board of directors.

7.4.1   Size

According to a study prepared by Spencer Stuart (2002), analysing 78 listed companies among which 31 are included in the IBEX 35 index:

- the number of directors of the companies analysed ranged between 5 and 29 and the average was established at 12.6;
- 20 per cent of the companies had fewer than 10 directors;
- 61 per cent of the companies had between 10 and 15 directors;
- 19 per cent of the companies had more than 15 directors.

7.4.2   Composition

A basic distinction is made between internal or executive directors and external directors. There are two types of external directors: 'domanial' and 'independent' directors.

The internal or executive directors are those in charge of the management functions of the company. Additionally, these are the directors who have some capacity to decide on some parts of the company's or group's business through a stable delegation or proxy granted by the board of directors or the company respectively.

The domanial external directors are those appointed by shareholders who individually or collectively own a stable participation in share capital which, regardless of whether or not this entitles them to have a seat on the governing body, the board has estimated it to be sufficiently significant to propose their appointment at the shareholders' meeting.

Finally, the independent external directors are those persons of an acknowledged professional prestige who can contribute their experience to governing the company, satisfying the conditions of impartiality and objectivity such as:

- are not presently employed or have not been in the recent past nor have a direct or indirect commercial or contractual relation with the company, its managers, domanial directors or credit institutions with a significant position in the company's finances;

- do not hold the position of director of another listed company that has domanial directors in the company in question;

- do not have close relationships with the company's executive, domanial directors or senior managers.

The overall composition of boards:

Internal or executive directors	18%
External directors	82%
Domanial	(44%)
Independent	(36%)
Others	2%

The majority of companies have one or two executive directors:

- 5 per cent do not have any executive directors;

- 30 per cent have one executive director;

- 32 per cent have two executive directors;

- 33 per cent have between three and eight executive directors.

7.4.3 Diversity

The 'Olivencia Code' suggested a directors' age limit of between 65 and 70 years old for executive directors, and gave the possibility of being more flexible with respect to the others.

The Aldama Commission, after an extensive discussion, concluded, in contrast to Olivencia, that because of the increase in life expectancy there are no substantive reasons in terms of good governance to warrant a recommendation on this matter.

The Spencer Stuart report identified that the average age of a director is 56 years old. Furthermore, 44 per cent of the analysed companies do not have a time limit for the retirement of their directors, and the other 56 per cent have an age limit between 65 and 75 years old.

The study found that 36 per cent of the companies have women among their directors, the total ratio of women directors among the boards of directors being about 4 per cent. In the majority of cases there is one woman on each board.

Another study, in 2001, prepared by the Corporate Women Directors International organization, involving the three hundred biggest companies in Spain established that only 4.6 per cent of the companies have a woman on their board.

7.4.4 Separation of Roles of Chairman and Chief Executive

The 'Aldama Report' pointed out that one of the main issues that requires attention is the separation between the position of chairman and the function of chief executive of the company.

It seems that public opinion is predominantly in favour of separating these positions, considering that this would make the board more independent of the management team. At the same time the Commission considered the disadvantages of the dual solution, because:

- it might deprive the company of strong leadership;
- it might hinder the transmission of information between the management and the board; and
- it might generate additional coordination costs in the organization.

In Spain it is estimated that 70 per cent of the listed companies have an executive chairman, which means that the same person performs the office of chairman on the board of directors and chief executive of the company.

7.4.5 Committees (Commissions)

The Aldama Report also recommend that the following commissions should be created to improve corporate governance:

- executive or delegate commission;
- audit and control commission;
- appointment and remuneration commission; and if appropriate
- strategy and investment commission.

The Measures for the Reform of the Financial System Act introduced an amendment to the Securities Market Act and obliged listed companies to create an audit committee which must have a majority of non-executive directors appointed by the board of directors with the following functions:

- informing the general shareholders' meeting of the different matters brought by the shareholders;

- suggesting to the board of directors the appointment of the external auditors to be presented at the general shareholders' meeting;

- supervising the internal audit services, in the case where such services exist;

- knowing the financial information procedure and the internal control systems of the company.

The relationships with the external auditors when receiving information regarding these matters may cause their independence to be put at risk.

7.5   Codes, Standards and Good Practice Guidelines

7.5.1   Olivencia Code

In 1997, the Commission for the Study of a Code of Good Governance was created. Commonly known as the 'Olivencia Code', its Code of Good Governance was published in February 1998. It stated that it was probable and desirable that much of the Anglo-Saxon tradition of good governance should be taken on board by Spanish listed companies and capital markets.

The Olivencia Commission's report led to a number of precise and carefully considered recommendations that comprise the Code of Good Governance, whose adoption by the companies was voluntary.

Companies adopting the code should undertake to comply fully with the code or to explain why they do not, on the expectation that the markets, upon receiving the information, would reward good governance practices and punish non-compliance.

In summary, the recommendations of the Olivencia Code are the following:

1. The board of directors should expressly assume the general supervisory function as its core mission, exercise the appropriate responsibilities and establish a catalogue of its exclusive competence.

2. The board of directors should be formed by a reasonable number of independent directors who must be prestigious professionals with no links to the management team or the significant shareholders.

3. The non-executive directors (both domanial directors and independent directors) should have an ample majority over executive directors, and the proportion between domanial directors and independent directors should take account of the ratio between the significant holdings in capital between shareholders.

4. The board of directors should adjust its size to achieve more efficiency and participation. In principle, the size could range from five to fifteen members.

5. If the board chooses to combine the positions of chairman and CEO in the same person, it should adopt the necessary safeguards to mitigate the risks of concentrating power in a single person.

6. The figure of secretary of the board should be made more important by giving him or her more independence and stability.

7. The composition of the executive committee, if there is one, should reflect the same balance between the various classes of directors as the board, and the relationships between the two bodies should be inspired by the principle of transparency.

8. The board of directors should create sub-committees for control purposes, composed exclusively of non-executive directors, to deal with matters of accounting information and control (audit committee), the selection of directors and senior executives (nomination committee), the determination and review of remuneration policies (remuneration committee) and the evaluation of the governance system (compliance committee).

9. To ensure that the board works well it should meet as often as necessary to fulfil its mission.

10. The board's participation in the selection and re-election of its members should conform to a formal and transparent procedure based on reasoned proposals from the nomination committee.

11. Companies should establish in their regulations the obligation on behalf of directors to resign upon the appearance of an event that may cause a detrimental impact on the functioning of the board of directors.

12. An age limit should be established for the position of director, which could vary from 65 to 70 for executive directors and the chairman, while being more flexible with respect to the other members.

13. The directors' remuneration policy, the proposal of which and evaluation and review should be assigned to the remuneration committee, must be done in accordance with the principles of moderation, the relationship with the company's performance and total disclosure on an individual basis.

14. The company's internal regulations should detail the obligations arising from the directors' general duties of diligence and loyalty, with particular attention to conflicts of interest, the duty of confidentiality, and the use of the company's business opportunities and assets.

15. The board of directors should foster the adoption of appropriate measures to extend the duties of loyalty to the significant shareholders and, in particular, establish safeguards to cover transactions between significant shareholders and the company.

16. Measures should be taken to provide greater transparency in the delegation of voting rights mechanism and to promote communication between the company and its shareholders, particularly institutional investors.

17. The board of directors should be responsible for the provision of accurate and reliable information to the markets, particularly with regard to the shareholder structure and substantial modifications in the governance rules.

18. The periodic financial information released to the markets, in addition to the annual report, should be drafted under the same professional principles and practices as the annual accounts and should be verified by the audit committee.

19. The board of directors and the audit committee should monitor situations which might jeopardize the independence of the

company's external auditors and specifically verify the percentage of the audit firm's total revenues represented by the fees paid to it.

20. The board of directors should include information about its corporate governance in the annual report.

7.5.2 Measures for the Reform of the Financial System Act 44/2002 of 22 November

The Spanish government introduced, through the Measures for the Reform of the Financial System Act, an amendment to the Securities Market Act stating that listed companies should include, in the information disclosed every six months with respect to their complementary financial statements, all relevant information regarding the operations carried out by the company.

Additionally, with respect to the privileged information regime it stated that:

1. Any concrete information that refers directly or indirectly to any securities or companies in the context of the Securities Market Act which has not become public and, upon becoming public, could significantly influence its price shall be considered privileged information.

   Those who have privileged information shall abstain from:

   - preparing or carrying out any transaction on the securities in question, which are referred to in the information, or any other financial instrument that may have those securities as underlying;

   - communicating the information to third parties;

   - recommending a third party to acquire or sell the securities in question.

   These prohibitions are applicable to any person who has privileged information since they know or should have known that this information is privileged.

2. Any information, the knowledge of which may cause an investor to acquire or sell securities and as a consequence may influence its price, shall be considered relevant information.

The companies which issue securities are obliged to immediately disclose to the markets any relevant information, through notification sent to the CNMV.

3. Every company or group of companies that renders investment services within the securities market has an obligation to establish all necessary measures to avoid disclosure of privileged information.

4. Every individual or company that participates in the securities market shall abstain from practices that may distort the free formation of prices such as:

- transactions that give or may give false evidence with respect to an offer, demand or price of securities;

- transactions that guarantee the price of a security to an abnormal or artificial level;

- transactions that used false mechanisms or any other similar devices;

- the diffusion of information through the media, including the Internet, that gives or may give false evidence with respect to the securities, when those who gave the information had known that it is false.

7.5.3 'Aldama Report'

The Olivencia Code had been in full force for four years but in 2002 it was not really clear to what extent it had been applied.

For this reason, the Spanish Cabinet appointed a new commission in order to study the criteria and guidelines that should apply to companies that issue securities and instruments admitted to listing on organized markets in their relations with consultants, financial analysts and other companies, persons or entities which assist them or provide professional services to them, in order to increase the transparency and security of the financial markets.

The result was the issue of the 'Aldama Report' on 8 January 2003. This was a further step in the transformation of the Spanish capital markets, continuing with the Olivencia tradition as it assumed the basic philosophy of self-regulation and transparency. Like its predecessor, this Commission also considered that its function was neither to take the place of the legislature nor to curtail companies' capacity for self-regulation.

The Aldama Report proposed the following:

1. a yearly report has to be drafted and published by the board of directors of public companies regarding the structure and governance practices within the corporation;

2. independent directors should not be terminated before the period for which they were originally appointed except in extraordinary circumstances;

3. the majority of the board should be composed of external directors (that is, not executives) and, within this majority, a significant number should be independent;

4. companies should create an audit committee, a remuneration and appointment committee and an executive commission;

5. the disclosure of the amount of remuneration received by each director, and that each item of this remuneration should be broken down, including the delivery or assignment of shares, stocks, options or systems referenced to the share price, which must be approved by the shareholders' meeting;

6. annual accounts should be certified by the chairman, the CEO and the CFO (before being approved by the entire board); and

7. additional independence rules have been included as regards auditors, financial analysts and rating agencies, recommending, for example, the non-participation of financial analysts in meetings between the financial institution and the governing bodies of the companies.

The Aldama Report also recommended that the legislative body should complement the above self-regulation proposals with the enactment of certain substantive rules such as:

1. companies should comply, or explain non-compliance, within a code of ethics;

2. the concept of fiduciary duties should be developed in order to solve issues in which the interests of the corporation conflict with the interests of management; and

3. the duty to have corporate governance provisions that include at least a board of directors' regulation and a shareholders' meeting regulation. Within the latter, for example, the notice of the meeting, the agenda, the disclosure of the motions and information given to the shareholders during the preparation of the shareholders' meeting should be included.

7.5.4 Transparency Act 26/2003 of 17 July

The Spanish government welcomed the recommendations set forth by the Aldama Report and decided to legislate by approving the Transparency Act.

The regulatory reform amended certain articles of the Joint Stock Companies Act.

The most important amendments include:

1. Publication of shareholders' agreements in relation to listed companies.

2. The obligation for the general shareholders' meeting to draw up a specific regulation for the general shareholders' meetings.

3. Duties of directors:

   - The directors shall perform their functions with the diligence of an orderly businessman and a loyal representative.

   - The directors shall perform their duties imposed by laws with fidelity to the corporate interest.

   - Directors shall not use the name of the company to perform operations for their own account.

   - Directors shall make known any situation of conflict of interests that may arise with the interest of the company.

   - Directors shall communicate their stake in the capital of a company with the same, analogous or complementary line of business as the business purpose, and offices or functions exercised therein, as well as the performance, for their own account or for that of a third party, an analogous or complementary line of business as the business purpose. That information shall be included in the annual report.

- Directors, even when they cease to be in their position, shall observe the secrecy of confidential information, and shall undertake to observe the secrecy of information, data, reports or antecedents of which they are aware as a result of their position, without communicating it to third parties when this could jeopardize the corporate interest.

- Until the seventh day prior to when the general shareholders' meeting is to be held, shareholders may apply to the directors in relation to the issues included in the agenda, reports or clarifications deemed necessary. Shareholders of listed companies may apply for reports or clarifications or raise queries in writing in relation to information available to the public that may have been furnished by the company to the Securities Market Commission since the last general shareholders' meeting was held.

4. The new legislation, which is to a great extent in response to Community provisions contained in the proposed 5th Directive, has involved a stricter regime of directors' liability by increasing the degree of diligence required on the one hand and, on the other, removing nuances in the degree of fault contained in the previous legislation.

5. There should be an annual corporate governance report, submitted to the Securities Market Commission by Order 3722/2003 of 26 December of the Ministry of the Economy. It should include:

- Structure of corporate ownership, significant shareholders, percentage of their holdings and relations of a family, commercial or corporate nature that may exist; shareholdings of members of the board, shareholders' agreements specifying the identity of the parties and, the percentage of the company holding of its own shares during the last accounting period.

- Structure of corporate administration, composition, rules and functioning of the board and its committees with the identification and remuneration of its members.

- Affiliated operations of the company with its shareholders and its directors and managers.

- Risk control systems.

- Functioning of the general shareholders' meeting.

- Degree of follow-up of recommendations on corporate management or explaining the absence of follow-up.

Additionally, the Order establishes that listed companies shall have a Web page with at least the following information:

1. Company bylaws.

2. General Shareholders Meeting Regulation.

3. Board of Directors Regulation.

4. Company's annual report and internal regulation of conduct.

5. Corporate governance report.

6. Documents of the General Shareholders Meeting ordinary or extraordinary.

7. Means of communication among the company and its shareholders.

8. Means and proceeding to confer powers to be represented in the General Shareholders Meeting.

9. Means and proceeding for the distance voting and the forms to vote through telematic means.

10. Relevant facts, in accordance with the Order.

Additionally the Order states that the company directors shall be responsible for keeping the Web page updated and for coordinating its content.

Finally, the Order entitled the CNMV to create a unique Code of Corporate Governance to rewrite the existent documents (Transparency Law, Olivencia and Aldama Report).

7.5.5 Circular 1/2004 of 17 March of the Securities Market Commission

The Securities Market Commission establishes through the above said Circular different aspects with respect to the annual corporate governance report as well as the information to be published in the Web pages of the listed companies.

Additionally the Circular reasserts the general principle of transparency stating that any information the company gives whether voluntary or obligatory shall be clear, complete, correct, truthful, without allowing to include partial information that may confuse the investors.

7.6 Disclosure and Transparency

7.6.1 Remuneration

This issue has been and still is one of the most discussed. The Olivencia Code stated that it was the shareholders' desire that the directors' remuneration does not exceed what is necessary to attract competent people.

The Aldama Commission recommended that remuneration comprising shares of the company, stock options or options referenced to the share price should be limited to executive or internal directors.

The amount of remuneration received by each director should be disclosed in the notes to the accounts and in the annual report. Additionally, all the items of the remuneration should be broken down, including the delivery or assignment of shares, stock options or systems referenced to the share price.

The Spencer Stuart study in 2002 identified external directors' remuneration as:

- 23 per cent of external directors received less than €24,000 per year;
- 29 per cent of external directors received between €24,001 and €42,000 per year;
- 48 per cent of external directors received more than €42,000 per year.

Additionally, the majority of the companies declared that committee members were also remunerated.

7.6.2 Reporting

Each year the board of directors are required to draft an annual report on the company's corporate governance structure and practices.

The annual accounts must be presented to the board of directors, having been previously certified by the chairman, the managing director and the chief financial officer. In addition, it must be disclosed that the consolidated annual accounts include the accounts of all the consolidated domestic and foreign subsidiaries, in accordance with the applicable legislation.

7.6.3 Audit

The Measures for the Reform of the Financial System Act 44/2002 of 22 November established the following provisions:

- Auditors in the exercise of their duties must be independent from the companies or audited entities. The auditor does not have sufficient independence in the following cases:

  a) Should the auditor hold an executive, management, labour or internal supervision position in the audited company.

  b) There is a direct financial interest in the audited company or significant indirect interest.

  c) The existence of blood relations as regards managers or the responsible economic heads of the audited companies.

  d) The auditor has prepared the annual accounts of the company.

  e) The auditor has provided audit services for the company.

  f) Legal advice has been provided in the previous three years.

  g) The auditor has participated in the recruiting of directors or important staff, in the case of government-supervised entities.

  h) The receipt of fees different to those of the audited services on behalf of the company, if they constitute a large percentage in relation to the total annual income of the auditors.

- Three years after the ending of its functions, the auditors should not form part of the corporate or management bodies of the companies.

- Auditors must rotate after a period of seven years in listed companies that are subject to public supervision or companies with a net income higher than €30,000,000.

7.7 Shareholder Rights and Stakeholder Relations

There are three categories of shareholder dispersion amongst the Spanish listed companies:

(i)   Companies in which the majority of the share capital is 'free float'. Despite being very few in number in Spain, those are the biggest companies in terms of capitalization. They include the largest banks and the principal public companies that arose from the privatization process, in which its share capital was placed, through IPOs, among a large number of investors.

(ii)   Companies in which the share capital is distributed between a reduced number of investors that generally restrict the entry to other investors outside the group. This covers the majority of listed companies in Spain.

(iii)   Companies in which the share capital is distributed among a large number of shareholders but a minority group have sufficient voting rights to control it.

The corporate governance reports recommend that the institutional investors and the individual shareholders become more involved in the governance of companies.

7.7.1   Stakeholders

The ancient doctrine in Spain has always regarded the corporate interest as the common interest of the shareholders, understood as the maximization of company value.

However, as mentioned in the Olivencia Code, the interests of other stakeholders should be taken into consideration concerning the requirements imposed by the laws and complying with their contractual obligations according to the good faith principle.

The amendment to the Joint Stock Companies Act regarding the directors' liability states that the prime objective of the company should be to pursue its mission within the general framework of the law. It should not only regard the legal duties of its mission but also take into account traditional ethical values which are vital for human society.

In the context of the company's social responsibility in managing its business, each company can freely adopt additional ethical or social obligations within a general framework of sustainable development, such as presenting a triple balance sheet (economic, social and environmental perspectives) in order to disclose those obligations to shareholders, employees and society in general.

7.8   Director Development Activity

The ICA has formed an agreement with the Institute of Directors (IoD) in the UK to develop board-level director training in Spain. This is based on the IoD's flagship Company Direction Programme and will be contextualized to local market conditions and laws. The training programme was launched in 2004 and focuses on the professional development needs of directors, addressing issues such as:

- the role of the director;
- legal compliance;
- strategic business direction; and
- board decision making.

The programme will be jointly accredited by the ICA and the IoD and is analogous to the IoD's Certificate and/or Diploma in Company Direction.

7.9   Useful Contacts

- Banco de España – www.bde.es
- Bolsa de Valores de Madrid – www.bolsamadrid.es
- Comisión Nacional del Mercado de Valores (Securities Market Commission) – www.cnmv.es
- Dirección General de Seguros y Fondos de Pensiones – www.dgseguros.mineco.es
- Gobierno Español – www.la-moncloa.es
- Instituto de Consejeros-Administradores – www.iconsejeros.com
- Instituto Nacional de Estadística – www.ine.es
- Mercado Español de Futuros Financieros – www.meff.es

- Mercado Español de Renta Fija – www.aiaf-ecn.com
- Ministerio de Economía – www.mineco.es

7.10 Further Reading

Aldama Report (2003) *Informe de la comision espacial para el fomento de la transparencia y seguridad en los mercados y*

Olivencia Code (1998)

United Kingdom | 8

Table 8.1

Population	60 million (2003)
Gross National Income (GNI)	US $1.5 trillion (2002)
GNI per capita	US $25,250 (2002)
Total number of companies	1.8 million (April 2004)
Number of companies listed on Stock Exchange	2,700 London Stock Exchange including 809 on AIM (April 2004)
Market capitalization	US $2,567.7 billion (2001)
Key corporate laws	● Insolvency Act (1986)
	● Financial Servcice and Market Act (2000)
	● Enterprise Act (2002)
	● Companies Act (1989)
	● Company Directors Disqualification Act (1986)
	● Companies Act (1985)
Key corporate governance codes	● Combined Code (2003)

8.1 Corporate Structure and Ownership

The United Kingdom has a plethora of company structures including:

● companies limited by shares:

- private companies;
- public limited companies;
- companies limited by guarantee;
- unlimited companies.

Economically the most important are the two types of company limited by shares, and for the purposes of this chapter, all references to a company are either to a private company limited by shares ('private company') or to a public limited company ('plc').

There are different governance requirements for each type of company, with more stringent requirements for plcs. United Kingdom company law is drafted on a top-down basis drafted as applicable to the plc, with exceptions and exemptions for all or some private companies.

There are over 1.8 million active companies in the UK and of these 12,400 are public limited companies and some 2,700 are listed on the London Stock Exchange. This includes around 800 companies listed on the Alternative Investment Market (AIM) for new companies not eligible for the Official List. Given the numbers of registered companies it is no surprise that a large majority of them are very small businesses. Their corporate structures are and will remain very different from those of the listed company. While the major principles of good corporate governance are of relevance to all companies, it would be a mistake to believe that every aspect of the detail of what is promulgated for large listed companies is relevant across the corporate spectrum. In order to achieve acceptance and eventually enthusiasm for corporate governance the principles must be relevant to the size, structure and nature of the business entity.

Ownership patterns have changed radically over the past few decades. Direct shareholder involvement in the management of larger companies has diminished until there is almost entire separation of the two. From 54 per cent of shares being owned by individuals in 1963, this had fallen to 14.3 per cent by the end of 2002. Overseas ownership has grown over the same period from 7 per cent to 32.1 per cent.

Alongside this, the growing concentration of share ownership into the hands of institutional investors had a very real effect. Institutional shareholders, comprised mainly of insurance companies and pension funds, accounted for 49.4 per cent of UK ordinary shares in December 2001 according to the National Statistics 2002 Share Ownership Survey. The institutions are able to use the concentration of ownership to influence boards, since it is more difficult for boards to ignore significant shareholders in circumstances where they have a common interest, than a group of disparate individuals with differing requirements.

In recent times institutional investors have increasingly turned to using their votes at annual general meetings. There are a number of reasons for this; one factor is probably the current state of the stock market, where many investors are holding stocks at a very large loss. Increasingly, it is seen as a role of corporate governance to attempt to align the interests of shareholders and boards. Having said that, it is noticeable that the average duration of institutional holding in the United Kingdom is no longer than two years. Companies find it hard to regard this as shareholders taking a long-term interest in the company.

8.2   Legal Framework

The legal framework of the United Kingdom is essentially a common law system. While there is a large amount of legislation, important aspects of the law applicable to directors of companies is at present still almost entirely based on precedents, which are continually evolving. Two main areas are fundamental to the relationship between the director, the company, the shareholders and others. They are: the duty of care and skill; and the director's fiduciary duties.

It is important to note that there is not one single United Kingdom system of law, but three systems: England and Wales, Scotland and Northern Ireland. In the area of company law the same legislation generally applies to England and Wales and to Scotland but there are some procedural differences. Northern Ireland has its own companies legislation which has the same basis, but is not identical.

The legal provisions relating to companies and their governance derive from a number of sources:

- statute and subsidiary legislation;
- directly applicable European Union law;
- regulation including accounting standards;

- listing rules applicable to quoted companies;
- takeover rules;
- specific legislation applying to companies operating in specific sectors (eg banking and insurance);
- decisions of the courts; and
- extra-legislative codes.

The current basis of company legislation is the Companies Act 1985 and the Companies Act 1989. Together these will be referred to here as the 'Companies Acts'.

8.2.1 Company Law Reform

European Community law has been the main source of amendment to United Kingdom company law since accession in 1973 and is expected to continue to be a significant factor. Because the European Union Directives address specific subject areas and each has to be incorporated into the national law there was, for a long period, no time for overall review and reform of company law to shape or even reflect modern corporate reality. In 1998 the Company Law Review Steering Group was set up under the instructions of the Secretary of State for Trade and Industry and after extensive consultation and investigations it issued its final report in June 2001.

In July 2002 the government published a White Paper, *Modernizing Company Law*, which contained provisions which, if enacted, would make radical changes to the governance of United Kingdom companies.

Some of these measures would bring in a more relaxed regime for private companies, others would bring in more stringent requirements, particularly for plcs. The premise is that, unlike now, the legislation should be drafted from the viewpoint of the smallest companies, with additional requirements for larger companies. The present law is drafted for large companies, with a series of exemptions for smaller companies. The new approach recognizes the realities of the structure of companies. For private companies the requirement to hold an AGM would be removed. The members of plcs would also be able to elect to dispense with the AGM. There are proposals for the company to bear the cost of circulating member resolutions, but this could lead to problems with dissident shareholders requiring extensive diatribes to be circulated.

United Kingdom companies legislation is based on the premise that the registered holder of shares is the owner. Increasingly, particularly for quoted companies, behind the registered holder are the beneficial owners. Procedures for providing information to beneficial owners and making provision for the registered holder to act on the beneficiaries' instructions are cumbersome and expensive. The proposed regime would enable companies, if they wished, to recognize the rights of beneficial owners. The *Company Law Review* recommended that such recognition be mandatory and the government is looking into the practicality of this.

Alongside empowering beneficial owners, there are concerns that institutional investors do not always exercise their powers. In part this is due to failures in the vote execution system and lack of transparency. Possible conflicts of interest can also inhibit institutions from exercising their governance role. The government is proposing that companies should make greater disclosure of voting, but is not convinced that company law is the place to resolve the issues of conflicts of interest.

Probably the most radical corporate governance proposals in the White Paper are in the area of directors' duties. In the United Kingdom the law on directors' duties (both the duty of care and fiduciary duties) is entirely based on common law. It is proposed that many of these duties should be codified. The fundamentals of the current common law duties would be retained; hence, the unitary board is recognized, with all directors being subject to the same general duties. Equally, the shareholder model is retained (ie directors must act in the way they decide would promote the success of the company for the benefit of the members as a whole). However, in doing this they must take account of all material factors involving:

- the interests of employees, suppliers and customers;
- the impact of operations on communities and the environment; and
- the company's reputation for high standards of business conduct.

The draft does not indicate how conflicts between these factors might be resolved.

The *Company Law White Paper* covers only a small part of company law. When the *Companies Act 1985* was enacted it was the largest and most complex single piece of legislation ever passed. There is no reason to suppose that its replacement will be any shorter or less complicated. The remainder of the proposals are awaited. The government may choose to split up the legislation into a number of statutes that would then be consolidated and it has already announced that it is going to bring forward certain elements in advance of others. These include the Operating and Financial Review (OFR), which is currently being considered for secondary legislation and would enforce directors to decide what information is material to their particular business.

The government recently consulted on a proposed new corporate vehicle called the Community Interest Company (CIC) (*Enterprise for Communities*) March 2003. The government has decided to bring forward legislation to introduce these in advance of reforming company law. The legislation will be included with the legislation on accounting and auditing which is discussed in more detail in Section 8.6.

8.2.2 The European Union

The EU is very active in company law and in 2001 appointed a High Level Group of Company Law Experts to make recommendations for a modern regulatory framework for company law in the EU. Among the topics considered was corporate governance. In November 2002 this Group published their final report (the *Experts' Report*) and in May 2003 the EU Commission issued a communication to the EU Council and the European Parliament, *Modernizing Company Law and Enhancing Corporate Governance in the European Union – A Plan to Move Forward* (the *Company Law Action Plan*).

Between the EU member states there have been some 40 corporate governance codes over the last decade (with the United Kingdom having a clear numerical lead). An EU-wide corporate governance code was not proposed; however, the report stated that '*some specific rules and principles need to be agreed at EU level*'.

The EU Commission has divided the work into short-, medium- and long-term areas. The short-term objectives are proposed to be achieved over the period 2003–05. A considerable number of the areas are suggested as targets for a legislative approach, including:

- disclosure requirements;

- exercise of voting rights;

- cross-border voting;

- enhanced disclosure by institutional investors; and

- enhancing responsibilities of board members.

Alongside the *Company Law Action Plan* sits the *Financial Services Action Plan*. A number of measures with corporate governance implications fall within its remit. These include the draft *Transparency Directive* which, if enacted in its present form, would, among other provisions on disclosure requirements, introduce quarterly financial reporting.

8.3   Legal, Regulatory and Institutional Bodies

Much of the United Kingdom's corporate governance structure is determined by a series of regulatory bodies. Between them they cover a whole range of duties, from setting accounting standards and policing their compliance to the listing of company securities.

8.3.1   Financial Services Authority (FSA)/UK Listing Authority (UKLA)

The FSA was given statutory authority by the Financial Services and Markets Act 2000 (FSMA). Under the FSMA the Board of the FSA is appointed by Her Majesty's Treasury (HMT). Under various EU Directives each member state had to identify a single competent authority for listing. The United Kingdom named the FSA which, when acting as the competent authority, is referred to as the UK Listing Authority (UKLA). The UKLA has taken over the listing function from the Stock Exchange. It has adopted the Listing Rules put in place by the Stock Exchange in 1998, which are now published as part of the '*UKLA Sourcebook*'. In this capacity the FSA is responsible for the listing requirements relating to the *Combined Code*.

8.3.2   Financial Reporting Council (FRC)

The FRC with its subsidiaries, the Accounting Standards Board (ASB) and the Financial Reporting Review Panel (FRRP), together make up an organization whose purpose is to promote and secure good financial reporting. The FRC has played a key role in corporate governance and is the body charged with oversight of the *Combined Code*; in this capacity it took forward the recommendations of the Higgs Review and the Smith Report. The FRC provides general policy guidance to its operational bodies, the ASB and the FRRP. The ASB makes, amends and withdraws accounting standards. The FRRP examines apparent departures from the accounting requirements of the Companies Act 1985, including applicable accounting standards, and if necessary seeks an order from the court to remedy them. Although the FRC is the parent company of both bodies, each is independent both of the FRC and of the other in exercising its functions.

8.3.3   London Stock Exchange (LSE)

The London Stock Exchange provides a regulated primary and secondary market for securities. The official List had 1,521 companies listed, as of April 2004, plus an additional 370 international listed companies. The Alternative Investment Market had 809 companies listed. The distinction between a full listing and an AIM listing is important, since the *Combined Code* (and its predecessors) applies only to companies with a full listing. AIM companies are not admitted to the Official List of the *UKLA*. The AIM market is comprised of younger, smaller companies not yet eligible for the Official List.

8.3.4   National Association of Pension Funds (NAPF)

The NAPF is the principal UK body representing the interests of the employer-sponsored pensions movement. Among its members are both large and small companies, local authority and public sector bodies. The member organizations provide pensions for over 10 million employees and 5 million people in retirement. They account for 75 per cent of occupational scheme assets in the UK and control 20 per cent of the shares of the London Stock Market.

8.3.5   Confederation of British Industry (CBI)

Founded in 1965, the CBI is a non-profit-making, non-party political organization funded by the subscriptions paid by its corporate members. The CBI's objective is to help create and sustain the conditions in which business in the UK can compete and prosper. It exists to ensure that the government of the day, the European

Commission and the wider community understand both the needs of British business and the contribution it makes to the well-being of UK society.

8.3.6 Institute of Chartered Secretaries and Administrators (ICSA)

ICSA is the professional body for Chartered Secretaries. The Institute has 44,000 members in the UK and 28,000 students in over 70 countries. A Chartered Secretary is qualified in company law, accounting, corporate governance, administration, company secretarial practice and management.

8.3.7 Institute of Directors (IoD)

The IoD is a politically independent membership organization for over 55,000 individual directors. It was established in 1903 and granted a Royal Charter in 1906. The Institute's motto is *'enterprise and integrity'*. The Institute is highly regarded for its insight into board-related issues. Within its remit to develop director professionalism the Institute's main activities are to:

- educate and enhance the professionalism of directors and boards through development programmes, certification and evaluation;
- develop, set and monitor standards of director professionalism;
- represent and advocate the interests of members to government and civil society;
- research, publish and formulate policy on issues of relevance to directors; and
- support directors through the provision of information and advice relevant to the strategic direction of companies.

8.4 Board Structure

8.4.1 Composition

In the United Kingdom all directors have the same basic duties and liabilities whether they are executive (full-time employed) or non-executive. The existence of non-executive directors and the split of the

Table 8.2

Type of company	Chairman	Executive directors	Non-executive directors	Total
Largest 100 companies listed on the stock exchange (FTSE 100)	1	4.5	6	11.5
101–350 companies listed on the stock exchange	1	4	4	9
Other companies listed on the stock exchange	1	2.8	2.3	6.1
Average for companies listed on the stock exchange	1	3	2.7	6.7

Source: *Higgs Report*, 2003

roles of chief executive and chairman depend, to a certain extent on the size and type of company.

The importance of good non-executive directors in improving both accountability and company performance has long been recognized. Among the top 100 companies (the FTSE 100) the average percentage of non-executive directors (excluding the chairman from either executive or non-executive categories) is just over 57 per cent. The exception is one FTSE 100 company with an all-executive director board. The percentage falls depending on the size of company. Companies outside the top 350 companies have on average only 45 per cent of the board being non-executive directors.

The question of the independence of non-executive directors has been of increasing concern in the UK in recent years and is essentially considered an attitude of mind and a matter of personality. Different measures have been adopted by different organizations, institutions and associations to measure independence. This has been a problem for companies in two main ways. Firstly, they have had to deal with sometimes conflicting criteria; secondly, a 'tick-box mentality' has arisen where standardized checklists have been used by analysts and commentators.

In relation to composition, there is concern that the limited range of appointees to boards, particularly non-executive directors and chief executives, has resulted in the boards of United Kingdom companies being less effective than they could be. While there is little support for notions of diversity for its own sake, there is strong recognition that traditional methods of recruitment of directors through personal contacts have tended to act as a barrier to expanding the diversity of boards. Since the publication of the *Original Combined Code* in 1998, one of the principles has been that companies should have a 'formal and transparent procedure for the appointment of new directors to the board'. They must, unless 'the board is small', establish a nomination committee.

The average age of non-executive directors in the UK is 59 years, and of chairmen 62 years. Less than 20 per cent are under the age of 45. Only 4 per cent of all UK listed company directorships are held by women, and women comprise only 1 per cent of listed company chairmanships. This is in stark contrast to the 30 per cent of women managers. The percentage of women directors increases with the size of company. The ethnic composition of boards shows even less diversity. Only 7 per cent of directors are not British, with just 1 per cent from ethnic minority groups.

These statistics have to be contrasted with public sector boards where, of those appointed or re-appointed to such boards in the year to 31 March 2002, 38 per cent were female (chairmen 34 per cent), with 9 per cent from ethnic minorities.

8.4.2 Separation of the Roles of Chairman and Chief Executive

The recommendation that the roles of the chairman and chief executive should be separated first came to prominence in the code of best practice in the *Cadbury Report*. This has been a contentious issue in

Table 8.3 *Percentage of companies with joint chairman/chief executive*

Company type	%
Largest 100 companies (FTSE 100)	5
Largest 101–350 companies listed on the stock exchange (FTSE 250)	8
Other companies listed on the stock exchange	11
Average	10

Source: Higgs Report, 2003

some quarters in the UK. However, the figures show that although there are still joint role holders there is in general a high level of compliance, particularly among larger listed companies.

Another issue concerning the roles of chairman and chief executive is the circumstance of a chief executive going on to be the chairman of the same company. This has been an issue of concern to investors for some time, and the practice of the chairmanship being a reward for a successful chief executive is diminishing. By 2002 less than 25 per cent of the largest 100 companies had a chairman who had formerly been chief executive.

8.4.3 Committees

Since 1998 the *Original Combined Code* has required nearly all listed companies to have audit, remuneration and nomination committees or explain why not. Of the three committees the remuneration committee is the most universally adopted, followed closely by the audit committee, with the nomination committee lagging some way behind.

The audit committee frequently encompasses risk within its remit. Where it does not, companies tend to have a separate risk committee. Individual companies may also have other committees, either standing or ad hoc.

Table 8.4 *Percentage of companies with an audit committee*

Company type	%
Largest 100 companies (FTSE 100)	99
Largest 101–350 companies listed on the stock exchange (FTSE 250)	100
Other companies listed on the stock exchange	85

Table 8.5 *Percentage of companies with a remuneration committee*

Company type	%
Largest 100 companies (FTSE 100)	99
Largest 101–350 companies listed on the stock exchange (FTSE 250)	100
Other companies listed on the stock exchange	86

Table 8.6 *Percentage of companies with a nomination committee*

Company type	%
Largest 100 companies (FTSE 100)	94
Largest 101–350 companies listed on the stock exchange (FTSE 250)	81
Other companies listed on the stock exchange	29

8.5 Codes, Standards and Good Practice Guidelines

Although there is a strong basis of legislation and regulation, at the heart of the United Kingdom's approach to corporate governance is self-regulation backed by codes and guidelines. Widespread interest in the subject really took off in the early 1990s. There was increasing concern about the standards of corporate reporting and the accountability of boards. There were continuing scandals; the collapse of Polly Peck and Coloroll involved published accounts that did not give a true indication of the state of finances. It was recognized that if published information could not be trusted there would be serious consequences for the reputation of the United Kingdom as a business and financial centre.

A number of reports have been published over the last 15 years. These include the following.

8.5.1 The Cadbury Report (1992)

The first corporate governance code in the UK was developed by the *Committee on the Financial Aspects of Corporate Governance*. It was set up in May 1991 and sponsored by the London Stock Exchange, the Financial Reporting Council and the accountancy profession, under the chairmanship of Sir Adrian Cadbury. Key recommendations included the separation of the role of Chief Executive and Chairman, balanced composition of the board and selection processes for non-executive directors. The resulting report, widely known as the *Cadbury Report*, was issued in December 1992. The *Cadbury Report* included a Code of Best Practice and the recommendations were incorporated into the London Stock Exchange Listing Rules.

8.5.2 The Greenbury Report (1995)

The Confederation of British Industry set up a group under the chairmanship of Sir Richard Greenbury to examine the remuneration of directors, particularly compensation packages, large pay increases and share options. The *Greenbury Report* put forward a code of best practice and established the remuneration committee composed of non-executive directors being responsible for executive director remuneration. Again, the majority of the recommendations were endorsed by the Listing Rules.

8.5.3 The Hampel Report and Original Combined Code (1998)

Not long after the *Greenbury Report* was published, a number of institutions (the London Stock Exchange, the Confederation of British Industry, the Institute of Directors, the Consultative Committee of Accountancy Bodies, the National Association of Pension Funds and the Association of British Insurers) decided that the time was right to review the extent to which Cadbury and Greenbury had been implemented and whether their purposes were being achieved. The *Hampel Report* of the Committee on Corporate Governance was published in 1998, together with a summary of conclusions and recommendations. These, following further consultation by the London Stock Exchange, became the Combined Code on Corporate Governance (the *Original Combined Code*), which has applied to all listed companies from 31 December 1998, and will do so until reporting years commencing on or after 1 November 2003.

8.5.4 The Turnbull Report (1999)

An important aspect of the *Original Combined Code* are the provisions relating to internal control. These are translated into the Listing Rules which require listed companies to include a narrative statement in their Annual Report of how the internal control provisions have been applied. However, there was little guidance in the *Combined Code* as to how these provisions should be applied by companies. This led to the establishment of a working group under the auspices of the Institute of Chartered Accountants in England and Wales, chaired by Nigel Turnbull. The resulting *Internal Control: Guidance for Directors on the Combined Code* was issued in September

1999 and endorsed by the London Stock Exchange as consistent with the *Original Combined Code*.

8.5.5 The Higgs and Smith Reports and the Revised Combined Code (2003)

In July 2002 a review of the *Combined Code* was commenced. This was at the instigation of the Department of Trade and Industry (DTI) and Her Majesty's Treasury (HMT) following a review of company law. The subject was a *Review of the role and effectiveness of non-executive directors* and it was conducted by Derek Higgs (the *Higgs Review*).

Some two months into Derek Higgs' review the Financial Reporting Council set up a group under the chairmanship of Sir Robert Smith to develop guidance Audit Committees in the Combined Code (the *Smith Report*). Both the *Higgs Review* and the *Smith Report* were published on 20 January 2003. The *Tyson Report* on the Recruitment and Development of non-executive directors was commissioned by DTI following the publication of Higgs and Smith. All three provided recommendations for the revised *Combined Code* which emerged on 23 July 2003.

The *Revised Combined Code* applies for reporting years commencing on or after 1 November 2003. It applies only to companies on the Official List of the UKLA, but companies listed on the Alternative Investment Market (AIM) are recommended to have regard to its provisions. The *Combined Code* does not form part of the UKLA Listing Rules, but is appended to them. It is a voluntary code, but since a statement of compliance with it is required by the Listing Rules to be included in each annual report, there is an element of compulsion.

The *Combined Code* contains main and supporting principles and provisions. The distinction between them is that for both main and supporting principles, companies must report how they are applied. There is deliberately no prescribed form, the intention being to allow companies a free hand to explain their governance policies. For the provisions companies must either confirm that they have complied with them or, where they have not, provide an explanation. This is the 'comply or explain' basis of the *Combined Code*. It offers a degree of flexibility, but must be treated with care by both companies and investors. The expression has now become common parlance but companies should not use it as an excuse to ignore the provisions. If they do this or provide unconvincing explanations they rightly run the risk of investors attacking their standards of governance. On the other hand, analysts and investors must get away from a 'box-ticking' approach and have regard to proper explanations of 'non-compliance'.

The main principles and provisions in the revised *Combined Code* (2003) include:

A. Directors

The Board (A.1): The main principle addresses the collective responsibility of the unitary board. This is backed up by supporting principles identifying the board's role, particularly that of the non-executive directors. The underlying code provisions require greater detail about how the board operates, including provisions about meetings of non-executives without executive directors present. This section recognizes that being a director is not a sinecure and that directors are coming under increasing threat of litigation. For the first time, there is a code provision that says the company should provide insurance cover in respect of legal action against its directors.

Chairman and chief executive (A.2): The role of the chairman in relation to leadership of the board is recognized. There is a code provision explicitly stating that the roles of chairman and chief executive should be split. There is also a code provision stating that a chief executive should not go on to become chairman of the same company.

Board balance and independence (A.3): The main principle emphasizes the independence of non-executive directors. This is backed by supporting principles relating to the size of the board, the need for both executive and non-executive board members and refreshment of committee membership. There is a definition of independence for non-executive directors. This has been a contentious issue and, while it will not stop debates about individual directors, it provides a single basis against which the arguments take place. The percentage of non-executive directors and of those required to be independent has increased. At least half the board (excluding the chairman) should be independent non-executive directors. For companies outside the FTSE 350 the requirement is two independent non-executive directors. A senior independent director is required.

Appointments to the board (A.4): The recognition that the best people should be on boards is taken up here. The need for appointments to be on merit and against objective criteria forms a supporting principle. These are backed by detailed code provisions, including those designed to tackle the issues of availability of time to do the job. Companies have to explain if they use a search consultancy or advertisement in the recruitment of non-executive directors or a chairman.

Information and professional development (A.5): As well as the provision of information, the importance of the induction and training of directors is included for the first time.

Performance evaluation (A.6): This requires that boards should formally and rigorously review their own performance and that of individual members.

Re-election (A.7): The main provision has been strengthened by reference to continuing satisfactory performance of an individual director, and also planned and progressive refreshment of the board. The code provisions have been enhanced by laying down provisions on re-election of non-executives including the length of time on the board.

B. Remuneration

The level and make up of remuneration (B.1): Within the context of the continuing debate about levels of remuneration the code provisions recommend contractual notice periods of one year or less and place emphasis on the need to reduce compensation to reflect the duty on a departing director to mitigate loss.

Procedure (B.2): There have been few substantive amendments to the provisions on procedures for developing remuneration policy. The previous provisions on disclosure of directors' remuneration have been deleted from the *Combined Code*. The reason for this is that they have been superseded by the statutory requirements of The Directors' Remuneration Report Regulations 2002 (SI 2002 no. 1986).

C. Accountability and Audit

Financial reporting (C.1): These provisions are based on the principle that the board should present a balanced and understandable assessment of the company's position and prospects.

Internal control (C.2): There is a requirement to maintain a sound system of internal control and to review it at least annually.

Audit committee and auditors (C.3): Audit committees require at least one member to have 'recent and relevant financial experience'.

The duties of the audit committee are set out in some detail. There are provisions on whistle-blowing and the review of the effectiveness of internal controls. Important provisions concern the role of the audit committee in the appointment or removal of external auditors and the requirement for explanation of how auditor objectivity and independence are safeguarded if the auditor provides non-audit services.

D. Relations with Shareholders

Dialogue with institutional shareholders (D.1): The responsibility for ensuring that this is satisfactory is clearly placed on the whole board. The code provisions back up the role of different elements of the board in securing the overall purpose.

Constructive use of the AGM (D.2): All directors should attend the AGM.

These are the provisions against which the company has to report. There is also a Section 2 to the *Combined Code* addressed to institutional shareholders. This section is not subject to any sanction, but it does stress the need for institutional shareholders to consider carefully explanations for departure from the *Combined Code* and make a reasoned judgement in each case.

8.6 Disclosure and Transparency

8.6.1 Remuneration

Directors' pay has long been an issue in United Kingdom boardrooms. It first came to prominence following the privatization of utility companies in the early 1990s. At the time of privatization, many directors were awarded large pay increases and made large amounts of money from share options. These were sometimes coincident with staff reductions, pay restraint for staff and price increases. They led in some cases to shareholder revolts. At the same time, there was public concern about payments to departing directors. It was these issues that led to the establishment of the committee under the chairmanship of Sir Richard Greenbury which produced the *Greenbury Report* on directors' remuneration in 1995.

The lasting legacy of the Greenbury Report was the establishment of the remuneration committee. Other aspects of the report included:

- the approval of shareholders to new long-term incentive schemes (including option schemes);

- notice periods being reduced to one year or less; and

- terms of directors' contracts avoiding rewarding failure.

In essence, these provisions form the basis for the *Combined Code* provisions, which has built on them and strengthened them, but not radically altered them.

The next change in the area of remuneration was in the reporting of directors' pay with the introduction of The Directors' Remuneration Report Regulations 2002 (SI 2002 no. 1986). These Regulations apply to quoted companies with financial years ending on or after 31 December 2002. They increase the amount of information shareholders are given on directors' remuneration and prescribe comparative information and performance graphs. The aspect that has received most publicity has been the introduction of a vote by shareholders to approve the directors' remuneration report. Individual directors' entitlement to remuneration is not affected by the vote, so it is an advisory vote. However, the first 'reporting season' since the introduction of the regulations in 2003 saw significant shareholder activity which included a vote against the directors' remuneration report of Glaxo Smith Kline plc.

In the wake of these regulations the Association of British Insurers and the National Association of Pension Funds published *Guidelines on Executive Remuneration* in December 2002, including best practice on contracts and severance.

8.6.2 Reporting

There are a number of proposals in the Company Law Reform White Paper related to areas of company reporting and accounts. Most companies would simply have to produce a short supplementary statement to their accounts to comply with EU law and would not be required to include a narrative directors' report. The most economically significant companies would have to produce an Operating and Financial Review (OFR). On size grounds alone it is estimated that, under the proposed size criteria, this would cover about 1,000 companies. It will be interesting to see if the United Kingdom Listing Authority (UKLA) will require all quoted companies to produce an OFR even if outside the size criteria. The *Company Law Review* suggested that much of the decision on matters to be included in the OFR should be left to companies. The government's proposals are more prescriptive and will probably tend to a more 'boilerplate' approach, thus reducing the value of the OFR.

8.6.3 Audit

Using primary legislation, certain measures will be introduced in the United Kingdom on accounting and auditing based on recommendations from reviews instituted following US corporate collapses in 2001 and 2002. These will cover:

- auditor independence and qualifications;
- extending the powers of auditors to obtain information;
- a requirement for directors to state that they have not withheld information from auditors;
- a gateway for the Inland Revenue (the UK government office responsible for Income Tax) to pass information to the Financial Reporting Review Panel;
- a power to require companies to publish details of non-audit services provided by their audit firm; and
- greater powers for the Department of Trade and Industry (DTI) to obtain information in cases of suspected fraud and misconduct.

8.7 Shareholder Rights and Stakeholder Relations

Shareholder activism is an expression that sometimes has negative connotations: single-issue pressure groups, class actions and the like. On the other hand, companies frequently complain that shareholders, particularly many institutional shareholders, do not play an active role, and are only interested in short-term performance. This is the subject of much discussion and debate between companies and investors and it was highlighted as being of concern in the preamble to the *Combined Code*. It is not a simple matter to resolve. Some institutional investors have taken a particular interest in corporate governance. Prominent among these is Hermes, whose *Hermes Principles* were published in 2002. The five headings under which the *Hermes Principles* are grouped are:

- communication;
- financial;
- strategic and social;
- ethical; and
- environmental.

Linked to the interest shareholders take in the affairs of the companies in which they invest is the problem of short-termism. Investors are accused of short-termism; the average institutional holding in the United Kingdom is no longer than two years. This is not surprising as the majority of investors are traders who perceive shares as a commodity to make money from through taking profits at the optimum time. This has an effect on company attitudes. There is a tendency for short-term market pressures either to take precedence over longer-term strategy or, at the least, influence strategy. Linked with this is the pressure then put on individual directors to perform over comparatively short periods, with consequences not only for remuneration packages but also for the duration of executive directors in post. In the United Kingdom the average life-cycle of a chief executive is less than four years. This is another factor leading to short-term pressures coming to the fore.

8.7.1 Corporate Social Responsibility

Corporate social responsibility has over recent years been as ubiquitous a subject for debate in the United Kingdom as directors' remuneration. There has been a trend for many pressure groups and some investors to try to introduce the 'stakeholder' model into the United Kingdom. When considering United Kingdom companies it has to be remembered that at law directors' duties are owed to the shareholders as a whole, not to any other group or groups. Therefore, even if a particular investor or investors has particular social interests the directors would be in breach of their duty to promote these unless they coincided with the interests of the shareholders as a whole. However, United Kingdom companies increasingly recognize that trust and respect are vital for a successful company and these factors have to be taken into account and integrated into business operations. In the United Kingdom what most companies are looking for is improved competitiveness.

8.8   Director Development Activity

There are three professional bodies focusing upon developing board competency and effectiveness:

- The Institute of Directors;
- 3i; and
- The Institute of Chartered Secretaries and Administrators.

8.8.1   The Institute of Directors (IoD)

The IoD is strongly committed to raising directors' professional standards by encouraging directors to attain high levels of expertise and effectiveness and developing professional standards in boardroom practice. Below is a list of some of the courses and services offered by the IoD.

Courses for Directors

The IoD produce a range of over 30 short courses (1-, 2- and 3-day duration) formulated and developed from a director's perspective which are designed to be immediately relevant. They are led by business experts with considerable experience in the facilitation of training. All of the courses provide an excellent opportunity to meet other directors and expand personal networks.

Programmes for Directors

Programmes of study are available from the IoD (9- and 15-day duration), including the Company Direction Programme which can lead to the award of a professionally recognized Diploma.

Board Development Services

The IoD provides services to main, subsidiary and business unit boards from all types of organizations. The service helps boards to improve their structure, procedures and performance for enhanced success. These services are expertly delivered in the context of the organization's own industry, culture and addressing its key issues.

Director Coaching

The IoD provide an executive coaching service that is available to deal with a range of personal and professional issues.

Books and Publications

A range of books and publications on director development issues are available from the IoD.

The Chartered Director

In 1999, a milestone was achieved in the UK when the Privy Council agreed to the creation of the Chartered Director qualification. Chartered Directors are allowed to use the C Dir designation. Admission to the Chartered Director profession is open to IoD members and fellows who satisfy all the requirements and subscribe to the Code of Professional Conduct. Chartered Directors are required to undertake continuing professional development.

8.8.2   3i

3i invests to help boards realize their plans to grow their business. 3i provides a mixture of equity and loan capital tailored to fit each company's needs. The company is Europe's leading venture capital company and has a network of over 30 offices in Europe, Asia, Pacific and the USA. 3i has invested over £11 billion in over 13,000 businesses and has a portfolio of over 3,000 companies with a combined valuation of £4.5 billion.

3i launched its independent director programme (IDP) in 1986. The programme has become the leading placer of independent directors. IDP members are now on the boards of over 1,200 3i-backed businesses.

3i also organizes quarterly events for IDP members to get together, draw upon the experience of others and discuss best practice. The company also conducts research into independent director issues and regularly publishes information for members.

8.8.3 The Institute of Chartered Secretaries and Administrators (ICSA)

The ICSA is strongly committed to raising company secretaries' professional standards by encouraging company secretaries to attain high levels of expertise and effectiveness.

ICSA runs professional courses for its students. Courses include:

- corporate finance and taxation;
- corporate financial management;
- management practice;
- professional administration;
- administration of corporate affairs; and
- company secretarial practice.

8.9 Useful Contacts

- 3i – www.3i.com
- Association of British Insurers (ABI) – www.abi.org.uk
- Accounting Standards Board – www.asb.org.uk
- Association of Chartered Certified Accountants – www.acca.co.uk
- Bank of England – www.bankofengland.com
- British Bankers Association – www.bba.org.uk
- Companies House – www.companieshouse.gov.uk
- Confederation of British Industry (CBI) – www.cbi.org.uk
- Department of Trade and Industry – www.dti.gov.uk
- Financial Reporting Council (FRC) – www.frc.org.uk
- Financial Reporting Review Panel – www.frrp.org.uk
- Financial Services Authority (FSA)/UK Listing Authority (UKLA) – www.fsa.gov.uk

- Governance – www.governance.co.uk

- Her Majesty's Treasury – www.hm-treasury.gov.uk

- Hermes Pension Management Ltd – www.hermes.co.uk

- Institute of Chartered Secretaries and Administrators (ICSA) – www.icsa.org.uk

- Institute of Chartered Accountants in England and Wales – www.icaew.co.uk

- Institute of Directors (IoD) – www.iod.com

- London Stock Exchange (LSE) – www.londonstockexchange.com

- National Association of Pension Funds (NAPF) – www.napf.co.uk

- Pensions & Investment Research Consultants Limited (PIRC) – www.pirc.co.uk

8.10 Further Reading

ABI/NAPF (2002) *The Responsibilities of Institutional Shareholders and Agents – Statements and Principles*, ABI-NAPF, London

Cadbury, A (1992) *Report of the Committee on the Financial Aspects of Corporate Governance*, Gee, London

Cadbury, A (2002) *The Chairman and Corporate Governance*, London

Financial Reporting Council (2003), *Revised Financial Code*, FRC, London

Greenbury, R (1995) *Study Group on Directors' Remuneration*, Final Report, Gee, London

Hampel, R (1998) *Committee on Corporate Governance; Final Report*, Gee, London

Hermes Pensions Management Ltd (2002) The Hermes Principles

Higgs, D (2003) *Review of the role and effectiveness of non-executive directors*, The Department of Trade and Industry, London

Institute of Chartered Accountants in England and Wales (1999) *Internal Control: Guidance for Directors on the Combined Code* (known as the 'Turnbull Report')

ICSA (1996) *A Guide to Best Practice for Annual General Meetings*, ICSA, London

ICSA (1999) *A Guide to the Statement of Compliance*, ICSA, London

ICSA (1998) *Duties of a Company Secretary*, ICSA, London

ICSA (1998) *The Appointment and Induction of Directors*, ICSA, London

IoD (2001) *Standards for the Board*, IoD, London

Developed countries

London Stock Exchange (1998) *Combined Code: Principles of Good Governance and Code of Best Practice*, LSE, London

London Stock Exchange (2003) *The Combined Code on Corporate Governance*, LSE, London

Myners, P (2001) *Institutional Investment in the UK: A review*, HM Treasure, London

Pierce, C (2001) *The Effective Director: An Essential Guide to Director and Board Development*, Kogan Page, London

Smith, R (2003) *Audit committees – Combined Code guidance*, FRC, London

Tyson, L (2003) *The Tyson Report on the Recruitment and Development of Non-Executive Directors*, Department of Trade and Industry, London

9

United States

Table 9.1

Population	288 million (2002)
Gross National Income (GNI)	US $10.1 trillion (2002)
GNI per capita	US $35,060 (2002)
Total number of registered companies	15 million (est)
Market capitalization	US $15,500 billion (2001)
Number of companies listed on the stock exchange	15,000
Key corporate governance laws	• The Public Accounting Reform and Investor Protection Act (also known as Sarbanes–Oxley) (2002)

9.1   Corporate Structure and Ownership

The United States has nearly 15,000 public companies (including the smallest 'shells') and another 15 million or so unlisted private companies, including sole-proprietorships and 'mom and pop' stores. Under state law, all corporations must have boards.

In the case of public companies, the boards are functional, having, for example, an audit committee that performs certain functions in order to be listed on a stock exchange. In the case of private companies, the boards may be in name only, although many private companies do have working boards.

The ownership of US shares is as follows, according to US Federal Reserve statistics (June 2003):

Individuals	37%
Mutual funds	18.9%
Corporate and union private pension funds	12%
Foreign	10%
State and local pension funds	8.4%
Life and general insurance	7%
Other	6.7%

9.2 Legal Framework

Under state law in the US, expressed with various nuances, certain powers of the corporation are reserved to the board. Only the board has these powers. These include the power to sell the corporation or substantial assets, to declare dividends, to declare bankruptcy and so forth. In addition, there are certain functions normally expected of the board, under state law, such as overseeing management of the corporation, reviewing strategic plans and so forth.

The current governance system in the US is still based largely on the laws of incorporation enacted in each of the 50 states. These state corporation laws resemble each other closely – thanks in part to the so-called Model Business Corporation Act (MBCA) published and regularly updated by the American Bar Association (ABA). State laws and the influential MBCA set forth the fundamentals of corporations and the fiduciary duties of directors, namely the 'duty of care' and the 'duty of loyalty', also known as the duties of 'due care' and 'due loyalty'.

The duty of care is a duty to act in good faith with the amount of care that directors would exercise in a similar situation. This means making decisions after obtaining all reasonably available information required to make an intelligent decision. The duty of loyalty means making decisions in the interests of the corporation and its owners, rather than in one's own personal interest. It also means making decisions without conflicts of interests, excusing oneself from votes where such conflicts are present, and disclosing all known potential conflicts whenever they arise.

Courts are constantly giving new shades of meaning to the duties of care and loyalty, and as such these duties are always worth director attention. Today, however, directors of the 15,000 public companies in the US are focusing on two other sources of mandated practices: the law known as Sarbanes–Oxley passed in 2002 and the listing rules for each of the Self Regulating Organizations (SROs), approved in 2003.

9.2.1 Sarbanes–Oxley

On 2 July 2002, President George W Bush signed into law the Public Accounting Reform and Investor Protection Act of 2002, known as Sarbanes–Oxley after its sponsors Paul Sarbanes (a Democrat representing Maryland) and Michael Oxley (a Republican representing Ohio). The law has been hailed as a landmark comparable to the securities and securities exchange acts that created the Securities and Exchange Commission (SEC). As Senator Phil Gramm (a Republican representing Texas) declared after the bill passed, 'No one sitting on a corporate board or audit committee will ever be the same.'

With nearly a dozen sections and more than 80 subsections, the law covers many topics – from analyst conflicts of interests to document shredding. Among other goals, the law has created a publicly funded oversight board, The Public Company Accounting Oversight Board, to monitor auditors, strengthen auditor independence, increase CEO accountability for financial statements, make CEOs and Chief Financial Officers (CFOs) sign off on financials, ease private securities litigation, and give the SEC more resources and authority to enforce securities laws. It has also mandated increased criminal penalties for fraud, disbarring of directors and officers found guilty of fraud, longer prison sentences for certain types of white-collar crime, and disgorgement of ill-gotten gains to benefit defrauded shareholders.

Perhaps most notably for boards, Sarbanes–Oxley has strengthened the role of the audit committee. The law defines the audit committee as the 'committee (or equivalent body) established by and amongst the board of directors of an issuer for the purpose of overseeing the accounting and financial reporting processes of the issuer and audits of the financial statements of the issuer [or] if no such committee exists with respect to an issuer, the entire board of directors of the issuer'.

The audit committee's new strength comes from several aspects of the new law. Sarbanes–Oxley set new standards for auditor independence, banning certain types of consulting services that auditors had been able to provide in the past, namely:

- bookkeeping or other services related to the accounting records or financial statements of the audit client;
- financial information systems design and implementation;
- appraisal or valuation services, fairness opinions, or contribution-in-kind reports;
- actuarial services;
- internal audit outsourcing services;
- management functions or human resources;
- broker or dealer, investment adviser, or investment banking services; and
- legal services and other expert services unrelated to the audit.

Some tax consulting is still permissible.

The law also requires a new section of the annual report on internal control, describing the responsibility of management for this function and assessing its effectiveness. This regulation has raised board awareness of internal control, defined by The Institute of Internal Auditors as 'the process, effected by an entity's board of directors, management and other personnel in order to provide reasonable assurance regarding the achievement of objectives in the following categories: effectiveness and efficiency of operations; reliability of financial reporting; and compliance with applicable laws and regulations. This includes the safeguarding of assets.'

Under Sarbanes–Oxley, auditors must give reports to the audit committee on all *critical accounting policies and practices* to be used, as well as reports on the auditors' discussions with management about accounting policies and any material matters.

Furthermore, Sarbanes–Oxley requires that audit committees of companies listed on stock exchanges disclose the presence or absence of at least one member who is 'an audit committee financial expert'. In its final rule implementing this provision of the law, the SEC provided a detailed definition consistent with the one in the law. A 'financial expert' for the purposes of audit committee service is a person with understanding of generally accepted accounting principles and financial statements, experience in the preparation or auditing of financial statements of generally comparable issuers, and the application of such principles in connection with the accounting for estimates, accruals and reserves, experience with internal accounting controls and an understanding of audit committee functions.

The SEC has issued a number of rules implementing the major governance provisions of Sarbanes–Oxley. Of note are rules in the following areas:

- **Standards relating to listed company audit committees.** This rule addressed the independence of audit committee members; the audit committee's responsibility to select and oversee the company's independent accountant; procedures for handling complaints regarding the issuer's accounting practices; the authority of the audit committee to engage advisers; and funding for the independent auditor and any outside advisers engaged by the audit committee.

- **Implementation of standards of professional conduct for attorneys.** This rule sets more stringent reporting obligations for attorneys who suspect legal violations. If lawyers (whether internal counsel or outside counsel) see wrongdoing they must warn the company about it and, if the company fails to respond, must report the wrongdoing and make a 'noisy withdrawal' by stating that they are resigning for 'professional considerations'.

- **Strengthening the Commission's requirements regarding auditor independence.** This rule sets forth detailed restrictions on non-audit services provided by auditors.

- **Disclosure required by Sections 406 and 407 of the Sarbanes–Oxley Act of 2002.** This rule sets standards for ethics codes and the audit committee financial expert.

In addition to these four broad areas, the SEC has acted on other, narrower, aspects of Sarbanes–Oxley. Furthermore, as mentioned earlier, the SEC has approved new listing rules for the SROs pertaining to governance. Directors have a full agenda mastering all these new rules affecting corporate governance.

9.2.2 Private Company Regulation in the Aftermath of Sarbanes–Oxley

Private companies have been sheltered from the governance storms described above. They do not sell shares to the general public in the USA, so they are not listed on any stock market, and are not covered by Sarbanes–Oxley, although the full text of the law does include a suggestion to this effect. But private companies are hardly immune from the changes sweeping governance. These changes are arriving via *state corporation laws*. A number of states have passed laws that are similar to Sarbanes–Oxley, and, in some cases, even more stringent. Also, accounting practices of private companies are affected by the opinions expressed by CPA organizations such as the National Association of State Boards of Accountancy (NASBA) and the American Institute of Certified Public Accountants (AICPA).

9.3 Legal, Regulatory and Institutional Bodies

9.3.1 US Securities and Exchange Commission (SEC)

The primary mission of the US Securities and Exchange Commission (SEC) is to protect investors and maintain the integrity of the securities markets. The laws and rules that govern the securities industry in the United States derive from a simple and straightforward concept: all investors, whether large institutions or private individuals, should have access to certain basic facts about an investment prior to buying it. To achieve this, the SEC requires public companies to disclose meaningful financial and other information to the public, which provides a common pool of knowledge for all investors to use to judge for themselves if a company's securities are a good investment. The SEC also oversees other key participants in the securities world, including stock exchanges, broker-dealers, investment advisers, mutual funds, and public utility holding companies. Here again, the SEC is concerned primarily with promoting disclosure of important information, enforcing the securities laws, and protecting investors who interact with these various organizations and individuals.

9.3.2 American Stock Exchange (Amex)

The American Stock Exchange is a floor-based auction market where trading is conducted through a centralized specialist system supported by trading information technology. The overwhelming majority of buy and sell orders meet on the floor without specialist intervention. Amex regards itself as being well placed through its market structure and personalized services to offer growth opportunities to small and medium-sized companies seeking access to capital. In a typical year, several hundred companies list their shares on this exchange.

9.3.3 NASDAQ

NASDAQ is the world's largest electronic stock market and transmits real-time quote and trade data to more than 1.3 million users in 83 countries. With its unique framework NASDAQ provides listed companies' securities with ready access to investors, visibility in the marketplace and market conditions that promote immediate and continuous trading. In a typical year, approximately 4,000 companies list their stocks in this market.

9.3.4 New York Stock Exchange (NYSE)

The New York Stock Exchange is a self-regulated exchange and the designated examining authority for the major securities firms in the USA servicing 93 million customer accounts. It is committed to strong and effective regulation of its member firms to protect investors, the health of the financial system and the integrity of the capital-formation process. Obviously, the most important responsibilities for directors are the ones that are mandatory. In a typical year, approximately 3,000 companies list their shares on this exchange. In November 2003 the NYSE and the NASDAQ (the two largest US stock markets) received approval for new listing rules pertaining to governance (cited at the end of this chapter).

9.3.5 National Association of Corporate Directors (NACD)

Founded in 1977, the National Association of Corporate Directors (NACD) is the premier educational, publishing and consulting organization in board leadership and the only membership association for boards, directors, director-candidates and board advisers in the USA. The NACD promotes high professional board standards, creates forums for peer interaction, enhances director effectiveness, asserts the policy interests of directors, conducts research and educates boards and directors concerning traditional and cutting-edge issues. The NACD is focused primarily on the responsibilities of the board, including the scope and limits of that responsibility. Ten Blue Ribbon Commission reports on board responsibilities have been published so far, and the series is not yet complete.

9.4 Board Structure

9.4.1 Composition

Boards of US companies are unitary in structure. That is, most companies have only one board, rather than having a board of owners and a board of managers or employees, as some nations do. To say 'unitary' is somewhat simplistic, however. In the case of holding companies, there is a central board, with additional boards for subsidiaries. And in mutual funds – technically known as investment companies – fund families may have a single board (overseeing all funds) or multiple boards (one per fund or fund subgroup).

For over a decade, most recently with the Institutional Shareholder Services (ISS), the National Association of Corporate Directors (NACD) has conducted extensive research on board composition. We have seen a gradual growth in the presence of independent outside directors. At first, most of these outside directors were CEOs. In recent years, we have seen an increase in non-CEOs, including women and minorities who are senior executives of corporations, leaders of non-profit organizations, or professionals with specialized expertise.

9.4.2 Audit, Compensation and Nomination Committees

US boards vary in their use of committees. The most common committees are audit, compensation, and nomination (also called variously governance committee or committee on directors).

Audit committees of public companies must ensure that the companies they oversee have procedures in place that ensure compliance with generally accepted accounting principles as determined by the Financial Accounting Standards Board (FASB), the entity that sets accounting standards for US companies. In addition, conforming to Sarbanes–Oxley, now audit committees of public companies must:

● assume responsibility for the appointment, compensation, and oversight of the auditor;

- meet strict new independence requirements (having no affiliations and accepting no fees);

- establish procedures for the 'receipt, retention, and treatment of complaints received by the issuer regarding accounting, internal accounting controls, or auditing matters'; and the 'confidential, anonymous submission by employees of the issuer of concerns regarding questionable accounting or auditing matters';

- have authority to engage 'independent counsel and other advisers, as it determines necessary to carry out its duties';

- receive any necessary funding from the company, 'as determined by the audit committee in its capacity as a committee of the board of directors', for payment of compensation to the auditor or any advisors to the committee;

- furthermore, the SEC prohibits the listing of any company, after giving it a chance to 'cure defects' that do not comply with these standards.

Sarbanes–Oxley does not cover the duties of the other two key committees. However, the new NYSE and NASDAQ listing rules include requirements for all three committees. NACD has published guidance on the functions of all three committees, most recently compensation committees, the subject of its 2003 NACD Blue Ribbon Commission report.

9.5 Codes, Standards and Good Practice Guidelines

Standards for voluntary practices come from literally dozens of groups and include:

- the National Association of Corporate Directors (NACD), for directors of public and private organizations;

- the American Bar Association (ABA), for practising attorneys both internal and external;

- the Association of Corporate Council (ACC), for internal counsel;

- the Business Roundtable (BRT), for CEOs of the largest public companies;

- the Council of Institutional Investors (CII), for institutions investing in public companies; and

- the Institute of Internal Auditors, for internal auditors – to name just a few.

The voluntary best practices have also had a notable impact on changes over time on *mandated practices* which come primarily from federal and state governments (emanating from the legislative, executive, and judicial branches of the US government and the government of each state). For public companies, mandated practices also come from the SROs listing stock, including the Amex, the NASDAQ and the NYSE.

Together, US voluntary and mandatory standards – best practices and legal or listing requirements – offer guidance and incentives for an ethical and compliant tone at the top in US boardrooms.

In recent years, however, the delicate balance between the voluntary best practices and the mandates in the USA seems to have shifted to the latter direction. Directors have experienced a new governance 'paradigm', one that has shifted from a governance system largely composed of voluntary best practices, to one currently focused on mandatory practices.

There is good news here, but there are also urgent headlines. In the wake of corporate scandals such as the December 2001 bankruptcy of the Enron Corporation and the June 2002 bankruptcy of the Worldcom Corporation, many practices that were traditionally considered to be voluntary have become mandatory for public companies and, in some states, for private companies as well.

Boards that had already mastered the 'best practices' recommended by NACD, the BRT, the CII, and others, have had little trouble following all the new standards now imposed on them. Some boards, however, have found a need – almost overnight – to educate their boards in a number of areas previously left unattended. The need for director information and education, always valuable, is now vital.

9.6 Disclosure and Transparency

A primary goal of US securities laws is transparency – a term describing the ability of an investor to see the value of an investment as clearly as possible. Disclosure is the main means of achieving transparency. For this reason, US securities laws centre around disclosure.

Traditionally, disclosure focused almost exclusively on quantitative matters. Today, however, there is increasing interest in disclosure of qualitative matters. Sarbanes–Oxley and the new stock listing rules include new requirements to disclose procedural matters, such as how committees operate. Also, a number of organizations, such as the AICPA and the FASB, are studying ways that financial reports can reflect non-financial developments. Recently, a subgroup of the AICPA helped launch a consortium for enhanced business reporting.

Accurate and full disclosure of both quantitative and qualitative matters helps investors hold company officers and directors accountable for financial results.

9.7 Shareholder Rights and Stakeholder Relations

In the US, state corporation laws emphasize the director's duties of care and loyalty to the corporation's owners. Additional laws protect the interests of other stakeholders such as creditors (in the case of insolvency) and employees (in the case of response to takeover offers). Governance focus shifts back and forth between these two concerns over time.

Currently, the hottest topic is shareholder rights. The SEC is considering (as of mid-2004) a new rule that would permit shareholders, under certain conditions, to nominate directors. At present, nominations occur through independent nominating committees.

In early 2004, NACD published *Framework and Tools for Improving Board-Shareowner Communications: The Report of the Council of Institutional Investors – National Association of Corporate Directors Task Force on Improving Board – Shareowner Communications*. The report is available free of charge on the Web sites of both organizations (www.nacdonline.org and www.cii.org).

9.8 Director Development Activity

The NASDAQ and NYSE are encouraging their listed companies to educate their directors. Furthermore, organizations such as ISS, which advises institutional shareholders, are including director education in their corporate governance standards. The ISS includes education in its 'Corporate Governance Quotient' as follows:

Corporate Governance Quotient Explained *(excerpted from the Institutional Investor Services Web site)*

The widespread view that 'governance matters' necessitates the creation of metrics that allow investors to quickly and accurately identify the relative performance of companies. To meet this rising demand, Institutional Shareholder Services (ISS) – with input from a panel of advisory board members – spent 18 months developing a new tool for monitoring and comparing the corporate governance structures of America's leading publicly-traded companies.

CGQ (shorthand for Corporate Governance Quotient) ratings will appear on the front page of each ISS proxy analysis along with information that provides some context for the rating. A table on the second page of each analysis provides details about the key factors that drive the rating. ProxyMaster.com, ISS's electronic platform for delivering research to institutional investors, allows users to screen portfolio companies on the basis of their CGQ.

Seven core topics comprise the CGQ rating:

(1) board structure and composition,

(2) charter and by-law provisions,

(3) laws of the state of incorporation,

(4) executive and director compensation,

(5) qualitative factors, including financial performance,

(6) D&O stock ownership, and

(7) director education.

The score for each core topic reflects a set of key governance variables. The current list comprises 51 of these sub issues. In addition, some variables are analyzed in combination with other provisions. For example, a board with a majority of independent directors and all-independent key board panels (audit, nominating and compensation) receives a higher rating for each of these attributes than it would if it had either one of them in isolation.

ISS hopes CGQ will foster progressive governance practices. Many governance experts advocate continuing education for board members, for example, companies often have little reason to encourage (or pay for) such training. Going forward, directors who participate in 'ISS-accredited' director education programs will boost the CGQ scores for the boards where they serve.

Accredited education programs include those offered by the National Association of Corporate Directors, the University of Wisconsin/State of Wisconsin Investment Board, the Wharton/SpencerStuart Directors' Institute, Dartmouth's Center for Corporate Governance, and the Stanford Directors' College.

9.8.1　The Importance of Networking, Research and Education

NACD has been educating corporate boards and researching and publishing valuable tools on governance issues for more than 25 years. Its funding comes primarily from its membership (including local chapters for networking), publications, and educational programs. It receives research support from the Center for Board Leadership, a not-for-profit entity composed of leading professional services organizations.

NACD has been recognized by NYSE, NASDAQ and ISS as a quality education resource for corporate boards. NACD seminars capitalize on NACD's years of experience inside the boardrooms of some of the nation's most influential public and private companies. NACD conducts in-boardroom programmes, and helps boards develop processes and practices unique to their own industries and challenges.

9.9　Useful Contacts

- American Bar Association – www.aba.org
- American Institute of Certified of Public Accountants – www.aicpa.org
- American Stock Exchange – www.amex.com
- Business Roundtable – www.brtable.org
- CALPERS – www.calpers.ca.gov
- Caux Round Table – www.cauxroundtable.org
- Conference Board – www.conference-board.org
- Corporate Library – www.thecorporatelibrary.com
- Council of Institutional Investors – www.cii.org
- Governance Metrics International – www.governancemetrics.com

- Institutional Shareholder Services – www.issproxy.com

- NASDAQ – www.nasdaq.com

- National Association of Corporate Directors – www.nacdonline.org

- National Association of Securities Dealers (NASD) – www.nasd.com

- National Association of State Boards of Accountancy – www. nasba.org

- New York Stock Exchange – www.nyse.com

- Public Company Accounting Oversight Board – www.pcaobus.org

- Securities and Exchange Commission – www.sec.gov

9.10   Further Reading

American Bar Association, Committee on Corporate Laws, Section of Business Law (2001) *Corporate Director's Guidebook*, ABA, Washington

American Law Institute (1994, revised 2002) Principles *of Corporate Governance: Analysis and Recommendations*, ALI

Breeden (2003) *Restoring Trust: The Breeden Report on Corporate Governance for the Future of MC/Inc*, United States Court for the Southern District of New York

The Business Roundtable (2002) *Statement on Corporate Governance*, Business Roundtable

CALPERS (1998) *Corporate Governance Core Principles and Guidelines: The United States*, CALPERS, California

Conference Board (2003) *Commission on Public Trust and Private Enterprise Findings and Recommendations; Part 2*: Corporate Governance, Conference Board

Council of Institutional Investors (2003) *Corporate Goverannce Policies* ,CII, Washington

NASDAQ (2003) *Qualititative Requirements of the NASDAQ Stock Market: Corporate Goverannce*

National Association of Corporate Directors (1995) *Director Compensation: Report of the NACD Blue Ribbon Commission*, NACD, Washington

National Association of Corporate Directors (1996, with subsequent updating) *Director Professionalism: Report of the NACD Blue Ribbon Commission*, NACD, Washington

National Association of Corporate Directors (1998) *CEO Succession: Report of the NACD Blue Ribbon Commission*, NACD, Washington

National Association of Corporate Directors (1999) *Audit Committees: Report of the NACD Blue Ribbon Commission*, NACD, Washington

National Association of Corporate Directors (2000) *Role of the Board in Corporate Strategy: Report of the NACD Blue Ribbon Comision*, NACD, Washington

National Association of Corporate Directors (2001) *Board Evaluation: Report of the NACD Blue Ribbon Commission*, NACD, Washington

National Association of Corporate Directors (2002) *Risk Oversight: Report of the NACD Blue Ribbon Comision*, NACD, Washington

National Association of Corporate Directors (2003) *Executive Compensation: Report of the NACD Blue Ribbon Commission*, NACD, Washington

NYSE (2003) *Final NYSE Corporate Governance Rules*, http://www.nyse.com/pdfs/finalcorpgovrules.pdf

Part 2

Developing Countries

10

Argentina

Table 10.1

Population	37.9 million (2002)
Gross National Income (GNI)	US $154 billion (2002)
GNI per capita	US $4,060 (2002)
Total number of companies	4,500
Number of companies listed on the stock exchange	90
Market capitalization	N/A
Key corporate laws	● Decree 677 (2001)
	● Business Companies Law (1972 & 1983)

10.1 Corporate Structure and Ownership

There are approximately 4,500 companies in Argentina with a capital of US $700,000 or over. Of these, only 90 are quoted on the local stock market.

There is a high level of ownership concentration within Argentinian companies. In 2003 the largest shareholder owned 61 per cent of the shares of the 15 companies sampled, the 3 largest shareholders held 82 per cent of the shares and the 5 largest shareholders held 90 per cent of the shares (OECD, 2003: 53).

The OECD also states that among the 20 largest listed companies, controlling shareholders hold 65 per cent of the equity. The very high levels of ownership concentration in Argentina have created a situation where corporate control is tightly exercised by majority shareholders.

Of the 40 largest Argentinian companies, 25 are foreign controlled, 14 are controlled by a local family and there is one state-owned company (OECD, 2003: 48).

Pyramid structures are widely employed in Argentina. The OECD (2003: 54) examined 24 Argentinian firms that had issued American Depository Receipts and found 93 per cent affiliation to groups through pyramids. Little use of no-voting shares was also noted (3.9 per cent). The OECD estimates that in these companies, the controlling group had, on average, rights over 68 per cent of the company's cash flows.

10.2 Legal Framework

Argentina is a civil law country. Its corporate governance system is based on the Business Companies Law No. 19.550, promulgated in 1972 and amended in 1983 by Law 22.903. Although this law was not originally conceived in terms of developing corporate governance, it included a series of provisions that involved corporate governance principles. The Business Companies Law governs all business companies, from general partnerships to listing corporations. It does not provide a separate treatment for listing corporations but does contain specific provisions applicable to corporations in general. More recently, Decree 677 dated May 2001 introduced corporate governance principles into Argentine law applicable to listed corporations. The system has been further supplemented through other rules, such as:

● the Securities and Stock Exchanges Law No. 17.811;

● the Bankruptcy Law No. 24.522 – recently amended by Laws 25.563 and 25.589; and

● the regulations issued by the agency, Argentine Securities Commission (*Comisión Nacional de Valores*), that oversees public offerings.

The Business Companies Law establishes that managers must fulfil their duties with the loyalty and diligence expected of a good business-man. Decree 677 (2001) determines that such duty of loyalty includes:

- the prohibition to use corporate assets or confidential information for private purposes;
- the prohibition to take advantage – whether by action or omission – for their own or third parties' benefit of the corporation's business opportunities;
- the obligation to use their powers only for the purposes for which they were granted; and
- the obligation to make sure that their conduct never leads to a direct or indirect conflict of their own interests with those of the corporation.

Particularly important is the provision reversing the burden of proof for directors whose observance of the duty of loyalty is being questioned.

Decree 677 (2001) also imposes on directors, managers and statutory auditors of issuers the duty to have the corporate interests of the issuer and the common interest of all members prevail, without exception, over any others, including those of the corporation's con-trolling company(ies), it being their duty to adopt and implement preventive measures to protect the corporate interest in order to reduce the risk of any conflict of interest involving the issuer.

Directors have joint and unlimited liability for the corporation, shareholders and third parties for:

- the non-compliance with their duties;
- for violation of the law, regulations or by-laws, and
- for any other damage caused by their wilful misconduct, abuse of powers or gross negligence.

Actions against directors for damage caused to the corporation may be brought by the corporation itself or, failing that, by any shareholder. In addition, shareholders and third parties may file lawsuits for any damages sustained in their own assets due to the above.

10.3 Legal, Regulatory and Institutional Bodies

10.3.1 Instituto Argentino para el Gobierno de las Organizaciones (IAGO)

In 1999, FUNDECE (Business Foundation for Quality and Excellence) and IDEA (Instituto para el Desarrollo Empresarial), which together represent over 400 local and international companies operating in Argentina, decided to join forces in order to promote board best practices and train professional directors. These two leading organizations founded the IAGO (Argentine Institute for the Governance of Organizations) in April 2002.

IAGO's objectives for 2003 and beyond are:

- Align with regional organizations committed to corporate governance to promote the implementation of recommendations of the Latin America 'White Paper' coordinated by OECD and IFC.

- Keep boards of directors abreast of major governance issues.

- Act as enabler and referents in Argentina to develop the concept, spirit and practice of corporate governance.

- Communicate with the media, investors, educators, companies, non-government organizations, business world leaders and directors to improve their understanding on corporate board matters.

- Incorporate corporate governance into the curricula and research at leading business and public administration schools.

Major ongoing activities are:

- creation of a Web site www.iago.org.ar;
- a quarterly electronic newsletter distributed to over 1,500 incumbents in Argentina and abroad;
- two IAGO committees: Audit and Best Practices, preparing a Best Practices Code as well as audit procedure recommendations.

10.4 Board Structure

Most boards in Argentina serve mainly in an advisory function for controllers.

The typical composition of the boards of companies quoted on the stock market include shareholders and family members. Most are 'amateur' directors. There are so far very few professional boards. But in the past few years there have been a few trend-setter companies (eg YPF, Perez Companc, Zucamor and CCI).

Argentina has a dualistic governance system (ie two-tier board system), in which the company's oversight is provided by the Statutory Auditing Body or Oversight Council (*Sindicatura* or *Consejo de Vigilancia*), rather than the Board of Directors.

The OECD (2003: 55) estimates from American Depository Receipt (ADR) filings that the average board size for large companies in Argentina in 2002 was 8.1 and that 38.8 per cent of board members were independent.

Few companies have functioning committees. However, Decree 677 (2001) establishes that all listing companies shall have an audit committee consisting of at least three directors, most of whom should be independent. To be considered as independent, the respective member shall fulfil no executive duties within the company and such independence needs to be not only from the corporation but also from its controlling shareholders. The CNV has determined the degree of independence required. Moreover, the regulation of the Decree provides that members of the audit committee shall be financial or accounting experts. This obligation will become effective in May 2004.

Included among the duties of the audit committee are the following:

- to issue opinions on the appointment of the external auditor and to ensure that such external auditor is and remains independent;

- to oversee the internal control and administrative-accounting systems;

- to monitor compliance with corporate risk management information policies;

- to disclose information to the market on any events giving rise to a conflict of interest;

- to express an opinion on the company's compensation policy and stock options plans;

- to determine compliance with any applicable standards of conduct; and

- to offer an opinion on any eventual contracts with related parties.

10.5 Codes, Standards and Good Practice Guidelines

Decree 677 (2001) has been the major corporate governance change in Argentina. This decree is discussed in other sections of this chapter.

10.6 Disclosure and Transparency

10.6.1 Disclosure of Material Information

The Business Companies Law provisions on Books and Records are supplemented by Decree 677 (2001) and regulations issued by the CNV.

Specifically, the Decree makes it mandatory for managers and members of the statutory auditing body to issue direct, accurate, adequate and timely disclosure on all material matters regarding the corporation. All issuers must appoint an Officer in Charge of Relations with the Market. Additionally, their officers and controlling shareholders and other participants in the system of public offerings are bound to disclose their share ownership and voting rights. Purchases or sales which may result in a change of control of the issuer, or grant at least 5 per cent of total issued votes at the shareholders' meetings, should also be disclosed.

10.6.2 Independent External Auditors

Decree 677 (2001) provides that the financial statements of companies listing their securities must be audited by independent certified public accountants. The CNV states that auditors are not to be considered independent if they provide other services to the issuer that, at the CNV's sole discretion, suggest an unsuitable participation in management responsibilities, making their independence questionable. The regulation also establishes that, if external auditors or the accounting firms of which they are members render other services or sell or provide other goods to the issuer or their controlling or controlled entities, the audit report should contain the different ratios. These ratios would indicate the relation between the amounts charged for audit services and non-audit services.

Within the powers that the Decree grants to the CNV, an external auditor may be appointed at the request of minority shareholders representing no less than 5 per cent of the corporate capital.

10.7   Shareholder Rights and Stakeholder Relations

10.7.1   Shareholders

Shareholders' Ownership Rights

There are no restrictions on the shareholders' ownership rights. All securities listed on the local stock exchanges are deposited or registered with the *Caja de Valores* (national securities depository), without any restrictions attaching to their transfer or conveyance.

When a company makes a new issue of shares, shareholders are given a pre-emptive right to acquire the new shares. That right may only be restricted under exceptional circumstances.

Shareholders' Right to Information

Before an ordinary shareholders' meeting can be held to consider a company's fiscal-year documents, shareholders representing no less than 2 per cent of the corporate capital may make statements or submit proposals concerning the conduct of the corporate business during that fiscal year. The board of directors shall then circulate such proposals or statements to the other shareholders.

In addition, during such meetings, shareholders may make direct requests to the board of directors for information on any item to be discussed. Shareholders representing at least 2 per cent of corporate capital) may also request information from the statutory auditors on matters within the auditor's area of responsibility.

Twenty days before the ordinary shareholders' meeting, the board of directors shall make available to the shareholders:

- all relevant information;
- the documents to be reviewed; and

- the board's proposals for that meeting.

The board shall also inform in their report on the status of the principal activities of the company during the fiscal year and the forthcoming prospects for the company.

Additionally, Decree 677 (2001) provides that information shall be furnished on:

- proposed business plans and other considerations involving business, financial and investment issues;
- the company's decision-making structure and internal control system;
- the dividends policy proposed by the board of directors; and
- the compensation for board members and the compensation policy for management staff, stocks options plans, etc.

Shareholders' Right to Participate and Vote at Shareholders' Meetings

All shareholders are entitled to participate and vote in shareholders' meetings provided they notify their decision to attend at least 3 days prior to the date of the meeting. Notice of meetings must be published not less than 20 days nor more than 45 days before the meeting. Such notice shall include the agenda, and the meeting may consider no items except those contained in the agenda.

Shareholders representing at least 5 per cent of the corporate capital (this percentage may be reduced by the by-laws) may request the board or the statutory auditors to call a shareholders' meeting indicating the items to be considered.

Shareholders may participate at a meeting in person or by proxy, without any restrictions, but directors, statutory auditors and company employees could not represent shareholders in such corporate meetings.

Shareholders' Agreements

Decree 677 (2001) requires participants in public offerings to disclose any kind of agreements, including voting agreements, to the CNV.

The referred disclosure does not judge over the validity of the above mentioned agreements.

Corporate Control Market

Whenever someone intends to purchase a 'significant interest' in an issuer's shares, that person is required to launch a mandatory bid (*Oferta Pública de Adquisición* or OPA), in order to ensure fair conditions to every shareholder. The OPA is mandatory, unless the issuer decides not to come under that system, which must be expressly decided by the Shareholders' Meeting and disclosed to investors. If the issuer decides to de-list its shares from the stock exchange, the OPA procedure becomes mandatory.

10.7.2   The Equitable Treatment of Shareholders

Equitable Treatment Within Each Class of Shares

According to the Business Companies Law, all shareholders have the same rights within any class of shares. Argentine laws make no difference between majority or minority, domestic or foreign shareholders.

The Business Companies Law allows companies to issue non-voting shares. However, these shares may regain their voting rights in certain circumstances and always entitle the holder to vote on the appointment and removal of the company's statutory auditor(s).

The company can issue shares with plural voting rights (up to 5 votes per share), but no plural vote shares may be issued after the company has filed its registration statement prior to a public offering.

The Argentine Securities Commission regulations allow depository entities to cast dissenting votes, if it is necessary to comply with the express wishes of the beneficial owner of the shares.

Insider Trading

Decree 677 (2001) prohibits the use of privileged information by insiders. The price differential obtained by insiders should belong to the corporation, which must file legal action against the insiders. Any shareholder may bring or continue such action if the corporation fails to do so. The law also prohibits any market manipulation or misleading practices.

Prohibitions Imposed on Directors Regarding Conflicts of Interest

Company directors, statutory auditors and officers who are also shareholders should abstain from voting at shareholders' meetings on the approval of their performance or their removal with cause.

The Business Companies Law provides that directors who have an interest that is contrary to that of the corporation should:

- abstain from taking part in discussions;
- not vote; and
- should make their contrary interests known to the board and statutory auditor(s).

There are also restrictions concerning the contracts that directors may enter into with the corporation. Decree 677 (2001) established the obligation to follow a special procedure for legal acts or contracts with related parties involving a significant amount.

Possibility of Obtaining Effective Redress for Violation of Shareholders' Rights

Shareholders may resort to the remedies granted by the Business Companies Law to obtain effective redress for violation of their rights. However, to guarantee such effectiveness and to secure a quicker response, Decree 677 (2001) makes it mandatory for the issuer to submit any dispute regarding public offerings to arbitration.

10.7.3 Liability of Shareholders for Null Resolutions by the Shareholders' Meetings

The rule providing shareholders' responsibility for any damages caused by decisions adopted by the shareholders' meetings subsequently declared to be null and void for being contrary to law, regulations or by-laws, may be considered as limiting their voting rights.

10.7.4 Stakeholders

Argentine law does not include any provision on the participation of stakeholders in corporate governance. Although the Argentine Constitution grants workers the right to participate in corporate profits, control production and to cooperate with management, that right has not been regulated beyond the Business Companies Law provision for participation bonuses for the staff and Law 23.696 which established the Joint Ownership Programme (*Programa de Propiedad Participada*) for privatized companies.

10.8 Director Development Activity

Research on corporate governance has been undertaken in Argentina by FUNDECE (Business Foundation for Quality and Excellence) and IDEA (Instituto para el Desarrollo Empresarial) since 1999. It includes:

- identifying corporate governance trends in several selected countries (USA, UK, Brazil, EU, Canada, Japan and Mexico); this involves assessing how governance practices were introduced in the selected countries and evaluating their success;

- recommending what should be done in Argentina; and

- interviewing incumbents: banks, pension funds, investment funds, stock market, securities and exchange commission, auditors, private and government companies' CEOs and independent board members.

Initial conclusions, from interviews with over 100 individuals, are modest but encouraging. They indicate that corporate governance and director development activity need to be initiated in Argentina.

10.9 Useful Contacts

- Argentine Institute for the Governance of Organizations (IAGO) – www.iago.org.ar

- Business Foundation for Quality and Excellence (FUNDECE) – www.fundece.org.ar

- Instituto para el Desarrollo Empresarial (IDEA) – www.ideared.org

- Latin American Corporate Governance Network – www.confecamaras.org.co/CG

10.10 Further Reading

OECD (2003) *White Paper on Corporate Governance in Latin America*, OECD, Paris

11

Brazil

Table 11.1

Population	174 million (2000)
Gross National Income (GNI)	US $497 billion (2002)
GNI per capita	US $2,850 (2002)
Number of registered companies	n/a
Number of companies listed on the stock exchange	400 (Bovespa)
Key corporate laws	⦿ Law 10,303 (2001)
	⦿ Law 9,457 (1997)
	⦿ Law 6,404 (1976)
Key corporate governance codes	⦿ Recomendacoes sobre Governanca Corporativa (2002)

11.1 Corporate Structure and Ownership

The very high levels of ownership concentration in Brazil have created a situation where corporate control is tightly exercised by majority shareholders. In 2002, the largest shareholder owned 51 per cent of the 459 companies sampled, the three largest shareholders held 65 per cent of the shares and the five largest shareholders held 73 per cent of the shares (OECD, 2003: 53). The OECD (2003: 49) estimates that of the 100 largest non-financial companies in Brazil, 2 have dispersed ownership, 29 are controlled by a family, 37 are controlled by a foreign firm and 32 are controlled by the government.

The OECD (2003: 49) quotes a study by Khanna and Yafeh (2000) involving 38 conglomerates participating in the ownership of large listed Brazilian companies. They found 89 per cent of affiliations were through pyramids.

Brazilian companies widely use non-voting shares. In Brazil companies are allowed to issue shares without voting rights up to two-thirds of the total capital stock. Almost 90 per cent of 459 listed Brazilian firms have non-voting shares that represent 120 per cent of total voting capital (OECD, 2003: 49).

11.2 Legal Framework

The basic corporate governance principles were established by the Brazilian Corporations Law (Law 6,404 of 15 December 1976). This law was amended by Law 9,457 of 5 May 1997 and by Law 10,303 of 31 October 2001).

Brazilian corporations have two decision-making bodies: the shareholders and the board of directors – the board of directors is optional for unlisted corporations with no authorized capital.

Brazilian corporations must have at least two officers, resident in Brazil, elected by the board of directors (if there is one) or by the shareholders' meeting (if there is no board). Up to one-third of the members of the board may serve as officers.

The day-to-day management is incumbent upon the executive management appointed by the directors (or by the shareholders if there are no directors).

11.2.1 Fiduciary Duties

The general rule is that directors and officers are not personally liable for actions taken on behalf of the company. However, they may be held personally liable if they act beyond their power, in violation of the law or the company's by-laws or if they act with negligence or wilful misconduct.

Fiduciary duties include:

(i)   the duty of loyalty;

(ii)   the duty of care;

(iii) the duty to pursue the company's interest with no deviation of power;

(iv) the duty to avoid conflict of interests; and

(v)   the duty to inform.

11.2.2   Fiscal Council

The fiscal council is responsible for monitoring the acts of the board members and the officers and reviewing the management accounts and reports.

The fiscal council is not necessarily permanent, but must be installed if requested by holders of 10 per cent of the voting shares or 5 per cent of the non-voting shares. It should be composed of a minimum of three and a maximum of five members.

Preferred non-voting shareholders have the right to appoint one member of the fiscal council. Shareholders holding at least 10 per cent of the voting stock have the right to appoint another member. The remaining voting shareholders have the right to appoint an equal number of members, plus one.

11.3   Legal, Regulatory and Institutional Bodies

11.3.1   The Brazilian Securities and Exchange Commission (CVM)

The 'Comissão de Valores Mobiliários', or CVM as it is widely referred to, is essentially a Securities and Exchange Commission.

The Law that instituted CVM established that it should observe the following objectives:

● to ensure the proper functioning of the exchange and over-the-counter markets;

● to protect all securities holders against fraudulent issues and illegal actions performed by company managers, controlling shareholders, or mutual fund managers;

- to avoid or inhibit any kind of fraud or manipulation which may give rise to artificial price formation in the securities market;

- to assure public access to all relevant information about the securities traded and the companies which have issued them;

- to ensure that all market participants adopt fair trading practices;

- to stimulate the formation of savings and their investment in securities; and

- to promote the expansion and efficiency of the securities market and the capitalization of Brazilian publicly held companies.

11.3.2   The 'Novo Mercado' Created by the São Paulo Stock Exchange (Bovespa)

The São Paulo Stock Exchange (Bovespa) recently created a new listing segment called 'Novo Mercado' ('New Market'). Participation in the 'Novo Mercado' is voluntary, but companies willing to have their shares traded must undertake to comply with corporate governance standards and disclosure requirements more stringent than those already applicable to the traditional segment. The purpose of this new segment is to encourage the adoption of good corporate governance practices and foster a stronger securities market.

The 'Novo Mercado' has two entry levels, with varying degrees of adherence to good corporate governance demanded. Requirements to entry at 'Corporate Governance Level One' concern basically disclosure rules in addition to the regular listing and a free float of 25 per cent. The entry to 'Corporate Governance Level Two' requires the same conditions as 'Level One', plus annual reports according to US GAAP or IAS, a unified term of one year for board members and adherence to Bovespa's Arbitration Panel.

Currently (February 2003) there are 400 listed companies at Bovespa. Additionally, 26 companies are listed in 'Level One', 3 companies are listed in 'Level Two' and 2 companies are listed in the 'Novo Mercado'. The Brazilian national bank, 'Banco do Brasil', came close to joining the 'Novo Mercado' at the end of 2002, because of an almost 100 per cent adherence to the stipulated guidelines, but were denied access to this elite group because they failed to secure a 'free float' of 25 per cent of their shares. In a related case, Petrobras, the state petroleum giant, almost made it to 'Level Two' of the 'Novo Mercado' but couldn't because legalese meant they failed to formalize their practices of good corporate governance.

Bovespa computes regularly the 'IGC – Índice de Governança Corporativa' (Corporate Governance Index) which compares figures for 'Novo Mercado', Level One and Level Two with the general listing of the stock market. IGC evidences the higher valuations commended by companies that adhere to higher standards of corporate governance.

'Novo Mercado' companies normally trade with a premium and are subject to less market volatility. Research indicates that investors are willing to pay a premium of 23 per cent for Brazilian companies that adopt good corporate governance practices ('Investor Opinion Survey', McKinsey & Company, 2000).

The 'Novo Mercado' rules include the following, among others:

1. All shares must have voting rights (the Corporations Law allows the issuance of preferred non-voting shares up to a limit of 50%).

2. The purchaser of controlling shares must make a tender offer for the acquisition of the remaining common shares for the same price being paid for the controlling shares (the Corporations Law provides for a tag-along of 80 per cent of the price paid for the controlling shares).

3. The controlling shareholder must make a tender offer to purchase the minority shareholders' shares at their economic value when a company goes private (the Corporations Law establishes a similar right). Valuation must take into account: (i) book net worth value; (ii) net worth according to market value; (iii) discounted cash flow valuation; (iv) multiple comparisons; (v) market value of the shares; and (vi) other method accepted by CVM.

4. The board of directors must have at least five members and a term in office of one year (the Corporations Law establishes a minimum of three members for a maximum of three years).

5. After an IPO, controlling shareholders are prohibited from negotiating shares for six months. From the seventh to the twelfth month, only 40 per cent of the shares may be negotiated.

6. Consolidated audited financial statements must be made quarterly. The Annual Reports must be published in US GAAP or IAS.

7. Company must make public: (i) related party contracts; (ii) stock option plans; and (iii) transactions of management or controlling shareholder with securities of the company.

8. At least 25 per cent of the total outstanding shares must be kept in the market.

9. Adherence to a Market Arbitration Panel, designed by the São Paulo Stock Exchange (Bovespa) to settle disputes among listed companies concerning the Brazilian Corporations Law, instructions by the Brazilian SEC and corporate governance matters.

Petros Pension Fund

Petros was initially founded in March 1970 with the intention of ensuring the quality of life for Petrobras employees. As time moved on, other companies involved themselves with the scheme and the non-profit organization grew from strength to strength until today where it stands as the second largest pension fund company in the country and one of the largest corporate investors.

In December 2002 Petros issued its 'Manual of Governance of Investment', a document explaining its criteria for investment in a company's shares. In the opening paragraph of the introduction it states that: 'As an institutional investor Petros is constantly looking for ways in which to stimulate the good practice of corporate governance in the companies in which it participates.'

Petros's hope has been that in making it clear that their investment funds will be directed to companies adopting good corporate governance principles, the possibility of greater investment income will stimulate companies to implement good practice systems.

Firstly, it is hoped that companies will appoint well-informed and independent directors, and institute transparent management practices with the aim of maximizing the financial returns for shareholders. Above all, it states, it expects to see the development of practices that attack attitudes that negatively prejudice minority shareholders.

11.3.3 The National Economic and Social Development Bank (BNDES)

Another significant recent development in the implementation of good corporate governance practices in Brazil has been a move by the

BNDES, the 'Banco Nacional de Desenvolvimento Econômico e Social' (National Economic and Social Development Bank).

The mission statement of the BNDES makes it clear that their aim is: 'to promote the country's development, increasing the competitiveness of the Brazilian economy, while giving priority both to the reduction of social and regional inequalities and to the preservation of existing jobs and the creation of new ones'.

This they have always hoped to do through the direction of funds to projects in key areas where the private sector is unable to act alone, by helping to raise the technological content of Brazil's industrial production, giving priority to projects that contribute to reduce regional imbalances, prioritizing projects that have a significant multiplier effect on investment and lead to better social conditions and incorporating the concept of 'sustainable development' into their projects.

In addition to these admirable policies, they have declared that they will be establishing a lending policy on a criteria profile in accordance with good corporate governance policies.

BNDES's 'Strategic Plan 2000–2005' states that their 'involvement in capital markets is also expected to promote greater transparency in company management and an improvement in corporate governance, leading to a reduction in the average cost of capital and an increase in business competitiveness'.

This statement of intent has since been confirmed, meaning that the massive amount of support available for investment in Brazil – in 2005, BNDES expects to support investments of R$75 billion in the Brazilian economy – will only be directed to companies which have adopted 'best practice' policies.

11.3.4 The Instituto Brasileiro de Governança Corporativa (IBGC)

In 1994 a group of businessmen realized that their conversations turned time and again to the deficiencies of the company boards upon which they sat. With the aim of ridding these boards of the problems they could see at first hand, and of providing a model upon which other Brazilian boards could model themselves, they established the 'Brazilian Institute of Corporate Directors', which eventually became the 'IBGC' – 'Instituto Brasileiro de Governança Corporativa'. Since being officially founded on 27 November 1995, the eight years of its existence have seen it make a marked impact on the landscape of Brazilian corporate activity.

On a day-to-day basis, the IBGC provides a structural example to the Brazilian business community and also plays a practical role in highlighting the legal and professional steps that should be undertaken towards a transparent business climate. The Institute also serves as a forum for those already involved in the issues to come together and learn from each other, as well as providing somewhere for individuals and companies recognizing the benefits that corporate governance can bring them to find out more about the subject through seminars and monthly meetings.

Perhaps the most important development in the steps taken by the IBGC to spread the ideas of corporate governance in Brazil came with the publication in May 1999 of a first version of a 'Brazilian Code of Best Practice'. This first version focused essentially on the role of corporate director and was followed, in April 2001, by a second edition that was extended to cover the roles of the shareholder, the CEO, the fiscal council and the independent auditor besides the board of directors. Using the codes which had already been published elsewhere in the world as their basic guideline, the Institute's council drew up what is now recognized as being one of the most comprehensive codes of best practice of corporate governance anywhere in the world to date. Many copies of the code have been distributed since, and the effects have been tangible in both the attraction of new members to the Institute and the establishment of good governance practices throughout the country.

Although membership in 2002 reached almost 400 and continues to rise, it has until now been made up almost exclusively of representatives from small to medium-sized businesses, which although representing the category making up the majority of Brazilian registered companies, do not represent a majority of corporate capital investment. One of the next aims of the Institute is to attract the large corporations to the ethic of corporate governance as, in so doing, Brazil's economic base will be brought into the global advance towards a clear and ethical way of doing business by heightening the respect and marketability of all involved in trade, industry and commerce in Brazil.

11.4 Board Structure

The management of a Brazilian corporation is the responsibility of the board of directors and the officers. A board of directors is mandatory for:

- listed companies;
- companies with pre-authorized capital; and
- certain companies with government participation.

A board must have at least three members, appointed by the shareholders' meeting. The OECD (2003: 55) estimates from American Depository Receipt (ADR) filings that the average board size for large companies in 2002 was 8.5 and that 28.6 per cent of board members were independent. It suggests that fewer than 20 per cent of directors would qualify as independent using US standards.

The board is responsible for:

- defining strategies for the company;
- electing and dismissing officers and establishing their compensation;
- inspecting the activities of officers and their performance;
- calling shareholders meetings;
- reviewing management reports and accounts; and
- appointing independent auditors.

Many Brazilian companies are family-controlled businesses and there has been a tendency in Brazil to concentrate the power of family companies in one individual or a small group of individuals. Typically the board of directors is made up largely of family shareholders, and there is frequently an unwritten, perhaps unconscious, unwillingness to accept the influx of professional and recognizably competent outside board members. This might be in part due to the family's mistrust of outside interference or may be an inability to accept that business expertise is not necessarily inherited.

The problem with this kind of structure is that ownership and management tend to become concentrated in the same person, which can create minority shareholder abuse. The controlling shareholder normally takes the important decisions and the board of directors exists only to comply with the law (phantom boards).

11.4.1 Committees

Committees are not common in Brazilian companies. The OECD (2003: 51) states that only 17 per cent of Brazilian companies have a standing board committee.

11.5 Codes, Standards and Good Practice Guidelines

In 2002, CVM published a set of Recommendations on Corporate Governance, partly based on the Code of Best Practices published by the Brazilian Institute of Corporate Governance (IBGC) but aimed specifically at publicly listed companies. Compliance with the recommendations is voluntary. However, CVM is adopting a 'comply or explain' posture: a company must explain, in its annual filings, the reasons for not complying with a certain recommendation.

The recommendations include, among others:

1. Extended deadlines for calling shareholders meetings: 30 days when there are complex issues on the agenda and 40 days when the company has foreign depositary receipt programmes (the period normally required by the Corporations Law is 15 days).

2. By-laws should establish clear guidelines for representation of shareholders in the shareholders' meetings. Formal irregularities should not be reasons to impede voting.

3. Board of directors should be composed of 5 to 10 members, at least 2 of them with expertise in finance and accounting, and as many independent members as possible. A director's term in office should be one year (the Corporations Law established a minimum of three members for a maximum of three years).

4. The chairman of the board and CEO should not be the same person.

5. The audit committee should be composed of board members with experience in finance and include at least one board member elected by minority shareholders.

6. Preferred non-voting shareholders should have the right to vote in the following cases: (i) approval of evaluation reports of assets

to be incorporated into the corporate capital, (ii) change in the corporate purposes, (iii) reduction of mandatory dividends, (iv) merger or spin-off, and (v) related party transactions.

7. The purchaser of controlling shares must make a tender offer for the acquisition of any remaining common shares for the same price being paid for the controlling shares (the Corporations Law also provides for tag-along rights, but minorities are entitled to only 80 per cent of the price paid for the controlling shares).

8. Related party contracts must be disclosed in the financial statements and carried out on an arm's length basis.

9. Shares with fixed or guaranteed minimum dividends will immediately attain the right to vote when a company does not declare payment of dividends. Non-voting shares will permanently acquire voting rights if the company does not distribute dividends for three consecutive years.

10. By-laws should establish arbitration as the dispute resolution system.

11. The board should restrict the hiring of independent auditors for other services to the company.

12. Financial statements should adopt US GAAP or IAS.

11.6 Disclosure and Transparency

Financial statements, including an annual balance sheet, accumulated profit and loss statement, income statement and source and application of funds statement, must be prepared under the direction of the board of directors, audited in the case of a listed corporation, approved by the shareholders and published. Unlisted corporations with net worth of less than one million reals are not required to publish financial statements.

11.7 Shareholder Rights and Stakeholder Relations

The shareholders' general meetings may be annual or special. Annual shareholders' meetings must be held within the first four months from the end of the fiscal year and review the financial statements and dividend distribution and appoint members of the board of directors or officers.

The special shareholders' meeting may be held whenever deemed appropriate.

Shareholders' meetings may be called by the board of directors or by shareholders holding at least 5 per cent of the capital stock when the board does not call a shareholders' meeting. Matters that may be discussed in shareholders' meetings include amendments to by-laws, capital increases, mergers, spin-offs, liquidation and bankruptcy.

Decisions at general meetings are normally taken by majority vote. However, the Corporations Law requires supermajority in certain cases, including:

- the creation of new preferred shares or an increase in the number of existing classes of preferred shares, unless allowed in the by-laws;
- changes in the redemption or amortization terms of one or more classes of preferred shares or the creation of a new, more favourable class;
- a reduction in the mandatory dividend;
- a merger;
- a change in the corporate purposes;
- a spin-off; and
- a dissolution.

The by-laws of the company may include other matters subject to supermajority approval or increase the percentage of supermajority applicable to such matters.

Dissenting shareholders may have withdrawal rights under certain circumstances. In such cases the shareholders' meeting approves the items listed above and the by-laws may establish rules for the calculation of the reimbursement value. This value may only be inferior to the net worth indicated in the last balance sheet approved by the shareholders' meeting. The calculation is based on economic value and is made by three experts or a specialized company.

Minority shareholders can use a cumulative voting system to appoint members of the board of directors. This system allocates, for each share, as many votes as the number of members in the board, and such votes can all be used for the same person.

Another protection for minority shareholders allows the holders of at least 15 per cent of voting shares and the preferred shareholders holding at least 10 per cent of total outstanding shares, and who have been so for more than three months, the right to appoint, by separate voting, one member of the board of directors.

11.8   Director Development Activity

Director training has been recognized as one of the most important instruments to accomplish IBGC's mission 'to be the main reference in corporate governance in Brazil and to develop and disseminate best concepts and practices'. The importance of director training lies also in the fact that it has traditionally been the main source of funds for all other activities of the Institute.

IBGC's training activities achieved early visibility through two high-level international programmes. In 1998 in Boston and New York, and again in 1999 in London and Paris, the Institute ran a one-week seminar abroad.

In 1998 the first local course was offered in São Paulo to members of boards of directors. The course schedule amounted to 100 hours. The Institute's education committee defined the syllabus, and instructors were selected primarily, but not exclusively, from amongst IBGC members. All instructors agreed to waive all costs for this pilot course.

Since this initial experiment, more than 1,000 directors, shareholders, investors and executives of about 100 different companies have been trained in a number of different types of courses. The main director-training course covers essentially three parts:

- corporate governance concepts, legal framework and best practices;
- understanding financial statements, tax planning, capital budgeting, project evaluation, risk management and investor relations;
- strategy and ethics, case studies and practice simulations.

A special version of this main course was designed for heirs, shareholders and directors of family companies. A shorter version of just 16 hours is offered twice a year in other state capitals.

In 2001 a 'Board Case' was developed by IBGC in association with the director of COPPEAD, one of the leading graduate business courses in Brazil. The course, partially sponsored by Deloitte, Touche Tohmatsu and Spencer Stuart, is based on role-play techniques in which each student assumes the role of a board member, and takes part in board and committee meetings to discuss issues such as strategy, independent auditing and management succession. The underlying case study was based on a real, well-known Brazilian company.

In-house programmes are gaining importance and as they are normally offered on company premises, the costs can be greatly reduced, much to the advantage of both the company and the Institute.

Since the pioneer effort of the IBGC, several other courses are now offered in Brazil by business schools and private organizations. The IBGC supports these initiatives because they also help improve the performance of boards of directors and corporate governance overall.

IBGC's education committee strives to achieve differentiation by constantly updating syllabi and methods and maintaining links with IBGC's research committee, regulators and market institutions, both in Brazil and abroad. Differentiation is also achieved by a practical, hands-on approach and a faculty composed of experienced board members, investors, lawyers, auditors and top executives.

11.9   Useful Contacts

- Brazilian Institute of Accountants – www.inracom.org.br
- The Brazilian Institute of Corporate Governance (IBGC) – www. ibgc.org.br
- Deloitte – www.deloitte.com.br
- Korn/Ferry – www.kornferry.com.br
- Latin Corporate Governance – www.latincorporategovernance.net
- McKinsey – www.mckinsey.com

- National Economic and Social Development Bank (BNDES) – www.bndes.gov.br

- Petros Pension Fund – www.petros.com

- Securities and Exchange Commission

- Spencer Stuart – www.spencerstuart.com.br

11.10   Further Reading

The Brazilian Securities and Exchange Commission, Comissao de Valores Mobiliarios (CVM) (2002) *Reconendacoes sobre governanca corporativa*, CVM, São Paulo

Carvalhal, A, Lear, R, Valadares, S, Procianoy, J, Aloy, R, and Lapagess, G (2000) *Ownership, control and corporate valuation of Brazilian companies*, Latin American Corporate Governance Roundtable, São Paulo Stock Exchange, 26–28 April 2000

IBCG (2001) *Brazilian Code of best practice of corporate governance* (2nd ed) IBCG, São Paulo

McKinsey and Korn/Ferry (2001) *Panorama de Governanca Corporativa no Brasil*, McKinsey and Korn Ferry, São Paulo

OECD (2003) *White Paper on Corporate Governance in Latin America*, OECD, Paris

12

China

Table 12.1

Population	1,286 million (2003)
Gross Domestic Income (GDI)	US $5.7 trillion (2002)
GDI per capita	US $4,400 (2002)
Total number of companies	N/A
Number of companies listed on the stock exchange	1,187 (2002)
Market capitalization	US $443.5 billion (2001)
Key corporate laws	● Code of Corporate Governance for Listed Companies (China Securities Regulatory Commission)2002
Key governance codes	● Company Law (1993 revised in 1999)

12.1   Corporate Structure and Ownership

Since the mid-1980s China has embarked on a massive restructuring of its business environment. This restructure has involved:

● an ambitious privatization programme through which many state-owned and state-controlled companies have offered shares to the public;

- the reform of its stock market systems in 1990 with the redevelopment of the Shanghai and Shenzhen stock exchanges;

- the establishment of the China Securities Regulatory Commission in 1992 as the national regulatory authority over the securities industry;

- the promulgation of company law in 1993 (amended 1999);

- the formulation of the Code of Corporate Governance for Listed Companies in 2002.

The state is a controlling shareholder in about 25 per cent of publicly listed companies in China. These are often some of the largest companies by revenue, assets and employment, and usually have a strategic function in the economy, including air travel, telecommunications, banking, electricity, water and oil.

In 2001, the authorities allowed private companies to list on the Shanghai and Shenzhen exchanges. By 2003 there were some 1,200 listed companies, with a market capitalization of over $500 billion, second only to Japan in Asia. It is estimated that 30–60 million Chinese own shares.

Some of the largest Chinese state-owned enterprises were also listed on the Hong Kong stock exchange, and made up 35 per cent of its market capitalization.

12.2 Legal Framework

Although a relatively new concept to most Chinese people, corporate governance has received great attention in recent years as China marches from a planned economy towards a market economy. The development of the securities market in the 1990s served as a strong boost to better corporate governance. More than 1,200 large companies, most of them state-owned enterprises (SOEs), were incorporated and their ownership diversified through public offerings.

A basic framework was established to underpin the corporate form in China, including company law, accounting, and securities law. Since 2000, China's securities watchdog, the China Securities Regulatory Commission (CSRC), has intensified its efforts to improve corporate governance among listed companies, as exemplified by promulgating new governance rules such as the system of independent directors and the code of corporate governance (2002).

In China companies operate within the terms of The Company Law which came into force in 1994 and was amended in 1999. Its general purpose as stated in Article 1 was to 'to meet the needs of establishing a modern enterprise system, to standardize the organization and activities of companies, to protect the legitimate rights and interests of companies, shareholders and creditors, to maintain the socio-economic order and to promote the development of the socialist market economy'.

The law established a number of fundamental legal concepts that were already widely used in Western economies: 'limited liability company', 'joint stock company' and the company as a 'legal person'. The legalization of these concepts enabled two steps to be taken in releasing the business environment from domination by the political command structure. The first was privatization in part or in whole of state-owned enterprises and the second was the creation of privately owned companies as separate legal entities from their owners.

Article 5 requires a company to operate autonomously and be responsible for its own profit and loss. This means it has to organize its production and operation autonomously in light of market demand, with a view to improving economic return and productivity, and to accomplishing the preservation and increase of the value of its assets. Thus, decision making is the responsibility of the directors of the company who will appoint managers to undertake these duties.

Articles 14 and 15 set out conditions that reflect the local context. In addition to abiding by the law and observing industry ethics, a company must strengthen the development of socialist spiritual civilization, and subject itself to supervision by the government and the public. It must also protect the lawful rights and interests of its workers, strengthen labour protection, and achieve workplace safety. It must also strengthen the professional education and on-the-job training of its workers in various forms, so as to improve their quality.

The law provides also for the organization of a labour union to carry out union activities and safeguard the lawful rights and interests of the workers.

Chapter two of the law deals with the establishment and organs of a limited liability company.

It specifies the responsibilities of shareholders to contribute capital and prepare the articles of association. Limited liability companies may be established through joint investment of shareholders or be wholly owned by a state enterprise. Shareholders may contribute their capital in the form of cash, or tangible goods, industrial property, non-patented technology and land use rights. All of these must have been independently valued.

The law sets out the rights of shareholders to information and a share of any profit distribution. If a company is to increase its capital, its shareholders have the pre-emptive right to subscribe for the increased amount. Shareholders may not sell their holding unless agreed by all the other shareholders.

Rules for shareholder meetings include the relationship that must exist with the board of directors. The chairman leads board meetings. The board appoints a general manager to undertake overall management of the company's operations; to organize the implementation of board resolutions and of operating and investment plans; to plan the structure of the company's internal management; and to appoint officers of the company.

There is some flexibility for small limited liability companies to simplify these directorial and operational matters. Large-scale limited liability companies, however, should also have a board of supervisors, composed of representatives of the shareholders and the workers, that reviews the company's financial affairs and monitors the acts of directors. Small companies may just have one or two supervisors. The supervisors shall be present at board meetings.

The law provides all the expected limitations on officers of the company, including entitlement to the role in the first place, and business and financial requirements for those in post.

Wholly state-owned companies have a number of specific requirements that enable the state department or organization that is the owner to exercise certain rights and controls, for example passing some duties of the shareholders' committee to the board of directors.

Chapter Three deals with joint stock limited companies.

Whether they derive from a state or a private enterprise, such companies are established by sponsorship or by the public offer of shares. They start from a larger capital base than limited companies, but have similar constraints, structures and rules. The offering of shares to the public is subject to approval by the securities regulatory authority, which has to be satisfied that all its requirements have been met.

The law specifies the responsibilities and authority of the shareholders' general committee, and the annual meeting and its role in relation to the board of directors and to the board of supervisors, together with the financial decisions that fall within their remit.

The establishment and functions of the board of directors are extremely important and clearly stated. The board must have between 5 and 19 members, and is accountable to the shareholders' general committee. Its authorities include:

(i) being responsible for calling meetings of shareholders' general committee, and presenting reports thereto;

(ii) implementing resolutions adopted by the shareholders' general committee;

(iii) determining the company's operating plans and investment programmes;

(iv) preparing annual financial budget plans and final accounting plans of the company;

(v) preparing the company's profit distribution plans and plans to cover company losses;

(vi) preparing plans for increasing or reducing registered capital by the company, and plans to issue company bonds;

(vii) drafting plans for merger, division or dissolution of the company;

(viii) determining the structure of the company's internal management;

(ix) appointing or removing the general manager of the company; appointing or removing, upon the general manager's recommendation, deputy general managers of the company and the officer in charge of finance; and determining the remuneration for those officers;

(x) formulating the company's basic management scheme.

The chairman is the legal representative of the company and has the following authorities:

(i) presiding over meetings of shareholders' general committee, and calling and presiding over meetings of the board of directors;

(ii) supervising the implementation of resolutions adopted by the board of directors;

(iii) signing the share certificates and bond certificates of the company.

The articles of association set out directors' terms, which may not exceed three years but are renewable. They determine that board meetings must also be held at least twice a year and that the minutes must be signed by all attending directors. Directors are liable to the company for damages if they participate in decisions of the board that violate any national statutes, administrative regulations or the articles of association, and cause the company to incur serious loss.

The board appoints the general manager to implement all their decisions.

The articles of association set out the structure and authorities of the board of supervisors who represent proportionately the shareholders and the workers. Among other things, the board reviews the company's financial affairs and monitors the directors' acts. Supervisors attend board meetings.

Chapter Four deals with all the technical matters involved in the issue and transfer of shares of a joint stock limited company, and situations that might cause the regulatory authority to suspend dealing. Chapter Five deals similarly with bond issues.

Chapter Six deals with the financial and accounting affairs of the company and states the requirement for the financial and accounting systems to accord with the relevant national statutes, administrative regulations and the stipulations of the finance authority under the State Council.

The company has to prepare its financial and accounting reports at the end of each fiscal year and they must include:

(i) balance sheet;

(ii) income statement;

(iii)   statement of cash flow;

(iv)   explanation of financial conditions;

(v)   statement of profit distribution.

A joint stock limited company established through public share offer must make public its financial and accounting reports.

The law specifies the distribution of its current year after-tax profit as 10 per cent to its statutory reserve fund, and 5 to 10 per cent to its statutory welfare fund. Allocation to the company's statutory reserve fund may be waived once the cumulative amount of funds therein exceeds 50 per cent of the company's registered capital. Requirements to cover previous year losses are given.

The reserve funds of the company are to be used to cover company losses, expand its production and operation, or be converted to the company's increased capital. In the case of conversion to capital, the law sets out the proportions to be allocated.

Chapter Seven sets out the legal requirements of a merger or division of a company.

Chapter Eight sets out the legal requirements of bankruptcy, dissolution and liquidation of a company. These are similar to those in use in many other economies.

Should this situation arise, after identifying the company's assets and preparing the balance sheet and schedule of assets, the liquidating committee must prepare a liquidating plan, which is submitted to the shareholders' committee or the relevant authority for ratification.

Where the company's assets are sufficient for payment of company debts, such assets must be paid out in the following order: payment of liquidating expenses, payment of wages and expenses for labour insurance of the workers, payment of taxes owed, and payment of company debts.

After such payments have been made, the remaining assets must be distributed to the shareholders in proportion to their shares of capital contribution in the case of a limited liability company, and in proportion to their share holdings in the case of a joint stock limited company.

If the liquidating committee discovers that the company does not have sufficient assets to fully repay company debts, the liquidating committee must immediately file a bankruptcy application with the People's Court. Once a company is adjudged bankrupt by a ruling of the People's Court, the liquidating committee shall transfer the liquidating affairs to the People's Court.

Chapter Nine specifies the requirements for branches of foreign companies to be set up to conduct business in China.

A company registered and established outside China may establish branches within China to conduct business. It must submit an application to the Chinese authority, together with the relevant documents such as its articles of association, the company registration certificate issued in its home country, etc. Upon approval, it must carry out registration with the company registration authority and be issued a business licence. It must also appoint a representative or agent in charge of such branch within China, and fund its branch as appropriate in light of the nature of its intended business.

A foreign company is a foreign legal person, and its branch established within China does not have the status of a Chinese legal person. It must bear civil liabilities in respect of the business conducted by its branch within China.

Chapter Ten deals with legal liabilities of both companies and their officers not to make false statements, conceal material facts or take action that constitutes a crime. Fines may be imposed on companies and criminal liability may be imposed on individuals.

The situations covered by this law include:

- the issue of company shares or bonds, where the prospectus, subscription form, or plan for company bonds offer is falsely prepared;
- the case of capital contribution, where the sponsors or shareholders falsify capital contribution by failing to pay money, to deliver tangible goods or to transfer property rights, thus defrauding the creditors or the public;
- the withdrawal of the capital contribution of the sponsors or shareholders of a company after the establishment of the company;
- the issue of company shares or bonds without approval by the appropriate authorities provided for in the law;

- the establishment of another set of accounting books besides those prescribed by law;

- the deposit of company assets into an account established under an individual's name;

- the provision by a company to its shareholders and the public financial and accounting reports which are false or which conceal material facts;

- the conversion of state-owned assets into shares at low prices or sale to individuals at low prices, or distribution to individuals without compensation;

- the abuse of their authorities by directors, supervisors, or the general manager by accepting bribes or receiving other illegal income, or converting company assets;

- the misappropriation by a director or the general manager of company funds or loan company funds to third parties;

- the giving by directors or the general manager of company assets as security for the personal debts of any director of the company or any other person;

- the engagement by a director or the general manager in the same business as the company either for his own account or for another person's account;

- the failure by a company to make allocation to the statutory reserve fund and statutory welfare fund;

- the failure by a company to notify creditors through notice or public announcement in accordance herewith while carrying out merger, division, reduction of registered capital, or liquidation;

- the action by a company, while in the course of liquidation, to conceal its assets, make false statements in its balance sheet or schedule of assets, or distribute company assets prior to full repayment of company debts;

- the failure of the liquidating committee to submit the liquidating report to the company registration authority in accordance herewith, or concealment of any material fact or any material omission in the liquidating report submitted;

- the abuse of his authority by a member of the liquidating committee to engage in fraudulent activity for private gain, to obtain illegal income or convert company assets;

- the provision of a false certificate by an institution conducting assets appraisal, capital verification, or testing and verification;

- the provision of a report with material omission due to its negligence by an institution conducting assets appraisal, capital verification or testing and verification.

The provisions of the law extend to the authorities that approve applications that fail to meet the legal requirements. These include the securities regulatory authority and the company registration authority, or a government department.

The law prevents an entity from passing itself off as a limited liability company or joint stock limited company while not registered as such. In addition, a foreign company establishing a branch within China without approval will be ordered to make rectification.

There is also the opportunity for a company that has been failed by the authorities to seek administrative review and redress.

12.3   Legal, Regulatory and Institutional Bodies

12.3.1   The China Securities Regulatory Commission (CSRC)

In the past three years, China's securities watchdog, the China Securities Regulatory Commission (CSRC), has intensified its efforts to improve corporate governance among listed companies, as exemplified by promulgating new governance rules such as the system of independent directors and the code of corporate governance.

Applications for public offerings are screened by the CSRC and then submitted to the Public Offering Committee for approval where the majority of the members are not from CSRC. The CSRC's guidelines for assessing IPOs require committee members to pay special attention to corporate governance issues such as whether:

- the company's shareholders' meetings, board of directors, and board of supervisors have been discharging their duties and exercising their rights independently accordingly to the law;

- the company's management structure is complete;

- the company is engaged in frequent related party transactions;

- its assets, personnel, governing organs, and financing are separated from its parent company; and

- a competitive relationship exists between the parent company and the controlling shareholder.

Lifting the quota system and the new listing requirements on corporate governance reflect the intention of CSRC to improve the quality of listed companies through reform of the regulatory approach and corporate governance.

12.3.2 The Stock Exchange

The development of modern stock markets in China only started in 1986. This is due to the fact that until the mid-1980s, the Chinese government still considered the shareholding system counter to the socialist economy. However, economic reform created a need for a new form of finance other than bank credit. Firms started to issue shares to their employees in 1986 and informal stock exchanges formed in some cities in the late 1980s, the largest in Shanghai and Shenzhen. In November 1990, the Shanghai Stock Exchange was formally established. The Shenzhen Stock Exchange was officially recognized in the spring of 1991. In addition, there are several regional exchanges in Shenyang, Wuhan, Tianjian and Dalian, which are linked to Shanghai and Shenzhen. The Shanghai and Shenzhen Stock Exchanges were established as non-profit entities with a membership system and governed by a Board of Directors.

Despite good intentions from the government and the public, the development of stock markets was slow until the mid-1990s. The level of stock market development, measured as market capitalization as a percentage of GDP, started with less than 1 per cent in 1990. The market capitalization grew and by 1999 it exceeded 30 per cent of GDP.

12.4 Board Structure

The Company Law sets out the requirement for both limited liability companies and joint stock limited liability companies to have a single-tier board of directors and a supervisory board that monitors its activities.

In line with the worldwide recognition that the independence of some members of the board is critical, CRSC has made changes since 2001. One of CSRC's major efforts of reform was the requirement of having independent directors on the board in order to overcome the management-control problem in many of China's listed companies. CSRC issued a regulation in August 2001 requiring each listed company to have at least two independent directors by June 2002 and to have one-third of the board independent by June 2003. At least one of the independent directors must be an accounting professional. Independent directors are required to serve as chairs of audit, compensation, and nomination committees (although these committees are not yet mandatory under current rules), and major related-party transactions have to be approved by independent directors.

A survey conducted by CSRC on independent directors of listed companies showed that, by the end of June 2002, a total of 2,414 independent directors had been appointed to the 1,187 listed companies in China. Seventy per cent of these companies have at least one accounting professional as independent director.

Independent directors have also started to play a positive role in expressing their independent opinion on issues such as whether a particular related-party transaction would cause damage to minority shareholders, and on the nomination of directors, as well as accounting and disclosure issues. These independent opinions have been widely publicized by the media and welcomed by investors.

To ensure that there are enough qualified independent director candidates for companies to choose from, the CSRC, in partnership with some of the top management schools in China, runs regular monthly training sessions in the cities of Beijing, Shanghai and Shenzhen for those who are interested in becoming independent directors. The curriculum for the training classes covers topics such as corporate governance principles and practices, duties and responsibilities of directors and independent directors, operations of audit, remuneration, and nomination committees, analysis of financial statements and related-party transactions. To date around 8,000 individuals have taken training and have been included in the pool of candidates for independent directors. All independent directors are required to attend the training sessions.

A recent survey on independent directors also indicates that the background of the independent directors has changed. When the system of independent directors first started in China, not surprisingly most of them were well-known university professors. However, this situation has changed and by June 2002:

- 55 per cent of the independent directors were from academic institutions;
- 30 per cent were from intermediaries such as law and accounting firms;
- 10 per cent were executives of other companies; and
- the remaining 5 per cent were retired government officials and from other professions.

Although the lack of experienced independent directors in China means that it will be a few years before the true effect of independent directors is evident, it is believed that this is a major initial step towards better understanding of corporate governance both among companies as well as among investors.

12.5 Codes, Standards and Good Practice Guidelines

The second important step that the CSRC has taken to improve corporate governance in China was the promulgation of a Code of Corporate Governance for Listed Companies in early 2002. The Code was jointly issued by the CSRC and the State Economic and Trade Commission (SETC). The SETC was the ministry in charge of many of the controlling shareholders of the listed companies. It was reorganized when the new government came into office in March 2003 and is now renamed as the State Asset Management Commission (SAMC).

The joint publication of the Code means that the Code is applicable not only to listed companies, but also to their controlling shareholders. The Code is developed according to the OECD Principles of Corporate Governance, taking into consideration the peculiarity of the Chinese market. The Code is mandatory for all listed companies to follow and puts the protection of shareholders' rights as the basic goal of corporate governance. In doing so, the Code asks for equitable treatment of all shareholders. Listed companies may adopt proxy voting and cumulative voting methods to protect the rights of minority shareholders; listed companies are required to be completely segregated from their parent companies; related-party transactions have to be fair and transparent and approved by independent directors. The Code also calls for shareholder activism and the increased participation of institutional investors.

To ensure that listed companies comply with the Code of Corporate Governance, the CSRC and the SETC held a joint inspection of all the listed companies during the second half of 2002. The first phase of the inspection was a self-assessment questionnaire by the companies on their own corporate governance practice. Based on the inputs of the self-assessment, areas of deficiency were identified and on-site inspection of selected companies was conducted by joint teams of the regional offices of the CSRC and the SETC. More than 200 firms went through on-site inspection. The purpose of on-site inspection was to meet with the management and board of the companies and work out remedial action for the deficient areas. The final phase of the joint inspection was to identify some of the companies that have good corporate governance practice. This gave recognition to the better-governed companies and shared their experience with others.

Most of the listed companies took the inspection seriously. Some independent directors took time to participate in the assessment and reported to the CSRC in writing where improvement would be needed. The regional offices of the CSRC used the inspection process to bring pressure to problem companies and local governments to correct some of the irregular practices among the listed companies and the controlling shareholders. The inspection programme has enhanced the understanding of good corporate governance practice among the listed companies, and exposed some of the problematic areas.

12.6 Disclosure and Transparency

The problems in corporate governance and disclosure attracted great attention in China in July 2001 when it experienced its own version of 'Enron'. A blue-chip high-tech company called 'Yin Guang Xia' was found to have forged customs receipts and fabricated its profit figures in order to support its extremely high stock price. Since then a few other blue-chip companies were also found to have falsified accounts and disclosed misleading financial information. The exposure of these scandals, among other things, greatly damaged investor confidence and caused the market index to drop by almost 30 per cent in the following 12 months. The case of Yin Guang Xia and other corporate scandals highlighted the importance of corporate governance reform in China.

The Securities Regulatory Commission (CSRC) considers that disclosure is an important measure toward better corporate governance of listed companies. In recent years, CSRC and the two stock exchanges have tightened up rules for disclosure. Publicly listed companies in China are required to publish an audited annual report as well as a half-year report. In addition, from 2002 listed companies are required to publish un-audited quarterly reports. The format of annual, half-year and quarterly reports has been simplified and streamlined so that they are more readable and easily understood by investors. The level of punishment for violation of disclosure rules has been raised and has become more severe in recent years. Annual reports are carefully examined by the stock exchanges and the CSRC every year.

Directors and officers of a listed company may be publicly criticized or condemned by the stock exchanges or the CSRC if they seriously violate listing rules or disclosure rules. Companies and directors that are suspected of violating the Securities Law may be investigated by the CSRC and may receive a monetary fine in addition to other punishments. It is believed that the disclosure rules in China are now very close to the international standards but enforcement of these rules is an area that needs further improvement.

12.6.1 Financial Reporting

Another important area for corporate governance reform is the accounting and financial reporting framework. In 2002, the Supreme People's Court took an important step in legal reform to protect shareholder rights when the Court issued an ordinance on the procedures for investors to sue directors and the management of listed companies for losses in their share investment caused by false disclosure by the listed company. The court system has started to accept such cases.

China has also stepped up its reform in the accounting and auditing areas. The Ministry of Finance (MOF), which is charged with setting accounting standards, made significant changes in 2002 in China's accounting rules to bring them more in line with the International Accounting Standards (IAS). The CSRC and the MOF have also strengthened the supervision of auditors. As an effort to deter future misconduct on the part of auditors, the CSRC revoked the licence for a securities business of one of the largest auditing firms in China in 2002 because of its involvement in the scandal of Yin Guang Xia. The firm was eventually broken up.

The OECD (2003) described the national auditing and accounting systems used in China as having similar basic principles to International Accounting Standards but noted that divergence existed in areas such as measurement based on fair market value.

12.6.2 Enforcement

Recognizing the importance of enforcement, the CSRC last year greatly strengthened its enforcement procedures. An Enforcement Bureau was established in the CSRC to specifically handle cases of market manipulation. In addition, the Ministry of Public Security established the Bureau for Investigation of Securities Crime on the premises of the CSRC in order to facilitate the handling of criminal cases in relation to securities crime.

The CSRC has also instituted de-listing procedures for companies which have incurred losses for three consecutive years. Up to 2003, 10 companies had been de-listed from the Main Board and moved to an over-the-counter (OTC) share transfer system commonly known as the Third Board (the Second Board is yet to be established). It is anticipated that there will be orderly de-listings of companies every year. This will further improve the overall quality of the Chinese stock market.

12.7 Shareholder Rights and Stakeholder Relations

There are also two classes of stocks traded in the markets: A-shares and B-shares. The A-shares are reserved for Chinese residents and are denominated in *renminbi* (the Chinese currency). The Shanghai and Shenzhen Stock Exchanges began offering B-shares to foreign investors in February 1992. The B-shares were exclusively reserved for non-residents in the beginning. However, starting from June 2001, the B-shares market also opened for Chinese residents as an effort to stimulate the market and to make use of the large amount of foreign currency deposits in the banks. Both B-shares and A-shares are settled and quoted in *renminbi* but B-shares are settled in US dollars in Shanghai, and in Hong Kong dollars in Shenzhen. The B-shares are not convertible to A-shares, and therefore they are not substitutable. Compared with the A-share market, the B-share market is much smaller. The value of B-shares makes up only about 5 per cent of total market capitalization. Thus, stock markets in China mainly served as vehicles for mobilizing domestic funds and channelling them to investment. Their roles in attracting foreign portfolio investment were still very limited.

In mature capital markets, institutional investors play an important role in the corporate governance of the companies in which they invest. In the past three years the CSRC has placed developing institutional investors as a high priority in its work. Since it began in 1998 the securities investment fund industry has been growing rapidly. The Chinese stock market is now open to insurance funds and social security funds, as well as to foreign institutional investors.

In December 2002, the CSRC and the People's Bank of China (PBOC) issued a joint regulation allowing qualified foreign institutional investors (QFII), including fund management firms, insurance companies, securities houses and commercial banks, to invest in China's A-share market. QFII schemes have been adopted by Taiwan and other emerging markets and have been successful in attracting foreign participation in the domestic market before its currency is fully convertible. Up to June 2003, six foreign institutional investors had been approved by the PBOC as custodians for the QFII and a number of large investment banks, such as UBS Warburg, had been approved for qualification as QFII.

12.8 Director Development Activity

To ensure that there are enough qualified independent director candidates for companies to choose from, the Securities Regulatory Commission, in partnership with some of the top management schools in China, runs regular monthly training sessions in the cities of Beijing, Shanghai and Shenzhen for those who are interested in becoming independent directors. The curriculum for the training classes covers topics such as:

- corporate governance principles and practices;
- duties and responsibilities of directors and independent directors;
- operations of audit, remuneration, and nomination committees;
- analysis of financial statements; and
- related-party transactions.

12.9   Useful Contacts

- Securities Association – www.s-a-c.org.cn
- Securities Regulatory Commission – www.csrc.gov.cn
- Shanghai Stock Exchange – www.sse.com.cn
- Shenzen Stock Exchange – www.sse.org.cn

12.10   Further Reading

OECD (2003) *White Paper on Corporate Governance in Asia*, OECD, Paris

Colombia

13

Table 13.1

Population	44 million (2002)
Gross National Income (GNI)	US $80 billion (2002)
GNI per capita	US $1,830 (2002)
Total number of companies	n/a
Number of companies listed on the stock exchange	109 (2003) but only 20 of these trade regularly
Key corporate laws	● Resolution 275 (2001)
	● Law 446 (1998)
	● Commercial Code (1995)
	● Resolutions 400 and 1200 (1995)
	● Financial Framework Law 35 (1993)

13.1 Corporate Structure and Ownership

The corporate sector in Colombia is largely owned and controlled by family groups and conglomerates. In 2002, the largest shareholder owned 44 per cent of the shares of the 74 companies sampled, the three largest shareholders held 65 per cent of the shares and the five largest shareholders held 73 per cent of the shares (OECD, 2003: 53).

Recent statistics from the Colombian Securities and Exchange Commission indicate that foreign investment in portfolio equity has progressively diminished over the past five years. Between January 2001 and July 2002, foreign investment declined from US $421 million to US $276 million.

The Colombian stock market represented 12 per cent of gross domestic product (GDP) (US $10.4 billion) in 2000, down from 21 per cent of GDP (US $22.6 billion) in August 1997.

13.2 Legal Framework

Efforts to institute corporate governance reforms in Colombia have been plagued by the following obstacles:

- a lack of awareness on the part of market participants such as bond and stock issuers, investors, analysts, regulatory and supervisory bodies, stock exchanges and intermediaries concerning the concept and usefulness of corporate governance;

- a profound level of distrust on the part of the international community in the domestic Colombian market;

- high sovereign risk index results and low confidence index results, stemming from domestic, national-level conditions including the degree of security, the effectiveness of economic management, the performance of enterprises, the current political situation, labour relations and investors' rights;

- the absence of the rule of law and the inability to protect private property;

- declining levels of foreign direct and indirect investment;

- a concentration of economic power in the hands of a few, thereby diminishing the power of, and incentive for, institutional investors to promote good governance.

Resolution 275 was enacted by the Colombian Securities and Exchange Commission in March 2001. This resolution established a legal obligation for issuers who intend to be the consignees of pension fund resources to adopt good governance norms. In particular, these issuers must establish policies to manage conflicts of interest, ensure information disclosure and protect minority shareholders.

Using CIPE funds, Confecámaras appointed Davis Global Advisors to survey corporate governance practices in Colombian companies. The survey results were published in 2000 and were used to shape Confecámaras' strategic plan to introduce corporate governance in Colombia. The survey sample involved 20 companies representing all sectors. Each company's corporate governance practices were assessed based on the following dimensions:

- the degree of independence of the board of directors;
- the voting system;
- shareholders' voting rights;
- the degree of information disclosure and accuracy;
- policies regarding hostile takeovers; and
- the existence and use of good governance codes.

The results of the Colombian companies were then compared with those from other developed economies. On a scale of 1 to 10, Colombia was ranked 3.4. This clearly indicated that Colombian companies needed to improve their corporate governance practices.

13.3 Legal, Regulatory and Institutional Bodies

13.3.1 Confecámaras

Confecámaras is the leading organization in promoting corporate governance in Colombia. Confecámaras, in its formative stage, formed important strategic alliances with key stakeholders that included:

- members of academia;
- representatives of key economic and financial groups;
- non-governmental organizations;
- the stock exchange;
- lead pension fund investors;
- auditing firms;
- chambers of commerce;

- mass media;
- the securities superintendent; and
- other representatives of the national government and independent activists.

Working with these groups, Confecámaras raised widespread awareness that corporate governance is an effective tool that benefits all segments of society through:

- preventing capital flight;
- enhancing competitiveness;
- stimulating economic growth;
- generating employment; and
- equipping Colombians to take advantage of globalization processes such as the impending Free Trade of the Americas (FTAA) agreement.

Confecámaras has been engaged on a project that consists of the following components:

- **A diagnosis** of the state of Colombian companies' corporate practices compared with those of eight other countries. This project was published in 2000.

- **A declaration of corporate governance principles designed for Colombian companies:** Based on the Organization for Economic Cooperation and Development's (OECD) Corporate Governance Principles, Confecámaras, together with important private and public sector stakeholders, formed a committee that is preparing a Declaration of Corporate Governance Principles that is tailored to the legal and entrepreneurial realities of Colombia. Committee members include representatives from KPMG, the economic magazine *Dinero*, Spencer Stuart Consultants, the Chambers of Commerce of Bogotá and Cartagena, academia, the Colombian Stock Exchange, and the National Association of Pension Funds.

The Principles outline the rights of shareholders, the functions and responsibilities of boards of directors, the relations with stakeholders, and obligations regarding information disclosure and accuracy.

Going beyond basic international standards, the declaration also obliges companies to uphold five new principles that advance market-oriented reforms. These include implementing:

- alternate dispute resolution mechanisms to improve the enforcement of the Principles;
- anti-bribery policies;
- anti-piracy policies;
- environmental policies;
- social investment policies; and
- conflict of interest policies.

13.3.2 Supervalores

The capital market regulator is Supervalores which reports to the Ministry of Finance. Resolution 275 of 2001 was the first regulation to address corporate governance. It established broad conditions with which companies must comply in order to be eligible for pension funds to invest in them.

13.4 Board Structure

The Commercial Code (1995) lists the following duties of directors:

- furthering the company's social purpose;
- ensuring strict compliance with the law;
- overseeing the revisor fiscal (see section 13.6);
- safeguarding commercial secrets;
- abstaining from disclosure of privileged information;
- treating all shareholders equitably;
- respecting shareholders' rights to inspection;
- abstaining from direct or indirect participation in activities that compete with the company or any act that could imply a conflict of interest.

The board is not required to meet regularly and the directors are not required to disclose their attendance.

Directors cannot serve on more than five boards at a time (Article 202 of the Commercial Code).

In Colombia, board members are elected by shareholders at the Annual General Meeting (AGM) through a system called 'electoral quotient'. In this system, holders of voting shares are requested to cast their votes for competing lists of board members, each list making up the entire board, rather than individual candidates. The selection of individual board members then takes place as follows.

First, the total number of votes present at the AGM is computed and the quotient is calculated by dividing this computed number by the total number of seats on the board up for election/re-election, and rounding down to the lowest integer number. Holders of voting shares are then asked to cast their votes for the competing lists of board members and a tally is prepared. Each list receives a number of votes.

The number of votes cast on each list is then divided by the quotient. The result for a given list is a number consisting of an integer and a fraction.

Seat allocation then takes place as follows. Each list of board members is first allocated as many seats on the board as its integer number. If the sum of the numbers is less than the total number of seats up for election/re-election, the remaining seat(s) are allocated on the basis of the highest fractions, in decreasing order.

Although the system was devised to introduce proportional representation, in practice, board candidates of minority shareholders are seldom elected because of the concentrated ownership structure of companies.

The OECD (2003: 55) estimates from American Depository Receipt (ADR) filings that the average board size for large Colombian companies in 2002 was 5.0.

13.4.1 Independence

Colombia's legal and regulatory framework does not include the concept of independence. Some large listed companies have independent directors but the IMF/World Bank ROSC (2003) noted that 'they are mostly trusted friends and acquaintances appointed by the controller' (p 14).

A large percentage of board members are related to controlling shareholders. This is because ownership is so concentrated and controlling shareholders are extremely powerful. In many cases, the controlling shareholders are the same from company to company. These controlling shareholders favour and support having relatives and their friends as board members. As a result, in the sub-indicator used in the Confecámaras Study (2000) that measured the number of employees who are board members, Colombia ranked second, scoring 8.5. This is higher than French, German, Japanese and UK companies. However, Colombian companies ranked last with a score of 1 regarding the degree of board members' independence.

A security bill is currently being drafted which proposes that 35 per cent of the board should be independent.

13.4.2   Separation of the Roles of Chairman and Chief Executive

The positions of chairman and CEO are normally separated. The CEO normally sets the board agenda, controls access to information and frequently dominates the board.

13.5   Codes, Standards and Good Practice Guidelines

As a result of the passing of Resolution 275 in March 2001, there are now over 100 Colombian companies with a corporate governance code. This is significant progress in a short time period. However, not all of the codes uphold international corporate governance principles and standards. Confecámaras is therefore currently working with the major stakeholders to draft a Declaration of Principles that will adhere to international principles, but will also be tailored to the local environment. This document will serve as an effective guide and benchmark for Colombian companies seeking to improve their corporate governance practices. Moreover, Confecámaras' training efforts are equipping companies with the tools to implement these principles effectively.

In August 2003 the Colombian Corporate Governance Code for Listed Companies was published. This code was drafted by a committee that included a broad range of private sector representatives, including:

- The Colombian Stock Exchange;
- The National Association of Pension Funds;
- The Chambers of Commerce of Bogota and Cartagena.

The overall coordination of the Code was managed by Confecámaras.

13.6   Disclosure and Transparency

Decree 2649 of 1993 defines Colombian GAAP. These principles differ significantly from International Accounting Standards. The World Bank/IMF published an Auditing and Accounting Report on the observance of standards and codes (ROSC) on this issue in 2003. They found Colombian accounting standards to be 'substandard' (p 11).

The ROSC recommends that a breakdown of auditing and consulting fees should be disclosed in the annual report.

Colombia was ranked in fifth place in terms of information disclosure in the Confecámaras Survey (2000), scoring 5 points. This is because there is no policy requiring disclosure of directors' compensation packages to partners or shareholders. Only in exceptional circumstances is the remuneration of managers or presidents revealed. Colombia is currently searching for mechanisms to conform to international standards without creating undue risk for company owners and leaders given Colombia's current insecure political and social climate, characterized by frequent kidnappings.

Also, few firms in Colombia use international accounting standards that, by law, are voluntary. This is an important shortcoming because these standards permit investors to conduct an accurate and timely analysis of a firm's performance, which in turn affects investors' investment decisions. This then affects the availability and cost of capital and thus a firm's competitiveness.

The Commercial Code (1995) defines the role of a revisor fiscal. The AGM appoints the revisor fiscal. The duties of a revisor fiscal are:

- to certify the quality of internal controls;
- to certify that the company complies with the law; and
- to sign financial statements.

The World Bank/IMF ROSC (2003) noted 'concern about the independent judgement of the revisor fiscal, especially in cases where his or her salary is paid by the company.' (p 11) and recommended that 'the functions of the revisor fiscal should be separated into internal audit functions and external audit. The external audit should be fully independent' (p 11).

The Commercial Code (1995) requires each company to publish an annual report that includes:

- a balance sheet;
- an income statement;
- a cash flow statement;
- a statement of changes in equity;
- the revisor fiscal's report;
- certification of internal control by the revisor fiscal;
- management discussion and analysis;
- a limited discussion of a company's objectives;
- risk management analysis.

13.7   Shareholder Rights and Stakeholder Relations

In 2003 the World Bank/IMF noted in a Report on the Observance of Standards and Codes (ROSC) that:

- there were secure methods of ownership registration;
- shares were freely transferable;
- relevant information on the company was given to shareholders on a timely and regular basis;

- participation and voting occurred in shareholders' meetings;
- members of the board were elected by shareholders.

The World Bank/IMF ROSC (2003) recommended that:

- the notice period for AGMs should be increased from 15 to 30 days;
- detailed agendas should be circulated;
- distance voting mechanisms should be made more practical;
- the annual report should disclose the board holdings;
- minority threshold rights should be reduced to 5 per cent from 20 per cent;
- Supervalores or the Bolsa should install an electronic surveillance system to monitor insider dealing.

The Confecámaras survey results (2000) revealed that it was extremely difficult for foreign investors to exercise their voting rights. Although the possibility of voting by proxy legally exists, it is hindered in practice because crucial information such as voting dates and issues to be voted on is not released in a timely manner. The legality of electronic voting remains an unresolved, contentious issue.

Nonetheless, Colombia does offer some important basic shareholders' rights. Unequal votes are illegal, ie each share is entitled to one vote. In addition, investors in Colombian companies have the right to approve financial statements and the issuance of new shares, and elect board members, auditors and fiscal supervisors.

Notwithstanding these rights, shareholders of Colombian stocks have little or no voice concerning many aspects essential to a company's governance. These include:

- company restructuring;
- acquisitions and mergers;
- negotiations between shareholders and controllers;
- remuneration of auditors, board members and fiscal supervisors;
- benefits or dividend distribution; and

● ratification of board decisions and policies concerning overall management, borrowing, credit and risk management, voting rights limitations, and measures to avoid hostile takeovers.

Colombia clearly needs to expand and strengthen shareholders' rights. To begin with, the rights that already exist need to be enforced. Moreover, additional shareholders' rights need to be granted and upheld so that they conform to international standards.

13.7.1 The Colombian Public Securities Market

Colombia urgently needs to reform its securities market or risk being excluded from global markets and growth opportunities. Despite numerous reform efforts, Colombia's current securities framework is incoherent, confusing and falls short of upholding international standards. This has deterred new issuers from listing on the market and scared potential investors, thereby perpetuating concentrated ownership patterns, low liquidity levels and non-competitive companies.

Recent studies by the International Finance Corporation (IFC) and the National Association of Financial Institutions (ANIF) have exposed weaknesses in the Colombian securities market and show that the situation is deteriorating. Stock ownership remains highly concentrated and is estimated at around 74 per cent. An international study ranked Colombia as having one of the lowest rates of capital formation; only Argentina, Nigeria and Indonesia had lower capital formation rates.

Colombian securities markets do not have the liquidity to fund the expansion of existing, let alone new companies. Hence, most companies are forced to obtain credit from the banking sector. The banking sector uses its monopolistic position to charge very high interest rates and restricts credit access to firms. A recent ANIF study indicated that in 2000 sources of finance included:

● internal cash generation (72%);

● payable accounts (12%);

● financial obligations (10%); and

● stock (5%).

Companies cannot issue syndicated bonds without a bank guarantee. This, in some senses, defeats the purpose of trying to raise funds from the capital market because, with a bank guarantee, one could just as well borrow from the bank. Yet borrowing from banks is not always easy or feasible. Banks use most of their funds to buy government bonds because they are considered less risky than private sector loans. In short, companies are dependent on the small amount of high-interest credit that banks are willing to extend to the private sector.

Another obstacle hindering the development of the Colombian securities markets is that company owners, managers, and major shareholders fear that by disclosing information and opening up their companies, they could reveal successful business strategies, lose their competitive advantage and control over the company. This is a serious challenge that reformers must overcome.

Other factors are responsible for the uninviting conditions of Colombia's securities markets, eg poor macro-economic policy and social and political insecurity.

There is no legal provision that requires a board to take into account stakeholder interests but Resolution 275 recommends that companies recognize stakeholders' rights.

13.8   Director Development Activity

13.8.1   Training

In order to raise awareness about the importance of, and to demonstrate how to implement, corporate governance, Confecámaras has developed training programmes for directors, consultants, issuers, investors, auditing firms and members of the mass media. To date, about 150 high-level representatives from these groups have been trained.

13.8.2   Dissemination

Confecámaras has developed an effective dissemination strategy that includes a Web site and monthly electronic bulletins. Through these means, the Declaration of Principles, legislative information, international and domestic corporate governance news, literature, events and study results, as well as contacts with other organizations are distributed to over 400 private sector subscribers. In addition,

Confecámaras has obtained commitments from several mass media organizations that have agreed to draw attention to corporate governance nationally and regionally.

13.9   Useful Contacts

- Confecámaras – www.gobiernocorporativo.com.co
- Latin Corporate Governance – www.latincorporategovernance.net

13.10   Further Reading

La Porta, R, Lopez-de-Silanes, F, Shleifer, A and Vishny, R (1996) *Law and finance*, NBER Working Paper No. 5661

OECD (2003) *White Paper on Corporate Governance in Latin America*, OECD, Paris

World Bank/IMF (2003) *Report on the Observance of Standards and Codes (ROSC) Corporate Governance Country Assessment: Colombia* (August 2003), Washington, World Bank

14

Kenya

Table 14.1

Population	31.3 million (2002)
Gross National Income (GNI)	US $11.3 billion (2002)
GNI per capita	US $360 (2002)
Total number of companies	100,000 approx (2002)
Number of companies listed on the stock exchange	54 (Nairobi Exchange)
Market capitalization	US $1.4 billion (2001)
Key corporate laws	● Sample Code for Best Practice in Corporate Governance, 1999
Key corporate governance codes	● Companies Act 1962

14.1   Corporate Structure and Ownership

Corporate governance is still a relatively new concept in Kenya. However, it is gaining widespread acceptance and many organizations and individuals are embracing it. It is hoped that the impetus for the promotion of corporate governance will be sustained and that even wider frontiers will be explored in the efforts to entrench corporate governance practices in Kenyan enterprises.

The Companies Act, 1948 differentiates between two types of companies: private and public companies.

There are three types of private companies:

1. Companies limited by shares – these have a restriction on the right to transfer shares and a limitation on the total number of members and debenture holders to 50. This type of company does not attract public interest because its shares are not for sale.

2. Companies limited by guarantee – these are non-profit-making companies which do not have a share capital. Most NGOs and associations fall into this category.

3. Unlimited liability companies – these do not have any limit on the liability of their members. Most professional bodies in Kenya are in this category.

Outside this category, any other company limited by shares is a public company. The Incorporated Private Partnership Act enables two or more individuals to engage in private business. The Regulations of the Nairobi Stock Exchange also provide the primary regulatory framework for the establishment and operations of companies in the practice of corporate governance. These regulations safeguard shareholders' rights and the transfer of shares. Regulation also provides shareholders access to information and enables them to participate in decision making.

14.2   Legal Framework

Corporate governance practice in Kenya is contained in the Companies Act 1948 which outlines:

- the role of the chairman;
- responsibilities of the board;
- responsibilities of individual directors;
- the functions of auditors;
- disclosure and transparency in the operations of the company; and
- equitable treatment of shareholders.

The Companies Act gives shareholders the opportunity to:

- participate and vote in general shareholder meetings;
- obtain information on their company's activities; and
- vote either in person or in absentia at meetings.

The procedure and requirements for the formation of companies are carefully outlined in the Companies Act. The Registrar of Companies is the sole registration organ for all companies in Kenya. Before commencement of operations, a company is required by law to register its regulations and state the nature of business it will operate, as well as obtain a Certificate to Commence Business, all issued by the Registrar General. The certificate to commence business must show the share capital, names of directors, and auditors.

Until recently, most statutory bodies in Kenya were state-owned, with most appointments of their directors and chief executives made by the government. Most of these organizations could therefore not operate under the Companies Act effectively. The Auditor General Corporations is the oversight agency of state-owned corporations.

The Companies Act provides guidelines for the formation of all companies in Kenya and defines the relationship between the board of directors and the company's shareholders, as well as the administrative functions and procedures which border on the statutory regulation of companies in Kenya. Companies are required by law to have at least two directors to direct the affairs of the company.

Public quoted companies are regulated by the Capital Markets Authority (CMA) under the following legislative instruments:

- The Capital Markets Authority Act;
- The CIS (Amendment) Regulations 2002;
- The CMA (Licensing and General) Regulations 2002 (are not gazetted);
- The CMA (Foreign Investors) Regulations 2002; and
- The CMA (Takeovers and Mergers) Regulations 2002.

The following rules of the Nairobi Stock Exchange also apply to listed companies:

- Management and Membership Rules;

- Trading and Settlement Rules; and
- The Listing Manual.

Newly gazetted regulations and guidelines include:

- The Capital Markets (Securities) (Public Offers and Listing requirements) Regulations 2002;
- Corporate Governance Guidelines 2002; and
- Rating Agency Guidelines 2001.

14.3   Legal, Regulatory and Institutional Bodies

14.3.1   Government

The Government, and specifically the Department of Government Investments and Public Enterprises (DGIPE), is demanding good corporate governance from all state corporations and appropriate policy and legislative changes are being implemented or initiated.

14.3.2   Capital Markets Authority (CMA)

The Capital Markets Authority requires all listed companies to comply with principles of good corporate governance.

14.3.3   Nairobi Stock Exchange (NSE)

There are 54 companies listed at the Nairobi Stock Exchange and an estimated 100,000 unlisted companies in Kenya. The listed companies are primarily large trading concerns, engaged in large-scale business in the following sectors of the economy:

- agricultural sector;
- commercial and services sectors;
- finance and investment sectors;
- industrial and allied sectors.

14.3.4   Central Bank of Kenya (CBK)

The Central Bank now demands good corporate governance for financial stability and sustainability from all licensed banks and financial institutions.

14.3.5   Centre for Corporate Governance (CCG)

The Centre for Corporate Governance (CCG), formerly the Private Sector Corporate Governance Trust (PSCGT), was established in September 1999 to carry out activities and programmes that aim at improving the quality of life of the people of Africa by fostering the adoption and implementation of the highest standards of corporate governance, so as to improve the strategic leadership of enterprises and enhance their profitability, effectiveness and competitiveness in the global market. CCG has done this through institution and institutional capacity building and national and regional activities.

14.3.6   The Kenya Shareholders Association (KSA)

The Kenya Shareholders' Association was registered in June 2002 and launched in June 2003 with the aim of creating awareness of the need for good corporate governance, and to mobilise shareholders from all over the country to demand good corporate governance from their organizations.

Other bodies that play a part in the regulation of business enterprises include:

- The Retirement Benefits Authority (RBA);
- The Attorney General's Office;
- The Auditor General; and
- The Kenya Revenue Authority (KRA).

14.3.7   Institute of Directors (Kenya)

On 9 April 2003 the Institute of Directors (Kenya) was launched. It promotes activities that enhance director professionalism in the country.

14.4   Board Structure

Most public companies in Kenya have boards of directors with membership ranging from seven to eleven. For most state-owned enterprises the board size is between six and fifteen directors; while in private companies the number is between three and seven directors; and for cooperatives between five and nine directors.

Most public companies in Kenya have unitary boards with a mixture of both executive and non-executive directors. Generally, a large proportion of the board is made up of non-executive directors. It is recommended that boards should have at least one third of the directors being independent. This is because independent directors bring in expertise in various fields of practice to bear on the board.

Separation of the roles of chairman and chief executive is recommended in the Act to ensure a balance of power. This enables the board to be accountable and exercise independence in its decisions.

Some statistics relating to board composition are as follows:

- The average age of board directors is around 45–55 years.
- Female directors on a board comprise around 10–15 per cent.
- On average, board meetings are held once every three months but the frequency is increasing.
- The main board committees are Finance, Staff and Technical. However, Audit and Nomination committees are now required for quoted companies.

For private companies, the boards are typically composed of small numbers and the directors are mostly executive. This is because such companies are mostly family owned or owned by groups of close associates who rarely feel the need to have directors from outside their small circle.

14.5   Codes, Standards and Good Practice Guidelines

There are a number of governance issues that are currently creating much public debate in Kenya. The debate is focusing primarily on areas where there have been problems of mismanagement and underperformance. There is now a concerted effort to break from the past and ensure that enterprises, both public and private, are run efficiently and sustainably for the benefit of stakeholders.

14.5.1   Reform in Parastatals

As in most developing economies, Kenya's economic framework is such that the role of the public sector cannot be ignored in the wealth creation process. Wealth creation will continue to be undertaken by the public sector, private sector and cooperative societies working in concert. State-owned corporations will continue to play an important role in the production and creation of wealth necessary for enhancing national development.

For state-owned corporations to play this role, it is important that they are governed efficiently, effectively and sustainably. This has not always been the case, particularly in the recent past. There are a number of parastatals that have been a burden on the Exchequer year after year due to mismanagement, while many others have been operating below their potential.

Much attention is now being focused on the privatization of non-strategic state-owned corporations in the country. The government is in the process of introducing a Privatization Bill to parliament for that purpose. The bill is intended to streamline the privatization process to ensure that it is done in a transparent and sustainable way.

14.5.2 The Banking Sector

In the period prior to the banking crisis of the late 1980s and early 1990s, corporate governance issues were largely low priority areas in Kenya's banking sector. Directors were never vetted, investors could establish banks almost at will, the role of the external auditors was not well defined, the prudential regulations were scanty and at some stage bank supervision was not playing a major role in ensuring prudence in the financial sector. These deficiencies resulted in laxity by some boards, and mismanagement of institutions. The effect was imprudent lending practices, excessive investment in fixed assets and inadequate systems to measure, identify and control risk.

The Central Bank subsequently undertook several measures to enhance corporate governance in the banking sector. An effective legal and regulatory framework is now in place, regulations have been developed and there is increased interaction with other regulatory authorities, directors of banking institutions, and external auditors. Among other factors, the following amendments to the Banking Act have contributed to the enhancement of corporate governance in the banking sector:

- Section 4 which requires vetting of directors and shareholders;

- Section 11 which requires that facilities to a director be approved by the full board of directors and further empowers the Central Bank of Kenya to remove directors from office if their loans are non-performing;

- Section 24 (5) which gives the Central Bank powers to arrange trilateral meetings with an institution and its auditor;

- Section 31 (3) which allows the sharing of information between institutions;

- banking regulations that require banks to publish their unaudited results and other disclosures concerning connected lending, and contingent liabilities;

- banking (penalties) regulations that empower the Minister for Finance and the Central Bank to levy penalties for non-compliance with corporate governance principles and other violations of the Banking Act.

All of the regulations were reviewed in 2000 to ensure enhanced corporate governance in the banking sector.

In response to the growing importance of corporate governance, the Capital Markets Authority issued a Gazette Notice in January 2002, making adherence to the guidelines mandatory for public listed banks. Many of the requirements are already provided for, either in the Banking Act or in various regulations. However, there are some other issues contained in the guidelines that the banking sector has yet to adopt, including:

- disclosure of the ten major shareholders of the company;

- the requirement that no person should hold more than five directorships in any public listed companies at any one time;

- the requirement that executive directors have a fixed service contract not exceeding five years, with provision for renewal;

- the requirement that no person should hold more than two chairmanships in any public listed company at any one time; and

- the requirement for the inclusion of a statement on corporate governance in annual reports and financial statements.

The Central Bank supports the Capital Markets Authority's efforts to foster corporate governance. In line with this, all banks, including those that are not publicly quoted, were requested by the Central Bank to include a statement on corporate governance in their annual accounts for the years 2001 and 2002. The Central Bank continues to encouraging all financial institutions and especially the private ones to adopt the Capital Markets Authority guidelines. Governance issues in the banking sector, if addressed, will not only support the implementation of good governance practices but also encourage good corporate citizenship, especially by banking sector customers.

14.5.3 Sample Code for Best Practice in Corporate Governance

In 1999 the Private Sector Corporate Governance Trust (PSCGT), now the Centre for Corporate Governance (CCG), reviewed various codes of best practice developed internationally, keeping in mind local circumstances relevant to Kenya, and drafted a set of principles and a sample code of best practice. The code was circulated to the corporate sector, regulatory authorities and other interested parties. The principles and sample code were drafted to:

- excite and incite debate on good corporate governance in Kenya;
- facilitate local ownership; and
- incorporate international standards.

While it is not mandatory, the code is intended to help business enterprises develop their own specific corporate governance codes. The Principles are summarized into 22 main headings covering a broad scope of corporate governance practices for enterprises, and they are as follows:

1. The authority and duties of members of enterprises

Members or shareholders [as owners] of the corporation should jointly and severally protect, preserve and actively exercise the supreme authority of the corporation in general meetings. They have a duty, jointly and severally, to exercise that supreme authority of the corporation to:

- Ensure that only competent and reliable persons, who can add value, are elected or appointed to the board of directors.

- Ensure that the board is constantly held accountable and responsible for the efficient and effective governance of the corporation so as to achieve corporate objectives, prosperity and sustainability.

- Change the composition of a board that does not perform to expectations or in accordance with the mandate of the corporation.

2. Leadership

Every corporation should be headed by an effective board which should exercise enterprise, integrity and judgement in directing the corporation so as to achieve continuing prosperity. The board should also act in the best interests of the enterprise in a manner based on transparency, accountability and responsibility.

3. Appointments to the board

Appointments to the board should, through a managed and effective process, ensure that a balanced mix of proficient individuals is made and that each of those appointed is able to add value and bring independent judgement to bear on the decision-making process.

4. Strategy and values

The board of directors should determine the purpose and values of the corporation, determine the strategy to achieve that purpose, and implement its values. This is to ensure that the corporation survives and thrives and that procedures and values that protect the assets and reputation of the corporation are put in place.

5. Structure and organization

The board should ensure that a proper management structure [organization, systems and people] is in place and make sure that the structure functions to maintain corporate integrity, reputation and responsibility.

6. Corporate performance, viability and financial sustainability

The board should monitor and evaluate the implementation of strategies, policies and management performance criteria and the plans of the corporation. In addition, the board should constantly review the viability and financial sustainability of the enterprise. This must be done at least once every year.

7. Corporate compliance

The board should ensure that the corporation complies with all the relevant laws, regulations, governance practices, accounting and auditing standards.

8. Corporate communication

The board should ensure that the corporation communicates with all its stakeholders effectively.

9. Accountability to members

The board should serve the legitimate interests of all members and account to them fully.

10. Responsibility to stakeholders

The board should identify the company's internal and external stakeholders; agree on policies determining how the corporation should relate to and with them, in creating wealth, jobs and sustainability of a financially sound corporation, while ensuring that the rights of stakeholders [whether established by law or custom] are respected, recognized and protected.

11. Balance of powers

The board should ensure that no one person or group of persons has unfettered power and that there is an appropriate balance of power on the board so that it can exercise objective and independent judgement.

12. Internal control procedures

The board should regularly review systems, processes and procedures to ensure the effectiveness of its internal systems of control so that its decision-making capability and the accuracy of its reporting and financial results are maintained at the highest levels at all times.

13. Performance evaluation for the board

The board should regularly assess its performance and effectiveness as a whole and that of individual members, including the chief executive officer. A summary of the major findings together with a statement confirming that the board has carried out a self-assessment exercise should be made to the annual general meeting.

14. Induction, development and strengthening of skills of board members

The board should recognize the need for new members to be inducted into their roles and for all board members to develop and strengthen their governance skills in light of technological developments, changing corporate environment and other variables. The board should accordingly organize for the systematic induction and continuous development of its members.

15. Appointment and development of executive management

The board should appoint the chief executive officer and participate in the appointment of all senior management, ensure motivation and protection of intellectual capital crucial to the corporation, ensure that there is appropriate and adequate training for management and other employees, and put in place a succession plan for senior management.

16. Adoption of technology and skills

The board must recognize that to survive and thrive, it has to ensure that the technology, skills and systems used in the corporation are adequate to run the corporation and that the corporation constantly reviews and adopts the same in order to remain competitive.

17. Management of corporate risks

The board must identify key risk areas and key performance indicators of the corporation's business and constantly monitor these factors.

18. Corporate culture

The board should define, promote and protect the corporate ethos, ethics and beliefs on which the corporation premises its policies, actions and behaviour, in its relationships with all who deal with it.

19. Social and environmental responsibility

The board should recognize that it is in the enlightened self-interest of the corporation to operate within the mandate entrusted to it by society and shoulder its social responsibility. For this reason, a corporation does not fulfil its social responsibility by short-changing beneficiaries or customers, exploiting its labour, polluting the environment, failing to conserve resources, neglecting the needs of the local community, evading taxation or engaging in other anti-social practices.

20. Recognition and utilization of professional skills and competencies

The board should recognize and encourage professional development and, both collectively and individually, have the right to consult the corporation's professional advisers and, where necessary, seek independent professional advice at the corporation's expense in the furtherance of their duties as directors. [This is in addition to and not a substitute for their personal duty to acquire competence, training and information that would help them make informed, independent and astute decisions on issues relevant to the corporation.]

21. Recognition of members' rights and obligations

Members of the corporation have a right to receive any information that would materially affect their membership, to participate in any meeting of members and to participate in the election of directors and be facilitated to fully participate in all other resolutions of interest to them as members.

22. Reporting

Corporations should ensure that they report effectively on their corporate governance practices.

14.5.4 Best Practice Guidelines for State-owned Corporations

The PSCGT produced a set of guidelines of best practice for state-owned corporations, through an all-inclusive process that incorporated the input of directors of state-owned corporations in Kenya. The guidelines were launched in April 2003 and presented to the government with the aim of having the recommendations therein implemented in the governance of state-owned corporations.

Among the key recommendations are:

- The need to privatize non-strategic state-owned corporations.

- The formation of a State Corporations Advisory Committee (SCAC), which will, among other duties, monitor the performance of boards of state-owned corporations. Boards of state-owned corporations have not always performed efficiently in the past and have been dogged by appointments based on political expediency and other unmeritorious considerations.

- The SCAC should ensure the proper selection, induction and development of directors of state-owned corporations.

- The need to reduce the burden of state-owned corporations on the exchequer.

- The transparent selection of members of boards of state-owned corporations.

- The independence of the boards of state-owned enterprises.

14.6   Disclosure and Transparency

The following are the applicable disclosure standards and corporate governance codes in Kenya:

- International Accounting Standards;

- International Auditing Standards;

- publication of financial statements every quarter by banking institutions;

- corporate governance principles adopted by the Centre for Corporate Governance (CCG); and

- accounting standards and governance codes enforced by the regulatory authorities concerned through reporting and disclosure requirements.

14.7   Shareholder Rights and Stakeholder Relations

Shareholder activism has broadened public awareness of shareholders' rights and corporate governance issues in Kenya and brought about changes that impact positively on business and investment. This is because when investors express their social and financial goals they help to influence the Capital Markets Authority and the Nairobi Stock

Exchange to respond to societal concerns. The Kenya Shareholders' Association (KSA) believes that sustained, strategic shareholder activism will help investors meet their goal of influencing corporate culture and performance. KSA will share information with, and create and maintain alliances with, people and organizations with objectives similar to those of the Association.

14.8 Director Development Activity

14.8.1 Training

The following are some of organizations engaged in training of directors in Kenya:

- Centre for Corporate Governance (CCG);
- Kenya Institute of Management (KIM);
- Kenya School of Monetary Studies (KSMS)

The CCG conducts five-day training courses for company directors, which leads to the award of a certificate of company directorship issued by the Commonwealth Association for Corporate Governance (CACG). In addition to these courses, CCG has entered into a collaborative agreement with the African Management Services Company (AMSCO) and the African Project Development Facility (APDF) to conduct three-day induction courses in corporate governance for company directors in both Uganda and Tanzania. This effort will be extended to cover a number of countries in the region.

KSMS trains directors of banking institutions on their role and responsibilities under the auspices of the Bank Supervision Department of the Central Bank of Kenya.

Other organizations such as KIM, the Institute of Certified Public Accountants of Kenya (ICPAK) and the Institute of Certified Public Secretaries of Kenya (ICPSK) also provide training to directors.

14.8.2 Research

The CCG has undertaken research and development programmes to contribute to the continued improvement of the principles of good corporate governance.

Programmes undertaken so far include the production of Guidelines on Good Corporate Governance in state-owned corporations and ongoing research in three key areas, namely:

- cooperatives;
- banking; and
- governance reporting and disclosure.

14.8.3   Recognition and Reward Schemes

Various other bodies have introduced recognition and reward programmes that seek to identify business enterprises that excel in performance. Examples include the Company of the Year Award coordinated by the Kenya Institute of Management, and the Best CEO and Company of the Year Award coordinated by the Nation Media Group and PricewaterhouseCoopers.

14.8.4   Monitoring and Evaluation

The monitoring and evaluation of the extent to which companies in Kenya embrace, apply and implement good corporate governance principles and practices is important. Effective evaluation systems provide tools for assessing the impact that corporate governance has on improving national efficiency and competitiveness and therefore enhanced wealth and employment creation.

14.8.5   Advocacy and Communications

Advocating and communicating the value of corporate governance serves to sensitize, motivate and influence policy-makers, corporate directors and community leaders. Advocacy also motivates the participation and involvement of the community in actively demanding good economic governance for sustainable wealth creation and increased employment opportunities.

14.9   Useful Contacts

- Capital Markets Authority (CMA) – www.cma.or.ke
- Central Bank of Kenya (CBK) – www.centralbank.go.ke

- Centre for Corporate Governance (CCG) – www.corporategovernance.co.ke

- Nairobi Stock Exchange (NSE) – www.nse.co.ke

- The Kenya Shareholders Association (KSA) – www.cma.or.ke/KSA-CMA

- The Pan-African Consultive Forum on Corporate Governance – www.corporategovernanceafrica.org

14.10   Further Reading

The private sector initiative for corporate governance (2000) *Principles for Corporate Governance in Kenya: a sample code of best practice for corporate governance*, PSICG, Nairobi

World Bank (2001) *Report on the Observance of Standards and Codes (ROSC) Kenya: Accounting and Auditing*, World Bank, Washington

15

Malaysia

Table 15.1

Population	24.3 million (2002)
Gross Domestic Income (GDI)	US $86 billion (2002)
GDI per capita	US $3,540 (2002)
Total number of companies	N/A
Number of companies listed on the stock exchange	757 (2000)
Market capitalization	US $11.3 billion (2001)
Key corporate laws	● The Securities Commission Act (SCA) (1993)
Key corporate codes	● The Securities Industry Act (SIA) (1983)
	● Companies Act (1965)
	● Malaysian Code on Corporate Governance (2000)

15.1 Corporate Structure and Ownership

The corporate ownership structure in Malaysia is concentrated. The World Bank (2000) took a sample of companies which had over 50 per cent of the Kuala Lumpur Stock Exchange's capitalization and found that:

- in 50 per cent of the listed companies the five largest shareholders typically own more than 60 per cent of the shares;

- 67 per cent of shares were in family hands;

- 37 per cent had one dominant shareholder;

- 13 per cent were state owned;

- 85 per cent of the public limited companies had owner managers.

Each ordinary share carries one vote. Non-voting preferred shares are rare.

Nominees normally represent the largest type of shareholder. They own about 45 per cent of all public limited companies. About half of the beneficial owners of nominee accounts are foreigners.

15.2　Legal Framework

The Malaysian legal system is based upon UK common law principles requiring directors to act bona fide in the interests of the company and with diligence.

Directors have a fiduciary duty not to place themselves in a position where interest and duty conflict. Directors must not profit through the exploitation or misuse of corporate opportunities. Directors also have common law duties of care and skill.

15.2.1　The Companies Act (1965)

This is the main legislation concerned with corporate activity. It deals with incorporation, operations, the duties and obligations of directors and the rights of shareholders.

15.2.2　The Securities Industry Act (SIA) 1983 and the Securities Commission Act (SCA) 1993

These acts comprise the legislative and regulatory framework for the capital markets in Malaysia.

15.3   Legal, Regulatory and Institutional Bodies

15.3.1   Kuala Lumpur Stock Exchange (KLSE)

The KLSE is responsible for market surveillance and enforces the listing requirements. When an individual becomes a director of a listed company or when a company applies for listing, they must submit undertakings to comply with the Listing Requirements.

The Listing Requirements also require that every listed company must provide every one of its directors with full and unrestricted access to information and independent professional advice.

15.3.2   Malaysian Institute of Corporate Governance (MICE)

The Malaysian Institute of Corporate Governance was established in 1998. The Institute has a mission to promote the awareness of corporate governance principles amongst corporations, corporate participants and the investing public with particular reference to enhancing shareholder value and business prosperity. The Institute also aims to raise awareness and create a pool of independent directors through education and training programmes.

15.3.3   The Securities Commission

The Securities Commission regulates the capital market in Malaysia. In recent years it has been particularly focusing upon disclosure, due diligence, corporate governance and self-regulation. It has wide administrative powers. It reports to the minister of finance.

15.3.4   Companies Commission of Malaysia (CCM)

The Companies Commission of Malaysia took over the enforcement of administration of the Companies Act (1965) in 2001. The Chief Executive of the CCM has powers to:

- review the effectiveness of existing laws relating to companies and firms;
- regulate directors and officers;
- conduct associated training activities.

15.3.5 The Minority Shareholders Watchdog Group

This group was set up in 2001 to provide a voice for minority shareholders of listed issuers, particularly in assisting minority shareholders in initiating legal proceedings against listed issuers who flout corporate governance principals.

15.4 Board Structure

Boards are one tier or unitary with a combination of executive and non-executive directors. The Malaysian Code on Corporate Governance (2000) recommends that the size of a company's board should be examined with a view to determining the impact of the number on its effectiveness. The roles of chairman and CEO should be separate but where they must be combined a strong independent element on the board must exist and the decision to combine these roles must be publicly explained. The board should include a balance of executive and non-executive directors so that no individual or group of individuals may dominate the board.

The Code on Corporate Governance (2000) recommends the formation of the following committees:

- a committee dealing with nomination of directors and evaluation of performance of directors;
- a committee dealing with compensation and remuneration of directors and senior management;
- a committee dealing with internal controls and the integrity of the internal audit.

The Listing Requirements require that an audit committee be established for all listed companies. The committee shall consist of at least three members of whom a majority shall be independent directors. There should be an independent non-executive chairman. The finance director, head of internal audit and a representative of the external auditors should normally attend meetings. At least one member of the committee must be a member of the Malaysian Institute of Accountants or have at least three years' work experience, have passed examinations or be a member of one of the recognized associations of accountants. Audit committees are obliged to bring to the attention of the Kuala Lumpur Stock Exchange any breaches of the Listing Requirements.

The nominating committee should be comprised exclusively of non-executive directors with the responsibility for proposing new nominees for the board and for assessing directors on an ongoing basis.

The remuneration committee should consist wholly or mainly of non-executive directors whose membership should appear in the executive report. Executive directors should have no say in decisions regarding their remuneration.

A due diligence working group should be formed to oversee preparations of submissions to the Securities Commission.

The Companies Act (1965) requires that any company in Malaysia must have at least two directors and at least two must be resident in Malaysia. It also states that only natural persons can be appointed director. Directors (both executive and non-executive) are normally selected for three years and generally one-third of the board retires at each AGM.

The Code on Corporate Governance (2000) recommends that every company should establish a committee consisting exclusively of non-executive directors, a majority of whom should be independent, to consider the recommended nominees for appointments to the board.

A survey by the Kuala Lumpur Stock Exchange (KLSE) and PricewaterhouseCooper (1999) identified that the average board composition for a limited company was:

Executive directors	2–8
Non executive directors	2–6
Independent directors	2–6
Average board size	8–10

The Malaysian Code of Corporate Governance (2000) lists six specific responsibilities of a board:

- reviewing and adopting a strategic plan;

- overseeing the conduct of the company's business to evaluate whether the business is being properly managed;

- identifying principal risks and ensuring the implementation of appropriate systems to manage these risks;

- succession planning, including appointment training, fixing the compensation of, and where appropriate, replacing senior management;
- developing and implementing an investor relations programme or shareholders' communications policy for the company;
- reviewing the adequacy and the integrity of the company's integral control systems and management information systems, including systems for compliance with applicable laws, regulations, rules, directives and guidelines.

At least one-third of the board should be non-executives who are independent.

The Kuala Lumpur Stock Exchange Listing Requirements define independence as:

> *a director who is independent of management and free from any business or other relationship which could interfere with the exercise of independent judgement or the ability to act in the best interest of an applicant or a listed issuer.*

Practice note 13/2002 provides further elaboration of this definition.

No fewer than two independent directors should sit on any board and independent status on the board should be disclosed annually.

Independent directors have the right to retain experts to advise them on problems arising at the company's expense provided that they reasonably believe that the retention is required for the proper performance of their functions and powers and that the amount involved is reasonable.

Board meetings should occur on a regular basis, with due notice of the issues to be discussed, and should record its conclusions in discharging its duties and responsibilities. Boards should disclose the number of meetings each year and the details of attendance at the meetings.

Since 30 June 2003 banks are required to have risk management, remuneration and nomination committees.

15.5   Codes, Standards and Good Practice Guidelines

The Malaysian Code on Corporate Governance (2002) was developed by the High Level Finance Committee comprising of the major corporate governance stakeholders in Malaysia. The Code applies to listed companies on the Kuala Lumpur Stock Exchange and focuses upon:

- legal reform and regulation;
- board processes;
- board structures;
- introduction of best practice;
- the training and education of directors and aspirant directors.

The Kuala Lumpur Stock Exchange Listing Requirements have been significantly revised in recent years. The requirements now include:

- quarterly reporting;
- having nomination, audit and remuneration committees;
- strengthening of content of annual reports to include a statement of internal controls and a statement on corporate governance.

15.6   Disclosure and Transparency

The Code on Corporate Governance (2000) recommends that boards must employ a communications policy that enables management to communicate effectively with shareholders, stakeholders and the general public. Listed companies are required to provide annual reports and quarterly financial statements. The annual report should contain general information on the company, audited annual accounts, details of directors, reports on operations and information on corporate governance.

The company should present a balanced and understandable assessment of its position and prospects to shareholders and financial regulators.

Directors are required to make statements regarding internal controls and auditors are required to review this statement with directors privately.

Periods of advance notice of AGMs require a minimum of 21 days and meeting summaries should be made available to all shareholders.

External auditors are appointed and removed by the AGM. The auditors' primary duty is to: confirm that the board's financial reports are consistent with actual accounts; and approve the overall integrity and probity of the results.

If any flaws are detected, the audit committee should possess a procedure for investigation and reporting, with options to bring the matter to the attention of the Kuala Lumpur Stock Exchange.

The OECD (2003: 80) notes that the national accounting and auditing practices in Malaysia are not materially divergent from international standards.

There is a requirement that all accounting information conforms to International Accounting Standards in all material aspects. Compliance is a statutory requirement.

15.7 Shareholder Rights and Stakeholder Relations

The memorandum and articles of association set out the rights and powers of shareholders in Malaysian companies.

Shareholders are entitled to 21 days' notice for the Annual General Meeting. The notice must contain an agenda, material facts and statements regarding the effect of proposed resolutions. Shareholders may vote by proxy.

Shareholders may appoint or remove directors, or authorize and issue share capital at general meetings by ordinary resolution.

Shareholders are required to approve by ordinary resolution major corporate transactions involving more than 25 per cent of net tangible assets.

Any change to company business or objectives requires a special resolution involving a 75 per cent majority.

Shareholders can place items on the agenda of a general meeting if they own more than 5 per cent of the voting rights or there are not fewer than 100 members holding shares in the company with an average sum per member of not less than RM 500.

Employees have no special rights to information about the company.

Two or more members holding at least 10 per cent may call an extraordinary meeting.

The Companies Act provides that each share may carry only one vote. Voting may be by show of hands or through a ballot.

The Securities Commission Act (1993) allows individuals the statutory right of action to those who have sustained loss or damage as a result of breaching the Act.

Insider dealing cases are extremely rare. Insider trading is a criminal offence. The Companies Act provides for a fine of RM 30,000 or imprisonment of five years. The SIA can fine not less than RM 1 million or three times the insider's gain and the imprisonment can be up to ten years.

15.8 Director Development Activity

The Kuala Lumpur Stock Exchange is responsible for a mandatory accredited programme (MAP) for all directors of listed companies, under the Listing Requirements. All directors of listed companies must have undergone the MAP training.

The Corporate Directors Training Programme (CDTP) was launched in 2001 and is the leading director development programme in Malaysia. It is estimated that 72,000 directors have undergone the CDTP to date. Directors who attend the CDTP are exempt from attending the MAP.

The CDTP comprises:

- the duties and responsibilities of directors;
- laws and practices of company meetings;
- corporate and economic crimes;
- corruption offences and their prevention;
- the importance of corporate governance;

- the common offences committed by company directors under the Companies Act 1965.

In addition, the KLSE is implementing Continuing Professional Education (CPE) that will require all directors of listed companies to attend regular training from approved training establishments.

15.9   Useful Contacts

- Central Bank of Malaysia (Bank Negara Malaysia) – www. bnm.gov.my
- Companies Commission of Malaysia (CCM) – www.ssm.gov.my
- Institute of Accountants – www.mia.org.my
- Institute of Chartered Secretaries and Administrators – www. miacsa.org.my
- Kuala Lumpur Stock Exchange – www.klse.com.my
- Malaysian Institute of Corporate Governance – www.micg.net
- Malaysian Institute of Economic Research – www.mier.org.my
- Minority Shareholders Watchdog Group – www.mswg.org.my
- Securities Commission – www.sc.com.my

15.10   Further Reading

High Level Finance Committee on Corporate Governance (March 1999) *Report on Corporate Governance*

JPK Working Group on Corporate Governance in Malaysia (March 2000) *Report on corporate governance in Malaysia*

Kuala Lumpur Stock Exchange/PricewaterhouseCoopers (1999) *Corporate Governance Survey Reports*, KLSE, Kuala Lumpur

OECD (2003) *White Paper on Corporate Governance in Asia*, OECD, Paris

Malaysian Exchange of Securities Dealing and Automated Quotation Bhd (October 1997) (MESDAQ) *Business and Listing Rules*

Securities Commission (2000) *Malaysian Code on Corporate Governance*, Securities Commission, Kuala Lumpur

World Bank (2000) *Malaysia: Corporate Governance Assessment and ROSC Module,*

16

Philippines

Table 16.1

Population	79.9 million (2002)
Gross National Income (GNI)	US $81.5 billion (2002)
GNI per capita	US $1,020 (2002)
Total number of companies	N/A
Number of companies listed on the stock exchange	219 (1998)
Market capitalization	US $49.2 billion (2001)
Key corporate laws	• The Corporation Code (2002)
Key corporate governance codes	• Code of Corporate Governance (2002)

16.1   Corporate Structure and Ownership

The major corporate activities in the Philippines are manufacturing (46 per cent), financial services (20 per cent) and trading (14 per cent). While there are a greater number of small and medium-scale businesses, the larger companies account for a high proportion of business activities in each industry sector.

Multinational companies have a significant presence in the Philippine corporate sector. In 1997, multinational companies accounted for 27 per cent of the number of corporations, and 33.5 per cent of the gross sales within the corporate sector.

The typical business structure in the Philippines is a privately owned company having significant, controlling shareholdings of publicly listed companies.

Publicly listed companies are not necessarily large companies. Among the 219 companies listed in the stock exchange in 1998, only 97 had sales revenues that allowed them to join the list of the largest 1,000 corporations. The share of publicly listed companies was only 22 per cent of the gross sales of the corporate sector in 1997. But together with the multinational companies, publicly traded companies accounted for about 55 per cent of sales in 1997 and 37 per cent of the top 1,000 companies in the Philippines.

It is common for large shareholders to set up pure holding companies to own operating companies and gain central control over many companies in a group. Pure holding companies are a means of pooling the ownership of family members over many companies. They enable families to 'better manage' the income taxes they pay to the government. The setting up of holding companies has been common practice among the dominant families in the Philippines.

Equity ownership is concentrated in a few hands. In 1997 the top five shareholders owned about 65.3 per cent of the equity of corporations in the non-financial sector and 59.2 per cent in the financial sector. Furthermore, the top 20 shareholders owned 76 per cent of the equity of corporations in the Philippine non-financial and financial sectors.

The Corporation Code (2002) requires approval of management decisions by a majority vote of the board of directors. Strategic decisions, because of their major impact on a company, require a two-thirds majority. However, the five largest shareholders usually hold a sufficient majority to approve all operating and strategic decisions of companies. Minority shareholders, therefore, hardly have any influence on decisions, and they can be disregarded should the majority owners choose to do so.

Based on publicly available shareholder information and other published reports, 39 corporate groups belong to a family or a group of closely interrelated families and account for 31 per cent of the total sales of the corporate sector in 1997. Twenty financial institutions were affiliated with these groups, including 16 commercial banks.

Members of corporate groups controlled by a single family or closely related sets of families tend to dominate or become major players in industries where they participate. Corporate groups dominate or are major players in industries that are capital intensive, difficult to enter owing to start-up barriers and economies of scale, highly regulated, and heavily subject to government restrictions. In some of these industries (eg mining, pipelines and beer/cola industries), groups of companies with dominant family shareholders claim from 80 to 98 per cent of gross sales.

Groups of companies in the Philippines operate at varying degrees of effective central control. Some members of the groups may have autonomous operations. They separate operating management from central control. They may even allow these companies to raise their own financing without cross-guarantees from other members of the group or the holding company. Nonetheless, central control may still be exercised in key strategic decisions, particularly on major investments and their financing. Groups of companies under central control also tend to take advantage of scale economies from central purchasing, logistics and personnel as well as management programmes. In general, these groups of companies are more likely to avoid management inefficiencies, but they also tend to over-borrow. They are generally expected to show higher profitability but also have higher leverage risks.

The landscape of corporate Philippines is marked by a few groups of companies with a large and family-based ownership structure. If each group of companies were taken as one economic entity, then 7 of the 10 top corporations in the country would belong to this category. By extending the count to the top 50 corporations, 25 of the top 50 corporations would belong to this category. A group of companies can be engaged in many industries. But significantly, they draw most of their profits from only two or three industries, which they tend to dominate or have large market shares in. They are also generally affiliated with a commercial bank. Moreover, the country's economic history, its legal and policy regime, and the resulting highly concentrated ownership of groups of companies by a few families make the challenge of adopting modern corporate governance a challenge. This may well limit future growth and lead to inefficiencies in investments and financing in the corporate sector.

16.2 Legal Framework

The Philippine Corporation Code (2002) and the main agency enforcing it, the Securities and Exchange Commission, are patterned after their US counterparts. The Securities and Exchange Commission requires all securities to be registered, with the public registry open for inspection by the general public. Corporate stock and transfer books are open for inspection by the company's stockholders.

In addition, the SEC Memorandum Circular No. 2 Series 2002 on the Philippine Code of Corporate Governance describes in detail the shareholders' rights and protection of minority shareholders' interests. It states that the board of directors should be committed to respect and promote the rights of all shareholders. It is the duty of the board to promote shareholders' rights, remove impediments to the exercise of those rights, and specify avenues for seeking redress for their violation.

Directors who wilfully and knowingly vote for, or assent to, patently unlawful acts of the corporation or who are guilty of gross negligence or bad faith in directing the affairs of the corporation or acquire any personal or pecuniary interest in conflict with their duty shall be liable jointly and severally for all damages resulting therefrom suffered by the corporation, its shareholders and other persons.

16.3 Legal, Regulatory and Institutional Bodies

16.3.1 Securities and Exchange Commission (SEC)

The SEC regulates and supervises all businesses that are the grantees of primary franchises and/or a licence or permit issued by the government. It draws up the legislation and recommendations on all aspects of the securities market. It ensures compliance with the regulations and can impose sanctions if they are violated. It also advises Congress on all issues regarding the securities market.

16.3.2 Stock Exchange (PSE)

The PSE is a private shareholder-based, revenue-earning company that provides a market for buying and selling securities. In 1998 it was given powers to enforce its own regulations and impose penalties by the SEC.

16.3.3 Institute for Directors

The Institute for Directors was launched in 1999. The founder of the Institute was Jesus Estanislao, a former finance minister.

16.4 Board Structure

Philippine corporations have a one-tier or unitary board system. The board of directors is defined as a collegial body invested with the corporate powers of all corporations formed under the Corporation Code (2002). It conducts all business and controls or holds all the property and assets of the corporation. The board is primarily responsible for the governance of the corporation.

The board is composed of at least 5 but not more than 15 members elected by shareholders. In practice, large public companies typically have a board composed of between 7 and 11 members representing the largest shareholders of the company. The Corporation Code (2002) mandates that every member of the board must own at least one share of the capital stock of the corporation of which he is a director, which share shall stand in his name on the books of the corporation. A majority of the directors must be residents of the Philippines. However, there is no requirement in law or in practice of getting various stakeholders represented on boards. A director is normally appointed for one year and there is no limit to re-election. Board meetings are normally held each month.

Directors are elected during the annual general shareholders' meeting. Outside directors are not common and not mandatory. Outside directors, if present, are brought in by controlling shareholders. Legal entities may not serve as directors.

16.4.1 Independence

The Code of Corporate Governance (2002) requires large public companies to have at least two 'independent' directors, or at least

20 per cent of the members of such board, whichever is the lesser. All other companies are encouraged to have independent directors.

'Independent director' refers to a person other than an officer or employee of the corporation, its parent or subsidiaries, or any other individual having any relationship with the corporation that would interfere with the exercise of independent judgement in carrying out the responsibilities of a director. This means that apart from the directors' fees and shareholdings, he/she should be independent of the controlling shareholder and management, and be free from any business or other relationship that could materially interfere with the exercise of his/her independent judgement. However, having several independent directors has not been warmly welcomed by most private family-owned companies in the Philippines. Family members and their close associates naturally and habitually prefer to discuss business issues of a highly confidential nature within the family.

16.4.2 Separation of the Roles of Chairman and Chief Executive

The Code of Corporate Governance (2002) suggests that the roles of the chairman and the CEO be separated to ensure an appropriate balance of power, increased accountability and greater capacity of the board for independent decision-making. The company shall disclose the relationship between the chairman and the CEO upon their election. Where both positions of the chairman and CEO are unified, there is clearly one leader to provide a single vision and mission. In this instance, checks and balances should be clearly provided to help ensure that independent, outside views, perspectives, and judgements are given proper hearing in the board.

The chairman's responsibilities in respect to the board proceedings may include:

- to schedule meetings to enable the board to perform its duties responsibly while not interfering with the flow of the company's operations;
- to prepare the agenda of the board meeting in consultation with the CEO;
- to exercise control over quality, quantity and timeliness of the flow of information between management and the board; and

- to assist in ensuring the corporation's compliance with the generally accepted guidelines on corporate governance.

16.4.3   Committees

The Philippine Code of Corporate Governance (2002) suggests that to ensure high standards of good corporate governance practices, boards of directors may create subcommittees. However, most companies do not have subcommittees of the board of directors. A few have management remuneration and audit committees.

The Audit Committee

The audit committee is composed of at least three board members with accounting and finance backgrounds. One of the members must be an independent director, and another should have related audit experience. Some of the committee's key specific functions are to:

- provide oversight of the senior management's activities in managing the corporation;
- provide oversight of the corporation's internal and external auditors;
- monitor and evaluate the adequacy and effectiveness of the corporation's internal control system;
- review the quarterly, half-year and annual financial statements before submission to the board; and
- be responsible for coordinating, monitoring and facilitating compliance with existing laws, rules and regulations.

The chairman of the audit committee should be an independent director. He should be responsible for inculcating in the minds of the board members the importance of management responsibilities in maintaining a sound system of internal control and the board's oversight responsibility.

Through the audit committee, the board could recommend to the shareholders a duly accredited external auditor who shall undertake an independent audit and shall provide an objective assurance of the way in which financial statements are prepared and presented. Such external auditor cannot at the same time provide the services of an internal auditor to the same client. The external auditor has to be rotated every five years or earlier.

The Compensation or Remuneration Committee

The Philippine Code of Corporate Governance (2002) suggests that the compensation or remuneration committee shall be composed of at least three members, one of whom should be an independent director. It may establish a formal and transparent procedure for developing a policy on executive remuneration and for fixing the remuneration packages of corporate officers and directors, and provide oversight of remuneration of senior management and other key personnel, ensuring that compensation is consistent with the corporation's culture, strategy and control environment.

Levels of directors' remuneration shall be sufficient to attract and retain the directors and officers needed to run the company successfully. Corporations, however, should avoid paying more than what is necessary for this purpose. A proportion of executive directors' remuneration may be structured so as to link rewards to corporate and individual performance.

In addition, the Philippine Corporation Code (2002) states that in the absence of any provision in the by-laws fixing directors' remuneration, the directors shall not receive any remuneration, except for reasonable per diems. Any remuneration other than per diems may be granted to directors by the vote of the shareholders representing at least a majority of the outstanding capital stock at a regular or special shareholders' meeting. The total annual remuneration of directors shall not exceed 10 per cent of the net income before income tax of the corporation during the preceding year.

The Nominations Committee

The Code of Corporate Governance (2002) suggests that the board may also constitute a nomination committee that may be composed of at least three elected members, one of whom should be an independent director. This committee shall review and evaluate the qualifications of all persons nominated to the board as well as those nominated to other positions requiring appointment by the board. It shall also provide assessment on the board's effectiveness in directing the process of renewing and replacing board members.

All members of the board must be elected in the presence, either in person or by representative, of the owners of a majority of the outstanding capital stock. The election must be by ballot if requested by any voting shareholder. Every shareholder entitled to vote should have the right to vote in person or by proxy the number of shares he or she holds. Candidates receiving the highest number of votes shall be declared elected as directors.

Any director of a corporation may be removed from office by a vote of the shareholders holding or representing at least two-thirds of the capital stock. Such removal shall take place either at a regular meeting of the corporation or at a special meeting called for the purpose, after previous notice has been issued to its shareholders of the intention to propose such removal at the meeting.

16.5 Codes, Standards and Good Practice Guidelines

It is the board's responsibility to foster the long-term success of the corporation and secure its sustained competitiveness in a manner consistent with its fiduciary responsibility, which it should exercise in the best interest of the corporation and its shareholders. The Code of Corporate Governance (2002) classifies the duties and responsibilities of the board into two categories: general and specific duties and responsibilities.

Some of the key general duties and responsibilities of the board are to:

- act in the best interest of the corporation in a manner characterized by transparency, accountability and fairness;

- assume certain responsibilities to different constituencies or stakeholders, who have the right to expect that the institution is being run in a prudent and sound manner; and

- ensure good governance of the corporation by establishing the corporation's vision and mission, strategic objectives, policies and procedures that may guide and direct the activities of the company and the means to attain the same, as well as the mechanism for monitoring management's performance. While the management of the day-to-day affairs of the institution is the responsibility of the management team, the board is, however, responsible for monitoring and overseeing management action.

The specific duties and responsibilities of the board, on the other hand, are among others to:

- conduct fair business transactions with the corporation, exercise independent judgement, and ensure that personal interest does not bias board decisions;
- devote time and attention necessary to properly discharge its duties and responsibilities; and
- have a working knowledge of the statutory and regulatory requirements affecting the corporation.

To ensure a high standard of best practice for the company and its stakeholders, the board should conduct itself with utmost honesty and integrity in the discharge of its duties, functions and responsibilities, which include, among others, to:

- install a process of selection to ensure a mix of competent directors, each of whom can add value and contribute independent judgement to the formulation of sound corporate strategies and policies;
- select and appoint the CEO and other senior officers;
- provide sound written policies and strategic guidelines to the corporation that will help decide on major capital expenditures;
- periodically evaluate and monitor implementation of such strategies and policies, business plans and operating budgets as well as management's overall performance to ensure optimum results;
- conduct a review regularly of the effectiveness of such a system, so that the decision-making capability and the integrity of corporate operations and reporting systems are maintained at a high level at all times; and
- properly discharge board functions by meeting regularly.

16.6　Disclosure and Transparency

Listed companies are required to produce annual reports and quarterly financial statements. The company's annual report must contain general information on the company, annual accounts, details of the company directors, a director's report on company operations and information on corporate governance.

The control environment is framed by:

- the board, which ensures that the company is appropriately and effectively managed and controlled;

- a management that actively manages and operates the company in a sound and prudent manner;

- the organizational and procedural controls supported by an effective management information system and risk management reporting system; and

- the independent audit mechanisms to monitor the adequacy and effectiveness of the organization's governance, operations, information systems, to include reliability and integrity of financial and operational information, effectiveness and efficiency of operations, safeguarding of assets, and compliance with laws, rules, regulations, and contracts.

The auditors are appointed by shareholders at the annual general meeting. The Code (2002) recommends that the audit firm is rotated every five years. In 2003, the OECD identified 25 areas of difference between national accounting and auditing practices from international standards.

Through the Code of Corporate Governance (2002), the Security and Exchange Commission has set out that the minimum internal control mechanisms for the board's oversight responsibility shall include:

- defining the duties and responsibilities of the CEO;

- selecting or approving an individual with appropriate ability, integrity and experience to fill the CEO role;

- reviewing proposed senior management appointments;

- ensuring the selection, appointment and retention of qualified and competent management; and

- reviewing the company's personnel and human resource policies and sufficiency, conflict of interest situations, changes to the compensation plan for employees and officers and management succession plan. Meanwhile, the minimum internal control mechanisms for management's operational responsibility shall centre on the CEO, being ultimately accountable for the company's organizational and procedural controls.

16.7   Shareholder Rights and Stakeholder Relations

The Corporation Code (2002) outlines the basic rights of shareholders. Shareholders are under the one-share-one-vote rule with proxy voting legally allowed and practised. They have the right to elect, remove and replace directors and vote on certain corporate acts in accordance with the Corporation Code. The Code mandates the use of cumulative voting in the election of directors. Although directors may be removed with or without cause, the Code prohibits removal without cause if this would deny minority shareholders representation in the board. Removal of directors requires an affirmative vote of two-thirds of total outstanding capital. The Code also requires the annual general shareholders' meeting to confirm decisions of management. Notice for convening the annual general meeting must be at least 15 working days. The notice must contain agenda, financial statements, major transactions, operation plans and details of officers, directors and auditors. A shareholder can voice his/her concern during the annual general shareholders' meeting without any required minimum shareholdings for such privilege. Minority shareholders have the right to propose the holding of a meeting, and to propose items to be included in the agenda of the meeting, provided the items are for a legitimate business purpose.

All shareholders have pre-emptive rights under the law but this right can be waived in a company's articles of incorporation. Specifically, all shareholders have the right to subscribe to the additional capital stock the corporation may issue. But the articles of incorporation may lay down specific rights and powers of shareholders with respect to the particular shares they hold. Given the family shareholder groups with dominant control of corporations in the Philippine corporate sector, a major concern has been the possible conflict of interest in corporate transactions involving managers and large shareholders.

Proper disclosure is another important aspect of good corporate governance. Shareholders can request periodic reports disclosing personal and professional information about the directors and officers and certain other matters about the holdings of the company's shares, the identity of persons holding them, and the dealings of directors and key officers with the company. Disclosure is also required concerning the compensation of directors and officers. However, although in principle shareholders have the right to information, the information released to them is on such an aggregate basis that it is oftentimes not very meaningful.

The Corporation Code (2002) mandates corporations to grant the power of inspection to shareholders. They are allowed to inspect corporate books and records, including minutes of board meetings and stock registries in accordance with the Corporation Code, and must be provided with an annual report, including financial statements, without cost or restrictions.

Shareholders have the right to receive dividends subject to the discretion of the board (right to dividends). However, the Securities and Exchange Commission may direct the corporation to declare dividends when its retained earnings are in excess of 100 per cent of its paid-in capital stock, except:

- when justified by definite corporate expansion projects or programmes approved by the board;

- when the corporation is prohibited under any loan agreement with any financial institution or creditor, whether local or foreign, from declaring dividends without its consent, and such consent has not been secured; or

- when it can be clearly shown that such retention is necessary under special circumstances obtaining in the corporation, such as when there is a need for a special reserve for probable contingencies.

The legal framework for shareholder rights is generally regarded as adequate. However, in practice, shareholder protection is weakened considerably or even rendered meaningless by the dominance of large shareholders generally owning more than two-thirds of the corporation's equity. In such a case, which is common in the Philippines, there is no deterrent on the majority shareholder and the management under his/her control against possible conflict of interest. Indeed, insider trading, prohibited by law, has been difficult to police against.

Employees have no special rights to information on the company they work for.

16.7.1 Major Corporate Governance Issues

Given the concentrated ownership of shares in a company with significant control over public listed companies and of others falling under one business 'group' that includes a commercial bank, several features of corporate governance practice can be highlighted as follows:

- The controlling shareholders, belonging to one family or one group of closely interconnected business interests, generally control both the board of directors and management.

- There are few, if any, outside independent directors in a corporate board.

- Management, which tends to be increasingly professional, has to clear with the controlling shareholders any major (and still, even minor) corporate decisions.

- Minority shareholders, in practice, have neither voice nor effective vote. Activism on the part of minority shareholders does not lead anywhere.

- Standards of disclosure are low. Based on recent experience, even audited financial statements by internationally connected public accounting firms cannot be taken at face value.

- The regulatory regime is weak to enforce an otherwise modern corporation law.

- Banks can serve as external controllers of companies, given the practice of relationship finance. But in practice, when payments are suspended or when a corporate rehabilitation has to be undertaken, banks have limited power under the law.

- There is no effective market for corporate control to discipline inefficient management and constrain self-dealing.

Given all these constraints, it is a challenge to introduce corporate governance reforms in the Philippines. The Code of Corporate Governance introduced by the Securities and Exchange Commission of the Philippines in 2002 is a useful first step. It provides a guide and starting point for companies to improve their corporate governance practices in line with international best practices.

16.8 Director Development Activity

In the Philippines, a national task force chaired by former finance minister Jesus Estanislao has mapped a reform strategy for the country which focuses upon the role of banks as providers of finance and their need to include corporate governance as a part of risk management. In a landmark ruling, the Monetary Authority requires that bank directors in the Philippines meet the 'fit and proper test' by completing orientation courses in corporate governance. The Institute for Directors provides the basic training and codes of conduct to meet the new requirements and is developing a regional board evaluation assessment tool which will be promoted across the region.

The Philippines has also played a leading role in developing a regional network, promoting corporate governance reform through idea.net – an innovative association that brings together leaders in reform from nine regional economies, including China. The group is committed to developing regional standards of professional ethics and conduct for directors.

16.9 Useful Contacts

- Institute of Corporate Directors – www.icd.ph
- Securities and Exchange Commission – www.sec.gov.ph
- Stock Exchange – www.pse.org.ph

16.10 Further Reading

OECD (2003) *White Paper on Corporate Governance in Asia*, OECD, Paris

Saldaña, Cesar G (2001) *Corporate Governance Environment and Policy: Their Impact on Corporate Performance and Finance in the Philippines*, OECD Publication on Corporate Governance in Asia, pp 333–51

Securities and Exchange Commission (2002) *The Corporation Code of the Philippines*, SEC, Philippines

Securities and Exchange Commission (2002) *Code of Corporate Governance*, SEC Memorandum Circular No. 2, Philippines

17

South Africa

Table 17.1

Population	43.6 million (2002)
Gross National Income (GNI)	US $113.5 billion (2002)
GNI per capita	US $2,600 (2002)
Total number of companies	600,000 approx (2001)
Number of companies listed on the stock exchange	418 JSE (2004)
Market capitalization	US $288 billion (2004)
Key corporate laws	● Close Corporations Act 1984
	● Companies Act 1973
	● Insider Trading Act, 1998
Key corporate governance codes	● King Report (2) on Corporate Governance (2002)
	● King Report (1) on Corporate Governance (1994)

17.1   Corporate Structure and Ownership

There are various forms of business incorporation in South Africa governed by the Companies Act, 1973. The most common form of incorporation under the South African Companies Act is either private limited or public limited.

There are marginally under 7,000 active public companies incorporated under the Companies Act, of which 415 are currently listed on the JSE. Approximately 290,000 active private companies are incorporated and there exist approximately another 16 types of companies that are recorded as 'active'.

An interesting feature of the JSE, is that its market capitalization stands at 1.65 times GDP (excluding cross-holdings). This is higher than many developed countries such as the United Kingdom, France, Germany and the United States.

In order to establish a private company, only one person is required. A private company is not required to file financial statements with the Registrar of Companies but its articles of association must:

- limit the transferability of shares;
- limit the number of shareholders to 50 individuals; and
- prohibit any offer to the public to subscribe for shares or debentures in the company.

At least seven members are required to establish a public company. A public company can raise capital from the public as there is no restriction on the number of members or the transferability of shares.

Public companies may choose to list on the JSE Securities Exchange South Africa (JSE) and must file annual and interim financial statements to the Registrar of Companies as well as meet the listings requirements of the JSE.

Another form of popular incorporation for businesses in South Africa is the close corporation, which falls under separate legislation and is designed to accommodate small businesses without the substantial administrative requirements imposed on companies incorporated under the Companies Act. Over 850,000 are incorporated in this manner.

Between 1997 and 2000, five companies (Billiton, South African Breweries, Anglo American, Old Mutual and Dimension Data), accounting for almost a quarter of the JSE's market capitalization, shifted their primary listing to the UK. A number of other major

South African companies, including Telkom, Anglogold and Sasol have shifted their primary listing to New York.

Historically, the corporate sector was dominated by mining finance houses. However, following the opening of the economy to global forces with the advent of democracy, mining houses, as they were originally constructed, have largely unbundled their stakes in non-core holdings or bought out minority shareholding interests. The restructuring has significantly transformed the control structures of South Africa's economy and broadened ownership.

This has also been led, more recently, by strong motivation at the official policy level to diversify control holdings in the corporate sector to 'historically disadvantaged' ethnic groups (otherwise more commonly known as 'black economic empowerment'). This provides, perhaps, an interesting dimension to corporate governance issues that are unique to South Africa and it is too early to anticipate the impact.

Outside of the banking and financial services sectors, though, many of South Africa's larger companies still have considerable interests owned by the founding families of these companies.

South Africa has a large private retirement funds sector and long-term insurance industry. Domestic institutional investors dominate the JSE and account for around 40 per cent of the total market capitalization. Since exchange control restrictions regulate the investment of domestic funds to a large extent, issuers quoted on the JSE essentially operate in a captive market for domestic institutional investors.

The level of foreign institutional investment is difficult to ascertain with accuracy, as it is usually deployed through local intermediaries as part of their overall funds invested, but is deemed to be low. However, this is not necessarily out of line with the withdrawal of global investors from the emerging markets on account of a number of financial crises that occurred during the latter part of the 1990s.

The dismantling of the racially based Apartheid political system in the early 1990s has brought about a profound transformation in the socio-economic fabric of South Africa. Prior to this, the proper functioning of market mechanisms and a sound corporate culture of transparency and disclosure was largely stifled and accompanied by excessive rent seeking on the part of government and management, often at the expense of employees and shareholders generally.

A significant feature of the democratic period since 1994 has been successive political reforms, admission to the World Trade Organisation, rejuvenation of foreign capital inflows and a series of domestic regulatory initiatives designed to foster a policy of economic liberalization with special emphasis on capital market development and corporate reform.

17.1.1   Public Sector Institutional Framework

A significant factor in the South African economy is the public sector. State-owned enterprises in South Africa control about a quarter of the country's capital stock, which makes this sector significant in the overall context of the South African economy.

Some SOEs rank among the largest of their kind globally, including Eskom (electricity utility serving not just South Africa but much of Africa) and Transnet (transport utility responsible for South Africa's ports, railway system, national airline, etc).

SOEs are responsible for generating approximately a third of all savings in the country (on a gross basis). This means that they play a critical role in the allocation of capital in the South African economy.

The standard of corporate governance in this sector, therefore, plays an important role in the South African economy. This sector is also regulated by some of the most advanced, and onerous, public finance legislation internationally under the Public Finance Management Act. This is administered by the National Treasury, falling under the Minister of Finance, and the Office of the Auditor-General (an independent Constitutional oversight authority).

This extends to the provincial and municipal government sectors and any commercial enterprise established at these levels.

17.2   Legal Framework

The legal system in South Africa is based on Roman-Dutch law and the Constitution formally introduced in 1996. It draws much of its reference from the English legal system in the commercial sector, constituted by the Companies Act promulgated in 1973 and the common law system of judicial precedent.

The institutional framework in South Africa is constituted by primary law represented by statute promulgated by the national Parliament, which in the commercial sphere is generally subject to criminal sanction in the event of breach, and a disparate regulatory oversight framework of institutional structures designed to enforce compliance.

Given the weak enforcement of these rules and regulations, in part due to availability of skills and resources and budgetary constraints and also because of a heavy burden on the judicial system dealing with conventional criminal prosecution, there is a relatively heavy reliance on self-regulatory measures.

All incorporated bodies in South Africa are required to register with the Registrar of Companies, which administers the Companies Act. A number of the recommendations for statutory amendments to the Companies Act from the first King Report (1994) have been promulgated. This has provided for companies to obtain liability insurance cover indemnifying their directors and officers, compelling disclosure of the identity of beneficial owners of shares held by nominees and making the appointment of the company secretary mandatory for public companies with a share capital.

The banking sector, regulated by the Registrar of Banks falling under the South African Reserve Bank, has been subjected to considerable regulatory reform requiring extensive corporate governance disclosure. This includes codification of the fiduciary duties of directors and certain categories of executive officers. A number of the provisions of the second King Report (2002) are now mandatory for banks and their boards of directors.

The Insider Trading Act, introduced in 1998, forms an important backbone to the regulatory environment, particularly in relation to companies quoted on the JSE. It falls under the FSB, and has powers to institute criminal prosecution and civil proceedings, and also follows a 'name and shame' policy in disclosing miscreants that have fallen foul of this legislation.

The JSE has undertaken a comprehensive revision of its listings requirements (the third time in seven years) to embrace both developments internationally and to make mandatory a number of the recommendations contained in the second King Report. These new listings requirements became effective on 1 September 2003 and allow for certain transitional provisions.

Another significant regulatory instrument is the Securities Regulation Panel, which supervises mergers and takeovers. While it is a statutory body, it is essentially self-regulatory in nature and applies the Securities Regulation Code based on the takeover code in London. This institution falls under the Minister of Trade and industry.

The Public Accountants' and Auditors' Act provides for statutory regulation of the audit profession and is funded by fees and levies paid by the registered accountants and auditors. An investigation has recently presented a report to the Minister of Finance in regard to recommendations for the reform of the institutional framework governing the accounting sector.

Recommendations contained in the second King Report calling for the legal backing for accounting standards has led to draft legislation that is currently under consideration. South Africa is, for the most part, fully compliant with International Financial Reporting Standards (IFRS). In advance of this, the JSE has introduced a GAAP Monitoring Panel to enforce compliance with its own listings requirements prescribing compliance with South African Statements of Generally Accepted Accounting Practice. Compliance with IFRS will be compulsory for companies listed on the JSE for financial years commencing during 2005.

The Public Finance Management Act introduced in 1999 was followed by regulatory directives issued in 2001 and updated in 2002 and probably provides some of the most advanced regulation of public sector enterprises in the world. This has been further supplemented by the updated Protocol on Corporate Governance for State Owned Enterprises. This adapted the principles in the second King Report into a format more appropriate for the public sector and, in some cases, with even more stringent requirements. This has been followed by similar legislation and regulations for local authorities and municipal structures.

Numerous other developments have taken place within the regulatory framework of South Africa, including legislation regulating whistle-blowing, access to information, and electronic communication. Further amendments have been made to the Companies Act to allow for more effective and timely communication between companies and their shareholders.

17.3 Legal, Regulatory and Institutional Bodies

17.3.1 Public Accountants and Auditors Board (PAAB)

The Public Accountants' and Auditors' Act provides for statutory regulation of the audit profession. The Public Accountants and Auditors
Board (PAAB), which was created under the Public Accountants and
Auditors Act, is the statutory body responsible for controlling registered accountants and auditors involved in public practice. Members
of the PAAB are appointed by the Minister of Finance from among the
State departments, members of the accountancy profession nominated
by the provincial societies of chartered accountants, and academics
nominated by the Committee of University Principals.

17.3.2 Financial Services Board (FSB)

The FSB is an independent statutory body created in 1990. It is
financed by levies and fees. The board of the FSB is appointed by the
Minister of Finance for three-year terms. The FSB employs 189 people.
It regulates the insurance and pension fund industries, the stock and
bond exchanges, the central securities depositories, insider trading but
not issuers of securities. It has formal powers of investigation, with
criminal conduct being referred to the national director of public
prosecution. Plans to create an integrated (super-) financial markets
regulator have been the subject of public speculation.

17.3.3 JSE Securities Exchange South Africa (JSE)

The JSE is the 14th largest stock exchange globally and is a member-
owned regulatory body that regulates brokerage members, trading
and issuers. The JSE has a 50 per cent interest in the clearing and
settlement business called STRATE. The board of directors has been
structured along the lines of the recommendations contained in the
second King Report and the JSE has set its own corporate governance standards and practices as the benchmark for companies listed
on its exchange.

The JSE amended its listing requirements in March 2003. These
Listing Requirements became effective on 1 September 2003 and have
been aligned with international best practice. A brief synopsis of the
major changes incorporated into the 2003 Listing Requirements is
outlined in section 17.5.

17.3.4   Institute of Directors Southern Africa

The IoD is a voluntary membership organization that was established in South Africa nearly 50 years ago to promote director professionalism and interests. It is affiliated, loosely, to the IoD in the United Kingdom and also enjoys a close affiliation with its well-established counterparts in Australia and New Zealand. Some 2,000 directors and professionals are members of the IoD in South Africa.

17.3.5   Department of Trade and Industry

The Department of Trade and Industry (DTI) assists in the development of industries, the building and expansion of trade relations, the promotion of foreign trade and exports from South Africa and the maintenance of competitive conditions in the domestic market. Since April 1995, the DTI has promoted an institutional support framework for small, medium-sized and micro businesses, including the Chief Directorate for Small Business Promotion, Ntsika Enterprise Promotion Agency, Khula Enterprise Finance and local Business Service Centres.

17.3.6   Other

There are various private-sector organizations in major towns and cities, including the:

- South African Chamber of Business (SACOB);
- Afrikaanse Handelsinstituut (AHI);
- National African Federated Chamber of Commerce (NAFCOC);
- Foundation for African Business and Consumer Services (FABCOS);
- Chamber of Mines;
- South African Foundation;
- Regional Chambers of Business and Commerce; and
- Business South Africa.

A number of these organs which, for historical reasons, have traditionally been segregated between white business and black business have been initiated or under an umbrella organization, Business Unity South Africa (BUSA).

17.4   Board Structure

Directors owe their duties to the company. These originate in common law, statutes, the memorandum and articles of the company, service agreements, resolutions passed at the AGM and board meetings, and the rules of regulatory bodies. There is a general concern that directors in small to medium-sized enterprises do not always fully understand their duties and obligations. Shadow directors have been an issue and King 2 highlighted this problem and subjected shadow directors to their statutory duties by declaring them directors.

Major shareholders commonly appoint their own board representatives and the violation of the fair treatment principle is a concern in holding company structures with listed subsidiaries.

With regard to compliance with the law, directors can be civilly or criminally liable for company failure to comply with obligations. Stakeholder issues such as black empowerment and corporate social responsibility (CSR) are well known and directors are generally aware that they must take stakeholder interests into account.

No 'delinquent director' register presently exists, and some directors associated with corporate failures are known to have moved to other boards. While IFRS and JSE rules require disclosure the issues associated with related party transactions are another area of major concern.

The concept of 'independence' is not well known, although it is addressed in the listing rules and in King 2. There is a general feeling that there are too few qualified directors spread across too many boards, a typical problem in emerging markets like South Africa. In practice, many issues are apparently decided informally outside board meetings and then ratified at scheduled meetings.

With regard to access to information, under King 2, the board should have unrestricted access to all company information, records, documents and property. This extends the principle contained in the Companies Act.

17.5 Codes, Standards and Good Practice Guidelines

17.5.1 King Report (1994)

Corporate governance reform in South Africa was established with the formation of the King Committee on Corporate Governance in 1992 under the auspices of the Institute of Directors. This was a private-sector-led initiative that culminated in the release of the first King Report on Corporate Governance in 1994 under the chairmanship of Mervyn King, a former judge and businessman.

The report used the UK's Cadbury Report as a base and guidance while 'having regard to the special circumstances existing in South Africa, more particularly the entrance into the business community of members of previously disadvantaged communities' at the time of the political transition to a fully fledged democracy. It focused on board composition, the board's role and processes, information provision and decision making. The Report also determined that audit and remuneration committees be established.

17.5.2 King Report (2002)

The King Committee was reconstituted in 2000 to undertake a comprehensive review of corporate governance in South Africa, which resulted in the second King Report being released in March 2002. It provides a significant compilation of corporate governance standards and principles that are not only applicable to South African companies in both the private and public sectors, and has gained recognition globally for its extensive examination of corporate governance standards and practices.

The second King Report was considered necessary for a number of reasons, including significant regulatory reform that had taken place in South Africa following the political transition and in order to take account of international developments in corporate governance as they related to South African companies. A significant feature of the second King Report was that it not only extended to companies in the private sector but was designed to include all forms of corporate enterprise that operate within the public sector structures.

The second King Report provides comprehensive guidance in the conduct of boards and directors and also defined new parameters in the areas of risk management and internal control assurance, as well as attendant issues of corporate citizenship and responsibility. The major changes are as follows:

- More rigorous tests of independence for non-executive directors, especially in relation to the constitution of board committees and around issues of delegation of authority. It also recommends full disclosure of any form of remuneration enjoyed by directors on an individual basis in support of requirements of the JSE which came into force in March 2002.

- Regular self-evaluation, on an annual basis, of the board and all board committees as well as the evaluation of board members individually.

- The separation of the roles of chairman and chief executive. Where this is not possible, this should be justified annually by the board and any combination of these two functions should be countered by the presence of a strong, lead-independent non-executive director in the position of deputy chairman.

- Much more stringent disclosure requirements are called for in regard to activities and functions of board committees, re-election of directors, resolutions proposed at shareholder meetings, and reporting of the management of risks and internal controls assurance.

- The board, collectively, and directors, individually, are ultimately responsible for risk management and full annual disclosure must be provided as to the steps taken by the board to obtain the necessary assurances as to identified operational and financial risks internally and external to the company.

- The importance of an independent, objective, internal audit function is reiterated with guidelines. The role of the audit committee is emphasized, with particular attention paid to issues such as going concern assessments, non-audit services, membership and structure of the audit committee itself, etc.

- Strategic non-financial issues for South African companies, taking into account international developments around the so-called triple bottom line approach. This involves taking into account a range of economic, social and environmental issues relevant to South African companies. These are blended with a number of specifically South African priorities such as HIV/AIDS, black economic empowerment, gender and ethnic mix on boards, etc.

● Twenty-four recommendations are given around issues of compliance and enforcement, ranging from changes to the Companies Act through to a more active participation by domestic institutional investors.

The significance of King 2 is that while it remains private sector led, the composition of the participants in the review was drawn from nearly all relevant sectors of society, including government and regulators. Hence, it achieved extensive buy-in voluntarily from across the broad spectrum of South African business and society. As has been observed, while self-regulation is encouraged, the regulators have chosen to enforce compliance of a number of the recommendations through mandatory legislation and regulations. Notwithstanding this, the code contained in King 2 is intended to remain self-regulatory in nature and the compliance with its recommendations will be reviewed by the King Committee from time to time.

17.5.3 Impact of King 2 and the Regulatory Environment

It would be unrealistic to anticipate that King 2 on its own, given its voluntary nature, would generate a significant transformation of corporate governance standards and practices in South Africa.

It was recognized that other interventions would be necessary to create the necessary climate for adherence to these guidelines, led by the regulators without unnecessarily imposing restrictive requirements that would inhibit commercial and entrepreneurial enterprise. This, clearly, represents a challenging dimension to corporate governance reform in any country, not just South Africa.

The King Committee identified 24 issues for regulatory or other official intervention. In response, legislation has been formulated with the intention of introducing rigorous provisions relating to delinquent directors and for the introduction of provisions that will give legal backing to accounting standards in South Africa.

King 2 came to the conclusion that insofar as principles of corporate governance co-exist with established legal principles, no new sanctions or remedies were necessary. Nevertheless, the King Committee recorded its concerns at the lack of enforcement of existing rules and regulations and has called for urgent dialogue between the business community and the authorities to enhance the resources and capacity of the State to handle more effectively breaches and offences of these rules and regulations. Given the many other priorities facing the economy and government, little progress has taken place in response to this call.

Of concern, certainly controversially in South Africa, has been the country's ranking under the so-called Corruption Perception Index developed by Transparency International which ranked South Africa 38 out of 91 countries. Steps at the official level continue to be taken to address this issue, resulting recently in new legislation with draconian consequences for acts of corruption. The main problem, as exists throughout the commercial sector, is the available capacity of the regulators and the judiciary to enforce this and a plethora of other important legislation.

Added to this, has been the introduction of advanced legislation regulating money laundering and other similar activities.

More recently, an interesting dimension to corporate governance in South Africa has been the growing number of South African companies that have shifted their stock exchange listings to a foreign bourse – primarily London and New York. This has had positive spill-over effects in the domestic environment.

Through an active and free media, corporate governance has been closely observed by the press and has given considerable attention to the conduct of directors, boards and companies that has in turn stimulated a level of shareholder activism not previously observed in the South African market. Nonetheless, the level of public activity of institutional investors remains low key despite some well publicized events of poor governance.

King 2 made a number of recommendations, among which included public disclosure by institutions of their voting policies and decisions, but little apparent response has been noted to date. Another area identified by the King Committee for attention, was the role of pension and retirement fund trustees and their own obligations in this regard but again little response has taken place thus far. It is in this area, apparently, that international investors are most concerned in relation to the governance environment in South Africa.

Notwithstanding these various issues, the regulators have responded in various ways:

- The JSE comprehensively revised and updated its listing require-ments in line with international standards. A number of important changes had been made to the South African Companies Act as a result of the recommendations contained in the first King Report, new insider trading regulations had been introduced, public sector finance reporting and accountability had been significantly strengthened, and a range of other legislation addressing social and labour priorities was increasingly impacting on existing governance standards and practices.

  The JSE listing rules were again comprehensively updated (for the third time in seven years) to incorporate certain elements of King 2 as mandatory requirements for quoted companies. The JSE continues to enforce its existing requirement for companies to 'comply or explain' their adoption of the King 2 guidelines.

- The banking regulator has introduced, arguably, extremely rigor-ous provisions around director accountability in amendments to the Banks Act that reflect a number of principles enshrined in King II. Greater powers have been conferred on the banking regulator to intervene on matters such as director and executive appointments.

- The FSB continues to give attention to enhancing the financial mar-kets legislation that falls under its supervision, embracing a num-ber of the King 2 guidelines. It is also reviewing a number of pieces of securities legislation, including the Insider Trading Act and Stock Exchanges Control Act, to give more integrated consistency to these provisions and with enhanced enforcement powers.

- The Protocol for State-owned Enterprises on Corporate Governance was comprehensively updated in line with King 2 and adopted by Cabinet in 2003, which forms the basis of corporate governance standards at all levels of public sector institutions and agencies. This supplements the already onerous requirements of the Public Finance Management Act and updated National Treasury Regulations (to align with King 2).

- A formal review of the existing corporate laws in South Africa is in the process of being commissioned by government and a strong foundation for this review will rest on the recommendations and guidelines contained in King 2, taken against international developments as well.

● A major response in all of this to the King 2 guidelines, has been the surge in director development and corporate governance training led by the IoD, private consultants, large auditing and accounting firms, and higher education institutions including business schools. Interactive e-learning courses on corporate governance have also been developed in order to make specialized education on this topic accessible to many more people.

17.6   Disclosure and Transparency

Accounting statements comply with generally accepted accounting practice (GAAP) issued by the accounting profession. JSE listing requirements specify compliance with IFRS but lack legal backing. An interim oversight body has been set up by the JSE to enforce compliance with GAAP.

With regards to annual independent audit, there is no statutory definition of independence and the same auditor sometimes performs internal and external audit functions for the same company. The fair and timely dissemination of information is largely observed and the Companies Act has been amended to permit electronic distribution of full annual statements, where shareholders consent.

There are no specific Listing Requirements to disclose material foreseeable risk factors but King 2 recommends that boards undertake annual formal risk assessments. The accuracy of ultimate beneficial ownership is difficult to verify. Under the structure of the dematerialized share registration system (STRATE) of the Companies Act, each director must issue a declaration regarding conflict of interest every year, and King 2 has highlighted practices to make this more effective.

17.7   Shareholder Rights and Stakeholder Relations

17.7.1   Rights of Shareholders

Basic shareholder rights are observed in South Africa, although share registration processes are inefficient. Holders of ordinary shares may attend/vote at the Annual General Meeting (AGM) but often are passive and do not. The rights of shareholders to participate in fundamental decisions are largely observed under the Companies Act. The Companies Act provides that shareholders may appoint proxies and unless the articles provide it, proxies cannot vote by a show of hands. Electronic voting is not currently permitted.

Share class information is disclosed in the annual report. With regards to control arrangements, directors may not frustrate an offer without shareholder approval and it is believed that some companies have golden parachutes or poison pill provisions.

Institutional investors are apathetic in respect to voting. They tend not to vote or participate in shareholder meetings or do not disclose voting policies notwithstanding King 2 recommendations in this regard.

17.7.2   Equitable Treatment of Shareholders

The principle that all shareholders should be treated equally is largely observed. Differentiated voting rights are prohibited for companies listed on the JSEs. Nominees or custodians are used extensively and the dissemination of relevant documentation to clients is not always ensured. Insider trading is prohibited in South Africa under the Insider Trading Act (1998). The enforcement of the law in the area of disclosure of interests of board members in transactions affecting the company is lax because the Registrar of Companies does not have the necessary resources.

17.7.3   Role of Stakeholders

Stakeholder rights are observed in South Africa with laws providing for affirmative action, employee skill development, and prevention of discrimination and harassment. Laws concerning redress for the violation of rights in court with appeal to the Compensation Commissioner are strongly observed. With regards to enhancing the performance of stakeholders, most employees participate in share incentive schemes etc provided at the firm's discretion and usually subject to shareholder approval. Laws and listing rules provide the right to access relevant information.

17.8 Director Development Activity

Director development and corporate governance training and development initiatives have been widely introduced by higher education institutions, large auditing and accounting firms, and the Institute of Directors Southern Africa in order to raise the awareness and understanding of corporate governance principles. All of the largest South African universities and major technical colleges have incorporated corporate governance education as part of the auditing and accounting, law or higher business management degrees and diplomas and some offer specialized corporate governance postgraduate qualifications.

Interactive e-learning courses on corporate governance have also been developed in order to make specialized education on this topic accessible to many more people.

The second King Report on Corporate Governance for South Africa (2002) stated that:

> *New directors appointed to the board should be made familiar with the company's operations, senior management and its business environment, be made aware of their fiduciary duties and responsibilities, and of the board's and chairperson's expectations. Since their responsibility carries with it significant personal liability, new directors with no board experience should receive the relevant education and development.*

In order to increase the knowledge and skills of directors in Southern Africa, the IoD initiated a Centre for Directorship and Corporate Governance at the beginning of 2001. The main thrust of the Centre is the One-Day Director Development Overview Programme run on a monthly basis throughout South Africa and neighbouring countries. It is offered to both the private and public sectors and is not exclusive to IoD members.

The course starts by dealing with the overall background to corporate governance both locally and internationally and provides an in-depth insight into the latest King Report. It then continues by addressing issues surrounding boards and directors, detailing the legal position of the board, and takes into account the board's construction, balance and collective responsibilities to the organization, the shareowners and all stakeholders. The appraisal and evaluation of the board committees and individual directors are also highlighted. Other issues covered are risk management and internal controls, accounting and auditing.

17.9   Useful Contacts

- Chamber of Mines – www.bullion.org.za
- Department of Trade and Industry South Africa – www.dti. gov.za
- Financial Services Board – www.fsb.co.za
- Institute of Chartered Secretaries and Administrators South Africa – www.icsa.co.za
- Institute of Directors in Southern Africa – www.iodsa.co.za
- JSE Securities Exchange South Africa – www.jse.co.za
- National African Federated Chamber of Commerce – www.nafcoc. org.za
- SA Reserve Bank – www.reservebank.co.za
- South African Chamber of Business – www.sacob.co.za
- South African Excellence Foundation – www.saef.co.za
- South Africa Institute of Chartered Accountants – www.saica. co.za

17.10   Further Reading

Deutsche Bank Securities Inc (2002) *Global Corporate Governance: Valuing corporate governance in South Africa*

Global Corporate Governance Forum (2003) *Presentation to the High Level Working Meeting and Consultation on the OECD Principles of Corporate Governance*, Philip Armstrong

Institute of International Finance, Inc (2003) *Corporate Governance in South Africa: An investor perspective*, IIF Equity Advisory Group

King Committee (1994) *The King Report on Corporate Governance for South Africa*, Institute of Directors in Southern Africa

King Committee (2002) *The King Report on Corporate Governance for South Africa (2)*, Institute of Directors in Southern Africa

Malherbe, S and Segal, N (2003) *South Africa: After Apartheid*, CIPE/OECD

United Nations Conference on Trade and Development (2002) *World Investment Report 2002*, United Nations, New York and Geneva

World Bank (2003) *Report on the Observance of Standards and Codes (ROSC); Corporate Governance Country Assessment: Republic of South Africa*, July 2003, World Bank, Washington

World Bank (2003) *Report on the Observance of Standards and Codes (ROSC); South Africa: Accounting and Auditing*, April 2003, World Bank, Washington

18

Sri Lanka

Table 18.1

Population	19.3 million (2003)
Gross National Income (GNI)	US $18.7 billion (2003)
GNI per capita	US $947 (2003)
Number of registered companies	40,000
Number of companies listed on the stock exchange	244 (Colombo)
Market capitalization	US $2.77 billion (2003)
Key corporate laws	● Sri Lanka Accounting and Auditing Standards Act No. 15 (1995)
	● The Companies Act of Sri Lanka (1982)
Key corporate governance codes	● Code of Best Practice (1997)
	● Code of Best Practice for Audit Committees (2002)
	● Code of Best Practice on Corporate Governance (2003)

18.1 Corporate Structure and Ownership

While there is a prevalence of unlimited partnerships and sole proprietorships in Sri Lanka, many of the small and medium enterprises
trade as limited liability entities.

There are 244 public listed companies on the Colombo Stock Exchange (CSE), with a cumulative market capitalization of US $2.77 billion as at 31 December 2003. All listed companies have to follow fairly comprehensive reporting and disclosure requirements. In addition, there are an increasing number of companies that make voluntary disclosures above the mandatory requirements, with some giving specific attention to triple bottom line reporting.

18.2 Legal Framework

18.2.1 The Companies Act (1982)

The Companies Act of Sri Lanka (1982) has many provisions that encourage good governance practices. Extensive sections of the Companies Act deal with:

- disclosures in the annual financial statements of companies;
- conduct of board proceedings;
- conduct of shareholders' meetings, particulars re. proxies;
- directors' reports;
- responsibilities of directors;
- auditors functions, etc.

The Companies Act also sets out the provisions relating to the winding up of companies, consolidation procedures and certain procedures and processes connected to borrowings by companies. The provisions may not be the most modern of provisions, but nevertheless they serve as a useful framework, which is reasonably formal and practical.

18.2.2 Sri Lanka Accounting and Auditing Standards Act No. 15 of 1995

In the late 1980s and early 1990s, Sri Lanka witnessed many failures of companies, especially finance companies. One of the underlying causes for these failures was the weak financial reporting and auditing structures at that time. As a response to this particular aspect of this wide issue, in 1992 the Institute of Chartered Accountants of Sri

Lanka (ICASL) took the preliminary steps to institutionalize a scheme whereby the application of Sri Lanka Accounting Standards could be monitored and enforced. To implement such a scheme, the ICASL set up a Task Force to look into all aspects relating to the enforcement of the Sri Lanka Accounting Standards, and the Task Force recommended the setting up of an 'Accounting Standards Monitoring Unit' which finally resulted in the government enacting the present Sri Lanka Accounting and Auditing Standards Act No. 15 of 1995.

The Act empowered the ICASL to adopt Sri Lanka Accounting Standards (SLAS) and Sri Lanka Auditing Standards (SLAuS) and provided for the setting up of an independent Sri Lanka Accounting and Auditing Standards Monitoring Board (SLAASMB). The Act also required all specified business enterprises (defined in terms of criteria based on turnover, share capital, net assets, number of employees, and loans taken from the banking system) to prepare their financial statements in accordance with SLAS and have their accounts audited in accordance with SLAuS.

The Sri Lanka Accounting and Auditing Standards Monitoring Board now monitors the compliance of Sri Lanka Accounting and Auditing Standards promulgated by the ICASL for specified enterprises as set out in the Act.

18.3 Legal, Regulatory and Institutional Bodies

18.3.1 The Institute of Chartered Accountants of Sri Lanka (ICASL)

In Sri Lanka the focus on corporate governance has been led by the Institute of Chartered Accountants of Sri Lanka who developed the first Code of Best Practice on Corporate Governance in 1997 and followed with a code of best practice on Audit Committees in 2002 and a revised Code of Best Practice on Corporate Governance in late 2003. Further, a Task Force set up under ICASL recommended the setting up of the 'Accounting Standards Monitoring Unit' which finally resulted in the government enacting the present Sri Lanka Accounting and Auditing Standards Act No. 15 of 1995.

Another significant initiative that was taken by the ICASL was the setting up of an Urgent Issues Task Force (UITF) in 1993 with a mandate to provide clarification and interpretation of the Sri Lanka

Accounting and Auditing Standards. Today, the UITF makes regular rulings at the request of corporates, auditors, and interested parties, and is perceived by the business and financial community as a useful body in promoting the understanding and application of the Sri Lanka Accounting and Auditing Standards. Its rulings are accepted as quasi-Standards, particularly where the Standard itself is not clear on a particular issue.

18.3.2 The Registrar of Companies (ROC)

The ROC in Sri Lanka has traditionally been perceived as a typical governmental bureaucratic institution. However, it has recently undergone a considerable reorganization and is now generally considered to be responsive. Technological developments have assisted in improving ROC's function as a quasi-judicial institution and have had an impact of enhancing the overall governance in the corporate sector.

18.3.3 The Securities and Exchange Commission of Sri Lanka (SEC)

The Securities and Exchange Commission of Sri Lanka was established through an Act of Parliament No. 36 of 1987. The Commission became quite active from the early 1990s and, since then, has been playing a leading role in financial reporting issues and the development and regulation of the capital market in Sri Lanka. The Commission was instrumental in initiating many innovations such as the setting up of the Central Depository System, the formulation of the Mergers and Takeovers Code, and the implementation of laws relating to insider trading. Today the Securities Exchange Commission possesses a team of highly skilled professionals who have been trained in gathering and analysing market information, keeping abreast of worldwide developments and enforcing the implementation of the provisions contained in the SEC Act and Regulations.

18.3.4 The Colombo Stock Exchange (CSE)

The Colombo Stock Exchange was established over a century ago. It is the only 'market' that is available for the trading of listed securities in Sri Lanka. It has comprehensive procedures benchmarked to international standards in dealing with initial public offerings, mergers and takeovers, disclosure, related party, insider dealing etc.

In that context, the Central Bank by its supervisory function helps to improve the overall corporate governance procedures and practices in a key and important sector, which has a tremendous impact upon the economy of the nation.

18.3.5 The Ceylon Chamber of Commerce (CCC)

In 2001/02, the CCC prepared and issued a booklet titled 'Corporate Governance'. This publication codified the key corporate governance initiatives, which are considered desirable for Sri Lanka, and has been useful in promoting corporate governance in Sri Lanka. In addition to this publication, the CCC has consistently promoted good corporate governance among its members.

18.3.6 Institute of Chartered Secretaries and Administrators (ICSA)

ICSA in Sri Lanka has published a *Handbook on Corporate Governance*. This handbook contains detailed principles and guidelines to best practices in Sri Lanka. This booklet serves as a useful explanatory note to those who are involved in promoting and practising corporate governance.

18.3.7 The National Task Force on Corporate Governance

In December 2001, a Task Force on Corporate Governance in Sri Lanka was set up under the facilitation and auspices of the Institute of Chartered Secretaries and Administrators of Sri Lanka. This Task Force, which is comprised of many eminent persons in the business, professional, banking, marketing and regulatory fields, has been driving corporate governance forward in Sri Lanka since its formation. It has also been in close contact with the Commonwealth Association of Corporate Governance. This group plays an important role in creating awareness as well as promoting good governance practices in the country.

18.3.8 Sri Lanka Institute of Directors (SLID)

The formation of the Sri Lanka Institute of Directors is a recent initiative, which has brought together a large number of company directors who have been actively focusing on administration and governance issues. The meetings of the Institute are held on a regular basis and methods of improving governance in their own organizations are discussed.

18.4 Board Structure

Many listed companies follow a unitary board structure with a mix of non-executive and executive directors and increasingly many are practising the separation of the roles of chairman and chief executive.

In an empirical study of the corporate governance practices in Sri Lanka, conducted in September 2002 and involving a representative sample of the listed companies in the CSE, the following results were obtained:

Separate chairman and chief executive	62%
Separate director responsible for finance	18%
Over 40% of the board being non-executive directors	68%
Established Audit Committee	54%
Established Remuneration Committee	32%

18.4.1 Non-Executive Directorships

Many non-executive directors are retired 'eminent persons' who are either ceremoniously adorning boards, or being rewarded with directorships because of some past favour he or she had rendered to the chief executive. Some non-executive directors were even referred to as being 'fat, dumb and comfortable'. Board meetings were usually 'cakes and tea' affairs with board members usually jostling amongst themselves to endorse whatever decisions the chairman or chief executive wished to take, as fast as possible.

Fortunately, events and initiatives of the recent past are changing this situation to some extent. Today's shareholders, especially some of the institutional shareholders and some rather vociferous minority shareholders, are concerned about directors' relationships with management and they are now demanding that non-executive directors really earn their fees. When companies decline, many non-executive directors are being held liable for *all* of the company's actions. Judges and regulators are also becoming tougher. These developments have resulted in creating a marked change in the overall functioning of non-executive directors. So much so, that some individuals are nervous about taking positions as directors and are even shying away from being directors. Some others may, however, say that it is a case of 'when the going gets tough, the not-so-tough run away'.

The general perception, however, seems to be that this attitudinal shift has been a good one for the companies in Sri Lanka and should be sustained and further encouraged.

18.5 Codes, Standards and Good Practice Guidelines

Corporate governance practice in Sri Lanka is influenced by a number of codes. They are highlighted below.

18.5.1 The Code of Best Practice by the Institute of Chartered Accountants of Sri Lanka (ICASL)

The first real effort at codifying the principles of corporate governance in a structured manner in Sri Lanka was in 1996 when the Council of the Institute of Chartered Accountants of Sri Lanka decided to set up a Committee to make recommendations on matters relating to Financial Aspects of Corporate Governance.

The Committee categorized their final recommendations for implementation through the following mechanisms:

a) possible amendments to the Securities and Exchange Commission Act;

b) possible amendments to the rules and regulations of the Colombo Stock Exchange;

c) possible amendments to the Companies Act;

d) possible amendments to the ICASL Act;

e) a Code of Best Practice, as applicable to all listed companies.

In addition, the Committee Report made a useful observation that the corporate regulatory system in Sri Lanka had many involved regulatory and semi-regulatory organizations, sometimes working in rather rigid, watertight compartments. These authorities were often seen to be performing overlapping functions and therefore an attempt to infuse an element of congruence within their respective activities seemed also to be necessary. The ICASL Committee has been hopeful that the setting out of the Code of Best Practice would lead to a greater degree of congruence and understanding within the above-stated organizations as well.

When carrying out an overview of corporate governance practices in any particular corporate governance regime, it is useful to examine such provisions against governance practices, which are considered to be best international practices. In this respect the corporate governance practices in place in Sri Lanka are set out against the principles recommended by the Organization for Economic Cooperation and Development (OECD) as follows:

18.5.2 Disclosure and Transparency

The corporate governance framework should ensure that timely and accurate disclosure is made on all material matters regarding the corporation, including the financial situation, performance, ownership, and governance of the company.

In Sri Lanka disclosure should include, but not be limited to:

a) *The financing and operating results of the company* – Financial statements must be prepared in accordance with Companies Act No. 17 and the SL Accounting Standards.

b) *Company objectives* – Concise statements must be provided as per the ICASL recommendations.

c) *Members of the board and key executives and their remuneration* – The annual report should contain a statement of remuneration policy along with the identification of CEO, non-executive directors etc.

d) *Material foreseeable risk factors* – Concise statements must be provided as per the ICASL recommendations.

e) *Governance structures and policies* – Directors should state the extent of compliance with the ICASL Code of Best Practice.

f) *Information should be prepared, audited and disclosed with the highest quality standards* – Directors are required to confirm that applicable SL Accounting Standards have been followed.

g) *Annual audit should be conducted by an independent auditor* – Requirement of SL Accounting Standards.

18.5.3   The Responsibilities of the Board

The corporate governance framework should ensure the strategic guidance of the company, the effective monitoring of management by the board, and the board's accountability to the company and the shareholders.

In Sri Lanka the responsibilities of the board include:

a) *Acting fully informed with due diligence with the best interests of the company and shareholders* – The ICASL recommends that external legal and financial advice be sought at the company's expense.

b) *Treating shareholders fairly* – There should be a statement of equitable treatment of shareholders.

c) *Ensuring compliance of applicable laws and take into account the interests of the shareholders* – The board should issue a compliance report setting out the extent that statutory payments have been made.

d) *Selecting, compensating, monitoring, replacing key executives and overseeing succession planning* – Appointment of a remuneration committee, appointment of a nomination committee, reviewing and appraising the performance of the board and CEO annually.

e) *Monitoring and managing potential conflicts of interest* – Appointment of an audit committee, internal control statement, declaration of all material contacts involving the company and refraining from voting in materially interested matters.

f) *Ensuring the integrity of the corporation's accounting and financial reporting systems* – Finance function should be the responsibility of a specific board director, statement of directors' responsibility for financial statements, periodical rotation of audit partners, statement of going concern.

g) *Monitoring the effectiveness of governance practices* – Corporate governance report.

h) *Exercise objective judgement of corporate affairs* – Separation of chairman and CEO.

18.5.4   The Rights of Shareholders

The corporate governance framework should protect shareholders' rights.

In Sri Lanka this includes:

a) While the OECD Guidelines list a number of basic shareholders' rights, the Sri Lankan guidelines only address the right to attend AGMs and the election of directors.

b) *Extraordinary transactions* – Directors should disclose all proposed corporate transactions which, if entered into, would materially alter/vary the company's net asset base.

c) Issues such as the opportunity for shareholders to ask questions of the board and place items on the agenda, ability to vote in person or in absentia are not addressed formally in the Sri Lankan guidelines, but are widely practised.

18.5.5 The Equitable Treatment of Shareholders

The corporate governance framework should ensure the equitable treatment of all shareholders, including minority and foreign shareholders. All shareholders should have the opportunity to obtain effective redress for violation of their rights.

The Sri Lankan Corporate Governance guidelines do not address the above OECD principle. While some companies may practise a mixture of these guidelines it is not done in a formal and regulated manner.

18.5.6 The Role of Stakeholders in Corporate Governance

The corporate governance framework should recognize the rights of stakeholders in creating wealth, jobs, and the sustainability of financially sound enterprises.

The Sri Lankan Corporate Governance guidelines do not address the above OECD principle. While some of companies may practise a mixture of these guidelines it is not done in a formal and regulated manner.

18.6 Disclosure and Transparency

There are approximately 40,000 registered companies in Sri Lanka. Most take the form of private limited liability companies and a significant number of them are family owned.

18.6.1 Audit

Over the past two decades or so, there has been a growing concern building up in the minds of investors about the quality and independence of the services rendered by auditors, and many auditors have been sued for large sums of money for negligence, connivance and fraud. These reactions have compelled auditors to take their duties and responsibilities more seriously and as a result the quality of the audits has improved.

The advent of Audit Committees also helped to improve the quality of the audit. Sri Lanka's Code of Best Practice, and the Code of Best Practice on Audit Committees issued by the ICASL in May 2002 that followed it, were initiatives that focused on the need to improve the quality of the audit.

However, the issue also surfaces as to whether audits are becoming so onerous today that many practitioners are gradually moving away from such services. If that happens, the companies will face a difficult issue, ie the non-availability of competent auditors, which may be another hindrance to achieving good corporate governance.

At the same time, many commentators believe that auditors are getting too cosy with their clients.

In Sri Lanka, the introduction of the Sri Lanka Accounting and Auditing Standards Monitoring Board Act in 1995 added a new dimension to this vexed issue about ensuring compliance with Sri Lanka Accounting and Auditing Standards in the preparation and audit of financial statements by specified business entities (SBEs). The Act requires SBEs to prepare their financial statements in accordance with Sri Lanka Accounting Standards. The Act empowers the Monitoring Board to take various measures to ensure compliance, and penalties specified for defaulters include heavy fines and even imprisonment. These stringent provisions have had an impact on the financial reporting standards and audit quality, and this initiative of the SLAASMB could perhaps be described as one of the high points in the Sri Lankan corporate governance landscape.

18.6.2 Reporting and Compliance

Over the past three or four years, many corporate entities proudly state in their annual reports that they are complying with a wide variety of corporate governance practices. They also state very diligently that, as good corporate citizens, they adhere to some Code of Best Practice or another. These statements are obviously very comforting to the shareholders and the community of investors, who are naturally interested as to how efficiently and effectively their companies are being managed, operated and governed.

In the course of the empirical study on corporate governance practices in Sri Lanka carried out in September 2002, one of the surprising findings was that there was insufficient evidence to confirm that the corporate governance practices that corporate entities said publicly that they were following were in fact being practised. In general, many of the statements were grossly exaggerated and/or largely unsubstantiated.

This outcome raises a very significant issue – when companies make 'price sensitive' statements and such claims are not subjected to any review as to their veracity, is the corporate community inadvertently exposing itself to a dangerous abuse of the system?

The Sri Lankan survey identified that a number of Sri Lankan companies assessed during the survey were selecting extracts from the Institute of Chartered Accountants of Sri Lanka (ICASL) Code of Best Practice or the Cadbury Guidelines without a clear reference to the rest of these Reports. There was no clear disclosure as to how those guidelines were actually being followed. A number of relatively smaller companies reported on certain aspects of corporate governance within their corporate governance reports or directors' reports on an ad hoc basis and it seemed that they were merely mimicking the reports of others. Some of the larger companies obtained advice from specialized annual report production firms and seemed to be following a set template with a pre-configured checklist of reporting topics. All in all, the survey concluded that many companies were blindly following a framework or code on corporate governance without clearly comprehending the spirit in which it had been established.

This unsatisfactory situation is further compounded by the fact that an established mechanism of independently verifying the actual degree of compliance by different companies with the various Best Practice recommendations is not in place in Sri Lanka. For example, a company that has an audit committee that meets once a year for 15 minutes (perhaps just for the sake of meeting), and a company that has an audit committee with a number of non-executive directors, meeting once a month for a comprehensive review, would both be able to technically and truthfully disclose as having working audit committees. It is even possible that this wide latitude available in describing their practices has led some companies to have a somewhat lacklustre attitude towards corporate governance disclosures. As one company quite casually remarked in their annual report, 'it is not mandatory to disclose corporate governance practices'. However, this kind of feeling is obviously not surprising because in actual practice there is no real onus on the companies to disclose their corporate governance practices in a credible environment and even it they were to do so, they know it could be done by using a varied number of measures which result in it being difficult or even impossible for anyone to make useful inferences and comparisons.

18.6.3   Independent Regulators

An issue that is also quite pertinent in Sri Lanka is the quality, integrity and independence of regulators. Especially in smaller economies, 'old boys' clubs' have taken root where individuals with obvious conflicts of interest sit on commissions, supervisory bodies and other regulatory authorities. Such blatant disregard of good governance principles hardly promotes confidence, and should be exposed and discouraged at every turn.

In Sri Lanka there is a plethora of regulators in many forms. There are many instances of conflict of interest, arrogant or arbitrary behaviour, poor understanding of issues, obvious bias and/or painful bureaucratic procedures. These shortcomings very often make those institutions less credible and effective. Therefore not only is it necessary to head-hunt outstanding persons to fill regulatory roles and invite them to carry out the tasks ahead with integrity and efficiency, but also to restore confidence in the regulatory system by ensuring that there is consistency in the decision-making processes.

18.7   Shareholder Rights and Stakeholder Relations

18.7.1   Institutional Investors

In Sri Lanka institutional investors are today playing a significant role in capital market activity. At the same time, however, their influence over corporate activity and in implementing good corporate governance practices, unfortunately, has not been correspondingly proportionate or encouraging. Other than a few institutional investors and mutual funds, which have been somewhat insistent about good governance practices, many have passively watched the emerging scenario without taking a proactive role to drive companies towards better governance practices. Initiatives involving good corporate governance practices have been driven in Sri Lanka mainly by the regulators and quasi-regulators (such as the ICASL). It is only during the past one or two years that the investor community has been showing some interest in these issues.

18.7.2 Stakeholders

There are very few governance policies or practices in Sri Lanka which address the concerns of stakeholders. While many practices are designed from the point of view of safeguarding corporate stakeholders, there appear to be few which are to protect the environmental, national and local communities, employers, customers, suppliers and contractors. This wide gap is being felt by many, and today several civil groups are questioning the validity of the governance practices as they exist today.

18.8 Director Development Activity

The knowledge and appreciation of governance practices is very limited amongst many directors. Unfortunately, there are very few who could train such directors either! For example, in the case of the implementation of practices such as independent board appraisals, CEO appraisals, CEO succession, nominating committee processes, remuneration committee processes, etc, many directors are not sure as to how those processes could be worked or even how they should work.

It is therefore very necessary that experts in these fields start to offer specialized services to assist boards to carry out such appraisals as well as to develop functional and practical methods and models for the successful implementation of various governance procedures, processes, etc.

18.9 Useful Contacts

- Central Bank of Sri Lanka (CB) – www.lanka.net/centralbank
- Ceylon Chamber of Commerce – www.chamber.lk

- Colombo Stock Exchange – www.cse.lk
- Institute of Chartered Accountants of Sri Lanka – www.icasrilanka. com
- Institute of Chartered Secretaries and Administrators (ICSA) – www.icsa.org.uk
- Registrar of Companies – www.drc.gov.lk
- Securities and Exchange Commission of Sri Lanka – www.sec. gov.lk
- Sri Lanka Accounting and Auditing Standards Board – www.ped. gov.lk
- Sri Lanka Institute of Directors (SLID) – www.lanka.net.slid

18.10   Further Reading

The Institute of Chartered Accountants of Sri Lanka (ICASL) (1997) *Code of Best Practice: Report to the committee to make recommendations on matters relating to financial aspects of corporate governance* (December 1997)

The ICASL Code of Best Practice on Audit Committees (2002)

The ICASL Code of Best Practice on Corporate Governance (2003)

19

Turkey

Table 19.1

Population	65 million
Gross National Income (GNI)	US $240 billion
GNP per capita	US $2584
Total number of companies	85,000 joint stock companies, 634 public companies
Number of companies listed on the stock exchange	Istanbul Stock Exchange, 310 (including temporarily delisted companies)
Market capitalization	US $74 billion (2004 April)
Key corporate laws	• Capital Markets Law (1981)
	• Commercial Code (1956)
Key corporate governance codes	• Corporate Governance Principles (2003)
	• TUSIAD Corporate Governance Code of Best Practice, Composition and Functioning of Board of Directors (2002)

19.1 Corporate Structure and Ownership

The Turkish corporate governance system is an 'insider system'. Ultimate owners of listed companies are individual family members who exercise control through pyramidal structures and/or inter-company shareholdings. Families, directly or indirectly, own 75 per cent of all companies and maintain majority control. In 2000, families ultimately controlled 198 of the 257 listed companies with an average 53.8 per cent holding of the equity, although the pyramidal structures meant that average direct ownership was only 27.1 per cent.

Business in Turkey is organized into group structures. Corporations are affiliated with each other around a holding company whose purpose is to hold stock of other companies and manage them. Holding companies are the most significant majority shareholders of Turkish listed companies. All major groups also have a bank that is ultimately owned and controlled by the same family.

19.1.1   Inward Investment

In its long march for integration with Europe, Turkey made substantial improvements to achieve macroeconomic stability by:

- restructuring and monitoring of the financial industry;
- establishing independence of the Central Bank;
- deregulating the monopolized sectors and reducing the role of state in economy; and
- implementing a tight fiscal policy finally taking double-digit inflation under control.

As a result, higher than expected growth rates were recorded during 2003, but they fell short of the required growth rates if Turkey were to close the income gap with the EU. Turkey needs accelerated entry of foreign capital to reach its potential growth rate of 7–8 per cent. Macroeconomic instability, accompanied by corrupt business practices and highly concentrated family ownership, was the most important factor that kept Turkey off investors' radar screens, with the lowest FDI flows compared to its peers for the past few decades.

One of the undertakings to improve the investment climate in Turkey was the development of the Capital Markets Board's Corporate Governance Principles which were preceded by substantial improvements in the regulatory framework in the areas of accounting and audit as well as in protecting investors and enforcing the rules. The Principles, which borrow from the US Sarbanes–Oxley Act, set very high standards for publicly traded Turkish companies. The Principles are voluntary but companies are required to 'comply or explain'. If the efforts of the government to converge Turkey's institutions with Europe are to continue, the rate of injection of low-cost capital to Turkish economy in the form of FDI is likely to increase and help fuel the growth Turkey desperately needs.

19.2 Legal Framework

Turkey is a civil law country in the French tradition. One of the building blocks of the corporate governance legislative framework, the Commercial Code (CC), was originally taken from France in 1850. The Commercial Code underwent various revisions. The 1956 version, with its evidently eclectic nature, forms the basis of equity contracts and provides the general legal framework for incorporation, general assemblies, ownership rights and the definition of shares and bonds and their issuance. It is important to note that the fundamental document governing the rights of shareholders is the company's articles of association. The commercial code is currently undergoing a maor revision in persuit of harmonization with the EU legislation and the capital market.

The Commercial Code does not impose limits on the extent to which privileges may be granted. As a consequence, out of 30 companies listed on the Istanbul Stock Exchange (ISE), 11 have different classes of shares with multiple voting rights and variations for dividend entitlement. Contrary to the Commercial Code, Capital Market Law (CML) borrows from the Anglo-Saxon legal system. It provides the legislative framework for the securities market activities and establishes the Capital Markets Board (CMB).

According to the CML, insider trading, the dissemination of misleading or false information and manipulative practices are criminal offences punishable by fines and imprisonment. It is believed that a high percentage of suspected cases of insider trading and manipulative practices are not prosecuted owing to the difficulties in proof given the lack of effective surveillance, technical capacity, and enforcement. The most important flaw of the legal system is weak enforcement. The Capital Market Board of Turkey has recently launched a major technical infrastructure project which will drastically change its monitoring capabilities.

19.3 Legal, Regulatory and Institutional Bodies

19.3.1 Capital Markets Board (CMB)

The CMB develops, regulates and supervises Turkey's securities markets under the authority of a State Minister. It drafts statutory laws to be submitted to parliament for approval and issues rules of regulations. These rules require approval of the related ministry before they are issued.

19.3.2 Istanbul Stock Exchange (ISE)

The ISE is a public, non-profit organization established in its present state in 1986. It does not have a share capital, but it owns its assets and is financially independent. The ISE's members are brokerage houses and banks and it is governed by a General Assembly, a board of directors, auditing and other committees, and the chairman's office. The CMB closely supervises the exchange. The ISE has recently announced plans to float itself on the ISE in 2004.

19.3.3 Corporate Governance Forum of Turkey and The Corporate Governance Association of Turkey

Professional bodies do not have self-regulatory powers. There are a few NGOs promoting good governance and ethical behaviour, such as Corporate Governance Forum of Turkey (CGFT) and Corporate Governance Association of Turkey.

The Corporate Governance Forum of Turkey was founded by Sabanci University (SU) and the Turkish Industrialists' and Businessmen's Association (TUSIAD). Its mission is 'to support improvement of corporate governance practices and legal and institutional framework in Turkey through research and educational programmes as well as to be actively involved in advocacy of good corporate governance'.

19.3.4 Banking Regulation and Supervision Agency (BRSA)

The BRSA, in addition to the Capital Markets Board, defines accounting standards in Turkey for the banking sector. The BRSA issued a completely new set of standards to converge local accounting standards with International Financial Reporting Standards (IFRS) with effect from July 2002.

19.3.5   Turkish Industrialists' and Businessmen's Association (TUSIAD)

Founded in 1971, the Turkish Industrialists' and Businessmen's Association (TUSIAD) is an independent, non-governmental organization dedicated to promoting public welfare through private enterprise. TUSIAD supports independent research and policy discussions on important social and economic issues in Turkey and abroad. Much like the US Business Roundtable, TUSIAD is comprised of the CEOs and executives of the major industrial and service companies in Turkey, including those that are among global Fortune 500 companies.

19.4   Board Structure

According to the Commercial Code, companies have unitary boards comprising at least three directors appointed for three years. The board has to meet at least once a month, although the members may agree not to meet physically. Board members have to be shareholders or represent legal entities that are shareholders. There are no specified qualifications for the directors other than minimum legal qualifications. Directors are liable to the company and they have a general duty of due diligence, care and loyalty. The board can delegate its powers to executives. Those executives with 'signatory rights' and shadow directors are personally liable.

The boards are usually formed of owners and/or their family members and/or trusted advisers. In case of holdings, which are usually structured in business groups consisting of companies operating in the same industry, holding representatives sit on the board of group companies. In 80 per cent of the boardrooms of the listed companies, at least one board member is a family representative and 30 per cent are direct shareholders. Most members and executives are family associates.

In more institutionalized groups, anecdotal evidence suggests the existence of shadow directors, whereas the statutory boards rubber-stamp the decisions already made by the family. Interlocking directorships between allied families further damages the 'independence' of the boards. The rate of cross-directorships in ISE listed companies in 2001 was 56 per cent.

Companies that had a separate chairman and CEO listed on the ISE amounted to 12.8 per cent, although such separation will not deliver the intended benefits if both the chairman and the CEO represent the controlling shareholders' interests and in some cases have the same family name.

Non-executive board positions are usually occupied by the holding employees, with the exception of some professional executives whose independence is also dubious. Non-executive directors are appointed on recommendation of the controlling shareholders and are replaced at their will. Nevertheless, a few companies with a significant foreign shareholdings have appointed independent board members. This structure has not yet proven to work in practice when and if conflict of interests may be observed.

Board committees are rare and individual remunerations are never disclosed. There are no requirements to form an independent compensation committee or a nominating committee; however, listed companies have to establish audit committees chaired by a non-executive Board member. The Capital Market Board also recommends that listed companies should establish a Corporate Governance Committee to oversee remuneration and nomination.

19.5 Codes, Standards and Good Practice Guidelines

TUSIAD was the first organization to issue a best practice code. A task force set up by TUSIAD consisting of representatives of member companies developed a Code of Best Practice focusing on the composition and functioning of the boards. A year after its publication, no members have yet openly declared their compliance or intentions to comply. TUSIAD also has a Code of Ethics which seems to be adopted by most members; however, there is no evidence of its actual implementation. Some individual companies or holdings have developed their own Codes but they are rarely disclosed as a part of statutory reporting.

The Capital Markets Board's Principles of Corporate Governance were developed by a committee consisting of CMB, ISE (Istanbul Stock Exchange) and CGFT (Corporate Governance Forum of Turkey) representatives. The draft was opened to public consultation and the final version was issued in July 2003. The demanding nature of the Code requires a broader framework of incentives and harmonization of the Commercial Code before it can be widely adopted by corporations.

The framework disclosed by the regulator foresees establishment of a separate index within ISE consisting of companies complying with the Principles. According to the public announcements of the CMB, compliance will be qualified by rating agencies whose operations will be regulated by the CMB. The Principles address shareholders' rights, public disclosure/transparency, stakeholders and the board of directors.

19.6 Disclosure and Transparency

Turkey's reporting and accounting standards for non-listed companies are far from providing the basis for accountability. First of all, there are no national accounting standards except a presentation format for tax purposes. The CMB sets accounting standards for publicly held companies, financial intermediaries, and institutional investors. The standards are in line with international accounting standards, with the exception of a lack of mandatory consolidation and inflation accounting which will be enforced in 2005. Nevertheless, 70 per cent of public listed companies have adopted IAS standards internally, but their disclosure is not a common practice. Publicly held companies are required to file financial reports with the ISE and the CMB on a quarterly basis. Ad hoc reporting requirements include changes in ownership or management; purchase, sale or lease of assets with a value above a certain threshold; changes in investments; ownership interests in other companies; managerial problems such as strikes or labour disputes; block sales; and unusual share price fluctuations. Companies comply with these disclosure requirements quite promptly. The ISE and the CMB have the power to issue private and public warnings, impose financial penalties or suspend trading in case of non-compliance. These powers are regularly exercised. The ISE may also decide to put companies on a 'watch list' for non-compliance.

Disclosure requirements for ownership are well established. The CMB and the ISE must be immediately notified of any change of ownership resulting in ownership of 1 per cent of the share capital by any acquirer or group of acquirers acting in concert who already hold 10 per cent or more of the share capital or of voting rights, or who cross the 10 per cent threshold upward or downward. The board and the management must comply with the 1 per cent disclosure rule. Directors must also inform the board of directors of any conflicts of interest between themselves or their relatives and the company and they may not participate in the deliberations of the board on issues where a conflict of interest is observed.

Under the CML, transfer pricing is forbidden in related party transactions, with penalties; however, the procedures to be followed and the type of disclosure required in related party transactions are not clearly specified. There is strong evidence that insider expropriation and violation of shareholder rights through related party transactions are common. Only the most serious cases are brought before the public prosecutor; however, the average time required for the courts to reach a verdict is about 18 months.

Publicly held companies are required to have their year-end and half-year results independently audited by CMB-certified auditors. Rotation of auditors every five years is mandatory. The CMB requires independent audits in public offerings and may require one in mergers and acquisition transactions. Auditors are liable to civil action if they mislead investors. The CMB's list of approved auditors is long, ranging from the 'big four' to small local companies of unknown track record. The CMB recently established an accounting standards board, and new regulations aiming to improve the effectiveness of independent audit have been enacted.

The statutory audit, whose function is to audit the company's accounts on behalf of the shareholders and ensure compliance with the law and the company's articles of association, does not seem to work effectively. Anecdotal evidence suggests that auditors are often employees of related companies and appointment of auditors has been regarded as a formality.

A new regulation requires authorized officers to sign off the financial statements.

19.7 Shareholder Rights and Stakeholder Relations

According to the provisions of the Commercial Code and the CML, minority shareholders representing 5 per cent (10 per cent for non-public companies) of the share capital of a publicly held company can:

- veto the release of management;
- demand that the company or the company's internal auditor take legal action against members of the board of directors;
- demand that a special controller be appointed;
- call an extraordinary General Assembly or add an item to the agenda; or
- demand postponement of the discussions on the balance sheet for one month.

Cumulative voting is also recognized by the Capital Markets Board, although the implementation requires a change in the Articles of Association of the company.

Foreign investors in non-public companies can participate in annual general meetings (AGMs) provided their shares are registered with the Foreign Investment General Directorate of the undersecretaries of the Treasury. Any non-resident shareholder holding 10 per cent or more of a publicly held company is required to notify the Foreign Investment General Directorate of its investment in order to participate in a general meeting of shareholders and use their votes.

According to the Code, AGMs must be convened by the board of directors within three months after the end of the accounting period, although in practice most AGMs take place two to three months later owing to the time needed to comply with the external audit requirement. The board of directors must submit the balance sheet and a summary of operations, as well as a report indicating the commercial, financial and economic situation of the company, and formulate a written proposal regarding dividend pay-out and reserves; every shareholder has the right to a copy of the financial statements upon request. Auditors or shareholders in a publicly held company representing at least 5 per cent of the share capital are also entitled to convene extraordinary general meetings.

Shareholder rights may not be altered without holding a meeting where shareholders holding at least half the share capital of the company are present and the majority of the shareholders present in such a meeting approve such a change. Founders and other shareholders desiring certain privileges may not vote during the discussions concerning the approval of these privileges. Shareholders who have taken part in the conduct of the business of the company are not entitled to vote on resolutions concerning the release of directors. This prohibition does not extend to auditors.

19.7.1 Stakeholders

Neither under the Commercial Code nor under the CML are there cited provisions with respect to the rights of employees, customers, suppliers, creditors and society as stakeholders or their relationship with the company; however, the recently issued Corporate Governance Principles of the CMB have strong recommendations for stakeholder-oriented governance. Nevertheless, the increased number of social responsibility theme-based public relations campaigns indicates that companies recognize the importance of the risks to their reputation associated with family-owned conglomerates. A growing number of 'green' NGOs are also likely to exert pressure on companies to adopt environmentally responsible business controls.

19.8 Director Development Activity

The pace of change in the corporate scene requires directors to be well and continuously informed. The only organization that offers director development courses and programmes is the Corporate Governance Forum of Turkey, co-founded by Sabanci University and the Turkish Industrialists' and Businessmen's Association in 2003. The Forum aims to:

- develop and offer training and education programmes for directors (board members) of joint stock corporations (Anonim Sirket) to help them appreciate the benefits of better corporate governance and understand the role and responsibilities of boards; and

- help develop and document professional standards, best practices and accreditation criteria for boards and board members.

Hosted by the Sabanci University, the Forum works closely with the UK's Institute of Directors and the Global Corporate Governance Forum to meet the training needs of Turkish boards.

A board training programme called 'Leaders of Corporate Governance' was launched in April 2004. The programme consists of a syllabus derived from the IoD's 'Company Direction Programme', adapted to Turkish business law and norms, and is delivered in a number of blocks, handling the core subjects of governance, law, strategy and finance. Initially, the programme is attendance only, with a view to developing some form of accreditation and assessment at a later date.

19.9   Useful Contacts

- Capital Markets Board (CMB) – www.spk.gov.tr

- Corporate Governance Forum of Turkey, Sabanci University, e-mail: cgft@sabanciuniv.edu

- Istanbul Stock Exchange (ISE) – www.ise.org

- Turkish Industrialists' and Businessmen's Association (TUSIAD) – www.tusiad.org

19.10   Further Reading

Ararat, M and Ugur, M (2003) Corporate Governance in Turkey: An Overview and Some Policy Recommendations, Corporate Governance, *International Journal of Business in Society*, **3** (1), download from www.corporatelibrary.com

Ararat, M (2004) Turkey, in ed G Dalls, *Governance and Risk*, McGraw Hill

Capital Markets Board of Turkey (2003) *Corporate Governance Principles*, Istanbul

Izmen, U (2003) Instituting Corporate Governance in Family Owned Firms in Turkey, *In Search of Good Directors, CIPE*, 2003

Taboglu, Esin (2002) *Corporate Governance Report*, download from www.taboglu.com

TUSIAD (2002) *Corporate Governance Code of Best Practice, Composition and Functioning of Board of Directors*, TUSIAD, Istanbul

World Bank (2000) *Report on the Observance of Standards and Codes (ROSC): Turkey*, World Bank, Washington

Part 3

Transition

20

Armenia

Table 20.1

Population	3.1 million (2002)
Gross National Income (GNI)	US $2.4 billion (2002)
GNI per capita	US $790 (2002)
Total number of companies	1,152 open joint stock companies (2002)
Number of companies listed on the stock exchange	129 (2002)
Key corporate laws	● Law on Joint Stock Companies (2001)
Key corporate governance codes	● The collection of rules regulating securities markets (2001)
	● The listing and de-listing rules of the Armenian Stock Exchange (2001)
	● Securities Market Regulation Law (2000)
	● Law on Accounting (2000)
	● Civil Code (1999)

20.1   Corporate Structure and Ownership

Armenian joint stock companies are either the product of the privatization process or newly established companies. There are two types of companies in Armenia:

- *Open joint stock companies.* There were 1,152 open joint stock companies in Armenia in 2002.

- *Closed joint stock companies.* Closed joint stock companies may not have more than 49 shareholders. If the number of shareholders of a closed joint company exceeds 49, the company must reorganize as an open joint stock company or reduce its shareholders to below 50 within one year. There were 3,109 closed joint stock companies in Armenia in 2002.

Many registered companies exist in name only. Many find that being an open joint stock company and listed on the Armenian Stock Exchange (which is the only stock exchange in the country) conveys no tangible benefit. They view the reporting requirements as onerous and costly, and the listing has not provided them with any increased access to capital or a clear view as to the tangible valuation of the companies. These companies are often operating at fractions of prior levels of activity, in struggling industrial sectors that are trying to reconstruct customer bases. They are often impaired by many of the obstacles that confront most Armenian companies, including:

- lack of access to working capital;

- transportation and logistical impairment arising from the blockade situation with neighbouring countries; and

- fragmented and non-empowered shareholder bases.

Many of these companies have stated that they see little benefit in continuing to exist as open joint stock companies and being listed on the Armenian Stock Exchange. They are exploring the process of 'taking the company private' by converting to 'closed' company status and de-listing from the stock exchange.

There is a high concentration of share ownership in Armenian joint stock companies. Most of the companies have a single controlling shareholder.

The shareholders of Armenian joint stock companies comprise:

- The State. Government ministries and state agencies are an extremely important shareholder in Armenian companies. In 2002, the state owned 100 per cent of 1,635 closed joint stock companies. In addition, the state possessed more than 50 per cent of the shares of 105 companies (out of a total of 129 joint stock companies) listed on the Armenian Stock Exchange.

- Armenian diaspora investment groups. These groups usually have a controlling position in companies.

- Local Armenian investment groups. These groups are normally holding companies.

- Foreign companies. Armenia has been attracting a small number of foreign companies that normally take a majority equity position in a local company.

- Managers and employees. As a result of the privatization process many shareholders are managers or employees.

Listed companies accounted for about 18 per cent of Armenian GDP in 2001 (OECD, 2003).

20.2 Legal Framework

The government of Armenia has been making some progress in several key areas of the corporate governance agenda. In particular, several core pieces of legislation were enacted, which included:

- The Civil Code (1999);

- The Securities Market Regulation Law (2000);

- The Law on Accounting (2000).

The Joint Stock Company Law (JSCL) is a key law that influences corporate governance practices in Armenia. The JSCL contains several fundamental provisions that support good corporate governance, including:

- the requirement that company managers must have less than half the seats on the company board;

- specific liability provisions for the board members and the company executives; and

- the requirement for independent audits for all open joint stock companies.

The strengths in the Joint Stock Company Law are undermined, however, by other weaknesses in the business environment and legal framework. For instance, with respect to liability for board members and company managers, the current legislation does not include a detailed description of specific roles and responsibilities of directors and managers, beyond the provision of official information. In the absence of such defined roles and responsibilities, it is difficult to determine the extent of liability of specific individuals.

Large transactions: The Joint Stock Company Law allows the company board to make decisions on the transfer of large parts of company assets without calling a shareholders' meeting. Up to 50 per cent of the total assets (book value) may be sold or transferred to other parties by a unanimous decision of the board. While the Law includes some mitigating provisions, such as identified procedures for determining asset values, international norms suggest that any transfer in excess of 25 per cent of the company's assets should require the approval of the shareholders.

Audit framework: The Joint Stock Company Law requires the shareholders' meeting to approve both the company's annual financial statements and the selection of an auditor. However, the Law authorizes the company board to determine the compensation level for the auditor. Because the quality of work undertaken by an external auditor may be affected by the allocated compensation level, it creates a possibility for the board to manipulate the quality of the audit. In Armenia, such a risk may be significant, given the current weaknesses of the auditing profession. Thus, certain commentators suggest that it is important to amend the Law and transfer the authority over auditor compensation to the shareholders' meeting.

The current legal framework makes outside investments in existing corporations complicated for investors, mainly because it over-regulates the investment process. It is a potential barrier for investments and also undermines the efficiency of capital market mechanisms (eg it would reduce the threat of a takeover). The emerging concentrated forms of control do not facilitate the development of capital markets in Armenia.

The Law contains several technicalities that combined can lead to a substantial increase in transaction costs. Infusion of new capital in the company is difficult, because making respective amendments to the charter can take up to three months. The delays derive from over-complicated procedures for holding shareholders' meetings, for registering the amended charter, for issuing the shares, etc.

The equity investment also requires a full pre-payment of any increase in charter capital, ie investments are expected to be frozen at the company's account until the charter has been re-registered and new shares are issued.

Another example of legal deficiencies relates to debt-for-equity swaps, which is a convenient investment and corporate restructuring instrument. The Armenian Law does not allow for this kind of transaction. Also, the debt–asset ratio of Armenian companies is low and limits opportunities for company financing, especially given the artificially low valuation of many companies derived from valuation methods used during mass privatization.

One of the necessary and most important laws for the further strengthening of economic reforms in corporate governance – the Law of the Republic of Armenia 'On Securities Market Regulation' – came into force in 1999. This Law created a new dimension for trading in securities, registration of ownership in securities and application of corporate governance principles. Furthermore, the Law was almost entirely oriented towards the creation of vigorous mechanisms for investor protection. For the first time, a self-regulatory system was applied.

The corporate governance regime in Armenia is also affected by a major inconsistency in bankruptcy legislation. This has significant negative implications for corporate governance, budget constraint and contract enforcement. The exit of non-viable companies is limited, and so far has been promoted through government-sponsored liquidation of bankrupt state enterprises (not through court-led regular bankruptcy procedures). The continuing presence of non-viable companies has delayed formation of an even playing field in the economy, as loss-making companies are permitted to accumulate arrears in their payments of taxes and energy/utility bills, while profitable firms are required to pay their obligations in full.

The corporate governance system in Armenia is characterized by concentrated ownership structures in the hands of a small number of individuals, families, managers, directors, holding companies, banks and/or other non-financial corporations. Insiders exercise control over companies in several ways. A common scenario is where insiders own the majority of the company shares and voting rights. If a few owners own shares with significant voting rights, they can effectively control a company even though they did not provide the majority of the capital.

The stock market is less developed owing to a large concentration of owners. The control over the company is executed by a small number of significant shareholders structured in relatively closed networks through planning and industrial policy mechanisms. Companies that are controlled by insiders enjoy certain advantages. Insiders have the power and the incentive to monitor management closely, thereby minimizing the potential for mismanagement and fraud. Moreover, because of their significant ownership and control rights, insiders tend to keep their investment in a firm for long periods of time. As a result, insiders tend to support decisions that will enhance a firm's long-term performance as opposed to decisions designed to maximize short-term gains. Under the circumstances of diffuse ownership, it enables insiders to strip assets and leaves little value for minority shareholders.

However, the insider system predisposes a company to certain corporate governance failures. One is that dominant owners and/or vote-holders can bully or collude with management to expropriate firm assets at the expense of minority shareholders. This is a significant risk when minority shareholders do not enjoy legal rights.

Similarly, when managers control a large number of shares or votes they may use their power to influence board decisions that may directly benefit them at the company's expense. In short, insiders who wield their power irresponsibly waste resources and drain company productivity levels; they also foster investor reluctance and illiquid capital markets. Shallow capital markets, in turn, deprive companies of capital and prevent investors from diversifying their risks.

20.3 Legal, Regulatory and Institutional Bodies

20.3.1 The Armenian Stock Exchange

The Armenian Stock Exchange sets special requirements for securities and their issuers for listing. The Armenian Stock Exchange sets up different levels of listing: the higher the level of security listing, the higher the quality and safety of the security is considered to be. No minimum requirements or criteria were established for the lower-level listing.

20.3.2   Securities Commission of The Republic of Armenia

The Securities Commission is an independent regulator of the financial markets. The European Bank of Reconstruction and Development has recently recommended (2003) that the enforcement powers of this commission should be enhanced.

20.3.3   Central Depository of Armenia

The European Bank of Reconstruction and Development has noted that few companies have transferred their shareholder registration to the Central Depository. Few shareholders are properly registered in Armenia.

20.3.4   Corporate Governance Centre

The Corporate Governance Centre is a non-profit organization founded in January 2002. The Centre aims to improve corporate governance in Armenia and thereby influence the processes of building civil society and a democratic state based upon social justice and the rule of law. The Centre is planning the following activities:

- To develop a corporate governance code and submit this to the state authorities for approval.
- To arrange corporate governance studies in Armenian universities.
- To develop and enforce professional standards for corporate secretaries.
- To develop corporate governance rating methodologies.
- To arrange courses, workshops and roundtables.

20.4   Board Structure

Board members are elected at the company's shareholders' annual general meeting for one year. Shareholders owning 10 per cent or more of the company voting shares are entitled to be included in the board without election. In a company with shareholders owning more than 500 voting shares, elections to the board are carried out through cumulative voting. During cumulative voting, each voting share has a number of votes equal to the number of members being elected and the voting shareholder is entitled either to grant the votes to one candidate or to distribute the votes among several candidates.

The management of the company is carried out by the company's executive body, which is the executive director alone or the executive director together with the company administration. If the company charter determines the existence of an administration, the charter should differentiate the authority of the executive director and the administration. In the case of the existence of an administration, the executive director carries out the responsibilities of the head of administration as well. The establishment of the company's executive bodies and the suspension of their authority ahead of schedule are carried out according to the decision of the board, if so authorized by the company charter. All management issues are within the authority of the company's executive body except those that, according to the company charter, are within the authority of the shareholders' general meeting or the board. The company's executive body organizes the implementation of the decisions taken by the shareholders' general meeting and by the board. The executive director and the administration are appointed by the company's board unless the charter states that the general meeting has this authority. The contracts with the executive director and the administration members are concluded by the board chairman or other person as defined in the charter.

The company executive director:

- disposes of the company's assets, including its financial resources, and carries out transactions on behalf of the company;
- represents the company in the Republic of Armenia and abroad;
- acts without a letter of authority;
- gives letters of authority;
- concludes contracts in accordance with defined procedures, including employment contracts;
- opens deposit and other accounts in banks;

- submits the company employment regulations, separate unit regulations, and the company's administrative and organizational structure to the board for approval;

- gives orders or commands within his authority, gives instructions subject to compulsory implementation and controls their implementation;

- hires and dismisses company employees in accordance with defined procedures;

- has other authority as defined by the charter.

The rights and responsibilities of the company executive director and the administration members are defined according to the present legislation, other legislative acts, and contracts concluded by them with the company. The company executive director and administration members can occupy paid positions in other organizations, but only upon agreement of the company board.

The general meeting is entitled to take decisions at any time on contracts concluded with the company executive director, administration members, a managing organization or individual manager unless the charter places settlement of that issue within the authority of the company's board.

20.4.1   Size

The composition of the board is determined by the company charter or by the decision of the shareholders' general meeting. In a company with shareholders owning more than 500 voting shares, the board cannot be less than seven persons.

20.4.2   Composition

A member of the board can be a shareholder. A person that does not hold shares may be a member of a board as long as it is not prohibited by the company charter.

20.4.3   Separation of the Roles of Chairman and Chief Executive

The chairman of the board is elected by the board members by a majority vote of the total number of board members (the company charter can define a bigger number). The board can re-elect the chairman or elect a new chairman at any time. In a company with shareholders owning more than 500 voting shares, the positions of board chairman and executive director cannot be combined.

The chairman of the board:

- organizes the work of the company's board;
- holds the sittings of the board and presides at them;
- organizes the protocol-making at the sittings; and
- presides at the company shareholders' general meetings unless the company charter has different provisions.

20.5 Codes, Standards and Good Practice Guidelines

The International Finance Corporation (IFC) assisted Armenia to develop its corporate governance between 1999 and 2001.

The development of corporate governance in Armenia is currently in an early stage of development. There are corporate laws and regulations which define the role and responsibilities of those charged with conducting corporate business but it may take some time before these mechanisms mature enough in Armenia to serve as effective controls of corporate activity. The practical impact of legal regulations depends not so much on what is regulated as on what can be enforced: if the enforcement infrastructure is missing, legal regulations are of little assurance to the owners.

However, the problems of corporate governance in Armenia are not limited to securing managerial accountability. The corporate sector in Armenia consists of companies formed as a result of mass privatization, without the simultaneous development of legal and institutional structures necessary to operate in a competitive market economy. Under the existing economic environment in Armenia most of the individual minority shareholders are passive.

The main corporate governance issues currently being debated in the country are:

- The effects of a high degree of concentration of ownership structure in corporations.

- Under the unpredictable economic circumstances currently existing in Armenia, managers see their positions as temporary and uncertain, which leads to maximizing their own profit instead of maximizing the company profit.

- Open joint stock companies avoid disclosing information concerning their activity. In particular, they do not disclose the financial results of their activities. The companies are 'closed' systems to investors, which undoubtedly reduces their confidence in the company and its activities. The companies operate under 'hidden' conditions, which have a negative effect on the development of an atmosphere of confidence which is so necessary in financial markets.

- The European Bank for Reconstruction and Development, in a corporate governance sector assessment project in May 2003, classified Armenia as having a high compliance level of corporate governance systems measured against the OECD Principles of Corporate Governance. It found that existing corporate-governance-related laws were 'relatively sound'.

- There has been a lack of state enforcement measures. Even the minimum requirements defined under the Armenian Law on 'Joint Stock Companies' have not been followed. Prior to the adoption of the Law on 'Securities Market Regulation', shareholders were deprived of information. The issuers and their managers did not bear any responsibility for not following the requirement of data disclosure and providing non-realistic data to investors. The outcome of this is the passiveness of investors in making investment decisions owing to poor quantitative and qualitative data.

- The rights of shareholders are frequently violated by management. The minority are not only deprived of their rights to participate in management, but also it is extremely common for them to be extensively ignored by the issuers. General meetings of shareholders are called, which often violates the legislation. The shareholders are not informed about the meeting agenda, adopted decisions and their possible consequences. Decisions are adopted despite gross violation of the voting rules, in particular proxy statement rules.

- Through reorganization (usually splitting or separating) the major shareholders often transfer the current assets of a company without adequate indemnification by the newly established company. As a result, the rest of the shareholders can remain in a company structure whose assets are not working, and their shares are 'devaluing'. The low level of the enforcement of laws excludes the proper performance of minority rights' protection.

20.6 Disclosure and Transparency

The control commission is the internal audit structure of the company. It has the mandate of the internal auditor to examine and evaluate the effectiveness of the applicable operational activities and the systems of internal financial control, so as to bring material deficiencies, instances of non-compliance and development needs to the attention of the board and shareholders' resolution. The elected members of the control commission perform the internal audit functions. In case of need the commission may act involving a team of appropriately qualified and experienced employees or through the engagement of external practitioners upon specified and agreed terms with equivalent access.

The control commission monitors that adequate and appropriate internal financial controls are in place; that statutory and financial risks have been identified and are being monitored and managed; and that appropriate standards of governance, reporting and compliance are in operation. The control commission also advises the board and the shareholders' general meeting on issues relating to the financial information.

The control commission is entitled to carry out the checking of the annual results of the company's financial-economic activity, at its own initiative; by the decision of the shareholders' general meeting or the board, as well as upon the requirement of the shareholders owning at least 10 per cent of the company voting shares.

The control commission is entitled to demand the holding of a shareholders' extraordinary general meting. The control commission members are elected at the shareholders' general meeting for a three-year term. The control commission cannot have fewer than three members.

20.6.1 Disclosure Requirements

All joint stock companies are required to publish selected information from their accounts, the auditor's opinion, and annual accounts in national newspapers every year. They must disclose information about the capital structure, management and activities of the company, directors' shareholdings and rights issues, audited annual reports, major corporate acquisitions and default events, among other things.

Armenian legislation also requires joint stock companies to publish a copy of their fiscal year-end annual report in a public newspaper. The required financial statements are the balance sheet and profit and loss statement. Annual audited financial statements must be filed with the appropriate requirements at the fiscal year-end. Copies must be distributed to shareholders within the same time period.

20.6.2 Large Transactions

The corporate governance issues also include regulations on carrying out large transactions, which are related to the company's assets acquisition and selling, and are crucial for the company's financial-economic activity. The following transactions are considered to be large:

- One or more interrelated transactions, which are directly or indirectly related to the assets of the company, and whose value is 25 per cent or more of the company assets' book value as of the date when the decision was made to carry out the transaction.

- One or more interrelated transactions, which are directly or indirectly related to the allocation of a company's common shares, or preference shares to be converted into common shares, and whose value is 25 per cent or more of the total face value of the common shares having been already allocated by the company.

The decision on carrying out large transactions, concerning assets of the company whose value is 25–50 per cent of the company's assets' book value at the date of the decision to carry out the transaction, should be taken unanimously by the company's board.

When the value of assets is more than 50 per cent of the company's assets' book value, the decision on carrying out the transaction should be taken by the company's shareholders' general meeting by 75 per cent vote of the shareholders participating in the meeting.

20.6.3 Conflict of Interest Considerations

When an interested party engages in a transaction with a company, certain steps must be taken to ensure there is no conflict of interest. The following persons are considered to be interested parties:

- a board member;

- a person engaged in the company management bodies;

- a shareholder or group of shareholders, owning 20 per cent or more of the voting shares of the company, in the case when the stated persons, their parents, husbands, children, sisters and brothers, as well as the persons cooperating with them, are to be parties or agents or representatives in the transaction.

The persons considered to be interested in the transaction should provide necessary data on the existence of a conflict of interest to the board, control commission and the external auditor carrying out the company audit. They should state that they or their relatives are interested persons in the transaction.

In a company having fewer than 500 voting shares, the decision to carry out the transaction, where interest exists, is taken by a majority vote of the company's board members who do not have an interest in the transaction. In a company having more then 500 voting shares, the decision on the transaction, where interest exists, is taken by the majority vote of company board independent members (who are not the company executive director or members of the administration). When the market price of a transaction, where interest exists, exceeds a value of 2 per cent of the company's assets, the decision is taken by the general meeting of shareholders, by majority vote of shareholders lacking an interest in the transaction. The person recognized as interested is responsible to the company for the size of loss caused to it. If several persons carry the responsibility, they are proportionally responsible to the company.

20.7   Shareholder Rights and Stakeholder Relations

Each common share of the company grants shareholders the same rights. Shareholders owning common shares are entitled to:

- participate with their voting right in the company general meeting on the issues within its authority;

- participate in the management of the company;

- receive dividends from the profit generated from company activity (although the payment of dividends for common shares is not guaranteed by the company);

- acquire the shares allocated by the company on a priority basis (if the present legislation and the company charter do not define different provisions);

- receive information on company activities according to procedures defined by the charter, except secret documents, including getting acquainted with the balance sheet and other accounting statements, and the company's economic activity. Shareholders owning at least 5 per cent of the voting shares of the company's equity can require the checking of the statements and secret documents referring to company activity by an external specialized audit firm. The checking expenses are reimbursed by the shareholders requiring the checking;

- authorize a third person to represent their rights at the company constituent meeting (the first annual general meeting of the company's shareholders);

- make proposals at the shareholders' general meeting;

- vote at the shareholders' general meeting according to the number of voting shares fully paid by them;

- appeal to the court regarding decisions taken by the shareholders' general meeting that contradict current laws and other legislative acts;

- in case of company liquidation, receive the part pre-determined for them;

- in the case of company charter capital accumulation, receive free of charge the relevant number of common shares at the expense of company funds;

- sell or transfer shares owned by them to other persons; and

- use other rights determined by the company charter.

20.7.1 Responsibilities of the Shareholders General Meeting

The responsibilities of the company shareholders' general meeting include:

- approving the company charter, making amendments and changes to it, approving a new version of the company charter;

- reorganization of the company;

- liquidation of the company, appointment of the liquidation committee, approval of the company's intermediate and summarizing liquidation balances;

- approval of the quantitative composition of the company board, election of its members and termination of their rights ahead of schedule;

- definition of the maximum number of authorized shares;

- increasing the company charter capital size through an increase in the share face value and the allocation of additional shares;

- decreasing the company charter capital through a decrease in the share face value, the acquisition of allocated company shares for the purpose of reducing the total number of shares, the cancellation of partially paid shares, as well as through the cancellation of shares acquired or bought back by the company;

- establishment of the company executive body (the executive director, administration), termination of its authority ahead of schedule;

- election of the company control commission members (internal audit) and termination of its authority ahead of schedule;

- approval of the person carrying out the company audit;

- approval of the company's annual statements, accounting balances, profit and loss statement, distribution of profit and loss; decision making on the annual dividend payment and approval of the annual dividend size; as well as approval of the annual activity results of the company's branches and representations;

- decision making on the non-implementation of the priority right of the company's shareholders owning company shares or other securities convertible to shares;

- approval of the procedures for holding the general meeting and setting up the counting commission;

- definition of the form in which data and materials from the company are disseminated to the shareholders, including the selection of the relevant means of mass media if the message is to be sent through public announcements;

- decreasing (splitting) and increasing (consolidating) the face value of shares;

- acquisition and buy-back of the company's allocated shares in cases defined by the legislation;

- definition of payment terms for the company's leading officials;

- creation of subsidiaries by the company and participation in subsidiary and dependent companies;

- creation of company branches and representations;

- adoption of other decisions defined by the present legislation and company charter.

20.7.2 Decisions of the Shareholders' General Meeting

Shareholders holding common shares are entitled to vote. Most decisions are made on the basis of a simple majority of votes, while certain important decisions such as changing the company's charter require a 75 per cent majority. The procedures for decision making at the general meeting are defined by the company charter or by the general meeting itself. The company's shareholders' meeting is not entitled to change the meeting agenda, or to take decisions on issues not included in the agenda. Shareholders should be informed within 45 days concerning decisions taken at the meeting, as well as voting results. A shareholder is entitled to appeal to the court a decision taken by the general meeting that is a violation of the requirements of legislative acts and the company charter if he or she has not participated in the meeting or has voted against it, and his or her legal rights and interests have been violated by the decision.

20.7.3 Rights of Minority Shareholders

Minority shareholders have the following rights to protect their interests and to influence the management of the company:

- Shareholders *owning at least 1 per cent* or more of common shares of the company are entitled to submit a claim to the court against the company's board members, the executive director and the administration members, demanding the reimbursement of the loss they have caused to the company.

- Shareholders *owning at least 2 per cent* of voting shares are entitled to submit not more than two proposals to the agenda of the company's shareholders' annual general meeting, as well as to propose candidates for the board and control commission membership.

- Shareholders *owning at least 5 per cent* of voting shares of the company can demand the checking of the financial-economic activity of the company by outside auditors. In that case the services of the auditor are paid for by the shareholders who demanded the audit.

- Shareholders *owning at least 10 per cent* of the company voting shares can demand the holding of an extraordinary general meeting.

- Shareholders *owning at least 10 per cent* of voting shares of the company have a right to require the Control Commission to check the financial-economic activity of the company.

The European Bank for Reconstruction and Development noted in its assessment (2003):

> *Many companies in the country have not registered their shareholders' property or have not transferred their shareholder registration to the required central register (ie the Central Depository of Armenia); many companies have never held a general meeting of shareholders; problems of insider trading and asset stripping by major shareholders are rampant (p 7).*

20.8 Director Development Activity

Director training programmes in corporate governance have not yet been implemented in Armenia.

20.9 Useful Contacts

- Securities Commission of the Republic of Armenia – www.sca.am
- Central Depository of Armenia – www.cda.am

20.10   Further Reading

Chen, H (2003) *Corporate Governance Sector assessment project May 2003*, European Bank for Reconstruction and Development, London

Jrbashyan, T (2003) *Privatization: the problem of passive shareholders and the formation of a joint investment system in Armenia*, Centre for Corporate Researches, Yerevan

Karapetyan, D (2002) *Shareholder rights: theory and practice in Armenia*, Proceedings of the 3rd Meeting of the Eurasian Corporate Governance Roundtable in Kyiv, Ukraine, 17–18 April, World Bank, Washington

21

Romania

Table 21.1

Population	22.4 million (2002)
Gross Domestic Income (GDI)	US $41.3 billion (2002)
GDI per capita	US $1,850 (2002)
Total number of companies	N/A
Number of companies listed on the stock exchange	Approximately 5,000 on the Bucharest Stock Exchange
Key corporate laws	● The Securities and Stock Exchange Law No. 52 (1994) ● The Privatization Law No. 58 (1991) ● Company Law No. 31 (1990) ● The Law on the Reorganization of State Enterprises No. 15 (1990)
Key corporate governance codes	● Corporate Governance Code: Corporate Governance Initiative for Economic Democracy in Romania ● Corporate Governance Code in Romania Law No. 99 (1999)

21.1 Corporate Structure and Ownership

Most of Romania's shareholders are 'imposed' shareholders resulting from the privatization of the 5,000 companies listed on the Bucharest Stock Exchange (BSE) or the over-the-counter market RASDAQ. They remain the passive actors within capital markets, with little knowledge of the basics of stock exchange.

Most powerful shareholders emerged from privatization contracts settled by authorities with strategic investors (usually foreign companies like Renault, Société Générale, Samsung Deutschland, Aker or Trinity Industry), Romanian based-investors and employees' associations. State-owned companies, companies with major investors and employee-managed companies make up almost 80 per cent of BSE companies.

Institutional investors hold majority stakes in 7 per cent of BSE companies (Table 21.2) and in combination with other entities they hold significant minority positions in 44 per cent of companies (at least one or two minority shareholders together hold a minimum 15–20 per cent stake).

Throughout the Bucharest Stock Exchange's history, only four new companies have been listed on private initiative (Banca Transilvania) the defunct Banca Turco-Romana (banking), M.J. Maillis (packaging) and Impact Bucuresti (builder).

Many listed companies are dominated by strategic investors who were trapped in the ownership structure from the privatization process. Many of these big listed companies are not currently satisfying the disclosure requirements and would like to de-list to rationalize the size of the minority shareholders. To de-list they need to reduce the number of shareholders to below 500.

Foreign strategic investors and minority shareholders, headed by institutional investors, have played a major role in the main developments

Table 21.2 *The ownership of companies listed on the Bucharest Stock Exchange*

Strategic or other privatization investors	43%
Employers' Association	21%
State owned	16%
Institutional investors	7%
Other	13%

Table 21.3 *Ownership of companies on the Bucharest Stock Exchange*

	Out of 107 BSE companies
>50% ownership	64%
>90% ownership	9%
Significant minority shareholders	44%
The state as minority shareholder	4%
Significant natural persons	12%

in corporate life in the past two years. As a result, the capital legal framework has suffered repeated revisions, but enforcement of legal provisions regarding minority shareholders' protection has failed in most cases and abusive ways that damage minority shareholders' interests remain.

Mandatory takeover bids for companies whose majority shareholders hold more than 90 per cent of shares are currently seen as an escape from corporate governance requirements and many have started to acquire the necessary stock in order to de-list the companies they manage. The 90 per cent level is attained in many cases by share capital increases that dilutes the stake held by minority shareholders.

The RASDAQ-listed companies follow the same ownership pattern. More than half of the top 100 companies have a majority shareholder, either a strategic investor or an institutional investor. The same institutional investors on the BSE are equally active on the RASDAQ.

There are more than 4,500 companies listed on the RASDAQ, with sporadic trading sessions, whose ownership did not change significantly from post-privatization stages. They are controlled by employees' associations or by the state and they hold captive tens of thousands of voiceless beneficiaries of the voucher privatization.

The private sector accounts for 65 per cent of Romanian GDP and listed companies accounted for 60 per cent of the GDP in 2001 (OECD, 2003).

Ownership structures in Romania are characterized by:

- significant control by insiders and by managers who have obtained control through direct ownership or through the control of employees' shares (Table 21.3);

- high levels of state ownership and control;

- the emergence of various forms of institutional investors.

These characteristics can lead to:

- insider domination, which in turn can lead to the abuse of minority investors, asset stripping and problematic handling of conflicts of interest;

- remaining state ownership and control can be an impediment to corporate restructuring.

The banking sector in Romania is fairly weak. Loans to the private sector are less than 15 per cent of GDP, compared to 50 per cent in the USA or 120 per cent in Germany (EBRD, 2002).

The stock market in Romania is also very weak. The Romanian stock market capitalization as a percentage of GDP is below 10 per cent (EBRD, 2002).

A lot of deals are still off-exchange, based on inside information, with market pricing problems due to lack of transparency.

21.2 Legal Framework

The Company Law (no. 31/1990) contains regulations governing the creation, organization and functioning, modification and liquidation of all types of commercial companies. It was based on French and Italian models. There are also special provisions that apply to companies operating in a certain area (banking, insurance, investment funds, etc) and to companies facing special circumstances (companies listed on stock exchanges, companies to be liquidated, etc).

Law no. 31/1990 has been modified several times, the last amendment being the Anticorruption Law (no. 161/2003) which attempts to harmonize Romanian legislation with EU regulations.

The EBRD (2002) evaluated Romania as having 4 out of 5 for legal extensiveness and legal effectiveness, the highest score in south-east Europe. The main legal difficulty lies with implementation rather than unsatisfactory legislation. The OECD (2003: 70) concluded: 'The underlying fundamental legal difficulty is the weakness of the judicial and administrative systems unable to enforce shareholders' rights or more generally commercial law.'

21.3 Legal, Regulatory and Institutional Bodies

21.3.1 Bucharest Stock Exchange (BSE) and RASDAQ

The BSE became operational in 1995 and the RASDAQ was launched in 1996 to trade stocks associated with the mass privatization programme. Both the BSE and RASDAQ use electronic trading systems.

21.3.2 National Securities Commission

The Commission was created in 1994 but only became active in 1996. A scandal in 2000 badly damaged its reputation when it was held responsible for the collapse of NFI, an investment fund. The president and some commissioners were arrested during the investigations.

21.4 Board Structure

The companies listed on the over-the-counter market, RASDAQ, tend to have a unitary board structure, while larger companies listed on the Budapest Stock Exchange embrace a hybrid board structure.

In larger companies the board delegates some of its powers to a directors' committee composed of some of the board members. Romania also has censors. The censors do not have any role in corporate decision making but monitor the company and the board. They ensure that decisions made by the board are lawful and check the financial statements. Censors are elected at the AGM and only one of the three censors must be a certified public accountant.

A board member is not allowed to be associated with a competing company (eg a shareholder, manager or director). A board member is not allowed to pursue the same business for personal benefit as the company of which he or she is a director.

The larger the company is, the greater the chance that an independent non-executive member of the board would be appointed.

Foreign companies in Romania are inclined towards a dual board structure, where the position of chairman of the board of administrators or that of general manager is offered to a representative of the majority shareholder, and the other position is offered to an independent professional, usually local.

Investment institutions usually have a dual board structure, the executive activities being totally separated from the surveillance role of the board of directors.

21.5 Codes, Standards and Good Practice Guidelines

The European Bank for Reconstruction and Development, in its corporate governance sector assessment project (2003), classified Romania as having a low compliance level of corporate governance systems measured against the OECD Principles of Corporate Governance.

21.5.1 The Bucharest Stock Exchange Code (I)

The Bucharest Stock Exchange Code promotes the principles of good faith practice, diligence and transparency on behalf of the issuers. The provisions of the code are applied to those companies listed on the 'Plus Tier' in compliance with the Listing Regulation no. 3 of the Bucharest Stock Exchange. There is one company listed on the 'Plus Tier' whose majority shareholder is an institutional investor.

21.5.2 The Bucharest Stock Exchange Code (II)

The Bucharest Stock Exchange second voluntary corporate governance code was initiated and adopted by the Strategic Alliance of Business Associations. This Code encourages the surveillance and strengthening of private property rights; it provides a set of rules and standards as guidelines for the management of a company with respect to its strategic planning and decision making in order to promote the interests of shareholders and associates, creditors, customers, employers and employees.

The Code encourages active cooperation between corporations and stakeholders in creating wealth, jobs and the financially sound enterprises.

Timely and accurate disclosure of operations involving company's assets, financial situations, performance, ownership and governance of the company, and strategies are all necessary.

The effective monitoring of management by the board, and the board's accountability to the company and shareholders, are likely to increase investors' confidence.

21.6 Disclosure and Transparency

Companies are required by law to maintain a register of shareholders or delegate this duty to an independent specialist registry. Every shareholder should be able to obtain information on shareholder ownership.

A directors' report as well as a censor's report has to be approved by the AGM. The contents of these reports are not specified in much detail in the law and in practice the quality of reporting is very low.

External auditing is not required in Romania (except for banks). Censors fulfil the role of auditors. However, only one-third of censors have to be certified accountants. The Securities Law (1994) requires the certification of accounts by an independent censor authorized by the Securities Commission.

Law 99 (1999) allows greater shareholder access to information. It also provides shareholders with the right to consult certain documents. If shareholders represent more than 10 per cent of capital they may ask for an independent expert, paid for by the company, to check specific transactions.

An analysis was carried out in 2003 comprising 25 representative public companies traded on the Bucharest Stock Exchange (BSE), selected on the basis of their market capitalization and transaction value. The market capitalization of the 25 selected companies represents more than 90 per cent of BSE capitalization.

The survey revealed that:

- Eighty per cent of companies were suspended from trading on the Bucharest Stock Exchange for less than one month in the past six months, as a result of some events that might have had a major impact on price evolution (Table 21.4).

- Infringements of shareholders' rights were observed in 28 per cent of companies.

- Most companies (64 per cent) provided adequate information to the public regarding their activities and financial data; 56 per cent

Table 21.4 *Period of suspension from trading*

1 week	36%
2 weeks	28%
3 weeks	12%
4 weeks	4%
More than 1 month	20%

of companies submitted their 2002 financial statements in the first two months of year 2003; 12 per cent of them did not submit this information at all.

- Fifty-six per cent of companies dealt with major unfavourable events, but only 57 per cent of them managed to offer adequate information in order to clarify and stabilize the situation.

- Nine companies out of 25 selected (36 per cent) were very active in providing the public with adequate information regarding their activities, financial data, reasons for being suspended on the BSE and any other events that required an official statement on their behalf. Also, they showed special commitment in supporting minority shareholders' rights.

- Overall, 64 per cent of companies offered sufficient information to their shareholders.

- Fifty-six per cent of companies were involved in problematic events, such as:

  - news regarding detachment of assets, fraudulent operations, privatization issues and sudden top-manager resignation (eg SNP Petrom, Banca Transilvania);

  - announced control of state authorities on public funds management (eg SIF1,2,3,4,5 – financial investments companies);

  - abusive and misleading share capital increases (eg Otelinox, BRD);

  - unfair and unchallengeable price offered in mandatory takeover bids (eg Dacia);

  - stock transfer outside Bucharest Stock Exchange (eg Alro, Astra Romana, Excelent);

  - transfer of authority from General Shareholders' Meeting to managers (eg Rafo).

- Only 57 per cent of these companies provided sufficient information in order to assure shareholders of proper handling of these situations.

- The majority shareholders within 7 companies (28 per cent) provoked infringements of minority shareholders' rights (eg Dacia, Alro, Astra Romana, Otelinox, Excelent, BRD). Minority shareholders from three of these companies (12 per cent) suffered serious material damage (eg Dacia, Otelinox, BRD).

Extended suspension from trading is usually generated by events such as complicated share capital increases or mandatory takeover bids that target the removal of companies from the stock exchange. That was the case of 20 per cent of companies (eg BRD, Dacia, Arctic, Silcotub and Rafo).

There is much evidence of many companies not complying with corporate governance principles, endangering the very existence of investments on stock exchanges and the development of the Romanian capital market. Incorrect share capital increases, abusive mandatory takeover bids and delay or lack of information and financial data indicate significant problems within the Romanian capital market.

21.7 Shareholder Rights and Stakeholder Relations

Rights of shareholders in Romania include:

- To be informed about company's standing, to participate and to vote the issues debated in the general shareholders' meetings.

- To receive dividends, to sell their shares and to be granted pre-emption rights.

- In the case of liquidation, to receive part of the remaining assets, proportional to their participation to the share capital.

Special minority rights include:

- Shareholders representing at least 10 per cent of the voting rights (or less if the by-laws of the company provide so) may ask directors/administrators to convene a general meeting.

- Every individual shareholder has the right to asks auditors to investigate facts deemed to be questionable. Auditors are supposed to consider such notifications and include them in the annual report.

- Shareholders have the right to challenge the decisions of general shareholders' meetings in courts and ask for redress.

Board issues include:

- Members of the board can be discharged by the shareholders convened in general shareholders' meetings at any time and with no mandatory explanation.

- In accordance with the provisions envisaged by Law 31/1990, the directors (administrators) 'can carry all the operations required in order to achieve the objectives of the company, within the limits specified in the By-laws of the company'. The main limitations to the powers of the board refer to the objectives of the business (administrators cannot undertake actions that are not within the objectives of a company's business) and the decisions taken in the shareholders' meetings.

- Managers are liable for not fulfilling their mandate in compliance with the management contract and the by-laws of the company. Legal action against managers can be initiated by general shareholders' meetings and also by creditors, if the company undergoes bankruptcy procedures. Administrators are held responsible on the grounds of criminal law for prejudice brought to a company or bankruptcy caused by fraud.

The second pillar of corporate legislation is given by the Government Emergency Ordinance (GEO) (no. 28/2002) enacted and amended by Law no. 525/2002 regarding securities, financial investment services and regulated markets. This framework contains more demanding provisions directed towards 'public companies' than the ones comprised by Law 31/1990.

The centrepiece of insolvency legislation is Law no. 64/1995 regarding insolvency and bankruptcy situations, last modified by GEO no. 38/2002. From the beginning, Law 64/1995 was disputed and has been inconsistently applied.

Secure methods of ownership registration and convey or transfer shares. Emergency Ordinance no. 28/2002 and Law no. 525/2002 regarding securities, financial investment services and regulated markets concede all powers to the National Securities Commission

(CNVM) in order to set up, supervise, organize and manage all markets that trade securities. CNVM establishes the rules of trading shares, how clearing operations are done and the entities allowed to keep track of registered securities.

Obtain relevant information on the corporation on a timely and regular basis. Companies listed on the first tier of the Bucharest Stock Exchange (BSE) must obey rigorous rules concerning the necessity of presenting information every time major events occur and timely financial data. Second-tier and so-called 'un-listed' BSE companies and companies traded on the over-the-counter market RASDAQ are less transparent and less motivated to offer the relevant information to their shareholders. Nevertheless, law provisions provide different instruments to shareholders to obtain such information. Shareholders that own individually or jointly 5 per cent of the share capital have the right to ask managers and financial auditors, on a quarterly basis, to draft reports about operations concluded by the company.

Participate and vote in general shareholders' meetings. Companies are requested to publish the announcement calling the general shareholders' meeting (GSM) and to send a notice to the CNVM and to the market to which they belong. Managers must call the GSM at the request of significant shareholders (individually or jointly owning at least 10 per cent of share capital) and to include on the agenda all matters requested. Access to the GSM is allowed after simple identification of the shareholders. If a shareholder is forbidden participation in a GSM, all decisions taken by that GSM will be cancelled.

Elect members on the board. At least one member of the board will be elected by cumulative voting, if a significant shareholder calls for this procedure.

Share in the profits of the corporation. The GSM establishes the reference date for the shareholders to receive dividends as convened in that specific GSM. The dividend payment period cannot go beyond six months from the date the GSM decided its distribution.

21.7.1 Equitable Treatment of Shareholders

All shareholders of the same class should be treated equally. Law no. 31/1990 clearly states that all shares belonging to the same category grant their owner equal rights.

Insider trading and abusive self-dealing should be prohibited. Brokerage houses are strictly prohibited from: performing orders from investors, knowing that there will be no real transfer of property rights or that the selling operation settled between an investor and an affiliated person or employee is followed by a buy-back operation; performing orders that imply simultaneous sell/buy operations from the same investor; publishing untrue information about listed companies.

Any privileged-information holder is prohibited from buying or selling in his/others' name, directly or indirectly, securities of the issuer that relate to that possession of privileged information, or seeking profit by distributing the privileged information to other parties.

Members of the board and managers should be required to disclose any material interests in transactions or matters affecting the corporation. Managers are requested to submit reports mentioning any transaction settled between the company and its managers or employees, majority shareholder or persons related to them, which amounts to an aggregated amount of ROL 50,000.

Information should be prepared, audited and disclosed in accordance with high quality standards of accounting, financial and non-financial disclosure and audit. Financial statements and any report on the operations of a company that have to be authorized, supervised and controlled by the CNVM will be drafted in accordance with CNVM regulations and they will be verified and certified by financial auditors licensed by CNVM. The audit and accounting standards will be established by CNVM in cooperation with the Romanian Auditors' Association.

21.8   Director Development Activity

There has been little training development in the area of corporate governance in Romania. The sole educational programme that comprises aspects of corporate governance is the Master of Science in Financial Management and Capital Markets offered by the Faculty of Finance-Banking within the Academy of Economic Studies, Bucharest.

A lecture on corporate governance has been offered since October 2000 and is conducted by Mrs Gratiela Iordache, Executive Director of the Romanian Shareholders' Association. This seminar provides students with information about economic and legal procedures used by share-holders to manage and monitor the companies they own.

Sporadic seminars have been organized by the OECD, Romanian and foreign stock exchanges and other international organizations in order to spread knowledge on corporate governance, make share-holders aware of their rights, and improve the analytical skills of investors and financial analysts, and this kind of lecture is likely to continue in the future.

21.9   Useful Contacts

- Bucharest Stock Exchange – www.bvb.ro
- National Bank – www.bnro.ro
- Romanian National Securities Commission – www.cnvm.rdsnet.ro
- Shareholders' Association – www.aaro.ro

21.10   Further Reading

Chen, H (2003) *Corporate Governance Sector Assessment Project May 2003*, European Bank for Reconstruction and Development, London

Dochia, A (2001) *Patterns of Corporate Ownership: Corporate Governance in Romania*, OECD, Paris

International Centre for Entrepreneurial Studies Bucharest University and Strategic Alliance Associations (2002) *Corporate Governance Code: Corporate governance initiative for economic democracy in Romania*, Bucharest University, Bucharest

OECD (2003) *White Paper on Corporate Governance in South East Europe*, OECD, Paris

Russian Institute of Directors (2002) *Corporate Governance Code in Romania*, RID, Moscow

22 The Russian Federation

Table 22.1

Population	144.1 million (2002)
Gross Domestic Income (GDI)	US $458.78 million (2003)
GDI per capita	US $2,140 (2002)
Total number of companies	20,400 open-ended joint stock companies (OAO) (2003)
Market capitalization	US $211.5 million (May 6, 2004)
Key corporate laws	• Corporate Governance Code (2002)
	• The Law 'On the Protection of Rights and Legal Interests of Investors on the Securities Market' (The Investor Protection Law) (1999)
	• The Law on Joint Stock Company (JSC) (1995)
	• The Civil Code of the Russian Federation (Parts one and two) (1994)

22.1 Corporate Structure and Ownership

Ninety per cent of Russian output is now produced by private enterprise. The Civil Code of the Russian Federation (1994) and the

Joint Stock Company Law (1995) recognize two types of joint-stock companies: closed-end joint stock companies (ZAOs) and open-end joint stock companies (OAOs):

- Closed end joint-stock companies (ZAOs): ZAOs have a maximum of 50 shareholders and the authorized capital cannot exceed 100 times the minimum monthly wage. ZAO shares can only be distributed among its founders and no open subscription is allowed.

- Open ended joint-stock companies (OAOs): The number of shareholders is unlimited and the authorized capital must be at least 1,000 times the minimum monthly wage. Shareholders may dispose of their stock at their discretion.

Both closed-end and open-ended companies may have individuals and legal entities among their shareholders. By mid-2002, there were over 66,000 registered open-end joint stock companies (OAOs) in Russia.

The ownership structure of many Russian companies has been relatively dispersed. However, since the second half of the 1990s a process of concentration of ownership has been developing at a high pace. By the end of 2002, most companies in industries as oil production and processing, communications, metallurgy, timber, machine-building, chemistry, car-manufacturing and food were controlled by a single controlling shareholder or a small group of shareholders. The *New York Times* identified in 2002 that eight business groups controlled over 60 per cent of the target companies.

In 1999, 38 per cent of the joint stock companies had one single shareholder owning more than 25 per cent of the shares, 13 per cent had a shareholder owning more than 50 per cent of the shares and 4 per cent had a shareholder with more than 75 per cent of the shares.

The ownership structure of the major Russian companies is characterized by top managers often owning or controlling very significant stock levels.

The separation of management from ownership began in Russian companies only in the late 1990s and is at an early stage. It involves only a small group of the largest companies. In the middle-sized companies the controlling powers of the top managers remain virtually unchallenged.

Since 2000, the owners and top managers of a few major Russian companies have begun to sell a portion of their companies' stock to outside investors, often to foreign investors. However, almost none of these owners and top managers were willing to release control of more than 25 per cent of the shares to outsiders. Owners of almost all major companies have repeatedly stressed that for the foreseeable future they want to keep the controlling stocks.

The insider owners of middle-sized companies are more willing to share their ownership and control rights with outside shareholders. But they prefer deals with direct major investors rather than letting large stocks of their companies go to unknown shareholders through the stock market.

Since the late 1990s, holding companies have been undergoing a process of transition from amorphous conglomerates towards more technologically and vertically integrated structures with more clear-cut organizational and legal boundaries. The holding companies are now characterized by high levels of corporate control over their affiliated companies.

The federal government still remains a significant shareholder in the industrial sector and infrastructure and the controlling one in several major companies. The government plays a dominant role in gas supplies (Gazprom), electricity (RAO UES), communications, primarily non-mobile (Svyzainvest), and railways (RAO 'Russians Railways'). For some of them (Gazprom, RAO UES, Russian Railways) the prospects for privatization of these companies remain uncertain. Most experts believe that the government will retain its control over them for the near future. But others are expected to be privatized in the near future.

The banking sector in Russia is fairly weak. Loans to the private sector are less than 15 per cent of GDP, compared to 50 per cent in the USA or 120 per cent in Germany (EBRD, 2000).

22.2 Legal Framework

The major federal laws governing joint stock companies in the Russian Federation are:

- The Federal Law 'On Joint-Stock Companies'. This law was passed by the State Duma in 1995 (amended in 1996, 1999 and

2001) and regulates the legal status of joint stock companies established in the Russian Federation. It also covers shareholders' rights, decision-making procedures and the authority within the company.

- The Federal Law 'On the Securities Market'. This law was passed by the State Duma in 1996 (amended in 1999, 2001 and 2002). The law regulates the issuing of shares and the circulation of securities.

- The Federal Law 'On Protection of Rights and Legal Interest of Investors on the Securities Market' (1999). This law identifies the provision of services to investors, the responsibilities of equity issuers and the measures for the protection of rights and interests of investors and the liabilities for any violations of these rights.

- The Federal Law 'On Insolvency'. This law was passed by the State Duma in 2002. This law regulates bankruptcy procedures and bankruptcy prevention measures. The law allows bankruptcy to be used as a tool for transferring companies from ineffective owners to effective ones.

In recent years, major improvements in corporate governance have been achieved. These achievements include:

- protection of shareholder rights when the authorized capital is increased (the existing shareholders have the right of first refusal to a rights issue);

- protection of shareholders from the policy of 'ousting' when consolidating shares;

- protection of the right to receive dividends;

- protection of shareholder rights while preparing and conducting general meetings; this includes information sharing, registration and voting procedures;

- procedures concerning major transactions, interested party transactions and disclosure of information about these transactions;

- the company's responsibility for the timely disclosure of full and accurate information about its operations;

- exchanges have stronger powers to ensure that the issuer companies comply with legislation.

22.3   Legal, Regulatory and Institutional Bodies

22.3.1   The Stock Exchange

As of 2003, there are 11 organizations licensed as stock exchanges in Russia. However, only five exchanges are operational, and the largest volume of trade is generated by two Moscow exchanges, the Moscow Interbank Currency Exchange (MICEX) and the electronic Russian Trading System (RTS).

Despite significant recent improvements in its infrastructure, the Russian stock market is characterized by low market capitalization, low liquidity and free floats. Consequently, the Russian market has served as a source of financing for very few Russian companies.

There has never been a significant volume of IPOs within Russia. In 1999–2003, there were only four fully fledged IPOs.

In sharp contrast, the market of corporate bonds has been growing. However, in general, external financing remains at generally low levels. Neither the banking sector nor the financial markets provide companies with significant financing and most Russian companies rely on their own revenue as the dominant source of investment.

In April 2004, the FCSM was reorganized into the Federal Service for Financial Markets (FSFM), with broader rights. It was announced that in future, the FSFM will take the functions of the 'megaregulator', somewhat similar to the FSA in the United Kingdom.

22.3.2   The Federal Commission on the Securities Market (FCSM)

The FCSM was established in 1994. It is the federal executive organization responsible for implementing government policy on the securities market, regulating activities of professional securities market participants and protecting the rights of investors and shareholders. The FCSM has been engaged in the following activities:

- oversight of issuers and professional securities market;
- licensing professional activities on the securities market and licensing investment funds, unit investment funds, management companies, etc;
- information disclosure on the securities market;

- development of the regulatory legal framework on the securities market;
- forming the legal framework for good corporate governance including drafting the Russian corporate governance code;
- public awareness and information campaigns;
- professional training on corporate governance;
- establishment of institutional infrastructure for good corporate governance.

The FCSM issued a regulation which prescribed that starting with their annual reports for 2003, joint stock companies will be required to disclose the main aspects of their corporate governance practices and their conformity with the Code's recommendations in accordance with the principle 'comply or disclose and explain the discrepancies'. The monitoring of the companies' corporate governance practices, analysis of their reports and drawing conclusions with regard to further improvement of the Code's implementation tools and updating of the Code based on the lessons learnt from practice will be a challenging job for the Federal Commission over the coming years.

22.3.3   The National Council for Corporate Governance

The National Council for Corporate Governance is a permanent non-government advisory body initiated by the largest Russian issuers and investors. Its members include government officials in charge of the development of the investment and capital markets. This non-government forum plays a major role in making the principles from the Corporate Governance Code a part of the leading Russian companies' daily practices.

22.3.4   The Russian Institute of Directors (RID)

The Russian Institute of Directors was founded in late 2001 as a non-profit partnership by a group of the largest Russian companies listed on Russian and foreign stock markets. RID was the Russian business community's response to the need to improve corporate governance with a view to increasing the efficiency of using financial resources and their investment attractiveness.

Activities of the RID include:

- running specialist courses for directors and company secretaries;

- drafting codes of practice and ethics;

- regular surveys of corporate governance practices of Russian companies;

- monitoring of corporate governance practices and regulations in advanced and other emerging markets;

- public events to discuss 'hot' issues of Russian corporate governance practices and those abroad;

- encouraging the consolidation of the professional community of corporate directors.

The RID has been active in developing cooperation with the Russian securities market regulator, the Federal Commission for Securities Market, on issues related to corporate governance:

- RID experts took an active part in developing the Russian Corporate Governance Code.

- The Institute believes that effective corporate governance requires high professional expertise of all members of the board as the main corporate governance body, regardless of whether they are executive or non-executive directors.

The RID has also acted as an expert and resources centre for the National Council for Corporate Governance.

22.3.5 Independent Directors Association (IDA)

The IDA is a non-commercial professional organization that was established by the Investor Protection Association and Ernst & Young. The Association is engaged in the development and support of independent directors. Its mission is to encourage joint stock companies to improve their performance through the introduction of best practices for independent directors.

22.3.6 The Investor Protection Association (IPA)

The IPA is a non-commercial organization established in 2000. Its purpose is to unite investors' efforts aimed at the protection of their rights and improvements of corporate governance in Russia.

22.3.7 Organization of Company Shareholders and Investors (OPIAK)

The OPIAK is a non-commercial public organization established in 1999. Its mission is to provide information to small private shareholders of Russian companies and help them to support their rights. The organization has been active in disseminating information on shareholder rights and their treatment by various companies.

22.4 Board Structure

All companies must have a single-person executive body. The Russian name for a CEO is 'general director'. Joint stock companies may establish a management board. A joint stock company might have either a collective executive body (management board) or a single-person executive body. The quorum for a meeting of the company's collective executive body (management board) is normally set by the company's charter and is at least half the elected members of the company's board. The management board is normally chaired by the general director.

Executive bodies report to the supervisory board ('board of directors') of the company and to the general meeting of shareholders. The general meeting of shareholders may issue a resolution to delegate the authority of the single-person executive body to the 'management organization' or an individual 'manager'. The executive body has the authority to take action on all daily management issues, except for the issues within the authority of the general meeting of shareholders or the supervisory board.

In general, Russian companies are built around the general director, who manages the other executives. If the company has both a single-person body ('general director') and a collective body (management board), the general director will play the leading role and outline decisions to be taken by the management board. Yet, the recent trend in the holding companies has been to transfer CEO powers to management organizations and nominating executive directors to act on direct instructions from management organizations.

The Joint Stock Company Law (1995) states that if the executive bodies are not appointed by the board of directors in accordance with the company's charter, the general meeting of shareholders may at any time terminate the authority of the general director, or members of the management board. Also, the general meeting of shareholders may at any time terminate the authority of the management board or general director. If the appointment of the executive bodies comes within the authority of the supervisory board under the company charter, the supervisory board may at any time adopt a resolution to terminate the authority of the company's general director or members of the management committee and appoint new executive bodies. In reality, the general director performs his functions under a contract which the board offers him and which outlines the terms and conditions of his employment. The turnover of executives in the Russian companies is usually not very high. This is mainly because CEOs in many Russian companies are large or even major shareholders.

The law stipulates that all companies with more than 50 shareholders must have a supervisory board.

A supervisory board has authority in the following areas:

- to define the principal direction of the company;
- to call annual and special general meetings, to approve the agenda and to establish the date for shareholders entitled to participate in the general meeting;
- to increase the company's authorized capital through issuing additional shares, bonds and other securities;
- to determine the monetary value of property;
- to purchase shares, bonds or other securities issued by the company;
- to appoint the executive body of the company and terminate these powers (if the supervisory board has authority under the company's charter);
- to give recommendations on the amount of remuneration to be paid to members of the internal audit commission of the company and the determination of the fees for services provided by the external auditor;
- to give recommendations regarding the amount of dividend to be paid on shares and the procedure for their payment;
- to use the reserve fund and other company funds;

- to approve the company's internal documents other than the internal documents to be approved by the shareholder general meeting;

- to establish branches and representative offices of the company;

- to approve major transactions specified in the Joint Stock Company Law (1995);

- to approve the company's registrar and the terms and conditions of the registrar's contract and termination. Issues that are the authority of the supervisory board may not be delegated to the company's executive body.

The procedure for convening and conducting meetings of the supervisory board are normally described in the company's charter. The charter may provide for the possibility to take into account at a meeting of the supervisory board the written opinion of an absent board member on matters included in the agenda of the meeting when making a determination as to the presence of a quorum or voting results, or for the possibility of approving resolutions of the supervisory board of the company by written consent.

The quorum for a meeting of the supervisory board must be specified in the charter but it may not be less than half of the number of elected members of the supervisory board. If the number of members of the supervisory board is reduced to a level below such quorum requirement, the supervisory board must adopt a resolution to hold a special general meeting of shareholders to elect a new supervisory board. The remaining members of the supervisory board may not approve any resolution other than a resolution to convene such a special general meeting of shareholders.

It is a rather widespread practice in Russian companies to leave the supervisory board to perform procedural tasks. Crucial decisions are most often taken outside the board, while its members have only to give their formal approval. Yet, since 2000, the role of boards has been steadily growing.

There have been a number of recent changes in law relating to the work of the board. These changes include:

- amendments to the law 'On Joint Stock Companies' and the law 'On Securities Market';

- new Federal Commission of the Securities Market regulations;

- the Code of Corporate Governance (2002).

All these changes are aimed at enhancing the role and responsibilities of boards and impose stronger penalties on companies and their members. Individuals and companies are increasingly litigating against joint stock companies for corporate governance abuse (eg in the preparation and holding of the general meetings and board meetings, information disclosure, etc). There is also a broadening practice of *greenmail* (corporate blackmail) by certain companies and small investors that use the threat of litigation in order to gain material benefits. In most cases the litigation is prompted by board decisions that failed to comply with current legislation (very often on procedural issues) or, in certain cases when the legislation is inherently conflicting, decisions that ignore the interests of some of the stakeholders.

Board members are elected by the general meeting of shareholders for a period of one year until the next annual general meeting of shareholders. There are no limitations on successive re-elections. Only a 'physical person' may be a member of the supervisory board. A member of a supervisory board does not necessarily have to own shares in the company.

Shareholders who own at least 2 per cent of the shares can nominate candidates to the board. Since spring 2004, the election of board members by cumulative voting is mandatory for all joint stock companies.

All elections are conducted on the basis of one-share-one-vote. There are no shares with multiple voting rights.

The general meeting of shareholders may vote to move a board member before his term expires but such a voting by the general meeting means the entire board shall be relected.

22.4.1 Size

The number of members of the supervisory board is normally determined by the company in accordance with the requirements of the Joint Stock Company Law.

The law requires that the board of directors of open joint stock companies shall not have less than five members and companies with more than 1,000 voting shareholders must have at least seven board members. The board in companies with more than 10,000 voting shareholders should have at least nine members. In reality, the boards of industrial companies have 8–12 members. The largest Russian companies might have up to 15 members.

22.4.2 Composition

The chairman of the board is elected by a majority of the members of the board, unless otherwise provided in the charter. The supervisory board may re-elect its chairman at any time by a majority vote of all members of the board, unless otherwise provided in the charter.

Members of the management board shall not make up more than a quarter of the total number of board members. The 'general director' shall not be the chairman of the board. Formally, these legal requirements are observed, but the majority of board members in most companies are still the company's senior managers. Nearly all of the managers on supervisory boards represent controlling shareholders.

There is a general practice that board members owe their allegiance to the group that nominated them and cast votes for them, which is equally true of board members elected by minority and majority shareholders. As a consequence, board members often tend to support decisions that suit the interests of particular groups of shareholders but do not represent all company shareholders.

In companies with a significant holding owned by the state, government agencies elect their own officials as board members to represent the government's interests. In the largest companies, the government-nominated board members are usually senior government officials (ministers, deputy ministers or department heads) and in the middle-sized companies with government-owned stocks, these are lower-ranking officials. The largest number of these types of directors is nominated by the Ministry of State Property. Others are nominated by the branch ministries (Ministry of Energy, Ministry of Transport, etc). Government-nominated board members often tend to support decisions motivated by political or fiscal considerations instead of on the grounds of commercial merit and they are passive while serving as directors. The federal government has recently embarked on reforming the system of state-nominated directors by gradually shifting the emphasis from officials to professional managers.

22.4.3   Independence

Article 83 of the Joint Stock Company Law (1995) defines an independent director as:

> *An independent director shall be any member of the supervisory board of the company who is not then, and has not been for the year immediately preceding such approval:*
>
> - *the person serving as single-person executive body of the company, including, without limitation, its manager, or as a member of the collective executive body or holding a position in the governing bodies of the management organization; or*
>
> - *a person whose spouse, parents, children, brothers and sisters by both parents or by one parent only, adoptive parents or adopted children hold a position in such governing bodies of the company or its management organization or are the company's manager; or*
>
> - *an affiliate of the company other than a member of the supervisory board of the company.*

Most investors see this definition as very narrow. In order to make this concept more consistent with 'best practices' international guidelines, the Corporate Governance Code (2002) recommends the following definition of an independent director:

> *It is advisable that an independent director should be a director who:*
>
> (1) *over the last three years has not been, and at the time of election to the board of directors is not, an officer or employee of the company, or an officer or employee of the managing organization of the company*
>
> (2) *is not an officer of another company in which any of the officers of the company is a member of the appointments and remuneration committee of the board of directors*
>
> (3) *is not an affiliated person of an officer of the company*
>
> (4) *is not an affiliated person of the company or an affiliated person of such affiliated persons*
>
> (5) *is not bound by contractual relations with the company, whereby the person may receive money with a value in excess of 10 per cent of their aggregate annual income, other than through receipt of remuneration for participation in the operations of the board of directors*

(6) *is not a business partner with an annual value of transactions with the company in excess of 10 per cent of the asset value of the company*

(7) *is not a representative of the government.*

The Code also contains the following recommendation on the number of independent directors on a board:

In order to enable independent directors to influence actively the decision-making process and ensure that the board of directors considers the widest possible spectrum of opinions on matters being discussed, their number should comprise at least a quarter of the total number of members of the board of directors. In any event, it is recommended that the company's charter should provide that the board of directors include at least three independent directors.

The Federal Commission on the Securities Market requires that Russian companies disclose major aspects of their corporate governance practices, including the number of independent directors on their boards and the definition of 'independence' that they employ.

The first independent directors appeared on the boards of Russian companies after the 1998 crisis when foreign portfolio investors suffered significant losses. The investor and brokerage companies which represented these investors spearheaded the campaign for electing independent directors to companies in which they held stocks. These companies nominated and voted their candidates in through the Investor Protection Association (IPA). In 2002, IPA representatives were elected as independent directors to the boards of over 30 companies. These are mostly in energy (subsidiaries of RAO UES, the electricity monopoly) and telecommunications companies (subsidiaries of Svyazinvest). Yet, the problem with these directors is their allegiance to a particular group of shareholders – in this case, to those portfolio investors who have voted for their election. Most of the IPA-supported directors are officers of investment or brokerage companies that elected them on to the boards and they receive remuneration directly from these companies.

In addition to this category, there are a number of outside directors who are not affiliated with the IPA. Most of them are prominent experts in business or former senior government officials.

Since 2001, a new trend has been seen among the major Russian companies, which involves the election of prominent foreign businessmen as independent directors to boards with the votes cast by the controlling shareholders.

Some Russian companies allow trade union officers or other representatives of employees and some other stakeholders such as regional authorities to sit on their boards of directors (these are elected mostly by votes of the controlling/major shareholders). However, this practice is not widespread.

The Corporate Governance Code (2002) recommends the setting up of committees. The Code specifically recommends that companies should set up the following board committees:

- a strategic planning committee;
- an audit committee;
- a human resource and remuneration committee;
- a corporate conflicts resolution committee;
- a business ethics committee.

The Code also recommends that board committees are headed by outside directors.

At present, few Russian companies have committees although their number has been growing since 2003. The ones that do have committees are primarily companies whose securities are traded on Western stock exchanges or those which seek to make an IPO on Western stock exchanges in the foreseeable future.

Under the new listing requirements, companies must have an audit committee and remuneration committees.

22.4.4 Remuneration

Remuneration practices have not been a major issue in Russia. Most companies have board members who are managers and they usually do not receive any additional remuneration for serving on boards. There is a general view that their executive remuneration covers their efforts as board members.

As far as outside directors are concerned, most of them only receive refunds for the direct expenses related to the performance of their duties. Company managers believe that these shareholders or shareholder groups, not the company, should pay their nominees themselves. Yet since 2001, a growing number of companies have begun to pay their outside/independent directors. The amount of annual remuneration of outside directors presently varies from US $10,000 to US $120,000.

In January 2004, Energy Intelligence, a US analytical agency, published a corporate governance rating based on board composition and performance of the top transnational oil and gas companies. YUKOS was rated 2nd, Sibneft was 8th and LUKOIL was 11th. The average score was 59.7 for the US companies, 53.9 for the European ones and 52.8 for the Russian companies. Typically, these three Russian companies were ahead of several leading Western corporations. Russian companies had a lower average score because the quality of corporate governance in such companies as Gazprom and Surgutneftegaz was substandard.

The Corporate Governance Code (2002) recommends that companies should pay remuneration to their board members. This remuneration should be equal for all board members regardless of whether the member of the board of directors is an executive, non-executive or independent director. It also recommends that the amount of remuneration payable should be determined by the human resources and remuneration committee on the basis of sound criteria and approved by the board of directors.

22.4.5 The Management Board

The Corporate Governance Code (2002) recommends that joint stock companies should establish a management board. The role of the management board is to:

- develop important documents of the company (eg guidelines detailing priority areas of operation for the company and its financial and business plan for approval by the security board) and to consider and approve the company internal documents that outline the authority of the executive bodies;

- approve the company's transactions that have a value equal to, or in excess of, 5 per cent of the total value of the company's assets and promptly notify the supervisory board about such transactions;

- approve transactions that involve real estate and loans received by the company in connection with its routine business operations and the value equals, or is in excess of, 5 per cent of the total assets of the company;

- approve any real estate transactions and loans, provided that the company does not usually engage in such transactions in the ordinary course of its business.

The size of individual remuneration of Russian CEOs and senior executives in most cases is not publicly disclosed (under the regulation, the companies may submit aggregated amount of remuneration for all top managers and board members). A small number of large listed companies have started to award stock options to senior management. These plans can be a useful instrument to align the interests of managers and shareholders, improve managers' incentives and thereby corporate performance. However, a legal framework for this new concept and practice needs to be developed.

Under the Joint Stock Company Law (1995), members of the supervisory board, the general director, members of the management board, or managers exercising their rights and performing their obligations must act in the interests of the company, exercise their rights and perform their obligations with respect to the company in a diligent and reasonable manner. Members of the supervisory board, the general director, members of the management committee, or managers are liable to the company for any losses which the company incurs because of their wrongful acts or failure to act, unless federal laws provide other reasons to limit their liability.

Members of the supervisory board or management board who voted against a resolution which caused the company to incur losses or did not participate in such voting are not liable.

When determining the reasons for and the extent of liability of members of the supervisory board or the general director and/or members of the management committee or managers, it is necessary to take into consideration customary business practices and other relevant circumstances.

If several people are liable, their liability to the company shall be joint and several.

The representatives of the state or a municipal entity on the supervisory board of an open company are liable to the same extent as any other member of the supervisory board.

22.5   Codes, Standards and Good Practice Guidelines

22.5.1   The Corporate Governance Code (2002)

The Corporate Governance Code was developed under the guidance of the Federal Commission for Securities Market with the support of the OECD and World Bank in April 2002. The Code sets the 'best practice' recommendations for all the main aspects of company corporate governance practices. Under the recently adopted regulations, joint stock companies shall include in their annual reports chapters on their corporate governance practices and conformity with the Code in accordance with the principle 'comply or disclose discrepancies'.

The Corporate Governance Code recommends that the duties of members of the supervisory board be clearly defined and incorporated into internal documents of the company. It also recommends that the internal documents of the company should contain a list of rights granted to board members, including, specifically, their right to demand information from executive bodies within the company.

The Code recommends that companies vest the following main functions within boards:

- to determine the development strategy of the company;
- to consider and approve its annual financial and business plan;
- to carry out efficient supervision of the financial and business operations of the company;
- to protect the rights of shareholders and facilitate the settlement of corporate conflicts;
- to ensure efficient operation of the executive bodies of the company by supervising their operations.

22.5.2   The Civil Code

The Civil Code of the Russian Federation (Parts One and Two) was passed by the State Duma in 1994 (amended in 1996, 1999 and 2001).

The Code sets the basic principles, legal status and organizational and legal forms of legal entities.

22.5.3 The European Bank for Reconstruction and Development Assessment

The European Bank for Reconstruction and Development, in a corporate governance sector assessment project in May 2003, classified Russia as having a high compliance level of corporate governance systems measured against the OECD Principles of Corporate Governance. It found that the existing corporate governance related laws were 'relatively sound'.

The report also identified constraints that are inhibiting corporate governance in Russia. These constraints include:

- lack of transparency in company management;
- lack of accountability to shareholders on the part of management;
- unfair treatment of minority shareholders;
- weak coordination and advocacy among shareholders and stakeholders;
- a weak corporate governance culture;
- poor enforcement and oversight of existing laws and regulations.

22.6 Disclosure and Transparency

Every joint stock company is required to have its financial statements and performance results audited annually by an external auditor. The external auditor is recommended by the board of directors and must be approved by the general meeting of shareholders. The general meeting also approves the remuneration for the external auditor. The external auditor summarizes the audit of financial and business operations in an opinion which must include:

- confirmation that the information in the company's reports and other financial statements is accurate;
- information about cases of the company's breaching accounting legislation.

By law every joint stock company shall have a revision (financial audit) commission that is independent of the board of directors, the CEO and management board and reports directly to the annual general meeting of shareholders on the completeness and accuracy of the company's accounts. Members of the revision commission may not be members of the supervisory board, nor may they hold office in any other of the company's governance bodies. The revision commission is often criticized for not being effective enough. The criticism usually focuses on:

- the commissioners' dependence upon company management because the commission includes company employees and insider shareholders;
- the commissioners' level of professionalism (eg the absence of clear methodologies and procedures);
- audits and reports made by the commission often contain little useful information.

No shares owned by members of the supervisory board or by persons holding positions in governing bodies of the company may participate in voting to elect members of the revision commission.

22.7 Shareholder Rights and Stakeholder Relations

The strengthening of shareholder rights is an important corporate governance issue in Russia. In October 2001, President Putin stated:

> *Russia has a strategic goal.... to become a country that makes competitive goods and renders competitive services. All our efforts are committed to this goal. We understand we have to solve questions pertaining to the protection of owners' rights and the improvement of corporate governance and financial transparency in business in order to be integrated into world markets.*

There are two types of shares:

- Common shares: Each common share has the same nominal value. The most important right of the shareholder is to vote and to receive a dividend. Common shares may not be converted into preference shares, bonds or other securities.

- Preference shares: Owners of preference shares do not have the right to vote (except on decisions that affect the interests of their holders) but instead these shares offer certain privileges concerning receiving dividends and the liquidation value of shares. The nominal value of placed preference shares must not exceed 25 per cent of the company's authorized capital. The company's charter may permit the conversion of certain types of preference shares into common shares or preference shares of other types.

In Russia, the law also recognizes the existence of fractional shares (fractions of a share) which usually emerge as a result of consolidation of shares. A fractional share confers on its owner the rights corresponding to the full share it represents.

In Russia, investor activism has become a vital spur to reform in corporate governance, as local investors join forces with overseas investors to take advantage of new rules allowing cumulative voting, which concentrates minority votes for candidates to the board who can provide direct oversight of management in the face of uncertain regulatory protection.

A company or a shareholder (shareholders) who in total own(s) no less than 1 per cent of the issued and outstanding shares of common stock in the company may sue a member of the supervisory board of a company, the general director, a member of the management committee, or the management organization or manager in a court of law seeking compensation for losses caused to the company in the instances specified in the JSC Law (1995). Under the law, a shareholder with at least 2 per cent of the company's voting (ordinary) shares has the right to put up to two items on the agenda of the general meeting of shareholders and to nominate candidates to the board of directors and the company's executive management. If the board refuses to include these items in the agenda or to include the list of candidates, the shareholder has the right to challenge this decision in court. A shareholder with at least 10 per cent of the voting shares has the right to call for an extraordinary general meeting of shareholders.

A shareholder with at least 1 per cent of the voting shares has the right to file a complaint against a member of the supervisory board or management board, the CEO or an outside managing company. In this complaint he may seek reimbursement for damages to the company caused by their actions or failure to act. Any shareholder has the right to challenge in court a decision of the general meeting of shareholders, if the shareholder did not vote or voted against a decision, and the decision violated the shareholder's rights and lawful interests. The complaint must be filed within six months from the date when the shareholder learnt or should have learnt of the decision.

Until recently, Russian companies seldom paid dividends to their shareholders. This is partly acceptable due to economic considerations whereby many companies need large funds to modernize worn out fixed assets. However, companies that had posted large profits to attract investors, have begun paying sizeable dividends in recent years. For example, Uralkalii paid over 40 per cent of its net profit as dividend in 2002 and Norilsk Nickel and Severstal also paid a large dividend in 2003. Analysts estimate that leading companies will pay over 40 per cent of net profit in dividends in the period ahead. According to a survey of Russian middle-size and small companies conducted by the IFC in late 2002–early 2003, less than 30 per cent of the regional Russian companies with turnover below US $10 million and more than 50 per cent of the companies with turnover above US $10 million paid dividends. The share of net profit spent on dividend by these companies increased from 16 per cent in 2000 to 21 per cent in 2001.

When dividends were paid, the delay between the decision and the actual payment was often quite long. The 2001 amendments to the JSC Law largely addressed this issue, and there is now a two-month cut-off date for companies that fail to establish a deadline during the general meeting.

The JSC Law requires all joint stock companies to maintain a register of their shareholders, and the 2001 amendments to the JSC Law make it mandatory for companies with more than 50 shareholders to transfer their registers to professional registrars licensed by the FCSM. Cases of manipulation and fraud in company registrars used to be flagrant a few years ago, thus jeopardizing the effective transfer of ownership. These included refusal to re-register the title or transfer shares, illegal strike-off of shares from registers, change of share status from common to preferred and accidental losses of records. The situation has improved over the past years and abuses have become less frequent and blatant. The most typical offence is now the refusal to give information to shareholders about the company's ownership structures or improper handling of share transactions due to negligence. These problems still occur, mostly in the regions.

The general meeting of shareholders is authorized to take action on the following matters:

1. amendments to the company charter or approval of an amended and restated company charter;

2. reorganization of the company;

3. liquidation of the company, appointment of a liquidation committee and approval of the interim and final liquidation balance sheets;

4. determination of the number of members of the supervisory board, election of its members and early termination of their powers;

5. determination of the number, par value and type (class) of, and the rights attached to, additional authorized shares;

6. any increase of the company's authorized capital through par value shares or through the issuance of additional shares unless approval of an increase of the company's authorized capital through the issuance of additional shares falls within the authority of the supervisory board of the company under its charter as permitted by the Federal Law;

7. any decrease of the company's authorized capital through a decrease in the par value of its shares, through the redemption of a portion of the shares by the company for the purpose of reducing their total number, or through the cancellation of shares redeemed or bought back by the company;

8. appointment of any executive body of the company and early termination of its powers unless the company charter delegates such authority to the supervisory board;

9. election of members of the internal auditing commission (internal auditor) of the company and early termination of their powers;

10. approval of the external auditor of the company;

11. approval of annual reports, annual accounts, including the profit and loss statement of the company, the distribution of its profits,

including the declaration of dividends and the distribution of its losses upon the close of each fiscal year;

12. establishing a procedure for the conduct of the general meeting of shareholders;

13. approval of any internal documents governing the activities of the company's bodies.

No matter falling within the authority of the general meeting of shareholders may be delegated to the executive body of the company.

Any shareholder(s) owning, in aggregate, at least 2 per cent of the voting shares in a company may propose items for the agenda of the annual general meeting of shareholders and nominate candidates for the supervisory board of the company and the company's collective executive body, revision (financial audit) commission and ballot counting commission, the number of such candidates nominated by each eligible shareholder shall not exceed the membership of the respective body, and a candidate for the single-person executive body.

A special general meeting of shareholders is held by a resolution of the supervisory board of the company on its own initiative or at the request of the internal auditing commission (internal auditor) of the company, the external auditor of the company, or a shareholder(s) who own(s) no less than 10 per cent of the voting shares in the company as of the date of such request.

If a special general meeting of shareholders is called at the request of the revision commission of the company, the external auditor of the company, or a shareholder(s) who own(s) no less than 10 per cent of the voting shares in the company, such meeting is convened by the supervisory board of the company.

If a special general meeting of shareholders is called at the request of the revision commission of the company, the external auditor of the company, or a shareholder(s) who own(s) no less than 10 per cent of the voting shares in the company, such meeting must be held within 40 days after the submission of the request to hold such special general meeting of shareholders.

Any resolution of the supervisory board of the company to deny the convocation of a special general meeting of shareholders may be appealed in court. If the supervisory board fails to adopt a resolution to convene a special general meeting at the request of shareholders who own no less than 10 per cent of the voting shares or denies its convocation, such special general meeting of shareholders may be convened by the bodies or persons requesting such meeting. The bodies or persons so calling a special general meeting of shareholders have the powers to call and hold a special general meeting of shareholders. As a result, conflicting groups of shareholders, each owning more than 10 per cent of the voting shares, may convene 'their own' meetings where they have the majority of votes, elect vested boards and appoint vested CEOs. This leads at times, to a situation where the same company may have two boards of directors and two CEOs elected by rival groups of shareholders. The company's normal operations would in this case be disrupted, and a solution would need to be found through a long series of court litigations and intense bargaining between the conflicting parties.

Persons eligible to take part in the general meeting of shareholders are entititled, under the law, to receive the following information from the company:

- annual accounting reports including the auditor's reports;

- the report of the internal auditing commission (internal auditor) of the company on the results of the audit of annual accounts;

- information regarding candidates for the executive bodies of the company, the supervisory board, the internal auditing commission (internal auditor) of the company and the company's counting commission;

- draft amendments and additions to the company's charter or the drafted and restated charter;

- proposed internal documents of the company;

- proposed resolutions of the general meeting of shareholders;

- annual report;

- a report of the internal auditing commission concerning the reliability of information included in the company's annual report;

- recommendations to the supervisory board concerning the distribution of profit, including the size of the dividend on the company's shares and the payment procedures, and the company's losses in the financial year.

If the agenda of a general meeting of shareholders includes issues the voting on which might entail the right for the company to buy its shares from the shareholders, the latter must receive the following additional information from the company:

- an independent appraiser's report on the market value of the company's shares, the claim on buying which could be produced to the company;
- the value of the company's net assets for the last complete reporting period;
- minutes of the meeting of the supervisory board which took the decision to repurchase the company's shares and the price.

If the agenda of a general meeting of shareholders includes the issue of reorganization, the shareholders must receive the following additional information from the company:

- a rationale of the terms and conditions of reorganization, stated in a decision on a split-up, spin-off or transformation or in an agreement on a merger or acquisition, approved by the company's authorized body;
- the annual reports and annual accounts of all organizations involved in the reorganization, for three completed financial years preceding the date of the general meeting, or for each complete financial year after the date when the company was established if the company has been operational for less than three years;
- the quarterly accounts of all companies involved in the reorganization, for the last complete quarter preceding the date of the general meeting.

The problems that the shareholders face when they try to obtain this information before the general meetings are related to the fact that all or almost all companies provide these materials in their headquarters but do not make them available in the publicly accessible information channels (eg corporate Web sites). Information pertaining to the general meeting is not always made available to the shareholders at their first request nor as fully as is required by the law and regulation. However, recent court cases have ruled general meetings invalid and shareholders have won their cases on the grounds that they had not received all the required information. Investors' disappointment with the quality of information is usually caused by the companies' understatement of their profits and the use of semi-grey schemes of posting the profit to their affiliates for tax minimization purposes. However, during the past two or three years in search for raising investment attractiveness Russian companies have begun to disclose their profits. However, the behaviour is still rare. As a rule, Russian companies prefer to share strategic information only with their major investors and only after rather long discussions. Russian companies treat much of their business information as confidential.

22.7.1 Stakeholders

The debate concerning the role of stakeholders in corporate governance in Russia has not occurred so far. In the foreseeable future, discussions on the role of company employees as stakeholders will very likely be focused on ensuring the effective enforcement of rights based on labour and trade union legislation. Outside of these legal obligations, only a small group of companies are starting to take voluntary measures to pay attention to their staff as a stakeholder and use it as a valuable resource for building competitive and profitable enterprises in the long term.

22.8 Director Development Activity

The work on developing professional and ethical standards for board members and training programmes was initiated in Russia by the Russian Institute of Directors (RID). The Russian Institute of Directors currently runs regular courses for board members and company secretaries. The Corporate Director course includes six 8-hour core modules:

- introduction to corporate governance;
- how to make an effective board;
- board's role in development and implementation of company strategy;
- board's role in risk management and restructuring;

- board's role in ensuring disclosure and transparency;
- finance for non-financial directors.

Over the period 2001–03, about 350 executive and non-executive board members have taken the course, both in Moscow and in some regions of Russia. RID experts are currently working on developing new modules.

In Autumn 2003, the RID drafted a professional and ethic code for corporate directors, 'Declaration of Professionalism and Ethic Rules', which provides a guideline for shareholders in selecting and nominating candidates to the boards. The Declaration was approved by the second congress of Russian corporate directors in November 2003. The document is available at www.rid.ru.

The RID has also initiated the development of the professional and ethical code for company secretaries and in cooperation with Expert Rating Agency and the support of the USAID and the National Council for Corporate Governance has launched the National Corporate Governance Rating.

The Higher School of Economics also offers training on corporate governance issues for undergraduate and MBA students. The programme is sponsored by the Canadian International Development Agency and supported by the Schulich School of Business at York University in Toronto.

In 2002–04 the IFC carried out a project on improvement of Corporate Governance which included a series of training programmes in four Russian regions.

In addition, the Institute of Professional Auditors of Russia, the Institute of Internal Auditors, the Organisation of Company Shareholders and Investors, the Association of Independent Directors and the Investor Protection Association are involved in the education of their members concerning corporate governance best practice.

22.9 Useful Contacts

- Central Bank – www.cbr.ru
- Federal Service for Financial Markets – www.fcsm.ru

- National Council for Corporate Governance – www.nsku.ru; www.nccg.ru

- Russian Institute of Directors – www.rid.ru

22.10   Further Reading

Chen, H (2003) *Corporate Governance Sector Assessment Project May 2003*, European Bank for Reconstruction and Development, London

The Coordination Council for Corporate Governance (2002) *The Russian Code of Corporate Conduct*, CCGC, Moscow, www.rid.ru

National Council for Corporate Governance (2004) *National Report on Corporate Governance*, www.nccg.ru and www.nsku.ru, Moscow

Radygin, A (1999) *Ownership and Control of the Russian Industry*, Institute for the Economy in Transition, Russia

Russian Institute of Directors (2003) *Disclosure of Information about Corporate Governance Practices and Compliance with the Code of Corporate Conduct by Russian Joint Stock Companies*, Moscow, www.rid.ru

World Bank (2003) *Corporate Governance in Russia; Regime Change Required*, Transition Newsletter, **14** (1–3) (Jan–March), World Bank, Washington, www.worldbank.org

World Bank (2002) *White Paper on Corporate Governance in Russia*, World Bank, Washington

23

Ukraine

Table 23.1

Population	48.7 million (2002)
Gross Domestic Income (GDI)	US $37.7 billion (2002)
GDI per capita	US $770 (2002)
Total number of companies	23,000 closed companies (CJSC)
	12,000 open companies (OJSC)
Number of companies listed on the stock exchange	300
Key corporate laws	• 1992 Law No 2544 – XII On Ownership in Ukraine
	• 1991 Law No 887 – XII On Enterprises in Ukraine
	• 1991 Law No 698 – XII On Entrepreneurship
	• 1991 Law No 1576 – XII On Business Companies
	• 1991 Law No 1201 – XII On Securities and Stock Exchange
Key corporate governance codes	• 2002 National Principles of Corporate Goverance Securities and Stock Market State Comission

23.1 Corporate Structure and Ownership

Reform in Ukraine has caused the establishment of approximately 35,000 joint stock companies in Ukraine over the period from 1992 to 2003. In 2002, approximately 17 million Ukrainians were shareholders. Joint stock companies play a dominant role in the economy of Ukraine; they produce approximately 60 per cent of the total industrial output and over 2 million Ukrainian citizens are employed in joint stock companies.

In Ukraine there are two types of joint stock companies, public (open, OJSC) and private (closed, CJSC) joint stock companies:

- in establishing a CJSC no open subscription for shares may be held, and all the shares must be allocated among the founders;
- shares of CJSC may not be traded at the stock exchange; and
- if any shareholder of CJSC decides to sell his or her shares, shareholders of this CJSC have the right of privileged purchase of the shares.

Virtually all other aspects of activities carried out by OJSC and CJSC are regulated by the same rules. Overall, the country has approximately 23,000 CJSC and 12,000 OJSC.

Approximately 300 companies are listed on the Ukrainian stock exchange.

Joint stock companies have been established based on the property of state enterprises in the process of privatization (there are approximately 19,000 such companies). These have a large number of shareholders (who are mostly employees and citizens of Ukraine who purchased the shares in exchange for privatization certificates). Large privatized companies may have as many as 5,000–10,000 shareholders and sometimes over 50,000 shareholders. Presently, approximately 8 per cent of shares of the Ukrtelecom OJSC have been privatized. Ukrtelecom has as many as 123,000 shareholders. On the other hand, start-up companies established over the past few years by the traditional method have a small number of shareholders, which even in large companies rarely exceeds 20–25. Most joint stock companies of Ukraine have one or several majority shareholders holding more than

50 per cent of the shares. Approximately 10 per cent of majority share-holders are foreign individuals and legal entities. The number of shares held by Ukrainian citizens is falling, and the number of share-holders in virtually all joint stock companies is fast decreasing. We believe that in a few years the ownership structure of most Ukrainian joint stock companies 'several majority shareholders'.

23.1.1 Open and Closed Joint Stock Companies

A number of specialists suggest eliminating the division of companies into open and closed, meaning that all joint stock companies should be public companies and their activities should be regulated by the same rules. Legislation stipulates such legal form of establishment as a limited liability company, which may be used to establish private companies.

Less radical proposals regarding the future fate of closed joint stock companies are more popular among legislators and businessmen. It is proposed to preserve this type of company, but to abolish state registration of their share issues and to make disclosure, audit, etc requirements for closed joint stock companies much less stringent. It is suggested that restrictions on the number of shareholders in closed joint stock companies should be introduced. According to the latest draft laws, CJSCs may not have more than 200 shareholders. There is no doubt that such companies, such as the Obolon CJSC, Svitoch CJSC, etc, which have several thousand shareholders each, are not private companies and should not continue as closed joint stock companies.

The private sector accounted for 60 per cent of Ukraine's GDP and listed companies accounted for 9 per cent of GDP in 2001 (OECD, 2003).

23.2 Legal Framework

The Law 'On business companies' was introduced in 1991 and covers the establishment and management of companies in Ukraine. It also lists the basic rights and obligations of shareholders.

Companies may not be criminally prosecuted. Instead, officers of companies guilty of criminal offences are held criminally liable in court. Civil lawsuits against defendants in criminal cases may be tried together as part of proceedings in such criminal cases.

The current system of corporate governance in Ukraine involves:

- current legislation;
- the Corporate Governance Code and best practices recommendations;
- the stock exchange and trade systems listing rules;
- charters and other by-laws of companies.

The legislation regulating issues of corporate governance may be divided into:

- general company law;
- legislation regulating the activities of joint stock companies, banks and banking as well as non-governmental pension funds;
- privatization law;
- securities law;
- bankruptcy law;
- antitrust law.

The general principles of establishment, functioning, reorganization and liquidation of all types of companies in Ukraine are stipulated by the Civil Code of Ukraine and the Business Code of Ukraine, which came into force on 1 January 2004.

The specifics of the setting up and functioning of companies owned by several owners (business companies) are stipulated by the Law of Ukraine 'On Business Companies' (19 September 1991, No. 1576-XII).

Business organizations include:

- joint stock companies;
- limited liability companies;
- additional liability companies;
- general partnerships;
- limited partnerships.

These organizations must observe the requirements of both codes and the Laws. In the case of conflict of laws (which happens quite often), special rules of the Law 'On Business Companies' prevail over the rules of the civil code and the business code that regulate activities of all business entities.

The Law 'On Business Companies', which is the principal corporate governance framework, has only 26 articles concerning joint stock companies. This is considered to be not enough. In addition, many of the rules of the Law are ambiguous, which allows for multiple interpretations. This generates very inconsistent case law. Different courts may return diametrically opposite judgments in similar cases. The Cabinet of Ministers of Ukraine has recently prepared a draft law of Ukraine on joint stock companies. In the near future, it will be submitted for consideration by the Verkhovna Rada. This is not the first attempt to pass a law on joint stock companies. On 29 November 2001 the Verkhovna Rada turned down the draft law submitted by the Cabinet of Ministers.

Any type of companies in Ukraine may be established by legal entities and individuals, by both residents and non-residents of Ukraine. However, there are strict rules restricting participation by governmental enterprises, state authorities and public officials in the establishment of companies together with non-governmental enterprises and individuals.

The laws regulating the activities of companies in Ukraine specifically provide that any company shall be entitled to carry out activities that are not directly prohibited by law, including:

- Enter into contracts and other transactions with business partners.
- Carry out any types of business activity.
- Obtain land plots for ownership, use or lease.
- Hire and dismiss personnel.
- Obtain credit and loans.
- Open bank accounts.
- Carry out other actions causing legal consequences.

Companies have been granted sufficient independence in choosing types of activity and carrying them out. However, there are certain rules restricting activities of companies in the public interest. Restrictions include licensing procedures regulated by the Law of Ukraine 'On Entrepreneurship' (7 February 1991, No. 698-XII). Licensable activities may be carried out only after the relevant licence has been issued. Article 4 of the Law 'On Entrepreneurship' stipulates the list of activities that may be carried out only by companies determined by the Cabinet of Ministers of Ukraine. The licensing procedure and licensable activities are stipulated in the Law of Ukraine 'On Licensing of Certain Business Activities' (01.06.2000 No. 1775-111).

The specifics of the setting up and functioning of banking institutions as joint stock companies (an absolute majority of Ukrainian banks have been established in the form of joint stock companies) are stipulated by the Law of Ukraine 'On Banks and Banking' (7 December 2000, No. 2121-III). For example, this Law stipulates that the management board of a bank may be appointed only by resolution of the supervisory board, while in all other joint stock companies this may be done by any general shareholders' meeting or the supervisory board (depending on the rules stipulated by the charter).

The Law of Ukraine 'On the Non-state Pension Provision' (09.07.2009 No. 1057-IV) was enacted now on 1 January 2004 and therefore non-state pension funds have become active players in the corporate governance area.

23.2.1 Privatization Law

As a result of the Ukraine's policy to privatize state property, the majority of government enterprises have already been converted or are being converted to public (open) joint stock companies. From the moment of approving the decision on privatization until final completion of all stages of the privatization plan, company activities are regulated by the laws stipulating the specific details of the legal status of the different companies that are being privatized, depending on their size, sector and 'depth' of privatization. The main law regulating legal, economic and organization issues of privatization of state property of large and medium enterprises is the Law of Ukraine 'On Privatization of State Property' (4 March 1992, No. 2163-XII) (as revised and updated by the Law of Ukraine of 19 February 1997, No. 89/97-VR).

The specific tasks in the field of privatization as well as general direction, objectives and methods of privatization are provided by the State Privatization Programme implemented by the Law of Ukraine. Presently, the State Privatization Programme for 2000–02 is in effect. The term of this Programme has been extended until the approval of the State Privatization Programme for the next period. The Verkhovna Rada is currently considering a draft new programme for the period to 2008. It is worth noting that some rules of the Privatization Programme are obligatory for companies established as a result of the privatization process, irrespective of whether or not the privatization process has been completed. For example, in the event of a reorganization of joint stock companies established as a result of the privatization process, it is stipulated that the company must repurchase the shares of the shareholders who voted against the decision on reorganization.

In pursuance of the above Laws, the State Property Fund of Ukraine has approved a number of normative documents regulating individual aspects of corporate governance at companies that are being privatized.

23.2.2 Securities Law

Two important laws, the Law of Ukraine 'On Securities and Stock Exchange' (18 June 1991, No. 1201-XII) and the Law of Ukraine 'On National Depositary System and Specifics of Electronic Circulation of Securities in Ukraine' (10 December 1997, No. 710/97-VR), stipulate the rules for the issuance and circulation of securities, requirements on issuers, including those regarding disclosure, as well as the main rights of shareholders. State control over observance of securities and stock market legislation is carried out by the Securities and Stock Market State Commission. Its legal status was determined by the Law of Ukraine 'On State Regulation of Securities Market in Ukraine (30 October 1996, No. 448/96-VR).

23.2.3 Bankruptcy Law, Antitrust Law

Unfortunately, Ukrainian bankruptcy law is not an effective tool in corporate control. The Law of Ukraine 'On Restoring Solvency of a Debtor or Recognizing it Bankrupt' (14 May 1992, No. 2343-XII) (as revised and updated by the Law of Ukraine of 30 June 1999, No. 784-XIV) does not lay down any mechanisms for forced transfer of a bankrupt company's corporate rights to its receivers as part of the bankruptcy proceedings. Nor have other mechanisms been stipulated for the acquisition of a bankrupt company's corporate rights in exchange for its debts. This creates a situation where the majority of bankruptcy cases result not in receivership but in company liquidations. Bankruptcy proceedings for large companies may drag on for several years.

Antitrust law also plays a role in the regulation of the corporate control market restricting economic concentrations – acquisitions of controlling blocks of shares in large companies and reorganizations in the form of mergers and/or acquisitions. The Law of Ukraine 'On Protection of Economic Competition' (11 January 2001, No. 2210-III) stipulates a general rule, in accordance with which all the above actions shall be subject to approval by the Antimonopoly Committee of Ukraine, if the total value of assets of all participants in a concentration exceeds €12 million.

23.2.4 Systematized Rules

World best practices have long included the introduction in listing rules of higher requirements on transparency and protection of shareholder rights for listed companies compared to the requirements established by legislation. Unfortunately, we cannot say that this practice is customary for Ukraine. For example, the listing requirements of the PFTS Securities Trading System, the largest national securities trading system, contain only the condition of 'observing the requirements of law concerning disclosure of information'. Neither the PFTS Securities Trading System nor the Ukrainian Stock Exchange or other securities trading systems contain any additional requirements on listed companies concerning corporate governance.

The new Civil and Business Codes of Ukraine which came into effect as of 1 January 2004, significantly improved the legal framework for the functioning of joint stock companies.

The passing of the Codes gives a green light to the passing through the Verkhovna Rada of the draft law on joint stock companies. In 2003, this draft did not pass but is likely to be passed in 2005.

The Codes and the draft law provide for the improvement of the procedure for forming supervisory boards, the introduction of a cumulative voting procedure when electing boards of large companies, the determination of supervisory board powers, the regulation of the procedure for entering into large transactions of the company or transactions with a conflict of interest, and the establishment of a clear procedure for reorganizing companies.

The introduction of new legislation, which is in line with the main guidelines of the European Union, will speed up the process of stratification of Ukrainian joint stock companies. Most small companies are expected to change their legal form and re-register themselves as limited liability companies, while the largest Ukrainian joint stock companies, which strive to attract financing using stock market instruments, will bring their corporate governance practices into compliance with generally accepted rules.

The European Bank for Reconstruction and Development (2003) suggests that the following areas of improvement are required in Ukraine:

- The role of shareholders' meetings needs to be strengthened.
- The role of supervisory boards needs to be defined.
- Related party transaction regulations need to be enhanced.
- Disclosure of company information requires further rules.
- Rules preventing shareholder dilution need to be strengthened.

23.3 Board Structure

The supervisory board is elected by the shareholders. The supervisory board controls and regulates the activity of the management board of the company and acts within the authority granted to it by the charter or delegated to it by resolution of the general shareholders' meeting.

In accordance with Article 46 of the Law of Ukraine 'On Business Companies', the creation of the supervisory board is mandatory for joint stock companies with over 50 shareholders.

In accordance with the Law of Ukraine 'On Business Companies', members of the supervisory board may be neither members of the audit commission nor members of the executive body (the management board). Ukraine has adopted the 'two board' system similar to the German model: one board (the supervisory board) includes

423

non-executive directors representing mostly majority shareholders; the other board (the management board) includes executive directors, who are elected by the supervisory board or by the general shareholders' meeting.

Unfortunately, during the 12 years that have passed since the creation of the first Ukrainian joint stock company, Ukraine has failed to develop generally accepted standards applicable to the functioning of company supervisory boards, nor has it created requirements regarding the professional and personal qualities of candidates to the board or set up a system for their training, re-training, certification, etc. In this connection, the supervisory boards of many companies perform poorly and often are merely nominal, or they do not work at all.

23.3.1 Size

In Ukraine members of the supervisory board may be re-elected indefinitely. Current legislation of Ukraine does not stipulate an obligatory number of members of the supervisory board. In practice, this number may vary from 3 to 9 members.

23.3.2 Composition

Legislation of Ukraine does not prohibit the election to the supervisory board of a legal entity which is a company shareholder. In such an event, the head or an employee of the elected legal entity can be a member on the supervisory board.

23.3.3 The Procedure for Electing Members of the Supervisory Board

Current legislation does not lay down any special mechanisms for electing members of the supervisory board. They are elected at the general shareholders' meeting by a simple majority vote of the shareholders attending the meeting. The 'one share, one vote' principle applies. This allows the holder of a 50 per cent stake to make autocratic decisions as to the election of members of the supervisory board, which happens in practice quite often. In such a situation, minority shareholders cannot influence the board's decision making and often they do not even know what decisions are being made. This causes serious conflicts within joint stock companies.

The introduction of cumulative voting for the election of members of the supervisory board can help solve the problem. This provision has been included in the draft law on joint stock companies.

23.3.4 Committees

Audit committees must exist in all joint stock companies. The audit committee may be requested by holders of more than 10 per cent of the shares to audit the financial and business operations of the company's management.

23.4 Codes, Standards and Good Practice Guidelines

The European Bank for Reconstruction and Development, in a corporate governance sector assessment project in May 2003, classified Ukraine as having a very low compliance level of corporate governance systems measured against the OECD Principles of Corporate Governance.

In 2002, the Securities and Stock Market State Commission approved the 'Recommendations on Corporate Governance Best Practices for Joint Stock Companies in Ukraine' (Resolution of 2 June 2002). The Recommendations were the first document that, on behalf of a state authority, sets goals for companies based on the OECD Principles and best practices of Ukrainian and foreign companies. This document contains the following sections:

- protection of shareholder rights;
- disclosure of information;
- general shareholders' meetings;
- work of supervisory boards;
- regulation of company transactions.

The Recommendations provided momentum for drafting in Ukraine of National Standards (the Code) of Corporate Governance. The Decree of the President of Ukraine 'On Measures to Develop Corporate Governance in Joint Stock Companies' (21 March 2002, No. 280/2002) directly instructed the Securities and Stock Market State Commission to draft and approve the National Principles (the Code) of Corporate Governance. The Instructions of the Cabinet of Ministers of Ukraine 'On Approving the Measures to Implement the Priority Steps in Developing Corporate Governance in Joint Stock Companies' (18 January 2003, No. 25) ordered the SSMSC to approve the Code in 2002–04.

The Task Force on Corporate Governance and Protection of Shareholder Rights actively participated in drafting the National Principles (the Code) of Corporate Governance. The Task Force was created in 1998 at the Cabinet of Ministers of Ukraine in accordance with the Memorandum signed by the Governments of Ukraine and the USA and consists of representatives of the SSMSC, the State Property Fund of Ukraine, the Ministry of Justice of Ukraine, the World Bank, the International Finance Corporation, international organizations, shareholder rights protection associations, investment companies, banks, and large joint stock companies.

In 2003, the Securities and Stock Market State Commission finally approved the National Principles (the Code) of Corporate Governance (SSMSC Resolution No. 571 of 11.12.2003). The Code of Corporate Governance is structured as following:

- objective of the company;
- shareholder rights;
- supervisory board and executive body;
- disclosure and transparency;
- control over financial and business activities of the company;
- stakeholders.

The Code is a recommendatory document and suggests guidelines for companies regarding the development of their charters. The Code provides for specific implementation mechanisms, eg recommendations on disclosure in the annual report regarding Code compliance and/or reasons for non-compliance.

23.4.1 Charter of the Joint Stock Company

In accordance with the Law of Ukraine 'On Business Companies', each company must have a charter. The charter is the principal document of a joint stock company, having legal force and regulating, the issues of the company's activity and the main rights and responsibilities of shareholders. The requirements of the company charter are obligatory for all company bodies and their shareholders. The charter lists the objectives of the company, the types of activities and its governance bodies. To establish a company, its founders must register the charter with the executive committee of the local Council of People's Deputies (at the location of the company) in accordance with the requirements of law. The charter is an important source of information for third parties who wish to become shareholders of the company.

In accordance with the Law of Ukraine 'On Business Companies', the charter contains information about:

- the type of business activity of the company;
- name and location of the company;
- objectives and subject of the activity of the company;
- founders of and participants in the company;
- size of the charter capital of the company and procedure for setting up the charter capital;
- types and categories of the issued shares, their par value, correlation between different types and categories of issued shares, number of shares issued by the founders, and consequences of non-fulfilment of the obligations to purchase the shares;
- procedure for distributing profits, including payment of dividends and the covering of losses;
- composition and powers of company governance bodies and the procedure for their approving decisions;
- procedure for introducing changes to the constituent documents of the company;
- procedure for reorganizing and liquidating the company.

Besides the above provisions, the charter may contain other additional information not contradicting current legislation of Ukraine.

23.4.2   Company By-Laws

Normally, the charter does not regulate in detail the procedure for the management of company activities by its shareholders, members of the supervisory board and members of the management board. These rules are stipulated by company by-laws approved by the general shareholders' meeting or the supervisory board. These documents supplement and elaborate the provisions of the charter. The procedure for introducing changes and amendments to company by-laws is simpler than the procedure stipulated for introducing changes and amendments to the charter. The main requirement that must be taken into consideration when developing company by-laws is that they must comply with the provisions of the charter. Rules of company by-laws that contradict the charter are not valid.

Virtually all large Ukrainian companies aim to attract large shareholders owning 50 or more per cent of company shares. The same privatization policy is being carried out by the state selling shares of former large governmental enterprises, offering large blocks aiming to attract strategic investors. Also, the managers of many companies actively purchase shares in their companies, thus becoming the holders of fairly large blocks of shares. According to some sources, executive managers of Ukrainian joint stock companies hold approximately 44 per cent of all shares.

In such a situation, the idea of protecting the rights of minority shareholders faces strong resistance from managers. The opponents provide the following rationale: 'By protecting minority shareholders we may seriously damage the rights of the effective owner who assumes responsibility for the fate of the company in crisis and who is ready to make additional investment.'

However, the issue of responsibility of majority shareholders entitled to determine the activities of the company to minority shareholders is not even raised. The possibility is not provided either for minority shareholders to sell their shares on acquisition of a controlling block of shares simultaneously with such acquisition and at the same price.

As mentioned above, Ukraine does not have many principles in place regarding the responsibility of supervisory board members as well as that of members of the executive body, nor does legislation stipulate the right of the shareholders to file lawsuits against company management to recover losses in the interest of the company. The issues of insuring corporate directors against liability have not been resolved either.

23.5 Shareholder Rights and Stakeholder Relations

Shareholders of joint stock companies have rights which include:

- the right to participate in general shareholders' meetings;
- the right to vote at general shareholders' meetings;
- the right to transfer attendance and voting to a proxy; and
- the right to review minutes of general shareholders' meetings.

General meetings require 60 per cent+1 of the shares to be present or in proxy for the meeting to be quorate.

To amend the charter of the company, to terminate activities of the company or to establish and terminate subsidiaries and branches requires at least 60 per cent of shares entitled to vote.

The shareholders elect a supervisory board of a company with more than 50 shareholders.

Shareholders with 10 per cent or more of the company's shares can:

- convene an extraordinary general meeting;
- put proposals on the agenda of the general meeting; and
- request the audit committee to audit company operations.

Companies in Ukraine frequently fail to provide adequate notice of a general shareholders' meeting. This is particularly true of privatized companies that have a large number of shareholders. Legally, notice is 45 days.

In Ukraine companies frequently fail to provide an agenda and documents to a general shareholders' meeting.

23.5.1 Control over Company Officers

There are few legal remedies for shareholders in the areas of:

- asset stripping;
- related party transactions;
- insider trading;
- share dilution;
- wrongful disposition of assets.

Shareholders can appeal to the company's supervisory board for protection of their interests and rights.

The supreme governing body of a joint stock company is its general shareholders' meeting. It has the authority to approve decisions on the following issues:

1. determining the main fields of the company activities and approving its plans and reports on their fulfilment;
2. introducing changes to the company charter, including those made in connection with the changing of the size of its charter capital;
3. electing and recalling members of the supervisory board, the management board and the audit commission of the company;
4. approving annual results, financial statements and the balance sheet of the company, including its subsidiaries, as well as approving reports and opinions of the audit commission;
5. approving decisions on the procedure to distribute profits, including payment of dividends and the covering of losses;
6. establishing, reorganizing and liquidating subsidiaries, branches and establishments, approving their charters and by-laws;
7. approving rules of procedure and other internal documents of the company, defining the organizational structure of the company;
8. determining labour compensation terms for company officers as well as those of its subsidiaries, branches and establishments;
9. approving decisions on holding officers of company governance bodies liable for their property;
10. approving decisions for the company to repurchase the shares it issues;

11. approving contracts (agreements) entered into, if the value of products or services to which they relate exceeds that specified in the company charter;

12. approving the decision on discontinuing company operations, appointing the liquidation commission and approving the liquidation balance sheet.

The company charter may include the resolution of other issues within the powers of the general shareholders' meeting. On the other hand, the charter or resolution of the general shareholders' meeting may stipulate the powers of the general shareholders' meeting delegated by the shareholders to the supervisory board or the management board. The powers stipulated by Sections 2, 4, 5, 6 and 12, which are the exclusive powers of the general shareholders' meeting, may not be delegated.

23.6 Director Development Activity

Interest in developing corporate directors in Ukraine is only just beginning to happen. Over the past 2–3 years a group of 150–200 people have been developed who are professional supervisory board members for several companies. Most of them are officers at large banks and investment companies holding large stakes of shares in several companies. Ukrainian corporate directors are characterized by a relatively young age (mostly, up to 40 years old), good education, high level of motivation, and a certain amount of experience of working with large joint stock companies. However, it is evident that there is a lack of the required knowledge of the general principles of corporate governance and best practices of the functioning of boards in developed countries.

The first and, so far, only such programme (with the exception of the programmes for representatives of the state on supervisory boards held periodically on instructions of the State Property Funds of Ukraine) is the five-day programme offered by the International Institute of Business (in Kiev). The programme includes the following topics:

● the main principles of corporate governance, international work experience of boards;

- organization of supervisory board work in Ukraine (powers, composition, election, meetings, committees, work evaluation, remuneration, conflict of interest);

- participation by the supervisory board in the formulation of the corporate strategy;

- crisis management;

- issues of the company's financial policy in the work of the supervisory board;

- why it is beneficial for companies to make their activities transparent.

This is the first year that the programme has been in existence, but it has already produced positive comments from its participants. The IIB plans to further improve the programme, to involve foreign experts and to obtain international certificates.

Another field for improving the functioning of supervisory boards is the implementation in Ukraine of the institution of corporate secretaries. Unfortunately, the structure of joint stock company governance effective in Ukraine does not include such a position. However, the experience of many Ukrainian companies shows that a member of the supervisory board or the management board is charged with these functions. The International Institute of Business is the first in Ukraine to offer, since 2002, a training programme for corporate secretaries.

The establishment of professional associations of corporate directors and corporate secretaries is very important for the formation of the professions of corporate director and corporate secretary, which are new to Ukraine. No such associations have been created so far.

23.7   Useful Contacts

- National Bank of Ukraine – www.bank.gov.ua/ENGL/DEFAULT. htm

- Securities and Stock Market Commission – www.ssmsc.gov.ua

- State Commission for Regulation of Financial Services Markets in Ukraine – www.dfp.gov.ua

- Ukrainian Association of Investment Business (UAIB) – www. uaib.com.ua

- Ukrainian Federation of Professional Accountants and Auditors – www.ufpaa.kiev.ua

23.8   Further Reading

Batyuk, O (2002) *Shareholder rights, equitable treatment and the role of the state*, 3rd Meeting of the Eurasian Corporate Governance Roundtable, 17–18 April

Chen, H (2003) *Corporate Governance Sector Assessment Project May 2003*, European Bank for Reconstruction and Development, London

Part 4

Lesser Developed Countries

24

India

Table 24.1

Population	1,049 million (2003)
Gross National Income (GNI)	US $501.5 billion (2002)
GNI per capita	£480 (2002)
Total number of companies	550,000 (approx) (2000)
Number of companies listed on the stock exchange	10,000 approx listed on 23 exchanges 5,874 (2001) Bombay Stock Exchange
Market capitalization	US $147.8 billion (2001)
Key corporate laws	● The Securities and Exchange Board of India (SEBI) Act (1992) ● Companies Act (1956)
Key corporate governance codes	● Narayanmurthy Committee Report (2003) ● Report of the Naresh Chandra Committee on Corporate Audit and Governance (2002) ● Report of the Kumar Mangalam Committee on Corporate Governance (2000) ● Desirable Code of Corporate Governance: A Code Confederation of Indian Industry (1998)

24.1 Corporate Structure and Ownership

There are around 550,000 companies in India of which around 72,000 are publicly limited (as of January 2000). This sizeable market comprises of the following company forms:

- *Private limited company and public limited company.* Nearly 80–85 per cent of Indian companies are small scale, family-managed enterprises and are either:
  - publicly held companies (public limited) – companies listed on one or more of the stock exchanges;
  - closely held companies (private limited) – closely held companies greatly outnumber publicly held companies and are largely made up of small to medium-sized enterprises. However, public limited companies account for almost two-thirds of the book value of equity.

- *Government companies.* The number of government companies, also known as 'public sector units' (PSUs), in 1999 was 1,240. This compares with 440,997 private limited companies and 71,064 companies in the same year. That said, while they account for a mere fraction (0.3 per cent) of the number of companies, PSUs represent 39 per cent of India's paid-up capital. Interestingly, whilst there were only 73 government companies listed on the Bombay Stock Exchange in 1999 (less than 2 per cent of the total listing) the stocks accounted for almost 15 per cent of the market capitalization.

India is actively pursuing a path of disinvestment and some major examples include:

- Videsh Sanchar Nigam Limited (VSNL): India's largest telecommunications company; the Tata Group, one of India's largest business groups, has taken over the control of this company;
- Bharat Aluminium Company (BALCO);
- Hotel Corporation of India (HCI): a subsidiary of AIR-India;
- Indian Tourism Development Corporation (ITDC): a chain of hotels under the brand name 'Ashoka Hotel'.
- Oil and Natural Gas Corporation Limited (ONGC), India's largest state owned enterprise, was the latest big public offering issue.

It made history on 5 March 2004 by having its IPO oversubscribed within just a few minutes of its opening. By the time the issue closed on 13 March 2004, the IPO was over-subscribed 5.88 times – a response of some 14 billion US dollars.

Family-controlled firms are in decline. According to a report from Goswani (2001), Chief Economist of the Confederation of Indian Industry:

> *The dominant characteristic of the top 50 companies in India (as of April 2001) is the preponderance of first generation enterprise or professionally run business. In 1991, 22 out of the top 50 companies were controlled by family groups that held their sway during the licence control regime. By February 2000, the roles were reversed: 35 were professionally managed, of which 14 were first generation businesses; only 4 out of the top 50 were run by older business families.*

Large family company groups have traditionally protected their interests through cross-shareholdings. This is slowly changing owing to alterations in the tax system which previously protected shareholders from high wealth and inheritance taxes. As this is no longer the case, cross-shareholding in India is unwinding.

A large proportion of the equity of private sector companies is held by development financial institutions (DFI), the General Insurance Company (GIC) and the Unit Trust of India (UTI), the latter being a government-owned mutual fund. To date, pension funds are not allowed to invest in the stock market and foreign institutional investors own approximately 24 per cent of the equity of traded companies.

24.2   Legal Framework

A common law system operates in India. Most entities are incorporated as a company governed by the Companies Act 1956, which has been amended many times over the years.

The Companies Act is administered by the Department of Company Affairs and enforces the powers, roles, and responsibilities of directors and shareholders as well as the operations and duties of companies. In essence, areas relating to corporate governance include the following:

- rules and procedures regarding the incorporation of a company (registration, articles of association, etc);

- prospectus and allotment of ordinary and preference shares and debentures;

- kinds of share capital (numbering and certification of shares, transfer of shares and debentures, reduction in share capital);

- registration of various types of charges;

- management and administration of a company (registration office, annual returns, shareholder meetings, boards of directors, etc);

- winding up, or liquidation, of companies.

Other key legislation and regulations regarding the governance of companies include:

- Securities Contracts (Regulation) Act 1956 (SCRA);

- Securities and Exchange Board of India Act (1992);

- Sick Industrial Companies (Special Provisions) Act 1985 (SICA).

The Securities and Exchange Board of India enforces the Securities Contract (Regulation) Act 1956 (SCRA) which covers all marketable securities issued by companies. It was enacted to 'prevent undesirable transactions in securities by regulating the business of dealings therein'. The SCRA also defines and regulates the stock exchanges.

The Securities and Exchange Board of India Act (1992) created the independent capital market regulatory authority known as the Securities and Exchange Board of India (SEBI). The body protects the interests of investors as well as regulating the securities market.

The Sick Industrial Companies (Special Provisions) Act 1985 (SICA) created the framework for bankruptcy restructuring companies which are suffering financially.

24.2.1 Directors Duties

In keeping with Common Law, in India directors are the fiduciaries of a company and owe a duty of care to the company. They should not act negligently in the management of the company's affairs. Directors are obliged to comply with shareholder resolutions and can be removed by them from the board. Directors can be personally liable if they:

- contract in their own name without disclosing that they are acting on behalf of the company;
- act beyond their powers; and
- knowingly enter into an illegal contract.

As is happening in other countries around the world, there are increasing numbers of independent directors in India who are taking out insurance against their personal liabilities as directors. The Naresh Chandra Committee on Corporate Governance and Audit (2002) outlined in its report that:

> *It would be very difficult to attract high quality independent directors on the boards of Indian companies if they have to constantly worry about serious criminal liabilities under different Acts.*

The committee therefore recommended that non-executive directors should be exempt from certain criminal and civil liabilities. These Acts are the Companies Act, Negotiable Instruments Act, Provident Fund Act, ESI Act, Factories Act, Industrial Disputes Act and the Electricity Supply Act. The Committee also recommended that independent directors should also be indemnified from costs of litigation etc.

The Committee went further to recommend that:

> *there were several weaknesses in Indian law (the Companies Act, 1956) which, the Committee feels, need to be rectified as an important step towards better corporate governance in India. The principle that ill-gotten gains must be disgorged from the wrongful gainer needs to be enshrined in the Companies Act.*

The Committee's recommendations were as follows:

- Wherever possible, penalties ought to be rationalized, and related to the sums involved in the offence. Fees, especially late fees, can be related to the size of the company in terms of its paid-up capital and free reserves, or turnover, or both.
- Disqualification under section 274(1)(g) of the Companies Act, 1956 should be triggered for certain other serious offences than just non-payment of debt. However, independent directors need to be treated on a different footing and exempted as in the case of nominee directors representing financial institutions.

24.2.2   Corporate Serious Fraud Office (CSFO)

The Committee also made recommendations regarding corporate fraud and suggested the setting up of a Corporate Serious Fraud Office (CSFO), without taking away the powers of investigation and prosecution from existing agencies. The recommendation as it appears in the report is as follows:

- A Corporate Serious Fraud Office (CSFO) should be set up in the Department of Company Affairs with specialists inducted on the basis of transfer/deputation and on special term contracts.

- This should be in the form of a multidisciplinary team that not only uncovers the fraud, but is able to direct and supervise prosecutions under various economic legislation through appropriate agencies.

- There should be a Task Force constituted for each case under a designated team leader.

- In the interest of adequate control and efficiency, a Committee should be set up to directly oversee the appointments to, and functioning of, this office, and coordinate the work of concerned departments and agencies.

- Later, a legislative framework, along the lines of the SFO in the UK, should be set up to enable the CSFO to investigate all aspects of the fraud, and direct the prosecution in appropriate courts.

24.3   Legal, Regulatory and Institutional Bodies

24.3.1   Securities Exchange Board of India (SEBI)

SEBI is the prime regulatory authority and, like the SEC of the United States, regulates all aspects of the securities market, including primary and secondary markets as well as stock exchanges. SEBI was established through the Securities Contract (Regulation) Act. It was set up in 1988 and was given statutory status and power to regulate and develop the Indian Capital Market in 1992. The board consists of six members, including a chairman, two members from the ministries of finance and law, two members appointed by central government and one nominated from the Reserve Bank of India. It is appointed for a five-year term and can only be removed by parliament. In October 2002 SEBI's powers were enhanced to check cases of insider trading, fraudulent and unfair trading practices in securities markets and market manipulation.

24.3.2 Reserve Bank of India (RBI)

The RBI was established in April 1935. Though originally privately owned, it is now fully owned by the Government of India. The objective of the RBI is 'to regulate the issue of bank notes and keep reserves with a view to securing monetary stability in India. It strives to operate the currency and credit system of India to its advantage.'

24.3.3 Stock Exchanges

India has 23 stock exchanges accounting for approximately 10,000 listed companies but the Bombay Stock Exchange (BSE) and the National Stock Exchange (NSE) are the biggest and most liquid. The other regional bodies are mostly surviving on annual listing fees existing because the law insists that any listed company must register at the stock exchange that is nearest to its registered address.

24.3.4 Bombay Stock Exchange (BSE)

The Bombay Stock Exchange is the oldest one in Asia, even older than the Tokyo Stock Exchange, which was founded in 1875. Originally named the 'Native Share and Stockbrokers Association', the BSE has evolved into one of the premier stock exchanges in the country. The governing board of 20 directors is comprised of 9 elected directors (one-third of them retire every year by rotation), an executive director and chief executive officer, three SEBI nominees, a Reserve Bank of India nominee and five public representatives. The board regulates the Exchange and decides its policies and regulates the affairs of the Exchange.

The number of companies listed at the Exchange as at the end of May 2001 was 5,874. This is the highest number of listed companies on a stock exchange in the world. In February 2000 the market cap of the BSE was $236 billion – making it the seventh largest exchange in the Asia-Pacific region and accounting for 53 per cent of India's GDP.

The BSE's Equity Stock Index, BSE SENSEX, is the barometer of the Indian Stock Market. The Exchange has also adopted the free float methodology for computation of the most popular and widely tracked index.

24.3.5 National Stock Exchange (NSE)

The National Stock Exchange of India Limited was set up in response to recommendations in the report of the High Powered Study Group on Establishment of New Stock Exchanges. The report recommended the creation of a National Stock Exchange by financial institutions to provide access to investors from all across the country on an equal footing. The NSE was promoted by leading financial institutions at the behest of the Government of India and was incorporated in November 1992 as a tax-paying company, unlike other stock exchanges in the country.

On its recognition as a stock exchange under the Securities Contracts (Regulation) Act, 1956, in April 1993, NSE commenced operations in the Wholesale Debt Market (WDM) segment in June 1994. The Capital Market (Equities) segment commenced operations in November 1994 and operations in the Derivatives segment commenced in June 2000. There were 883 companies listed on the National Stock Exchange as of September 2003.

24.3.6 Confederation of Indian Industry (CII)

The Confederation of Indian Industry was founded 107 years ago. It is a non-political and not-for-profit membership organization with over 4,800 company members from both the public and private sectors. The CII has been at the forefront of corporate governance in India and developed the Desirable Code of Corporate Governance, the first of its kind in India. The CII works closely with government on policy issues, enhancing efficiency, competitiveness and expanding business opportunities for industry through a range of specialized services and global linkages.

24.4   Board Structure

24.4.1   Size

The board structure in India is one-tier and the Companies Act, 1956 stipulates that it must comprise of at least three directors. The Naresh Chandra Committee recommended that the minimum board size of all listed companies in India (as well as unlisted public limited companies with a paid-up share capital and free reserves of Rs.10 crore and above, or turnover of Rs.50 crore and above) should be seven, of which at least four should be independent directors. However, these recommendations do not apply to:

- unlisted public companies that have no more than 50 shareholders and that are without debt of any kind from the public, banks, or financial institutions, as long as they do not change their character;

- unlisted subsidiaries of listed companies.

Most of the top listed companies already have a majority of independent directors and have an audit committee comprised of at least three independent directors. However, non-executive directors are often family members, retired chief executives, lawyers or nominees from DFIs, GIC and UTI.

24.4.2 Composition

The Kumar Mangalam Birla Committee on Corporate Governance Report (2000) mandated that the board of a company shall have an optimum combination of executive and non-executive directors with not less than 50 per cent of the board comprising of non-executive directors. The number of independent directors would depend on the nature of the chairman of the board. In the case where a company has a non-executive chairman, at least one-third of the board should comprise of independent directors and where a company has an executive chairman, at least half the board should be independent.

As a sequel to the Kumar Mangalam Birla Committee, SEBI appointed yet another committee called Narayanmurthy Committee on Corporate Governance. The committee gave it's report on 8 February 2003 and the term 'independent director' is defined as a non-executive director of the company who:

- apart from receiving director remuneration, does not have any material pecuniary relationships or transactions with the company, its promoters, its senior management or its holding company, its subsidiaries and associated companies;

- is not related to promoters or management at the board level or at one level below the board;

- has not been an executive of the company in the immediately preceding three financial years;

- is not a partner or an executive of the statutory audit firm or the internal audit firm that is associated with the company, and has not been a partner or an executive of any such firm for the last three years. This will also apply to legal firm(s) and consulting firm(s) that have a material association with the entity;

- is not a supplier, service provider or customer of the company; and

- is not a substantial shareholder of the company, ie owning two per cent or more of the block of voting shares.

The considerations as regards to remuneration paid to an independent director shall be the same as those applied to a non-executive director.

Further, an employee, executive director or nominee of any bank, financial institution, corporation or trustees of debenture and bond holders, who is normally called a 'nominee director', will be excluded from the pool of directors in the determination of the number of independent directors. In other words, such a director will not feature in either the numerator or the denominator.

Moreover, if an executive in, say, Company X becomes a non-executive director in another Company Y, while another executive of Company Y becomes a non-executive director in Company X, then neither will be treated as an independent director.

24.4.3 Remuneration

The Kumar Mangalam Birla Committee recommended that the remuneration of non-executive directors shall be decided by the board of directors. The company should further agree that the following disclosures on the remuneration of directors shall be made in the corporate governance section of the annual report:

- all elements of remuneration packages of all the directors (ie salary, benefits, bonuses, stock options, pension);

- details of the fixed component and performance linked incentives along with performance criteria;

- service contracts, notice period and severance fees;

- stock option details, if any, and whether issued at a discount as well as the period over which accrued and over which exercisable.

The report went on to impose the following mandatory recommendations relating to remuneration:

- The Remuneration Committee, which would determine the remuneration packages of the executive directors, should comprise of a minimum of three non-executive directors, the chairman of the committee being an independent director.

- The recommendations of the board of directors would need to be ratified at the General Body meeting of shareholders and in case the board disagrees with the recommendations of the remuneration committee, the matter should be decided at the General Body meeting of the shareholders who should be provided with sufficient information about the remuneration policy and package.

The Narayanmurthy committee made the following mandatory recommendations on compensation paid to non-executive directors:

- All compensation paid to non-executive directors may be fixed by the Board of Directors and should be approved by shareholders in general meeting. Limits should be set for the maximum number of stock options that can be granted to non-executive directors in any financial year and in aggregate. The stock options granted to the non-executive directors shall vest after a period of at least one year from the date such non-executive directors have retired from the Board of the Company.

- Companies should publish their compensation philosophy and statement of entitled compensation in respect of non-executive directors in their annual report. Alternatively, this may be put up on the company's Web site and reference drawn thereto in the annual report. Companies should disclose on an annual basis, details of shares held by non-executive directors, including on an 'if-converted' basis. Non-executive directors should be required to disclose their stock holding (both own or held by/for other persons on a beneficial basis) in the listed company in which they are proposed to be appointed as directors, prior to their appointment. These details should accompany their notice of appointment.

The Naresh Chandra Committee went on to recommend the following with regard to the remuneration of non-executive directors:

- The statutory limit on sitting fees should be reviewed, although ideally it should be a matter to be resolved between the management and the shareholders.

- In addition, loss-making companies should be permitted by the DCA to pay special fees to any independent director, subject to reasonable caps, in order to attract the best restructuring and strategic talents to the boards of such companies.

- The present provisions relating to stock options, and to the 1 per cent commission on net profits, is adequate and does not, at present, need any revision. However, the vesting schedule of stock options should be staggered over at least three years, so as to align the independent and executive directors, as well as managers two levels below the board, with the long-term profitability and value of the company.

24.4.4 Board Meetings

According to the World Bank Report on the Observance of Standards and Codes, the board of directors is legally bound to meet at least once every three months and to disclose board members' shareholdings and their interests in any transaction of the company. It must convene the annual general meeting, provide the directors' report attached to the annual report and ensure the accuracy of the statements made therein. The board is responsible for signing off the company's balance sheet and profit and loss statement, ensuring that these documents are filed with the registrar and sent to shareholders. Minutes of the shareholder and board meetings have to be prepared within 30 days, with every page initialized, and directors are liable for the statements made in the directors' report.

24.5 Codes, Standards and Good Practice Guidelines

In India, the corporate governance movement began in 1997 on the initiative of the Confederation of Indian Industry and listed companies wishing to embrace corporate governance – not in response to triggers such as financial crisis or shareholder activism.

In fact the governance of the top 30 private sector companies in India is very good, with most of them having a majority of non-executive directors, an audit committee comprising of a minimum of three independent directors, and a remuneration and nomination committee.

The main corporate governance initiatives in India are as follows:

- Narayanmurthy Corporate Governance Committee Report, 2003;

- Report of the Naresh Chandra Committee on Corporate Audit and Governance, 2002;

- Report of the Kumar Mangalam Birla Committee on Corporate Governance, 2000;

- Desirable Code of Corporate Governance, Confederation of Indian Industry, 1998.

24.5.1 Narayanmurthy Committee Report (2003)

This committee was set up as a sequel to Kumar Mangalam Birla Committee. The terms of reference of the Committee were to review the performance of corporate governance, and to determine the role of companies in responding to rumour and other price sensitive information circulating in the market, in order to enhance the transparency and integrity of the market. The Mandatory recommendations of the committee relate to:

- audit committees: review of information by audit committees;

- financial literacy of members of the audit committee;

- audit reports and audit qualifications: disclosure of accounting treatment;

- related party transactions: basis for related party transactions;

- definition of 'related party';

- risk management: board disclosures;

- training of board members (non-mandatory);

- code of conduct: written code for executive management;

- whistle-blower policy: internal policy on access to audit committees;

- subsidiary companies: audit committee requirements;

- evaluation of board performance: mechanism for evaluating non-executive board members (non-mandatory);

- analyst reports: disclosures in reports issued by security analysts.

24.5.2 Naresh Chandra Committee on Corporate Audit and Governance (2002)

In August 2002 the Department of Company Affairs, under the Ministry of Finance and Company Affairs, appointed the Naresh Chandra Committee to examine various corporate governance issues, particularly the definition of independence and the relationship between auditors and the company. At the time of writing, the government had not yet made any of the recommendations mandatory for Indian companies, but the main issues likely to have significant effect are as follows.

Independence

Following on from the Kumar Mangalam Birla Committee Report, the Naresh Chandra Report takes recommendations regarding independence a step further. It recommends that all listed and unlisted companies with a paid-up capital and free reserves of over Rs.10 crore or a turnover of at least Rs 50 crore should have half the board members as independent directors – whether or not the board has an executive or non-executive chairman.

Audit

The report recommends that all directors on the audit committee should be independent and relationship guidelines between the auditor and the company are outlined. Specifically the report recommends that, along with its subsidiary, associates or affiliates, an audit firm should not derive more than 25 per cent of its business from a single corporate client. Also, the committee recommended that the partners and at least 50 per cent of the audit team working on company accounts be rotated every five years. The report also outlines a number of prohibited non-audit services. In addition, the CEO and CFO will have to certify the company accounts.

In essence, the Committee was asked to examine and recommend changes, if necessary, in diverse areas such as:

- the statutory auditor–company relationship, so as to further strengthen the professional nature of this interface;
- the need, if any, for rotation of statutory audit firms or partners;
- the procedure for appointment of auditors and determination of audit fees;
- restrictions, if necessary, on non-audit fees;
- independence of auditing functions;
- measures required to ensure that the management and companies actually present a 'true and fair' statement of the financial affairs of companies;
- the need to consider measures such as certification of accounts and financial statements by the management and directors;
- the necessity of having a transparent system of random scrutiny of audited accounts;
- adequacy of regulation of chartered accountants, company secretaries and other similar statutory oversight functionaries;
- advantages, if any, of setting up an independent regulator similar to the Public Company Accounting Oversight Board in the SOX Act, and if so, its constitution; and
- the role of independent directors, and how their independence and effectiveness can be ensured.

The Committee also recommends a number of other steps that would contribute to a better corporate governance regime. These have been grouped under the heading 'miscellaneous' towards the end of the report and cover areas such as:

- preventing stripping of assets;
- random scrutiny of accounts;
- better training for articles; and
- propagation of an internal code of ethics for companies.

24.5.3 Kumar Mangalam Birla Committee Report (2000)

The first formal mandatory corporate governance framework for listed companies was established by the Securities and Exchange Board of India (SEBI) in February 2000, following the recommendations of the Kumar Mangalam Birla Committee Report.

The committee emphasized the rights of shareholders and distinguished the responsibilities of the board and the management in instituting corporate governance.

The enforcement of mandatory recommendations was effected through 'Clause 49' of the Stock Exchange listing agreements and refers to all companies seeking to be listed on Indian Stock Exchanges or that are already listed.

Specifically, the terms of reference for the Committee were to:

- suggest suitable amendments to the listing agreement executed by the stock exchanges with the companies and any other measures to improve the standards of corporate governance in the listed companies in areas such as:
  - continuous disclosure of material information – both financial and non-financial;
  - manner and frequency of such disclosures; and
  - the responsibilities of independent and outside directors;
- draft a code of corporate best practice; and
- suggest safeguards to be instituted within the companies to deal with insider information and insider trading.

The companies are required to disclose separately in their annual reports, a report on corporate governance detailing compliance with the recommendations. There are also non-mandatory recommendations that the committee felt would be desirable for companies to follow.

Further, non-compliance with any mandatory requirement, ie which is part of the listing agreement with reasons thereof and the extent to which the non-mandatory requirements have been adopted, should be specifically highlighted.

The main recommendations as summarized by Goswani (2000) are:

- Independent directors are defined as those who, apart from receiving director's remuneration, do not have any other material pecuniary relationship or transactions with the company, its promoters, its management or its subsidiaries, which in the judgement of the board may affect their independence of judgement.

- Not less than 50 per cent of the board should comprise of non-executive directors. The number of independent directors would depend on the nature of the chairman of the board. In case a company has a non-executive chairman, at least one-third of the board should comprise of independent directors and in case a company has an executive chairman, at least half of the board should be independent.

- Every listed company must, according to their size and a three-year time-table, set up a qualified and independent audit committee at its board level. The audit committee should have a minimum of three members, all being non-executive directors, with the majority being independent, and with at least one director having financial and accounting knowledge; the chairman of the committee should be an independent director, who should be present at the annual general meeting to answer shareholder queries; the company secretary should act as the secretary to the committee. To begin with, the audit committee should meet at least three times a year. One meeting must be held before finalization of the annual accounts and one necessarily every six months. The audit committee should have the power to:

  (i)   investigate any activity within its terms of reference,

  (ii) seek information from any employee,

  (iii) obtain outside legal or other professional advice, and

  (iv) secure attendance of outsiders with relevant expertise, if necessary.

- Among other things, the audit committee should:

  (i)   oversee a company's financial reporting process and quality of disclosure of financial information,

(ii) recommend the appointment and removal of an external auditor, and

(iii) review with management, external and internal auditors the adequacy of the internal audit function and the annual financial statements before submission to the board, including financial risks and risk management policies.

- The board of directors should decide the remuneration of non-executive directors.

- The following disclosures should be made in the section on corporate governance of the annual report:

  (i) all elements of the remuneration package of all the directors, ie salary, benefits, bonuses, stock options, pension etc.,

  (ii) details of fixed component and performance linked incentives, along with the performance criteria,

  (iii) service contracts, notice periods, severance fees, and

  (iv) stock option details – whether issued at a discount as well as the period over which they were accrued and over which they were exercisable.

- Board meetings should be held at least four times a year, with a maximum time gap of four months between any two meetings. This is a mandatory recommendation.

- To ensure that directors give due importance and commitment to their fiduciary responsibilities, no director should be a member of more than 10 board-level committees or act as chairman of more than five committees across all companies of which he is a director.

- In every company's annual report, there should be a detailed chapter on Management Discussion and Analysis. This should include discussion on industry structure and developments, opportunities and threats, segment-wise or product-wise performance, outlook, risks and concerns, internal control systems and their adequacy, relating financial performance with operational performance, and issues relating to human resource development.

- For appointment or re-appointment of a director, shareholders must be provided with the following information:

  (i)   a brief resumé of the director,

  (ii) nature of his/her expertise in specific functional areas, and

  (iii) companies in which he/she holds directorships.

- Information like quarterly results and presentations made by companies to analysts should be put on the company's Web site and set out in such a form so as to enable the stock exchange, on which the company is listed, to put it on its own Web site.

- A board committee under the chairmanship of a non-executive director should be formed to specifically look into the redressing of shareholder complaints like transfer of shares, non-receipt of balance sheets, non-receipt of declared dividends, etc.

- There should be a separate section on corporate governance in the annual reports of companies. Non-compliance with any mandatory recommendation, with their reasons, should be specifically high-lighted. This will enable the shareholders and the securities market to assess for themselves the standards of corporate governance followed by a company.

24.5.4   Desirable Code of Corporate Governance (1998)

Corporate governance initiatives in India began in 1998 with the Desirable Code of Corporate Governance – a voluntary code published by the Confederation of Indian Industries (CII). The code was developed in response to public concerns regarding shareholder protection, transparency and the need to keep up with international standards of corporate governance. It includes recommendations on the structure and composition of the board and disclosure.

The code is designed to encourage companies to provide more information about their boards. It focused on listed companies which took on board the recommendations very quickly, with 30 large listed companies accounting for over 25 per cent of India's market capitalization voluntarily adopting the recommendations. These companies disclosed information regarding the following in their annual reports:

- composition of the board;
- number of outside directorships held;
- family relationships with other directors;
- business relationship with the company, other than being a director;
- loans and advances from the company;
- remuneration;
- attendance of directors at board meetings;
- details of monthly high and low share price in various stock exchanges and comparison of these with the market indices;
- data on the distribution of shares across various types of shareholders and according to size classes;
- data of complaints received from shareholders regarding share transfers and how these have been addressed;
- economic value added, return on capital employed and return on net worth;
- details on risk factors, especially foreign exchange and derivative risks;
- details on contingent liabilities;
- data on outstanding warrants and their efforts on dilution of equity, when convened;
- segment-wise information in a chapter on management discussion and analysis.

24.6　Disclosure and Transparency

All companies are required to prepare statutorily audited annual accounts which are first submitted to the board for approval, then sent to all shareholders, and finally lodged with the registrar of companies. Listed companies have three other requirements. The annual accounts have to be submitted to every stock exchange where the companies are listed. Abridged unaudited financial summaries must be produced for every quarter. Listed firms are also required to submit a cash flow statement.

24.6.1   Auditor–Company Relationship

The Naresh Chandra Committee Report made many recommendations regarding the auditor–company relationship relating to the following key areas:

- disqualifications for audit assignments;
- list of prohibited non-audit services;
- independence standards for consulting and other entities that are affiliated to audit firms;
- compulsory audit partner rotation;
- auditor's disclosure of contingent liabilities;
- auditor's disclosure of qualifications and consequent action;
- management's certification in the event of auditor's replacement;
- auditor's annual certification of independence;
- appointment of auditors;
- CEO and CFO certification of annual audited accounts.

24.6.2   Quality Review Boards

The Committee deliberated long and hard on the issue of whether it was necessary to establish a new, independent Public Oversight Board (POB) for supervising the work of auditors – such as the one proposed in the US Sarbannes–Oxley Act. On balance, the Committee felt that there is no need at this point of time to set up yet another new regulatory oversight body. However, the Committee felt that there is a need to establish an efficient and professional body which can be entrusted to provide transparent and expeditious auditing quality oversight. This will be in the interest of investors, the general public and the professionals themselves. With these considerations in mind, the Committee has recommended the setting up of independent Quality Review Boards.

Recommendation 3.1: Setting up of independent Quality Review Board

There should be established, with appropriate legislative support, three independent Quality Review Boards (QRBs), one each for the

Institute of Chartered Accountants of India (ICAI), the Institute of Chartered Secretaries of India (ICSI) and the ICWAI, to periodically examine and review the quality of audit, secretarial and cost accounting firms, and pass judgement and comments on the quality and sufficiency of systems, infrastructure and practices.

In the interest of realism, the QRBs should, for the initial five years, focus their audit quality reviews on the audit firms, which have conducted the audit for the top 150 listed companies, ranked according to market capitalization as on 31 March. Depending upon the record of success of such reviews, the DCA may subsequently consider altering the sample size or criterion.

24.7 Shareholder Rights and Stakeholder Relations

There are two types of shares in India: preference shares and ordinary shares. Preference shares give the holder the right to a fixed dividend but no right to vote, so long as dividends are paid. Ordinary share owners run the risk of variable dividends, but have the right to vote. Shares cannot be granted multiple voting rights.

The Report of the Kumar Mangalam Birla Committee on Corporate Governance (2000) introduced the following mandatory recommendations regarding shareholders:

A The company agrees that in case of the appointment of a new director or re-appointment of a director the shareholders must be provided with the following information:

a) a brief resumé of the director;

b) nature of his expertise in specific functional areas; and

c) names of companies in which the person also holds the directorship and the membership of committees of the board.

B The company further agrees that information presented to analysts, such as quarterly results, shall be put on the company's Web site, or shall be sent in such a form so as to enable the stock exchange on which the company is listed to put it on its own Web site.

C The company further agrees that a board committee under the chairmanship of a non-executive director shall be formed to specifically look into the redressing of shareholders' and investors' complaints such as the transfer of shares, non-receipt of balance sheet, non-receipt of declared dividends etc. This committee shall be designated as the 'Shareholders/Investors Grievance Committee'.

D The company further agrees that to expedite the process of share transfers the board of the company shall delegate the power of share transfer to an officer or a committee or to the registrar and share transfer agents. The delegated authority shall attend to share transfer formalities at least once in a fortnight.

24.7.1 Minority Shareholders

According to the World Bank Report on the Observance of Standards and Codes (2000), minority shareholders are guaranteed the right to participate and vote in company meetings by the Companies Act which mandates an annual general meeting. The notice has to be posted to shareholders 21 days before the date of the meeting and must contain the company's reports and accounts, the agenda, all resolutions that are to be discussed in the meeting and a proxy form. Shareholders accounting for at least one-tenth of the paid-up share capital have the right to call an extraordinary general meeting.

24.8 Director Development Activity

The Naresh Chandra Committee (2002) acknowledged that non-executive directors should be aware of the rights, responsibilities, duties and liabilities of a legal, recognized fiduciary. Understanding such issues requires training. The Committee feels that if companies can afford to compensate their independent directors well, then they should be able to provide them with good training too. The Department of Company Affairs has a special role in encouraging and promoting training programmes in leading Indian institutions such as the Indian Institutes of Management, and in the Centre for Corporate Governance that they intend to set up.

More specifically, the Committee made the following recommendations regarding the training of independent directors:

- The Department for Company Affairs should encourage institutions of prominence, including their proposed Centre for Corporate Excellence, to have regular training programmes for independent directors.

- All independent directors should be required to attend at least one such training course before assuming responsibilities as an independent director, or, considering that enough programmes might not be available in the initial years, within one year of becoming an independent director. An untrained independent director should be disqualified under section 274(1)(g) of the Companies Act, 1956 after being given reasonable notice.

- Considering that enough training institutions and programmes might not be available in the initial years, this requirement may be introduced in a phased manner, so that the larger listed companies are covered first.

- The executing bodies must clearly state their plan for the year and their funding should be directly proportionate to the extent to which they execute such plans.

- There should be a 'trainee appraisal' system to judge the quality of the programme and so help decide, in the second round, which agencies should be given a greater role and which should be dropped.

In addition, the Department of Company Affairs set up the 'National Foundation on Corporate Governance'. They are also in talks with various Indian Institutes of Management (IIM) to encourage them to design and conduct training programmes for directors.

In order to continually improve board performance in India director development is considered vital and is being pioneered by:

- Leading business schools such as the Indian Institute of Management (IIM) in Bangalore which developed a programme called the 'Corporate Governance Orientation Programme for Corporate Directors'. The IIM has been conducting this programme once a year since 2001.

- Asian Centre for Corporate Governance (ACCG), a not-for-profit institution established by the Mahendra & Young Knowledge

Foundation, which launched the first Asian Director Development Programme in 2002. This was in joint collaboration with the Asian Institute of Manila (AIM). The ACCG conducts the programme twice a year.

24.9   Useful Contacts

- Academy of Corporate Governance – www.academyofcg.org
- Bombay Stock Exchange (BSE) – www.bseindia.com
- Confederation of Indian Industry (CII) – www.ciionline.org
- Federation of Indian Chamber of Commerce and Industry – www.ficci.com
- Institute of Chartered Accountants of India (IICAI) – www.icia.org
- Institute of Company Secretaries of India (ICSI) – www.icsi.edu
- Institute of Cost and Works Accountants of India (ICWAI) – www.icwai.com
- Indian Institute of Management (IIM) Ahmedabad – www.iimahd.ernet.in
- Indian Institute of Management (IIM) Bangalore – www.iimb.ernet.in
- Mahendra & Young – www.mahendraandyoung.com
- National Stock Exchange (NSE) – www.nse-india.com
- Reserve Bank of India (RBI) – www.rbi.org.in
- Securities and Exchange Board of India (SEBI) – www.sebi.gov.in

24.10   Further Reading

Anandrajah, K (2003) *Corporate Governance Compliance*, Butterworth, New Delhi

Confederation of Indian Industry (1998) *Desirable Corporate Governance in India – A Code*

Goswani, O (2000) *Tide Rises Gradually: Corporate Governance in India*, 2nd OECD, World Bank Corporate Governance Roundtable, Washington

OECD (2003) *White Paper on Corporate Governance in Asia*, OECD, Paris

Securities and Exchange Board of India (SEBI) (2000) *Report of Committee on Corporate Governance* (Kumar Mangalam Birla Committee)

The World Bank Group (2000) *Report on the Observance of Standards and Codes*, The World Bank, Washington

Yaga Consulting (2001) *The First Principles of Corporate Governance for PEs in India*, email yaga@hd1.vsnl.net.in

25 Indonesia

Table 25.1

Population	212 million (2002)
Gross National Income (GNI)	US $150 billion (2002)
GNI per capita	US $710 (2002)
Total number of companies	n/a
Number of companies listed on the stock exchange	293
Key corporate laws	● Government Regulation No 64 (1999) ● Law for limited liability companies (1995)
Key corporate governance codes	● Best practice guidelines (National Committee for Corporate Governance Policy) (2001)

25.1 Corporate Structure and Ownership

There are four categories of companies in Indonesia.

25.1.1 State-owned Enterprises (SOEs)

SOEs are enterprises owned by the government. Some of the bigger and better managed state-owned enterprises have successfully been privatized, but many of the remaining SOEs are characterized by low profitability, excessive red tape, lack of customer and market orientation, low productivity and low asset utilization. The State Ministry for Public Enterprises has issued mandatory rules and regulations to ensure good corporate governance in SOEs. The Ministry also offers training on corporate governance for managers and commissioners of SOEs. There are 162 SOEs in Indonesia in almost all business sectors. Many of the SOEs were originally Dutch companies that were nationalized in the late 1950s and early 1960s.

Many SOEs are perceived as being poorly managed. Their directors and commissioners are typically government appointees who often got their jobs due to political considerations rather than business competence.

25.1.2 Perseroan Terbatas (PTs)

PTs are firms incorporated as limited liability companies. They are subject to the law for limited liability companies (1995). Most of these firms are founded and owned by families. There are thousands of these firms. Some of them are quite large and many of the large conglomerates belong to this category. Their main source of funding comes from family wealth and bank loans.

25.1.3 Listed Companies

As of September 2002, there are 293 listed companies in Indonesia (185 in the Jakarta Stock Exchange, 108 in the Surabaya Stock Exchange, and 107 of them are listed in both Jakarta and Surabaya). All of them are incorporated as limited liability companies. They are subject to the limited liability company law (1995) and rules and regulations of the stock exchange and the stock market supervisory agency.

It is estimated that two thirds of publicly listed companies are family held. The concentration of share ownership is high. The Asian Development Bank (2000) estimated that the top five largest shareholders control 60 per cent of company shares.

25.1.4 Banks and Financial Institutions

Deregulation within the banking sector in the early 1980s resulted in the incorporation of more than 200 banks. People who had not been served by government banks before deregulation rushed to deposit their savings in the newly established banks, which practised aggressive marketing. In spite of strict supervision by the central bank, many of the banks were mismanaged and practised poor governance. The ones that were part of the conglomerates directed most of their lending to related companies. When the financial crisis struck the Indonesian economy in 1997 many of the banks collapsed. To prevent total chaos and social unrest, the government fully guaranteed all savings, re-capitalized the major bankrupt banks, and took over management of non-performing loans. Currently there are 145 banks operating in Indonesia. Only a few of them are listed. Most of the major private banks have been acquired by foreign investors. A few bankers have been criminally prosecuted, found guilty and sentenced with jail terms. Consequently the central bank has issued tighter rules and regulations for banks. All candidates for senior bank managers and commissioners have to go through a fit and proper test by the central bank. Every bank must have a vice president for compliance.

Share ownership in Indonesian corporations is often concentrated in the hands of a few owners, even in publicly listed companies. In conglomerates and groups, overlapping and pyramidal ownership are widely practised in the form of intricate legal webs that are hard to untangle. The OECD (2003) estimates that over 50 per cent of listed companies in Indonesia are involved in control pyramids and complex cross-shareholding.

When power is concentrated in this manner there is little incentive to treat all shareholders fairly and to practise accountability. The web of intricate overlapping ownership also provides opportunities for unethical practices of related party transactions and transfer pricing. These practices, although legal, are frequently not consistent with corporate governance principles of fairness.

25.2 Legal Framework

The Indonesian legal system is based on the Dutch legal system. However, many corporate governance rules that are supposed to regulate corporate governance are adopted and adapted from code-based and common law practices in the USA and the OECD countries. These rules are issued by government agencies:

1. for the banking industry, by Bank Indonesia (the central bank);

2. for state-owned enterprises by the State Ministry for State Enterprises and the Ministry of Finance (as the legal owners of the state enterprises); and

3. for publicly listed companies by the Bursa Efek Jakarta (Jakarta Stock Exchange), Bursa Efek Surabaya (the Surabaya Stock Exchange), and the Badan Pengawas Pasar Modal (the Capital Market Supervisory Agency).

25.2.1 The Limited Liability Company Law (1995)

The law separates management from governance. As a principle it requires commissioners on behalf of shareholders to independently supervise directors who run the company. The law defines the legal rights and responsibilities of the corporation, shareholders, directors and commissioners. In broad terms it also provides a legal framework for the issuance of company-specific rules and regulations that contain principles of corporate governance.

The law requires listed companies to produce annual reports and quarterly financial statements. The annual reports contain general information on the company, audited annual accounts, details of the company's directors and a report on the company's operations. Information on corporate governance is not required.

The notice for annual general meetings is 28 days and the notice should contain the agenda items.

25.2.2 Encoded Principles for Listed Companies

Principles of corporate governance are specified in the capital market and company registration laws and rules and regulations issued by the Stock Exchange and the Capital Market Supervisory Agency. Application of these principles is mandatory for publicly listed companies.

The 1997 crisis revealed that many SOEs and privately owned companies in Indonesia were extremely poorly managed, including the largest conglomerates.

Many commentators argue that three decades of dictatorial rule and crony capitalism have bred a culture of collusion and corruption. They argue that powerful people frequently disregard the law since they know that they can always buy their way out if they violate the law.

25.3 Legal, Regulatory and Institutional Bodies

25.3.1 Komite Nasional Kebijakan Corporate Governance (National Committee for Corporate Governance Policies)

A government-sponsored institution consisting of professionals, business executives, and government officers with a mandate to formulate national policies of good corporate governance.

25.3.2 Forum Corporate Governance di Indonesia (Forum for Corporate Governance in Indonesia)

A forum established by a group of professional associations, including the Indonesian Accounting Association, the Association of Security Companies, the Association of Internal Auditors, Indonesian Netherlands Association. The forum conducts seminars, dialogues, and training programmes to promote good corporate governance. It also initiated corporate governance self-assessment for corporations.

25.3.3 The Indonesian Institute for Corporate Governance

An institute founded by concerned individuals, professionals and business practitioners to promote good corporate governance.

25.3.4 The Indonesian Society of Independent Commissioners

The society was founded by a group of independent commissioners to enhance competence and professionalism amongst its members.

25.3.5 The Indonesian Institute for Corporate Directorship

An institute founded by a group of universities and graduate schools of management to promote training, research, and publications that enhance corporate governance practices in Indonesia.

25.3.6 Masyarakat Tranparansi Indonesia (Indonesian Transparency Society)

This society is the Indonesian watchdog against public and corporate corrupt practices.

25.3.7 Media

In addition, since the political reform in 1998, the free press promotes good corporate governance. In the past few years, the press has investigated and publicly exposed a number of unethical corporate governance practices in SOEs, privately owned, and publicly listed companies.

25.3.8 Indonesian Government

The Indonesian government is committed to developing the legal and regulatory framework for corporate governance according to universally accepted principles. The government has also established the necessary institutions to ensure the socialization and implementation of good corporate governance, eg the Capital Market Supervisory Agency, the Business Competition Supervisory Commission, and the National Committee for Corporate Government Policies.

25.3.9 World Bank and Asian Development Bank

The World Bank and the Asian Development Bank are actively involved in facilitating the development of universally accepted corporate government practices in Indonesia by empowering and enabling institutions. The World Bank actively facilitates and supports:

- drafting of laws and regulations by government agencies;
- emerging government and non-government institutions that are founded to promote corporate governance practices in Indonesia; and
- learning and networking with institutions globally to promote best practice of universally accepted principles of corporate governance through global video-conferencing and providing funding for global and regional cooperation and training programmes.

25.4 Board Structure

Indonesian limited liability companies have a dual board structure.

25.4.1 The Board of Commissioners (Komisaris)

This board performs the supervisory and advisory role. The Indonesian Company Law requires the board of commissioners to:

- supervise the performance of the board of directors and policies made by the board; and
- provide advice to the board of directors.

In many cases commissioners are appointed because of their close connection (including family ties) to the major shareholder.

25.4.2 The Board of Directors

Listed companies must have at least two directors. The board performs the executive role. The Indonesian Company Law requires the board of directors to:

- manage the company in the interests of the company consistent with the objectives of the company; and
- represent the company.

In practice it is often found that the duties of the two boards are not clear but blurred and overlap.

A director or board of directors is legally and operationally responsible to run the company. A commissioner or board of commissioners supervises and advises the director on behalf of the shareholders. Public corporations are mandated to have more than one director and commissioner.

In the case where there is more than one director or commissioner, they act collectively as a board. Structurally the management board is separate from the board of commissioners. The chief director (the CEO) is the first among equals of the management board and the chief commissioner (chair of the board of commissioners) is the first among equals of the board of commissioners. Shareholders appoint and discharge both boards.

Companies are not required to disclose attendance records of board meetings. There is no minimum number of board meetings that must take place each year.

There are no limitations on the appointment of non-residents to the board of listed companies.

25.4.3 Committees

The Jakarta Stock Exchange listing requirements specify that listed companies should have an audit committee.

The National Committee on Corporate Governance Guidelines (2001) recommends that listed companies should have a remuneration and a nomination committee.

25.5 Codes, Standards and Good Practice Guidelines

The National Committee for Corporate Governance Policy has published a guideline to benchmark best practice of corporate governance in Indonesia. This guideline includes universally accepted principles of corporate governance.

25.6 Disclosure and Transparency

Under Government Regulation No 64 (1999) companies are required to produce annual financial statements which must be audited. The external auditors are appointed by either the shareholders or the board.

It is very rare to find any disclosure of risk or internal control in Indonesian company reports.

The OECD (2003) identified that Indonesian companies' auditing and accounting practices did not materially diverge from international standards.

25.7 Shareholder Rights and Stakeholder Relations

Ten per cent of the voting rights can place items on the shareholders' meeting agenda or request an extraordinary general meeting.

- Shareholders can vote by proxy.

- Shareholders can appoint and remove directors and auditors. They can also authorize and issue share capital. The shareholders have the authority to amend company articles and approve any major corporate transactions.

- Related party transactions are required to be approved by the shareholders.

- Employees do not have any special rights to company information.

25.8 Director Development Activity

Currently, there are over half a dozen institutions that offer training programmes, workshops and seminars on corporate governance topics. In the past three years short courses and workshops have been conducted all over Indonesia, but mostly in Jakarta and Surabaya (the two largest business centres in Indonesia). The courses and workshops have taken the following formats:

- awareness seminars;

- discussions on special topics, such as the role of independent commissioners, audit committees, etc;

- discussion of cases such as Enron, WorldCom, Lippo (an Indonesian bank that was perceived by the public and the press as having violated corporate governance principles by disclosing misleading information);

- training for directors and commissioners on corporate governance;

- curriculum design and case writing for conducting university courses on corporate governance.

25.9 Useful Contacts

- Central Bank of the Republic of Indonesia – www.bi.go.id

- Indonesian Capital Market Supervisory Agency – www.indoexchange.com

- Jakarta Stock Exchange – www.jsx.co.id

25.10   Further Reading

Asian Development Bank (2000) The First Position Paper of the Forum for Corporate Governance in Indonesia, Forum for Corporate Governance in Indonesia

Claessens, S, Djankov, S and Lang, L H P (1999) *Who Controls East Asian Corporations?* World Bank Working Paper, Washington

National Committee on Corporate Governance (2001) *Code for Good Corporate Governance*, Jakarta Stock Exchange, Jakarta

OECD (2003) *White Paper on Corporate Governance in Asia*, OECD, Paris

26 | Uzbekistan

Table 26.1

Population	25.4 million (2002)
Gross National Income (GNI)	US $11.5 billion (2002)
GNI per capita	US $450 (2002)
Total number of companies	3,000
Number of companies listed on the stock exchange	6
Market capitalization	US $30 million (2001)
Key corporate laws	• The Law on the Protection of the Rights of Investors at the Securities Market (2001)
	• The Law on Joint Stock Companies and the Protection of Shareholders' Rights (1996)
	• The Law on Securities Market Functioning Mechanism (1996)
	• The Law on Securities and the Stock Exchange (1993)

26.1   Corporate Structure and Ownership

Over the past decade, privatization has created more than 3,000 private companies. The securities market infrastructure, including the Tashkent Stock Exchange (TSE), the electronic over-the-counter market operated by Elsis-Savdo and the two-tier depositary system, have been created to serve the needs of investors.

The state wants to attract foreign investors to newly privatized companies because most local investors lack both human and capital resources. However, the state's marketing effort in attracting foreign investors has faced the burden of implementing sound corporate governance principles suggested by foreign investors as a part of the restructuring effort. Most foreign investors have identified the need to improve the framework within Uzbekistan.

The current corporate governance framework in Uzbekistan is characterized by:

- weak securities, company, auditing and accounting laws;
- ineffective judiciary enforcement; weak securities regulator (not independent from the state committee representing state ownership);
- inadequate regulator enforcement (many cases of insider trading, corruption involved between companies and the state);
- concentration of ownership (management and employees);
- many cases of expropriation of shareholder rights where the state is a controlling shareholder;
- the state's inadequately designed privatization programme has led to such concentration of ownership;
- very limited transparency and disclosure is required by law; and certain laws contradict the general principles of corporate governance by allowing the state to hold special rights and privileges as a shareholder.

In 2001, ADB provided technical assistance to the State Property Committee to assess the corporate governance framework in Uzbekistan and design a corporate governance reform programme. The ADB project analysts examined corporate governance practices in all joint stock companies and 34 companies' practices were reviewed in detail. The analysis showed that:

- the ownership structure has extremely low transparency, as the published information on ownership structure is either not available or very limited;

- information about the supervisory council and executive body members is not published and available in the reporting;

- minority shareholder rights are not protected adequately from arbitrary actions of large block holders, they do not receive information for appropriate decision making at AGMs, and they are not protected adequately from a decrease in the value of their shares or dilution of capital;

- shareholders play a passive role in company oversight;

- the cumulative voting procedure for election of supervisory council members is not widely used;

- companies have not developed clear procedures for preparation and disclosure of information about their activities;

- investors and shareholders have limited access to information and they do not receive all required reports;

- the supervisory council is relatively passive, and ineffective in the discharge of its duties;

- independence of the supervisory council is not adequately ensured;

- the supervisory council members are not compensated and have little incentive to act in the best interest of the company; and

- no policies have been developed for compensation of company management; inadequate internal controls are in place.

As Uzbekistan has faced the hardship of being a country with its economy in transition, the state has gradually transferred its ownership to the private sector. Initially, the state had special rights and privileges as an owner of privatized companies by holding 'golden shares' and this status remained from 1991 until the end of 2002. The President's decree in January 2003 changed the status of the state's ownership. Therefore, it is clearly defined in the principle that 'the state should be considered as one of the shareholders without any special rights and privileges'. Although it would take time to fully implement this principle, some amendments to the laws

governing the ownership structure in companies with state ownership will be made in compliance with the above-declared principle.
At the end of February 2003, the Cabinet of Ministers prepared draft
amendments to the laws and submitted them to parliament.

The state has set a priority to attract foreign investments to the country.
It has declared the following principle which is reflected in various
legislative acts: that 'the companies should ensure equitable treatment of all shareholders, including minority and foreign shareholders'.
Although the state itself contradicted its principle in some instances,
the gradual implementation of the principle is in place. The state is
the main reformer in promoting sound standards of corporate governance in Uzbekistan because the private sector is not powerful
enough to lobby its interests. The National Association of Investment
Institutions, a not-for-profit organization, has recently started to
invite private companies to become members of the association in
order to form a forum of private institutions to address business-related
issues, including corporate governance. No other formally declared
corporate governance principles are declared in Uzbekistan. All parties representing the corporate governance framework, including the
private initiatives and the TSE, play a passive role in promoting sound
corporate governance.

Under the Company Law, the state guarantees protection of the
rights and interests of shareholders. Other than the state guarantee
on such protection, shareholder rights are protected by companies
(issuers), investment institutions and stock exchanges, various
associations, insurance agencies, the securities regulator, external
auditors and civil courts. Any disputes among parties involved in
such relationships can be resolved in the court. In fact, all corporate
governance principles are reflected in the securities laws, company
laws and other rules and regulations; however, the principles are
not clearly defined and communicated to all parties, including the
investors.

26.2 Legal Framework

After many years of having a centrally planned economy, Uzbekistan
has adopted a gradual and cautious approach in its transition to a
market economy. During the course of gradual transition following
the collapse of the Soviet Union, the legal framework for corporate

ownership has been developing in Uzbekistan. In 1991 Uzbekistan became independent. The Oliy Majlis (the Parliament of Uzbekistan) adopted:

- the Law 'On Securities and Stock Exchange' in September 1993;
- the Law 'On Joint Stock Companies and the Protection of Shareholders' Rights' (Company Law, 1996);
- the Law 'On Securities Market Functioning Mechanism' (1996);
- the Law 'On Activity of Depositories In the Securities Market (1998); and
- the Law 'On Protection of the Rights of Investors at the Securities Market' (2001).

These laws set formal procedures for establishing corporations, list the main rights of shareholders, determine securities market players and provide mechanisms for protecting the rights of market participants and investors.

The legal system in Uzbekistan is based on the Roman-German Law, according to which the codes are considered a basis for the laws. In particular, the Civil Code sets the main guidelines for corporate ownership.

Following the Company Law, the state established the Centre for Coordination and Supervision of the Securities Market under the State Property Committee, securities market regulator, to enforce effectively the laws and regulations pertaining to the securities market. The Bankruptcy Law (28 August 1998), the Accounting Law (30 August 1996) and the Law 'On Auditing Activity' (26 May 2000) were adopted to provide legal protection for investors, including creditors, and improve financial reporting in companies under the emerging market economy.

In addition to the laws enacted by the Oliy Majlis, the President of Uzbekistan has issued more than 10 decrees on regulating and developing the securities market and the Cabinet of Ministers has issued more than 29 resolutions affecting joint stock companies and the infrastructure of the stock market, especially relating to state ownership in joint stock companies. The Central Bank of Uzbekistan, the State Property Committee, the Ministry of Finance, the Centre for Coordination and Supervision of the Securities Market, the State Tax

Committee, and the Tashkent Stock Exchange have issued more than 70 normative acts governing joint stock companies and the infrastructure of the capital market in Uzbekistan.

In January 2003, the President's decree 'On measures to substantially increase the share and the importance of the private sector in the economy of Uzbekistan' made significant changes to the corporate governance system in Uzbekistan. Pursuant to the new decree, all shares of companies with state ownership not exceeding 25 per cent are to be sold, primarily to the private sector. Commencing in February 2003, the minimum charter capital for public companies registered in the country should be more than the equivalent of US $50,000 (19.2 times more than the previous limitation). The dividend income received from privatized companies is free of tax for a period of five years. The state trustees and management officials no longer have a power of veto with regard to supervisory council decisions and AGM decisions (ie the elimination of 'a golden share'). The associations of companies cannot interfere with the operations of companies (their members); they are responsible for setting up general technical policies in related industries which they represent. State ownership in companies with more than 25 per cent ownership will be managed only by management companies selected on a tender basis. The decision to appoint a CEO in a corporation must be made by the AGM. The employment contract with the CEO must be signed for one year and the AGM or the supervisory council makes a decision to renew the contract for another year. The business plan of a corporation must be approved by the AGM, or the AGM has the right to delegate its power to the supervisory council. The President's decree also sets a mandatory requirement for the CEO (executive body) to report to the supervisory council on a quarterly basis. The decree highlights the importance of proper remuneration policies for motivating executive body and supervisory council members in corporations.

The European Bank for Reconstruction and Development concluded in 2003 that 'the existing laws of Uzbekistan seem to have laid a good basis to develop sound corporate governance practices in the country' (p 10). However, the report also notes with concern the volume of resolutions and decrees issued by the Cabinet of Ministers and the President.

The Asian Development Bank approved further technical assistance to Uzbekistan in May 2003 to strengthen the legal and regulatory framework for the corporate sector and to improve regulatory oversight.

26.3 Legal, Regulatory and Institutional Bodies

In order to monitor the operations and financial position of the company, the revision (audit) committee is established at the AGM to audit company financial statements and all related information. The committee members are elected by the shareholders at the AGM. The request to audit financial statements of the company can be made by the revision (audit) committee itself, AGM decision, the supervisory council and shareholders holding more than 10 per cent shares outstanding. The members of the revision (audit) committee cannot be members of the supervisory council or executive board. Those shareholders who are members of the supervisory council and the executive board are restrained from voting in electing the revision (audit) committee members. By request of the AGM, an external independent auditor can audit financial statements of the company.

26.3.1 The Independence of the Securities Regulator

According to the experiences of many developed and developing countries, the securities market regulator should be independent from the executive branch of the economy and report directly to the legislative branch (parliament) in order to eliminate conflicts of interest. The Center on Coordination and Supervision of the Securities Market, the securities regulator in Uzbekistan, functions under the State Property Committee which is responsible for privatization, restructuring of state-owned enterprises, managing the state property and stimulating entrepreneurship in the country. The deputy chairman of the State Property Committee is also considered to be the General Director of the Center on Coordination and Supervision of the Securities Market.

The securities regulator is not capable of properly regulating the securities market owing to the lack of qualified specialists, financial resources and authoritative powers assigned pursuant to the securities laws. The state is cutting approximately 20 per cent of staffing resources in state agencies. Accordingly, the securities regulator, instead of increasing its number of staff as a result of the increase in the number of joint stock companies in the country, must cut its staff by the same percentage. Therefore, the enforcement and adequate state regulatory control mechanisms have not been placed in the securities market. Most professionals believe that principles of self-regulation should be implemented in the laws, allowing the state to

479

delegate certain powers to self-regulatory organizations to promote sound corporate governance practices.

Among recent developments in the field of corporate governance in Uzbekistan to promote private sector activism in resolving business-related issues is the establishment of the National Association of Investment Institutions (NAII), which was established in January 2000 as a non-profit, self-regulating organization to represent the interests of professional investment institutions (brokers, registrars, depositories, investment funds and other professional bodies) operating in the securities market in Uzbekistan. Among the Association's main priorities are to protect investor interests and improve corporate governance standards in Uzbekistan. NAII has recently established the Advisory Board which consists of 20 representatives of international organizations, foreign companies and financial institutions functioning in the country. The mandate of the Advisory Board is to contribute knowledge and experience in the development of the securities market of Uzbekistan. NAII is planning to establish a Committee on Corporate Governance to address the issues related to promoting sound corporate governance practices, including a review of a draft *Code of Corporate Governance for Joint Stock Companies in Uzbekistan.* The Center on Coordination and Supervision of the Securities Market under the State Property Committee, the NAII and the IBS Training & Consulting Centre hosted a conference called 'Promoting Corporate Governance in Uzbekistan' in May 2003 where representatives of corporations, government agencies, TSE, investment institutions and institutional investors adopted 19 principles of Corporate Goverance for Joint-Stock Companies. The code is non-mandatory.

26.4 Board Structure

The Tashkent Stock Exchange (TSE), established in 1991, set the listing requirements based on the lifespan of a company, the amount of paid-in capital, total assets, number of shareholders, years of profitability and number of shares issued. TSE has never adopted a code of ethics or code of best practice for listed companies. The shares of only four commercial banks (*Uzjilsberbank, Pahtabank, Uzpromstroybank, Gallabank*) and two companies (*Uzmetcombinat, Bukhoroteks*) are traded as listed companies. The rest of the companies (1,255 in 2002) are considered pre-listed.

TSE requires companies to comply only with the current legislation. Pursuant to the Company Law, the corporations are required to have a two-tier board system: the supervisory council and the executive board.

The main responsibilities of the supervisory council are to:

- set strategic guidance for company operations;
- organize AGMs and extraordinary shareholder meetings;
- prepare an AGM agenda;
- make decisions to issue securities;
- set the remuneration policies with regard to executive board members;
- make recommendations to the AGM on the compensation of the revision (audit) committee and external auditors;
- determine the market value of the assets;
- make decisions to purchase company treasury stock;
- make recommendations on the dividend payment amounts;
- use company reserve funds (accounts);
- approve all documentation related to functioning of the executive board;
- establish representative offices and subsidiaries;
- enter into certain major transactions (under the Company Law, 'a major transaction is an acquisition, selling or disposition of an asset valued at 25 per cent of the company book value'); and
- other matters indicated in the charter and approved by the AGM.

With regard to composition of the supervisory councils, Uzbekistan's governance system has unique requirements. The members of the supervisory council are elected at the AGM and can be re-elected without any limitations. The executive board members strictly cannot be members of the supervisory council. The election criteria for members of the supervisory council should be indicated in the company charter. The council size is determined by the AGM. However, for corporations with more than 500 shareholders, the minimum council size cannot be less than 7 and for corporations with more than 1,000 shareholders, the minimum size of the council cannot be less than 9. Cumulative voting is permitted under the law.

The chairman of the supervisory council is elected by members of the council by majority vote. The chairman of the council is responsible for organizing the council sessions and represents the council at the AGM. The supervisory council sessions can be called by:

- the chairman of the council;
- a council member;
- revision (audit) committee;
- external auditor; or
- the executive board.

The supervisory council quorum should not be less than 75 per cent of the total number of elected council members. All council and executive board members have an obligation to act in the interests of shareholders. Those council members who voted against any decision in the council sessions are not liable for the negative outcomes resulting from such decisions. Shareholders who have more than 1 per cent of total shares outstanding have the right to hold liable the members of the supervisory council and senior management and receive remedies for their wrongdoings.

26.4.1 The Role of the Supervisory Council

Most countries accept the role of the board as a body providing strategic guidance, monitoring top management activities, ensuring the integrity of the company's accounting and financial reporting systems and overseeing the process of disclosure and communications. Those tasks of the board are well defined in the OECD guidelines. Although Uzbekistan Company Law determines the supervisory council as a body providing strategic guidance in improving company performance, most supervisory councils of newly established and privatized companies are not competent to fulfil their responsibilities. This could be elaborated as:

- lack of highly experienced and knowledgeable supervisory council members;
- lack of shareholder activism;

● poor disclosure and inadequate transparency; and

● absence of director training etc.

Under the Company Law, a clear separation of responsibilities between the supervisory council and company executive board is set in order to eliminate conflicts of interest; however, the issues of real independence of council members is not clearly defined. In most cases, the members of supervisory councils are not independent by 'fact and appearance'. Therefore, a clear definition of independence is considered necessary.

Other issues currently debated in Uzbekistan that relate to corporate governance include:

● the need for various subcommittees (such as the nomination committee and remuneration committee);

● adequate remuneration for members of the council and senior management of companies;

● the degree of disclosure on the supervisory council and executive board concerning their composition and functioning;

● the need for a code of ethics for top management and employees of the company;

● the relationship between the company and the external auditors;

● auditor rotation;

● the separation of consulting business from auditing business;

● liabilities associated with performing audits;

● the major corporate actions such as takeovers, reorganization and liquidation;

● the level of corporate disclosure;

● the reliability of published corporate information;

● the importance of ongoing disclosure and effective ways of communicating information to all interested parties;

● the role of institutional investors and stakeholders in promoting sound governance practices in companies; and

● adequate mechanisms for protecting the rights of minority shareholders.

26.5 Codes, Standards and Good Practice Guidelines

The European Bank for Reconstruction and Development, in its corporate governance sector assessment project (May 2003), classified Uzbekistan as having a medium compliance level of corporate governance systems measured against the OECD Principles of Corporate Governance.

26.6 Disclosure and Transparency

Between 2000 and 2001 the Asian Development Bank (ADB) provided technical assistance to Uzbekistan to enhance transparency and disclosure and the safeguarding of investors' rights.

The European Bank for Reconstruction and Development (2003) noted that 'the existing rules are insufficient to prevent insider trading since they do not prevent or punish the trading of shares where the seller or purchaser is using important information that has not been disclosed to the general public' (p 10).

26.7 Shareholder Rights and Stakeholder Relations

Shareholders at AGMs have the following exclusive authorities:

- to make amendments to the company charter;
- to reorganize the company;
- to put the company into liquidation and elect a liquidation committee;
- to determine the composition requirements of the supervisory council;
- to determine the maximum number of shares outstanding; to set the charter capital;
- to buy back company shares;
- to elect the executive board members if this authority is not delegated to the supervisory council;

- to elect the members of the revision (audit) committee;

- to approve the contract with the external auditors;

- to approve the company financial statements;

- to approve an AGM agenda;

- to make decisions with regard to stock split or consolidation; and

- to make decisions on entering into major transactions if this right is not delegated to the supervisory council.

Company shareholders holding more than 1 per cent of ownership have the right to include important matters on the AGM agenda. Extraordinary AGM meetings can be called by the supervisory council, the revision (audit) committee, the external auditor or shareholders holding more than 10 per cent of ownership in the company. Voting through proxies is permitted under the law. The quorum at the AGM must be at least 60 per cent of the total number of shareholders. Voting at the AGM is based on 'one share, one vote' principle except for cumulative voting in electing the supervisory council members.

26.8 Director Development Activity

On 26 January 2003, pursuant to the President's decree 'On measures to substantially increase the share and the importance of the private sector in the economy of Uzbekistan', the Centre for Corporate Governance was established at the President's Academy. The Centre for Corporate Governance provides training courses in corporate governance, financial reporting and strategic management particularly designed for supervisory council members and the senior management of companies.

Since 1992 the Regional Banking Centre, the President's Academy, state universities and business schools have been running courses for company executive directors and senior management of commercial banks; however, supervisory council members have never received any formal training. The main focus has been senior management of companies. Owing to the absence of training and highly qualified council members, executive boards have been playing a primary role in company management.

The recent President's decree highlights the significance of director training, including the training of council members, in order to achieve high standards in company governance. The Centre will target both council members and senior management of privatized companies or state-owned enterprises. Other private companies will not be targeted.

26.9 Useful Contacts

● Tashkent Stock Exchange – www.uzse.com

26.10 Further Reading

Chen, H (2003) *Corporate Governance Sector assessment project May 2003*, European Bank for Reconstruction and Development, London

Karimov, I (1998) *Uzbekistan on the Threshold of the Twenty First Century*, St Martins Press, New York

Appendix I

International Bodies Concerned with Corporate Governance

- Asian Development Bank – www.adb.org
- Business for Social Responsibility – www.bsr.org
- Business Roundtable – www.brtable.org
- Calpers – www.calpers-governance.org
- Conference Board – www.conferenceboard.org
- Corporate Governance Portal – www.corpgov.net/links/links.html
- Corporate Library – www.thecorporatelibrary.com
- European Bank for Reconstruction and Development (EBRD) – www.ebrd.com
- European Commission – www.europa.eu.int
- European Corporate Governance Network – www.ecgn.ubl.ac.be
- Global Corporate Governance Forum – www.gcgf.org

- Global Reporting Initiative – www.globalreporting.org
- Institute of Directors – www.iod.com
- Institute of Internal Auditors – www.theiia.org
- International Corporate Governance Network – www.icgn.org
- International Accounting Standards Committee (IASC) – www.iasc.org.uk
- International Finance Corporation (IFC) – www.ifc.org
- OECD – www.oecd.org
- Standard & Poors – www.standardandpoors.com
- Sustainability – www.sustainability.com
- World Bank Group – www.worldbank.org/html/fpd/privatesector/cg/index.htm
- World Business Council for Sustainable Development – www.wbcsd.ch

Appendix II

International Corporate Governance Codes

Commonwealth Association for Corporate Governance (1999) *Principles of best business practice in the Commonwealth*, CACG

International Corporate Governance Network (1999) *Statement on Global Corporate Governance Principles*, ICGN

International Corporate Governance Network (1999) *Statement on Stock-Based Incentive Scheme Principles*, ICGN

International Corporate Governance Network (1998) *Global Share Voting Principles*, ICGN

Organization for Economic Cooperation and Development (1999) OECD *Principles of Corporate Governance*, OECD

Organization for Economic Cooperation and Development (2004) OECD *Principles of Corporate Governance,* OECD

European Codes of Corporate Governance

European Association of Securities Dealers (2000) *Corporate Governance Principles and Recommendations*, EASD

European Association of Securities Dealers Automated Quotation (1996) *Rule Book,* EASDAQ

European Shareholders' Association (2000) *Euroshareholders Corporate Governance Guidelines,* ESA

European Bank for Reconstruction and Development (1997) *Sound Business Standards and Corporate Practices: A Set of Guidelines,* EBRD

OECD Regional Roundtable Corporate Governance White Papers

- Russia (April 2002)
- South East Europe (June 2003)
- Asia (June 2003)
- Latin America (December 2003)
- Eurasia (December 2003)

All White Papers can be found on www.oecd.org/daf/corporate-affairs.com.

Index

NB: page numbers in *italic* indicate tables

Index